HISTORY OF RELIGION
Pre-Columbian American Religions

Pre-Columbian American Religions

WALTER KRICKEBERG
HERMANN TRIMBORN
WERNER MÜLLER
OTTO ZERRIES

translated by
STANLEY DAVIS

HISTORY OF RELIGION SERIES

General Editor: E. O. James

Holt, Rinehart and Winston
New York   Chicago   San Francisco

8764458

Printed in Great Britain

CONTENTS

ILLUSTRATIONS

(*between pages* 184 *and* 185)

MAPS

INTRODUCTION

Walter Krickeberg

Man reached the Americas from northern Asia some 10,000 years ago, during the period following the most recent glaciation.[1] During the subsequent slow process of diffusion from Alaska to Tierra del Fuego the presumed common cultural and linguistic characteristics of the original immigrant population inevitably disappeared; and the population of the Americas, never more than forty-five million (an average population density of about $2\frac{1}{2}$ people to the square mile), split into a bewildering variety of distinct cultural and linguistic units. Lengthy and detailed investigation is often necessary before a relationship between one American language and another can be established, while connections with Old World languages have very seldom been found despite a strong presumption that common roots exist. The distinguished ethnologist and philologist Paul Rivet once estimated that within the pre-Columbian population there were no less than 123 separate families of languages, and Franz Boas has since established that these do not even have such characteristics in common as poly-synthesis and incorporation, once thought to be universal in American languages. Thanks to the tireless work of a number of North American philologists, Rivet's conviction that subsequent research would drastically reduce the numbers of known families of languages has been borne out, at least for North and Central America. In South America, on the other hand, the total of linguistic families has actually increased, from Rivet's figure of 77 to Čestmir Loukotka's more recent estimate of 114.[2]

The first link between Europe and North America was established by Northmen sailing by way of Iceland and Greenland; but this brief episode had practically no lasting consequences for the native Americans. Influences from Asia seem to have been very much more lasting and significant. This aspect of pre-Columbian antiquity has recently been the subject of lively controversy.[3] The sinologist Carl Hentze and the Austrian ethnologist Robert von Heine-Geldern point to numerous common features in the art and religion of early Mesoamerican and Andean cultures and those of India and the Far East, and regard the former existence of trans-Pacific links as a demonstrated fact. According

I

to Heine-Geldern these links arose during the period from the seventh to the third century BC, when Indian, Indochinese and Chinese influences were spreading over a large area of Indonesia and the southwestern Pacific, and lasted until the twelfth century of our era.[4] Hentze believes that Asian influences also affected the fishing communities of the northern Pacific seaboard of North America, whose sophisticated wood-carvings, as well as certain features of their social and religious life, mark them out as foreign bodies on North American soil and suggest comparisons with Asia.[5] The most likely source of these external influences is eastern Asia, as the North American coast can be reached from Chinese and Korean ports without the necessity of crossing the open Pacific.

In the Arctic, contact between the peoples of America and Asia was never completely broken; this explains the decision to exclude the Eskimos from this account of the religions of America. Although in their language, way of life and material culture they have much in common with other peoples of North America, from an ethnic and religious point of view they are better dealt with in a survey of north-eastern Asia.

Between the Arctic and Tierra del Fuego there was as great a variety of cultures as there was of languages. There were nomadic hunters and gatherers, agricultural communities at various stages of development, fishing communities and urban cultures which, although still in the Stone Age technologically, were the equals of advanced Old World cultures in religious development, art and the religious use of science. Both North and South America fall into two fairly clearly defined ethnographical divisions; and this book has been divided into four sections accordingly. In North America a line running across Mexico, roughly along the Tropic of Cancer, divides Mesoamerica, the area inhabited in general by advanced indigenous peoples with a knowledge of agriculture, weaving, pottery, sculpture and writing, from a vast area whose inhabitants have left comparatively few material remains. Similarly, in South America a line running along the eastern slopes of the Andes separates the Andean civilizations in the west and north from the vast and complex ethnographical area which is primitive South America. There are inevitably cases in which such a division appears arbitrary, especially where the dividing lines cut across a large linguistic group. The linguistic group known as Uto-Aztecan, for example, consists of a northern branch, the Shoshonean, which has always been regarded as wholly primitive, and a southern branch, the Náhua of Mexico, which produced the last great urban civilization of Mesoamerica, that of the Aztecs. Similarly, in the southern part of Central America the Chibcha were a primitive agricultural people, while in the Cordilleras of Colombia they were the principal representatives of advanced culture.

The boundary between the southern Náhua and the northern Chibcha was the ethnographical frontier between North and South America; although it is hard to see whether the Chorotegans (Mangue), an ancient and culturally advanced people in Nicaragua and northern Costa Rica, should be included among the peoples of Mesoamerica or South America. They show linguistic links with a small tribe in the Mexican state of Chiapas, their archaeological remains show both northern and southern features, and their culture displays many South American features.

In South America outposts of the advanced Chibcha culture have been found all along the north coast of South America, on the remotest Caribbean islands and in the Amazon delta. These regions have been dealt with in the section devoted to the primitive peoples of South America, as they were peopled mainly by Arawakans, members of one of the major ethnic groups of eastern South America, which took over elements of advanced culture at a very early date not only in the areas named but also in the Bolivian province of Mojos, far to the south along the upper tributaries of the Río Madeira. In the southern Andean region the influences of early and late Peruvian civilization extended as far as the Atacama desert in northern Chile, the adjacent Puna de Atacama, and the valleys of the north-west Argentinian Andes. The Araucanians of central and southern Chile came under Inca influence shortly before the Spanish conquest, although enough indigenous cultural elements survived to justify their exclusion from the section of this book which deals with the Andean civilizations.

The immense variety of cultural forms in the Americas applies to religion as well as to other features of social life. As in the case of language, our written sources for the nature and development of Amerindian religion go back no further than four hundred years. But in this case we can draw on archaeological evidence which takes us back two or three thousand years more. Estimates based on carbon 14 dating give dates ranging from 1000 to 1500 BC for the earliest relevant finds.[6]

Even the earliest clay objects to be discovered provide some evidence as to the religion of their users. But only later, after about AD 300, can archaeological finds in Mesoamerica and Peru (stone carvings and frescoes as well as pottery and, in Peru, representational tapestries) be said to provide really useful material evidence for the historian of religion. For centuries this kind of material evidence has to supply the place of

3

written evidence; Historic times in Mesoamerica begin with the appearance of pictographic manuscripts, while the painted clay vessels of the Mochica and Nazca cultures serve a roughly similar function as far as Peru is concerned.

In dealing with the religions of primitive north and south America archaeological sources are of relatively little value (except in dealing with the Caribbean and Amazon areas where Chibcha cultural influence from the Andean region was strong). The emphasis here has been placed on the available written sources.

From the sixteenth century onwards, the ethnographic literature of America has been exceedingly rich. The numerous excellent first-hand accounts written by explorers, missionaries, travellers and colonial administrators are of special interest to the historian of religion because most of their authors came in contact with the Indians at a time when their religious life was still uncontaminated by outside influences. Among these early authors were such remarkable figures as the Franciscan Bernardino de Sahagún, without whom our knowledge of Aztec religion would be very incomplete; and there has been no lack of first-class observers in all parts of the Americas, most of them Protestant or Catholic missionaries. It was not long before literate Indians, too, were moved to record the beliefs and customs of their ancestors and their contemporaries, not least because they wished to defend them against the hasty and biased judgements of European observers.

This astounding wealth of good written source-material covers the whole period between the last items of archaeological evidence and the beginning of scientific investigation in the last decades of the nineteenth century, when ethnographical fieldwork began on a large scale all over the Americas. Once again the history of religion was the principal beneficiary. It became apparent at last that Amerindian religion possessed immense significance in the wider context of the religious history of the human race as a whole. This significance springs largely from the fact that the Indians (if one leaves out of account hypothetical influences from southern and eastern Asia) enjoyed thousands of years of freedom from Old World religious influences, only meeting the messianic religions of Europe and Asia at a time when the organic growth of their native cultures had been brought to a standstill on all fronts by the European intruder.

CHAPTER ONE

MESOAMERICA
Walter Krickeberg

The development of Mesoamerican religions could not be studied as a whole until archaeological excavations began on a large scale some forty years ago. Investigators who had hitherto had to rely on such ruins and other monuments as happened to have been preserved above ground, together with Indian pictographic manuscripts and the reports of Spanish travellers, found themselves face to face with a whole world of infinite cultural variety and complexity which had lain underground, out of the reach of destructive hands, for more than two thousand years. Countless finds testified to the radical transformations which not only material culture but also religious ideas and customs had undergone not once but many times in the course of Mesoamerican prehistory.

The father of Mesoamerican archaeology was the Mexican Manuel Gamio, whose first dig in the Valley of Mexico in 1909 revealed the existence of three successive and totally distinct cultures within the restricted area of the Valley. Excavations did not, however, really begin in earnest until about ten years later, when work in the Mesa Central revealed a series of well-preserved Aztec temples and, almost simultaneously (1917–22), the great ruined city of Teotihuacán, the metropolis of the Classic culture which preceded that of the Aztecs. Excavations at Teotihuacán since 1932 have brought to light remains which give us some idea of the immense significance of this site in the subsequent cultural development of Mexico: great palace complexes and friezes which, like the pictographs of later cultures, reveal a great deal about the religious attitudes of those who created them.

The so-called 'archaic' cultures, better referred to as Preclassic, which represent the earliest stages of the known development of civilization in Mexico, were brought to light largely through the work of George C. Vaillant between 1927 and 1935. The temple-crowned mountain of

Monte Albán, the religious centre of ancient Oaxaca, with its numerous pyramids, stone monuments and chamber tombs, was excavated by the Mexican archaeologist Alfonso Caso between 1932 and 1952. In the years 1940–5 Jorge Acosta brought to light the remains of Tula, home of the Toltecs, people previously lost in the mists of legend. The equally mysterious 'Olmecs' of the southern Gulf coast were investigated, at La Venta and other sites, by a team led by Matthew Stirling, head of the Ethnological Bureau of the Smithsonian Institution in Washington. The credit for proving that this La Venta culture influenced the art and religion of practically all Mesoamerican cultures goes to Miguel Covarrubias, whose excavations (1947–9) at Tlatilco, the principal Preclassic site in the Valley of Mexico, demonstrated the presence of La Venta influence at an early stage in Central Mexican cultural development.

Not long after this the ancient culture of the northern Gulf Coast came to light with the excavation by José García Payón of the great temple city of El Tajín in the jungles of northern Veracruz. The wide distribution of finds in the unmistakable El Tajín style shows that the El Tajín culture had close contacts with Teotihuacán and that its influence reached as far south as the Pacific coast of Guatemala and El Salvador.

The Maya region played its part in Mexican cultural development from Preclassic times onwards. Contacts between Maya territory and the rest of Mesoamerica were sometimes extremely close: Teotihuacán and Tula established colonies inside Maya territory at Kaminaljuyú in the Guatemala highlands and Chichén Itzá in Yucatán respectively. These were, however, only transitory influences on the cultural development of the Maya, who, over a period of seven centuries (AD 300–1000), elaborated their own impressively self-contained style almost entirely free from external influences.

It is estimated today that indigenous civilization in Mesoamerica lasted about three thousand years. Its development may be divided into three main periods: the Preclassic, from c. 1500 BC to between AD 100 and AD 300, the Classic, ending about AD 1000, and the Postclassic from AD 1000 until the Spanish conquest. Only a tenth of this immense span of time (from AD 1200 onwards) is covered by written sources, set down after the arrival of the Spaniards, and by native pictographic manuscripts. In the case of the Chichimecs and Mixtecs both kinds of written source go back as far as the seventh century; but all events before this are lost in the obscurity of myth. For our knowledge of religion in the Preclassic and Classic periods, and even the earlier part of the Postclassic

6

period, we must therefore rely almost exclusively on archaeological evidence.

I *Mexico*

1. PRECLASSIC CULTURES: ZACATENCO AND TICOMÁN

The earliest inhabitants of Mexico were hunters and fishermen who killed mammoth in the Valley of Mexico, and who left behind them little more than a few stone and bone implements. From this period, before the introduction of agriculture and pottery, no traces of religious life whatever have come down to us.

Even the Preclassic cultures of the Valley of Mexico, whose pottery, in particular, shows them to have been anything but primitive, have left very few signs of religious observance. This culture developed in two distinct phases named after two important sites, Zacatenco and Ticomán (a division which corresponds to ethnic as well as cultural changes within the culture), and reached its highest peak of sophistication between 1000 and 500 BC in Tlatilco, one of the principal sites of the Zacatenco phase. After about 500 BC a series of natural disasters took place which were still dimly remembered in late Aztec times, when it was believed that four former ages of the world had been successively destroyed by deluge, whirlwind, showers of ash and volcanic eruption.

The earlier of the two Preclassic phases, the Zacatenco phase, is characterized by an extremely varied range of crude but astonishingly lively pottery figurines. These most frequently represent nude female figures of ample proportions, often modelled with a touch of humour or grotesquerie, which carry small children on their hips or hold little dogs in their arms, or appear as dancers with smart little skirts and artful coiffures. Figures of men appear with masks on their faces or dressed for the ball game. All sorts of monstrosities appear as well; some figures with two heads, some with two noses, two mouths and three eyes, and masks consisting of half a normal face and half a skull.

It is altogether possible that the generously proportioned female figures represent fertility spirits, and were buried in the fields to increase the harvest, and that the various freaks, too, represent supernatural beings. But it seems more likely that these were human figures intended to accompany the dead on their journey into the other world and

7

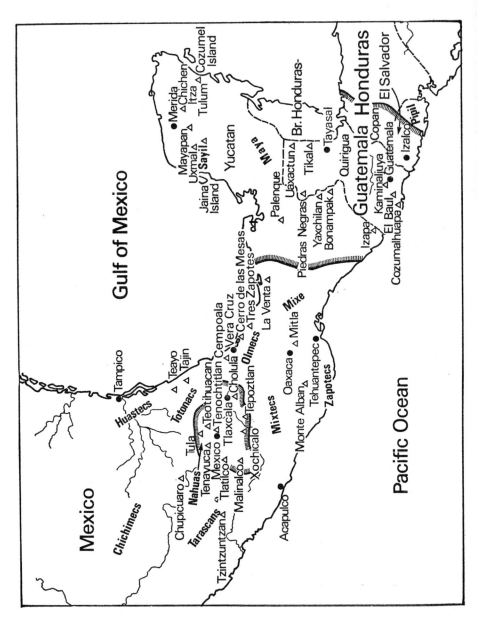

Map 1. Principal sites of Mesoamerica

entertain or protect them. Ritual burial was known in the Preclassic period in Mexico, and human remains have been found stretched out in shallow stone-filled graves which contain ornaments and stone implements as well as clay vessels and figurines.

In any case the highly individualized, purely naturalistic and unsymbolic style of the Tlatilco figurines makes it inconceivable that they were forerunners of the rigidly conventionalized gods of later Mexican art. It was not until the Ticomán Phase of the Preclassic period that a stereotyped pattern of figurines begins to appear which persisted far into Classic times. It represents an old, bent man sitting on the ground with a shallow bowl on his head. This is the god of fire whom the Aztecs called Huehueteotl, the 'old god', and whom they still depicted with a bowl for burning incense on his head.

In the Ticomán phase, from c. 500 BC onwards, appear the first sacred buildings, including the earliest example of a step pyramid. These structures were later built all over Mesoamerica; this early type retained the rounded shape of a natural hill but already had four terraces, a stairway on the east side, and a ramp on the west side leading to a terminal platform which carried a rectangular altar. This pyramid, at Cuicuilco (in the south-west of the Valley of Mexico), is built of packed earth and clad with undressed stone with a course of upright stone slabs round the base. A lava flow from the volcano Xictli later covered the bottom third of the structure.

In other respects, and especially in its pottery, the Ticomán Phase reveals a decline within Preclassic art. Ticomán Phase figurines look almost like mass-produced articles; perhaps because of this they are more widely distributed than their predecessors, being found as far afield as the state of Puebla to the east of the Mesa Central and the state of Morelos to the south. In the west of the Mesa Central, north of the Valley of Mexico, there was a renaissance of the art of clay modelling, reflected in the attractive polychrome figures of Chupícuaro in the state of Guanajuato.

1. LA VENTA

About 1000 BC the basically peasant Preclassic culture of Zacatenco underwent a rapid development as a result of outside influences. Larger, hollow clay figurines in a markedly more elaborate style appear among the finds, as well as vessels on which the predominantly geometrical ornamentation of the Zacatenco Phase is replaced by symbolic elements.

2

These innovations, characteristic of the so-called Tlatilco style, are believed by Covarrubias to be a consequence of the arrival of an aristocratic minority from the Gulf Coast or the south of Mexico who disappeared during the ensuing Ticomán Phase under the pressure of less culturally advanced groups from western Mexico. This *élite* undoubtedly had loose links with an ancient and mysterious Mexican civilization known to have existed in the southern Gulf Coast area, where its principal sites are La Venta (Tabasco) and San Lorenzo and Tres Zapotes (Veracruz). This civilization is generally known by the name of the tribes who inhabited this area in historic times, the Olmecs ('people of rubber country'), whom the Aztec historians believed to be the remnants of an ancient non-Nahuatl-speaking people, creators of the oldest civilization in Mexico, who had long since been assimilated into the ethnic groups which had subsequently settled in their territory. It is, however, preferable to refer to this culture by the neutral name of 'La Venta Culture', after its principal archaeological site, especially as it does not seem to have originated in Olmec territory, the 'rubber country', at all; its most archaic forms have been found in the valleys of the Pacific slopes of the Sierra Madre del Sur, in the states of Guerrero and Oaxaca,[1] and it is highly improbable that a culture characterized by large-scale sculptures in hard basalt can have sprung from a low-lying, almost stoneless coastline of swamps and jungles.

The basalt monuments of the La Venta culture comprise colossal human heads, the largest of which is almost ten feet high, with a diameter of over twenty feet; stylized human figures; rectangular stone altars each with a niche in the front containing a seated human figure; monolithic stone troughs and sarcophagi; and stelae, i.e. large, irregular upright carved stones. The altars, troughs, sarcophagi and stelae are decorated with bas reliefs, and there are also numbers of rock carvings. The architecture of the La Venta culture, in keeping with the nature of the terrain, consists largely of earthen structures, pyramids and platforms, arranged axially round rectangular plazas and only occasionally faced with stone. However, among the mounds of La Venta there is a rectangular enclosure, fenced with natural basalt columns, which contains a stone sarcophagus and a rectangular sepulchral chamber, walled and roofed with more basalt columns, in which three or four skeletons lay on a low platform. The fence of columns and the sepulchral chamber are unique among Mesoamerican antiquities. So too is a cache of serpentine axes, buried more than twenty feet below ground on top of a serpentine mosaic pavement. The only feature of this burial which reappears in another Mesoamerican context is the stone sarcophagus, of which we know of one example from Maya territory, in the famous crypt at Palenque.

If we are to judge from the colossal heads and the other sculpture, the creators of these monuments belonged to a very remarkable physical type; dumpy bodies and round heads with flat broad noses, often slanting eyes and a mouth with a swollen upper lip and downturned corners. Although somewhat similar types do still exist among the Indians of southern Mexico, this convention of representation, and especially the 'Olmec mouth', is at least partly based not on real models but on an attempt to make a human face resemble that of a jaguar. The people who produced the La Venta culture were clearly obsessed by this animal. In their sculptures every stage in the metamorphosis of the cat into a human being is represented; and their principal decorative motif is a stylized jaguar face. Another strange human type is associated with the first. It consists of infantile or dwarfish individuals with degenerative physical characteristics such as over-large, pear-shaped heads, short bandy legs, humps and club-feet; the so-called *Danzantes*, reliefs in the La Venta style from the earliest levels at Monte Albán in Oaxaca, show individuals of this type whose apparently deformed male genital organs suggest that they are eunuchs.

It is clear that the 'tiger face' or 'were-jaguar' figures and the 'baby face' figures owe their form to some underlying religious idea. In a tropical jungle where every rustle in the undergrowth, every cracking twig may betray the presence of the big cat, a belief in jaguar gods or spirits is only natural.

Proof that the jaguar was thought of as a god or spirit rather than a mere animal lies in the frequent appearance of its face in the incised and relief decorations on large and valuable jade, quartz, basalt and limestone 'votive axes', objects used for ceremonial purposes or as offerings. The creature appears in frontal view, with eyebrows that look like flames and a deep cleft in the crown of its head.

As far as the 'baby face' figurines are concerned, we know that many Indians in Veracruz, Guerrero and Oaxaca, the states which now include the former territory of the La Venta people, still believe in deformed jungle and mountain spirits, evil dwarfs who molest women and give men diseases. These dwarf spirits are also the 'lords of beasts', who protect the deer from extermination and grant permission to hunt in return for sacrifices.[2] Belief in such beings goes back to a very early stage in religious development; it is still found among many South American tribes.

An equally characteristic sign of La Venta culture is an evident love

of jade in all its varieties, from milky white to deep green. Like the
Chinese, another people who took delight in this rare and costly semi-
precious stone, the La Venta people endowed it with religious significance, doubtless because its smoothness and lustre and its colour,
usually blue-green, made it a symbol of water and of vegetation. Jade
preserved the same symbolic significance among later Mexican peoples,
but none of them employed it so lavishly (782 pieces in one cache alone)
or worked it with such delicacy as did the bearers of the La Venta culture. Quite apart from countless personal ornaments, the finest effigy
figurines from La Venta itself and other sites are made of jade. In the
basalt sepulchral chamber at La Venta these are present as offerings;
elsewhere on the site a group of fifteen jade figures have been found
clustered as if awaiting a sacrifice around an altar made of six large
jade votive axes.[3] The axe was revered as a religious emblem, as is
proved by the many large specimens that have been found decorated
with jaguar faces.

In contrast to the Preclassic cultures of the Mesa Central, the La
Venta culture paid much less attention to pottery than to stone-carving.
One La Venta clay figurine from the state of Morelos represents a naked
man with the pelt of a fantastic beast over his head and back. This was
a common way in ancient America of representing the *alter ego*, the
mysterious psychic double belonging to each individual.

The religious ceremonial of the La Venta culture is known from
crowded bas reliefs on stelae, altars and rocks. On a stela at Tres
Zapotes a religious ritual is shown framed in the jaws of a jaguar as an
indication that it is taking place not on earth but in heaven or in the
underworld, both of which are symbolized by a gaping jaguar mouth.
The large La Venta altars are also stylized representations of jaguar
heads, as their decoration shows; the niche in the front of the altar
represents the open jaws.

One religious custom in particular, which later spread to almost all
Mesoamerican cultures, seems to have originated in the La Venta culture: the ball game. On a stela in the La Venta style found near
Orizaba an attendant is shown dressing a ball player in the armour
which was worn as a necessary protection against the heavy solid rubber
ball.

The mythology of the La Venta culture is so far known only from the
bas reliefs on the four sides of a monolithic trough at Tres Zapotes,
which show numerous small human figures fighting in the coils of an
elaborate spiral pattern. If Stirling's surmise, that these spirals are
stylized cloud serpents, is correct, then the scene probably represents a

battle in heaven, in which the gods, like the Olympian gods of Greece, defeat and cast down their adversaries, the 'heaven-storming Titans'.[4]

The frequent juxtaposition, on monuments of the La Venta culture, of two different human types – one short, corpulent and flat-nosed and one tall, slender and narrow-nosed – suggests that the bearers of this culture belonged to more than one ethnic group and may have had more than one religion. Covarrubias surmises that the corpulent people had the jaguar as their totem or protective spirit and the thinner people the serpent. The thinner people were the ruling caste at whose behest the great monuments were constructed.

When the La Venta culture came under pressure on all sides from outposts of the rising Classic cultures, the short, fat people withdrew into the jungles of La Venta itself where they and their city soon disappeared. The slender people remained behind, perhaps to become the ancestors of the Mixtecs, who occupied a part of the old La Venta cultural sphere south of Veracruz in Aztec times and still preserved many features of the La Venta culture.[5]

All this took place towards the end of the Preclassic period and can be dated from a stela and a jade figurine, both belonging to the La Venta culture, which bear inscriptions, in the Long Count notation later used by the Maya, which correspond to the dates 31 BC and AD 162 respectively. The discovery of these inscriptions was a considerable surprise to archaeologists, who had previously believed that the first calendrical inscriptions in Mesoamerica were those of the Maya.

It is possible, then, that the La Venta culture bequeathed to the civilizations which came after it not only the jaguar and serpent cults, the religious importance of jade, the ball game and the custom of erecting stone stelae and altars in temple plazas, but also the greatest of all Mesoamerican cultural achievements, the invention of writing.

Nevertheless, La Venta had much in common with the Preclassic culture of the Mesa Central. The art of both cultures, with its realism, is as far removed from the hieratic severity of Classic Mesa Central art as it is from the fantastic exuberance of the art of the Maya and the later Gulf Coast peoples. Both Preclassic cultures also lack the all-pervading religious symbolism of the Classic cultures, the personified idols, the esotericism in worship and the priestly caste, versed in symbolic lore, which in Classic times ultimately developed into an all-powerful theocracy.

1. PRECLASSIC CULTURES: WESTERN MEXICO

With the rise of the Classic cultures the La Venta culture disappeared from all the areas of Mexico that it had previously dominated or influenced. The Preclassic culture of the Mesa Central, on the other hand, survived in the Pacific states of Colima, Jalisco and Nayarit, untouched by Classic influences, into Postclassic times.

Finds made in the north-west of the state of Michoacán, contemporary with the Zacatenco Phase of Mesa Central culture, form a transitional stage to these long-lived Pacific coast cultures whose clay figurines, both solid and hollow, and effigy vessels, retained their Preclassic variety and expressiveness to the last.

The pottery of the west coast cultures gives an inexhaustibly detailed picture of the people of the age, their environment, their family life and their social customs; but like the Preclassic art of the Mesa Central it contains no religious symbols and no representations of gods; it is entirely this-worldly. In its variety and vigour, although in nothing else, it recalls the pottery of the Chimú of the north of Peru, with whom the west coast cultures seem to have had maritime trading links. West coast burials, too, seem to show a link with Andean culture. As early as the Zacatenco Phase, burials were taking place in Michoacán in shaft graves, a form of grave otherwise unknown in Mesoamerica, although quite common in South America. A vertical or slanting shaft, sometimes with steps in it, leads down to a vaulted lateral tomb-chamber. The body lies on the floor of the chamber, or on a low platform, accompanied by pottery figurines representing either the deceased himself or the wives, slaves, domestics and animals that surrounded him in life. Sometimes the figurines are in groups representing either everyday activities or ceremonies such as temple rituals, ball games, royal progresses, funerals, mask dances and phallic dances.

One group of figurines from Nayarit seems to represent a blood ritual of the kind practised in Yucatán in Postclassic times: in it two men and two women are seen bound together by a cord passed through their cheeks.

Colima produced a characteristic type of very realistic figurines representing the fat little dogs which were bred in ancient Mexico to bury with the dead as companions and guides to the hereafter.

2. TEOTIHUACÁN

In the Valley of Mexico the transition from Preclassic to Classic culture took place almost imperceptibly. Here lay Teotihuacán, a great city covering three square miles, the largest and most influential centre of Classic culture in Mexico. All the other Classic sites lay to a greater or lesser extent under its influence: Cholula on the plateau of Puebla, with its huge pyramid which is contemporary with the oldest buildings at Teotihuacán if not earlier, Xochicalco in Morelos, Monte Albán in Oaxaca, El Tajín in Veracruz; there is even an outpost of the Teotihuacán culture at Kaminaljuyú in the Guatemala highlands.

The origins of Teotihuacán lie far back in the Preclassic period. The earliest small objects found are in the Ticomán style; and the city's two great pyramids, the Pyramid of the Sun, 700 feet square at the base and 200 feet high, and the somewhat smaller, oblong-based Pyramid of the Moon, could not have been built but for their modest earthen predecessor at Cuicuilco.

Before the collapse of Teotihuacán in c. AD 700 as a result of a series of wars and economic catastrophes, the city passed through three distinct architectural phases (Teotihuacán I, II and III), each of which corresponded to a rapid evolution in other branches of art. Even after the fall of the city, Teotihuacán culture lived on in a decadent form, particularly in the neighbourhood of Azcapotzalco on the western shore of Lake Texcoco, and was a fertile influence on the rising Postclassic culture of the Mesa Central.

Seven centuries after the fall of Teotihuacán the Aztecs believed that it had been built by a race of giants in the far distant past. Its temples they took for the tombs of bygone kings (hence the Aztec name Teotihuacán, 'where they become gods [by dying]') and they even believed that its two great pyramids were the birthplaces of the sun and moon. This is the origin of the misleading names still given to these two structures.

We do not know the tribal origin of the first inhabitants of Teotihuacán. We only know that they belonged to a brachycephalic type which was not found on the Mesa Central in ensuing periods but which is still the dominant strain on the Gulf Coast. Culturally, as well as racially, Teotihuacán culture is radically different from the culture of the peoples who inhabited the Mesa Central in Postclassic times (including the Toltecs), while showing clear links with other Classic Mexican cultures especially in religion, religious art and architecture.

The most important contribution to the development of Mesoamerican architecture made by Teotihuacán was the replacement of the round earth mound (rarely a tomb) by a truly architectonic form, the rectangular-based pyramid. In this early period each step of the pyramid consisted of two sections: a sloping 'batter' (*talud*) and a vertical panel with inset (*tablero*). Both sections were often richly decorated, either with reliefs and paintings or with purely abstract architectural ornaments.

This characteristic *talud-tablero* pattern reappears in stepped pyramids built throughout the Classic period; sometimes the sloping element is emphasized, sometimes the vertical panel.

A pyramid was not generally built all at once. At regular intervals another layer of masonry was added (generally following the original pattern), and the pyramid grew. In Teotihuacán the only structure which was not built in this way is the oldest and largest of all, the Pyramid of the Sun. In spite of its immense volume (nearly eight million cubic feet) it was built in one operation, whereas the great pyramid at Cholula, for example, received at least three layers of masonry in different styles on top of its original Teotihuacán-style structure.

This practice of adding extra layers to pyramids has a religious origin. In succeeding ages it was done mainly at the ends of 52-year Calendar Rounds, when a fresh start was made by man and nature.

The stepped dais at the foot of the Pyramid of the Sun, from which the great stairway rises, belongs to the second phase of Teotihuacán architecture. It has lost its sculptural decorations, but we can gain some idea of how it looked from the much smaller Temple of Quetzalcoatl, which later became the core of the large ramparted platform within a court known as the Ciudadela. The decorations here have survived intact and are of a massive richness unrivalled in ancient Mexican architecture. The vertical panels are carved in rectangular sections in which feathered serpents with their heads projecting at right angles to the surface of the pyramid alternate with grotesque stylized human faces which Alfonso Caso believes to represent a maize god.[6] The Temple of Quetzalcoatl stands on the east side of a wide ceremonial avenue lined with other temples. On the west side of this *via sacra* lies the so-called Temple of Agriculture, a low terrace with steps leading up to a wall decorated with paintings. Another temple is surmounted by a row of stone slabs bearing the stylized features of the rain god.

Teotihuacán is the earliest site in which religious symbolism plays a part in the decoration of temple buildings, and also the first to contain free-standing idols (an exception must be made for the clay and stone fire-god effigies of the Preclassic period, described above). In front of the Pyramid of the Moon at Teotihuacán there once stood a ten-foot basalt figure of a goddess weighing twenty-one tons; and in the bed of a stream to the east of Lake Texcoco there was found an unfinished stone figure, nearly twenty-three feet high. This is the water goddess which has been moved, and now stands outside the new Museum of Anthropology in Mexico City.[7] These figures, thought to represent the water goddess worshipped at Teotihuacán, are more like rectangular pillars with a relief on one side than statues. Their severe, archaistic cubic style contrasts strongly with the realism of the colossal heads of La Venta. A figure of a couchant jaguar, similarly stylized, with two hollows in its back, looks like an anticipation of the jaguar-shaped sacrificial vessel that once stood in the courtyard of the great temple in the Aztec capital, Tenochtitlán.

The small clay figures, just as numerous in Teotihuacán as they are in the Preclassic sites, here include types which must be regarded as images of gods. One rotund figurine, for example, resembles the Chinese god of luck; another, with its face covered by a rough mask with holes for mouth and eyes, is thought to be a prototype of the Aztec god Xipe, the 'flayed one'. (Another common symbol found on Teotihuacán clay vessels is the butterfly, which, like the human skin mask of Xipe, later played an important part in Aztec religious iconography.)

The stone masks, on the other hand, which are among the glories of Teotihuacán II art, do not seem to have represented the features of gods, although their features, like those of the gods, are generalized rather than individual. These masks, carved from basalt, andesite, jade and alabaster, were probably made to fit onto the heads of mummy bundles. We know this from certain clay incense burners on which mummy bundles are shown with masks of this sort; there was a similar burial custom in ancient Peru.

The richest source of information on the religious ideas and customs of the Teotihuacán culture lies in the numerous wall paintings which date from phases II and III. In these murals the figure of a rain god and food-provider assumes a dominant role for the first time.

This is a natural consequence of the geographical setting of Teotihuacán, in dry, treeless, thorny uplands which could be made to bear fruit only with great labour. The walls of the so-called Temple of Agriculture were covered with a brilliant array of frescoes representing flowing water, aquatic animals, seeds and flowering fronds: everything, in short, that was desired from the god of rain and agriculture.

In the two building complexes at Teotihuacán known as Tepantitla and Tetitla, both now believed to have been dwellings for priests, the god himself is to be seen rising from the sea and scattering his life-giving droplets of rain in handfuls upon the earth. On either side priests can be seen singing his praises and dispensing 'precious-jade rain' (water-drops with jade symbols) and grains of maize. The face of the god is partly covered by a mask which remained one of the attributes of the Aztec rain god Tlaloc ('he who makes things sprout') in Postclassic times; but although Tlaloc has the same functions as the great rain god of Teotihuacán, he is only one of many gods in the Aztec pantheon.

In Teotihuacán all the souls of the dead were believed to pass into the kingdom of the rain god; the Aztecs reserved the paradise of Tlaloc for those who had died by drowning. In the Temple of Agriculture, beneath the fresco of the god and his priests, the souls of the departed can be seen in paradise, savouring such delights, unknown in the arid environs of Teotihuacán, as fruit of all kinds and abundant water.[8]

The religion of Teotihuacán was thus very different from that of the subsequent Toltec and Aztec cultures, although related; thus, there are symbols common to both Classic and Postclassic religion, but their significance changes from one to the other. At Teotihuacán, the feathered serpent, for instance, represents the waters of the earth; and on the façade of the Temple of Quetzalcoatl it is consequently surrounded by sea-shells and snail shells. In the Postclassic cultures this same symbol represents the sky[9].

In the Teotihuacán period more attention was paid to earthly things than to heavenly bodies such as the sun and moon; blood sacrifice, a rite practised by later cultures in honour of astral deities, is therefore absent in Teotihuacán. Instead, as we can see from a badly defaced mural on the back wall of the Temple of Agriculture, the gods received offerings of objects which had a symbolic connection with rain (rubber balls representing raindrops) or with the fresh green of growing crops (jade beads and green quetzal feathers), and incense was burnt on high fire altars so that its smoke symbolized rain clouds.

Just as Teotihuacán religion lacks blood sacrifice, the Teotihuacán state lacks another typical feature of later Mesa Central cultures: the frequent waging of wars. The numerous finds made in Teotihuacán include no weapons, and the huge and wealthy city itself was unfortified. Warriors make only rare and isolated appearances in the frescoes. Priests, on the other hand, appear very frequently, usually in rich attire and with the head of the sacred feathered serpent as a headdress. The inference is clear. Teotihuacán was not ruled by warrior kings; it was a theocracy. The great power of the priesthood is evident from the number and size of the temples in this typical 'temple city', the construction of which must have involved the labour of many thousands of hands. Even the extensive complexes of buildings, discovered in outlying parts of the site by Sigvald Linné and Pedro Armillas and consisting of closely-packed small compartments, do not seem to have been dwelling-houses but pilgrims' hospices and temporary quarters or workshops for the many craftsmen needed to decorate the temples. It was beneath these structures that the dead were buried, in graves each consisting of a rectangular pit, with sides lined with clay tiles, closed with a stone slab. The skeletons, either flexed or supine, are accompanied by grave goods including elaborate clay ceremonial vessels.

Teotihuacán pottery reached its highest point of development in the cylindrical tripod vessels of Teotihuacán III, with their incised decorations or fresco paintings (on an added coating of stucco) representing religious subjects such as temples with high thatched roofs, masks of the rain god or of his attendant jaguar or butterfly spirits, and priests singing or making offerings.

The mask of the great rain god of Teotihuacán has already been mentioned more than once. Its upper lip curls inwards at each end and it has long fangs and a forked serpent's tongue; according to Covarrubias it can be traced back to the were-jaguar spirit of La Venta.[10] On wall paintings and clay vessels alike, the gods are accompanied by numerous symbols which may be regarded as immediate forerunners of a pictographic script; and true pictographs are indeed occasionally found at Teotihuacán. Similar but later inscriptions have been found on the walls of temples at Xochicalco and on some stelae at Monte Albán. When Teotihuacán itself was finally deserted, and its last inhabitants withdrew to the area round Azcapotzalco, the Teotihuacán culture went into decline. The buildings, with their reliefs and frescoes, disappeared, and the pottery showed a falling off in aesthetic and technical standards. The clay figurines now took on a stylized aspect, and if, as may be supposed, they represented gods, they show how quickly the belief in the great god of the Classic period had given place to uninhibited polytheism.

2. MONTE ALBÁN AND OAXACA

On the other side of the mountain range which forms the southern boundary of the Mesa Central lie the great sanctuaries of Xochicalco and Monte Albán, which developed over the centuries from primitive mountain settlements into great centres of religious life.

The site known as Xochicalco (Aztec: 'place of the flower-house') centres on a small single-storey temple on the summit of a hill south-west of the town of Cuernavaca, capital of the state of Morelos. This temple is faced with large andesite slabs carved, like the façade of the Temple of Quetzalcoatl at Teotihuacán, with great feathered serpents. These are stylized in a different way from those in Teotihuacán but they stand out in equally bold relief. Among their sinuosities sit priests accompanied by cartouches inscribed with hieroglyphs some of which seem to indicate that the temple was built as a result of a calendar reform.

On a very much larger scale than Xochicalco is the complex of buildings erected on the artificially levelled summit of Monte Albán, 1300 feet above the Oaxaca valley. Two huge terraces with wide projecting stairways and sunken courtyards, nine temple pyramids and a small block of dwellings (doubtless for the priests) surround and divide a longitudinal plaza. As at Xochicalco, there is also a ball court, a feature which is absent in Teotihuacán and which seems to have originated as an architectural form among the Maya, after they had taken the ball game itself over from the La Venta culture and made it the focus of a cult laden with religious symbolism.

As a similar court (Aztec: *tlachtli*) appears in almost any temple complex of any size right down to the Spanish conquest, it might be well at this point to give a short description of it.

The *tlachtli* was a court shaped like an H with an exaggeratedly long central limb generally orientated either north–south or east–west, on either side of which was a wall or platform which might serve for the spectators or be occupied by a temple. The two teams took up their positions at either end of the field of play. The object of the game was to propel the heavy rubber ball into the opponents' half of the court without touching it with any part of the body other than the knees, thighs or buttocks. Later, in Postclassic times, the decisive move in the game was to get the ball through one of two vertical stone rings set into the walls; the ball represented the sun (hence the taboo on touching it with the hands) and the rings represented either sunrise and sunset or the equinoxes.[11]

The façades of the temple pyramids on Monte Albán bear purely abstract ornaments. They are the first Mesoamerican structures to use circular columns – at first built up of masonry, later monolithic – to form colonnades, to support the ceilings of large rooms and to divide wide doorways.

These innovations gained ground slowly in the course of four architectural phases, the first and second of which (Monte Albán I and II) remained under the dominance of the La Venta culture, with façades decorated with the grotesque figures in bas relief known as *Danzantes* ('dancers') which recall the stunted 'baby face' jungle spirits of the Gulf Coast.

The Monte Albán III phase saw the finest flowering of the Monte Albán style, particularly in tomb design. Nowhere else in ancient Meso-america did the tomb develop into an independent art form.

The typical Monte Albán tomb, at first a simple stone box or cist, evolved into a rectangular sepulchral chamber hollowed out of the rocky ground and finally into a shaft grave with steps leading down to its narrow entrance. The walls were plastered, the roof consisted of horizontal stone slabs or a simple triangular corbelled vault, and the door, framed in massive blocks of stone, was a single slab. In three of the walls of the chamber there were niches, which in time reached down to the floor and gave the chamber a T-shaped or cruciform ground plan. On the walls were polychrome paintings similar in style and content to certain frescoes at Teotihuacán (third phase), and representing processions of gods. The door-slab was covered in glyphs and bas-relief figures.

Although the great period of Monte Albán was roughly contemporary with that of Teotihuacán, the two sites are laid out quite differently. There is, however, a close resemblance between the plan of Monte Albán and that of the Classic Maya centres, and the resemblance is enhanced by the presence, in front of the temples and in the courtyards or plazas, of inscribed stelae similar to those at Copán and Quiriguá. Some of these stelae are rectangular, one is round, and inscriptions and reliefs appear on one or two sides or all round them. The bar-and-dot system of numerals – although not the hieroglyphic script – is the same as that used by the Maya. Most of the human figures in the reliefs are surmounted by the stylized jaguar-mouth motif, symbolizing the sky, which originated in the La Venta culture. Under each figure appears a mountain symbol enclosing a hieroglyph which represents the name of a town. The figures are thus the gods or other representatives of conquered cities. Among the human-shaped figures appears the occasional jaguar god, a reminder of the were-jaguars of the La Venta culture.

The gods of Monte Albán appear even more clearly on the large clay 'funerary urns' which were set up either in the tomb chamber itself or in a niche above the entrance to receive votive offerings. The figure of the god, modelled in clay, appears on one side of the vessel only. In Monte Albán II tombs there are also clay figures and busts, with realistic and exquisitely modelled human features, which probably represent the dead rather than the gods. In Monte Albán III and IV the figures themselves became progressively obscured by quantities of garments, attributes and symbols, although the naturalistic rendering of the face persisted wherever the features were not those of a god. The god most frequently depicted on the urns is the rain god. His whole face is covered with a grotesque mask, its eyes bordered with thick folds of 'flesh', its nose a flat rectangle. From its wide mouth protrude fangs and a forked tongue. Other effigy vessels show: his companion the young corn god, whose strange face with its trunk-like upturned nose also appears on the façade of the Temple of Quetzalcoatl in Teotihuacán; the old god of fire with his wrinkled face; a jaguar god; and a bat god who is another of the oldest members of the Mesoamerican pantheon. A mask of this deity made out of twenty-five separate parts of dark green jadeite has been found in a Monte Albán II tomb. He also appears frequently in Maya territory.[12]

Cultural currents from many major centres in Mesoamerica – La Venta, Teotihuacán and the Maya cities – meet and unite at Monte Albán. Which ethnic group was it that achieved this synthesis? Monte Albán is usually thought to have belonged to the Zapotecs who still inhabit the Oaxaca valley. However, what we learn of their religion from Burgoa and the other historians of the Spanish conquest period is hard to reconcile with the material evidence found at Monte Albán. Many of their religious ideas and practices were undoubtedly introduced by the Mixtecs, who conquered the Oaxaca valley at the end of the Monte Albán IV phase and during the Monte Albán V phase. In one of the tombs at Monte Albán (of which the site contains more than a hundred and fifty), the famous Tomb 7 which was opened by Alfonso Caso in 1932, lies a Mixtec ruler surrounded with hundreds of the products of the sophisticated Mixtec craftsmen. The bones and grave goods of the previous Zapotec inmate of the tomb had been removed. Similarly the Mixtecs took possession of the palaces of Mitla, built in the Monte Albán IV phase, which lie further east, and decorated the stone lintels with frescoes in the style of their own pictographic manuscripts. These structures are no more Mixtec in origin than is Tomb 7; they are a continuation of the architectural traditions of Monte Albán; but their overall arrangement shows that they were influenced by the late Maya architecture of Yucatán, and their mural decorations copy Mixtec motifs. The palaces consist of halls built on low terraces round quadrangles; their walls are decorated with purely geometrical stone mosaics. Under two of these structures were found half-sunken chamber tombs showing the cruciform ground plan which typifies the last phase of Monte Albán tomb building.

2. EL TAJÍN AND VERACRUZ

The third region in which Classic Mexican culture developed to a high level corresponds roughly to the modern state of Veracruz, with the exception of the region in the far south of the state which was the seat of the Preclassic La Venta culture.

Just as it is difficult to establish a link between La Venta and the Historic Olmecs, the Classic culture of central and northern Veracruz cannot readily be identified with the Totonacs who occupied this whole area at the time of the Conquest – and who still occupy the northern part of it. This is true despite the fact that an early written source describes the Totonacs as old-established inhabitants and even credits them with the building of Teotihuacán. El Tajín, the main centre of Classic Veracruz culture, and the unique stone monuments elsewhere which show the same sculptural style, have nothing identifiably in common with the ruined city of Cempoala, which was the principal Totonac centre at the time of the arrival of the Spaniards.

The El Tajín culture was bounded on the north by the territory of the Huaxtecs, a Maya tribe which, in an almost undisturbed history of two thousand years, was influenced in turn by the Preclassic, the Classic and the Postclassic cultures of the Mesa Central. It was not until the last years of pre-Columbian history that the Huaxtecs attempted ambitious buildings, monumental stone carvings and coloured murals which throw light not only on their art but also on their original religion.

Huaxtec mural painting was strongly under the influence of the art of the Mixteca–Puebla culture; but the stone sculptures show a strong individuality which gives the Huaxtecs a particular interest to the historian of religion.

A well if rather stiffly carved statue from Huaxtec territory shows a man carrying a human skeleton on his back; this is reminiscent of the Janus-like double figures which represent Life and Death in certain pictographic manuscripts from Puebla.[13] Another Huaxtec sculpture shows a sky god, falling or floating downwards, who appears in the same pose above the portals of the late Maya temples of Yucatán. Two reliefs from near the southern borders of Huaxtec territory show priests piercing their tongues with thorns, a form of self-wounding which was also practised in southern Puebla and among the Totonacs. Like all priestly activities, it was thought to have been originated by the god and priest king, Quetzalcoatl. The cult of this deity, in his aspect as the wind god (in which he was known to the Aztecs as Ehecatl), began among the

23

Huaxtecs, as did the cult of the earth goddess Tlazolteotl. Like the Aztecs and Totonacs after them, the Huaxtecs built circular step pyramids in honour of the wind god, whom they depicted wearing the pointed cap and the vertical fan of feathers on the nape of his neck which are his special attributes.

In the year 1785, in the jungles of northern Veracruz, where countless oil-derricks now stand, a large ruined city was discovered. Its main temple pyramid was known to the Totonacs who lived in the surrounding area as Tajín (lightning), which would indicate that it was once sacred to a rain and thunderstorm god who bore the name of Tajín and corresponded to the Cocijo of the Zapotecs, the Tlaloc of the Aztecs, and the Chac and Tohil of the Maya, all of whom were rain gods closely related to the great god of Teotihuacán. The seven-tiered Pyramid of the Niches is one of the most beautiful pre-Columbian buildings in Mexico. Its tiers, like those of the temples in Teotihuacán, consist of alternately vertical and sloping elements built up of layers of sandstone slabs. The vertical panels are pierced by numerous square niches, and similar niches appear in shrine-like projections in the middle of the raised stairway which leads up the side of the pyramid. The niches are clearly purely decorative elements; they provide contrasts of light and shade which give the whole building life and grace.

Certain other buildings in El Tajín have walls compartmented in the same way as the Pyramid of the Niches. In some cases the niche encloses a key pattern or step-and-fret.

Pyramids with niches are found only at El Tajín and in the north of the state of Puebla; but carvings similar to those at El Tajín appear in many other sites not only in the neighbouring highlands but along the whole length of the Gulf Coast as far as Guatemala, El Salvador and Honduras.

Here as elsewhere in Mesoamerica, no temple precinct is complete without its ball court; both the ball courts at El Tajín have bas reliefs on their walls in the characteristic El Tajín style. Ellen Spinden considers that the reliefs on one of the courts depict the initiation of a young warrior into the order of eagle knights, a subsequent ceremony of some kind and his death by sacrifice in the ball court itself.[14] The great religious significance of this scene (and of the ball game in general) is apparent from the fact that it includes a skeleton apparently rising from an urn; perhaps this is one of the dead heroes of the tribe.

The El Tajín style in sculpture is characterized not so much by its representations of the human figure as by the ornamental frame in which they are set and the network of skilfully disposed scrollwork

24

ornaments which encloses them and which, in spite of its creeper-like appearance, is based on animal forms stylized almost out of recognition. In the linear friezes which run above and below the El Tajín ball-court reliefs, the animal forms can still just be recognized: above, a 'cloud serpent' and below an earth or water monster. We have already encountered this tendency on the part of ancient Mexican artists to depict all earthly human life in a framework of natural phenomena, on the stelae of Monte Albán; and it reappears in Toltec, Aztec and Maya art. Similar scrollwork ornaments spread from the coastal region to Teotihuacán, where they appear in frescoes and on clay vessels from a fairly early date. More important still is their use in a number of detached sculptures which represent ancient Mexican stone carving at its finest. These sculptures take strange forms which have no counterparts anywhere in the world, and which are known as *yugos* ('yokes'), *hachas* ('axes') and *palmas* ('palmate stones'). These names signify nothing with regard to the use or significance of the ornaments themselves, but they are universally used by archaeologists and I have therefore retained them here. The sculptures are not only outstanding works of art but also unique sources of information on the religion of the Classic period in Mexico.

The 'yokes', which are more like stone horseshoes than yokes, are carved from a hard, heavy, close-grained greenish stone (diorite, diabas, etc.). The outer side of the object usually depicts a frontal view of a stylized toad, its body either polished smooth or covered with scrollwork ornaments. Other motifs – an owl, a human being squatting like a toad – appear less frequently. Another type, almost equally common, has a human face in the centre of the horseshoe, facing outward, and a profile serpent's head at each end. As the toad was an earth symbol to the Aztecs, and the 'yoke', seen from above, resembles a cave (thought of in ancient Mexico as an entrance to the underworld), it may be supposed that these objects played some part in the burial of the dead. And indeed 'yokes' have been found with human skulls and other bones deposited inside them.[15] The 'yoke' must have served to enclose the dead man and protect the living against his dangerous magic powers. The owl too, as a nocturnal bird, had a connection with the underworld. As for the other type of 'yoke', with a serpent's head at each end, Covarrubias has pointed out that it is none other than the ubiquitous Maya sky symbol, the double-headed serpent.[16] The 'yokes' were probably stone reproductions of the stiff leather or wooden girdles worn by ball players. (Players wearing these girdles can be seen, hands raised to invoke a divine blessing on their game, on some stelae from Cozumalhuapa, in Guatemala, which are now in Berlin.) The ball game was a religious act. The ball court represented the sky; and the ball player was a man who stood under the special protection of Heaven. This is why he placed the sky serpent about his hips.

The *hachas* and *palmas*, too, seem to have had some connection with the ball game. They, or rather their wooden originals, can be seen attached to the girdles of the ball players on the frieze at El Tajín. We do not know what they signify; but the extraordinary variety of forms in which they appear suggests that they too played an important symbolic role.

The *hachas* are thin flat carvings, so called because most of them are shaped rather like an axe-head. They have a projection or a hole in the back which suggests that they were either set into a wall or attached to some larger object. They represent grotesque male faces with pointed features, the faces of old men, skulls, or whole human or animal figures. It has been suggested that they are heraldic emblems belonging to participants in the ball game.

The *palmas*, or 'palmate stones', show as much variety of form as do the *hachas*. They are carved from a softer stone and look more like paddles than palm fronds. They are always triangular in section, and have one concave surface on which they stand. They represent turkeys, pelicans, alligators, human figures; often the front is carved with a human figure and the back with a figurative relief. They are found only in the neighbourhood of the town of Jalapa, and they appeared only in the last phase of the El Tajín culture, when the *hacha* was already a thing of the past and the first Toltec influences were beginning to reach the Gulf Coast. Consequently they are often decorated with warriors, weapons and scenes of human sacrifice, subjects otherwise unknown in the art of the Classic cultures. One *palma*, which bears on the front a bust of a winged skeleton, has on the back a representation of a butterfly fluttering round a flower. In Aztec art this signifies the soul of a fallen warrior.[17] Nevertheless these late carvings do belong to the cultural sphere of El Tajín culture, as their scrollwork ornaments show.

Pyrites mirrors with carved slate backs, showing figures of gods surrounded by the tangled scrollwork ornaments of the El Tajín style, have been found as far afield as Guatemala. Together with the 'yokes', *hachas* and *palmas*, these give us a picture of an artistic style which although deeply imbued with religious emotion, was much closer to the baroque linear exuberance of early Maya art than to the hieratic severity of the Teotihuacán style. Strangely enough a closer parallel still is to be found in early stone and bronze vessels from China; this extraordinary fact must go on record without any immediate prospect of an explanation. It is probable that the El Tajín culture, like that of the Maya, has its roots in the La Venta civilization; the spiral ornaments on the great stone trough at Tres Zapotes, which coil about tiny figures battling against celestial adversaries, might well have evolved into the characteristic scrollwork of the El Tajín style.

A number of stone monuments which also date from the transitional period between Preclassic and Classic have been found at two sites in the coastal plain between the port of Veracruz and the Río Papaloapan. Significantly the stelae of Cerro de las Mesas, two of which bear dates corresponding to AD 468 and AD 593 respectively, carry representations of the were-jaguar mask of La Venta, while the stone of El Mesón bears the double-headed serpent of the stone 'yokes'.[18]

The Teotihuacán culture left its mark on the Classic Veracruz culture not in religious stone-carving but in the non-religious pottery figurines of the Remojadas style, named after a site in the vicinity of the subsequent Totonac capital, Cempoala.[19] These are well-modelled figurines, mostly of women dressed in skirts and *ponchos*, sitting on a sort of throne, standing on litters or joyfully dancing. The highest artistic achievement of Remojadas pottery lies in the 'laughing-face' figurines found around Cerro de las Mesas. With their heads broadened artificially by frontal-occipital compression, their filed teeth and their hair shaved into intricate patterns, they give the impression of being a population radically different from the highland tribes.

Neither the figurines nor the clay vessels of the Remojadas style, almost all of which are decorated with figures of animals, have anything in common with the pottery of the later, historical culture of this central part of the coast of Veracruz. Like the architecture of Cempoala, Postclassic Veracruz pottery stems from the Mixteca–Puebla culture. On the side of one of the pyramids at Cempoala, for instance, there are paintings incorporating sun, moon and star symbols, elements of the astral cult which was to dominate the religious life of Mesoamerica in the Postclassic period.

3. POSTCLASSIC CULTURES

For our knowledge of pre-Columbian Mexico in Postclassic times we still rely heavily on the evidence of the buildings, sculptures and other material remains of the age; but pride of place must of course go to the written sources.

The earliest of these in date are the relations of the Spanish *conquistadores*, explorers, missionaries and administrators; but these vary greatly in value. The most important from the point of view of the historian of religion are naturally those of missionaries, monks and secular priests such as Toribio de Benavente Motolinía (one of the 'twelve apostles' of Mexico), Olmos,[20] Mendieta, Torquemada and Burgoa, and of their successors Darán and Múñoz-Camargo, half-Indians who stood closer to the old traditions and found it easier to see things from the Indian point of view. Once a few natives had learned to read and write Spanish they felt the desire to tell the story of their forefathers and to speak up for them, especially with regard to their religion, which was regarded by the Spaniards as the work of the devil. These Indian chroniclers were mainly descended from the intellectual *élite* of their people. They therefore used the best available sources and wrote books in their own language, Náhuatl, which had proved its value as a literary medium in the hymns and epic poems of the previous age. Unfortunately not all the chronicles of native writers are known in the original Náhuatl versions; but several have come to light in the last few decades. Apart from Tezozomoc and Chimalpahin, two scions of ruling dynasties from the Valley of Mexico, there are several very important anonymous chroniclers such as the authors of the *Historia de los Reynos de Colhuacán y de México* and of the *Historia Tolteca Chichimeca*.

By far the most important source written from the native point of view is the monumental history compiled by the Franciscan scholar Bernardino de Sahagún. Sahagún arrived in Mexico City (Tenochtitlán) in 1529, five years after the Spanish conquest, and worked there until his death in 1590, first as a missionary and later as a teacher at the College of his order. During this period he gathered round himself a group of knowledgeable Aztecs whose accounts of pre-Columbian history he wrote down in Náhuatl with the help of his native pupils. Some parts of this huge mass of material he translated into Spanish himself, and parts of it have been published in Náhuatl, mainly with German translations. Sahagún's work is more important for our present purposes than any other Aztec text because of the many chapters dealing with Aztec gods, religious festivals, myths, magic, the priesthood and calendar lore.

The most important group of sources apart from the post-Conquest written texts consists of the pictographic manuscripts. Even after the Conquest the style of pictographic writing remained unchanged for some time; it was a long time before remembrance of the lost native civilization faded from men's minds. Often the native chronicles themselves base their accounts on these documents,[21] some of which deal mainly with history, some mainly with religious subjects such as divination and calendar lore. The manuscripts can be divided into two main groups:

(a) Aztec. The richest sources of religious information are the pre-Conquest *Codex Borbonicus* in Paris and two post-Conquest works, the *Codex Telleriano-Remensis* (also in Paris) and the *Codex Magliabechi* in Florence.

(b) Mixteca–Puebla. As the composite name suggests, these documents fall into two clear categories. The Puebla codices deal with religion, divination and the calendar: the inexhaustible *Codex Borgia*, discovered in Cholula and now in Rome, the *Codex Vaticanus* B in Rome, the *Codex Fejérváry-Mayer* in Liverpool and the *Codex Laud* in Oxford. The eight Mixtec codices now in Vienna, London, Oxford and Mexico City deal with the history of the Mixtecs themselves, a people still living in the north of the state of Oaxaca. They cover a period of some eight hundred years, only the earliest part of which appears in mythical disguise.

Until the end of the nineteenth century the meaning of these precious documents was largely unknown. The spell was broken by Eduard Seler in 1887–8 with his first commentaries on the *Codex Borgia* and the Aztec codices. Since then so much progress has been made that the interpretation of the representational and symbolic content of these codices (and pictographs carved on the monuments) no longer poses any major difficulty; it would of course be misleading to use the word 'read' in connection with these purely pictographic documents.

The predominantly historical information contained in the Mixtec codices was elucidated much later, by the English scholars J. Cooper Clark (1912) and Richard Long (1926), and above all by the great Mexican archaeologist Alfonso Caso (1946, etc.).

Hand in hand with the elucidation of the codices went a progressively deeper understanding of the nature of ancient Mexican religion. The Swiss theologian J. G. Müller, in a work on ancient American religions published in 1855, showed considerable insight into Aztec beliefs and customs; but very few authentic sources were yet available. No worker before Seler had the whole immense mass of extant source material at his disposal. Seler's own principal contribution was his work of exegesis on Aztec iconography and symbolism, which was successfully continued by Hermann Beyer. Especially in his later works, however, Seler has an unfortunate tendency to over-emphasize the elements of astral myth in ancient Mexican religion, neglecting the radical transformation which took place under the influence of priestly astrology and calendar lore. Konrad Theodor Preuss often falls into the same trap, but his study of two modern western Mexican tribes, the Cora and the Huichol, whose religion is closely related to that of the Aztecs, put an end to a great many misconceptions. Lewis Spence, in his *The Gods of Mexico*, offers an objective introduction to the facts and the problems of the subject.

The account of Toltec religion which follows is largely based on archaeological material. The religion of the Aztecs and that of the older but closely related Mixteca–Puebla culture are dealt with together; and what little we know of the religion of the Tarascans, Zapotecs and Totonacs, the direct heirs of the Preclassic and Classic Mexican cultures, is discussed in a third section. The religions of modern, mainly Christian-influenced peoples can be touched on only in passing.

3. THE TOLTECS

For the Aztecs, history begins with the Toltecs, the 'people of Tollan'. In Náhuatl, Tollan means 'place of the reeds' but its original meaning was probably 'royal city'; its name is now Tula, and it lies some fifty miles north of Mexico City, in the state of Hidalgo.

Of the two and a half thousand years of cultural development before the Toltecs, the Aztecs had only the haziest memories; instead they told the story of four defunct ages of the world which had preceded the Toltec empire, each of them terminated by a natural disaster which destroyed all living things. The surprisingly short historical memory of the Aztecs is as characteristic of them as is the holy number four which they believed to govern time and space, men and gods, earth and heaven.

In early Aztec records even the Toltecs are rather shadowy figures, although they were said to speak a language allied to that of the Aztecs and to have migrated from the same homeland in north-western Mexico. It was not until archaeologists excavated Tula itself that the legendary empire of Tollan became a solid historical reality, and it became apparent that the Aztecs were in many respects the direct heirs of the Toltecs, especially in their religion and religious art.

The chronology of the Toltecs now also received a factual basis. According to the *Historia de los Reynos*, the Toltecs had ten kings whose reigns (taking into account the constant error of two 52-year Calendar Rounds which has been detected in this chronicle) span the period from

AD 856 to AD 1168. The fifth ruler, Ce Ácatl, was a priest-king who assumed the name of the god Quetzalcoatl ('feathered serpent'). Ce Ácatl-Quetzalcoatl was an outsider invited to assume the kingship in 977, and his arrival ushered in the greatest period of Toltec history. After a short time he was expelled by 'hostile spirits' – by which is clearly meant a strong religious opposition – migrated with his adherents to the Gulf Coast and thence to the Yucatán peninsula, and spent many years among the Maya. He died on his return to Tollan in AD 997. Five reigns later, in 1168, the Toltec kingdom came to an end under a secular king called Huemac. The end came as a consequence of famine, epidemics and the sack of Tollan itself by barbarian invaders; according to the Aztecs the Toltecs brought these disasters upon themselves by sinning against divine and human laws. The Toltecs dispersed and founded smaller city-states in the Valley of Mexico and on the Puebla plateau.

This version, contained in several different written sources, is confirmed by a rock relief near Tula which gives the dates of Ce Ácatl's accession and the fall of Tollan as 980 and 1171 instead of 977 and 1168, and by the Maya chronicles which place Ce Ácatl's stay in Yucatán between the years 977 and 999, and which give him the name of Kukulcán, an exact Maya translation of Quetzalcoatl.

This agreement between Maya and Aztec sources has more than a purely chronological importance. It confirms the appearance, for the first time in Mesoamerican cultural development, of a historical figure of some stature. Quetzalcoatl-Kukulcán is described by Aztec sources as a religious reformer who introduced into Tollan the exclusive veneration of the two primordial deities Ometecuhtli and Omecihuatl, and who allowed only bloodless sacrifices, founded traditions of sacerdotal lore and ritual, promoted the development of the arts and crafts and erected major religious buildings. In Yucatán, although his principal achievements were as a statesman and city-builder, he was also a great founder of temples. All this information is confirmed by the numerous parallels which exist between the art and religion of the cities of Tula in central Mexico and Chichén Itzá in Yucatán; although it must be remembered that the original Toltec settlements in Yucatán were not only extended and developed under Maya influence but also enriched by many alien Maya cultural elements.

The art and architecture of the Toltecs, and above all the religious factors on which they depend, cosmology, theology and ritual, are better known than those of many other civilized Mesoamerican peoples. It is even thought that the personal influence of Quetzalcoatl-Kukulcán

31

can be detected particularly in the buildings which have traditionally been attributed to him.

Thus the oldest Toltec building at Chichén Itzá is a round temple, the Caracol, a form previously unknown in Maya territory but in common use in Mexico for temples of Quetzalcoatl. The principal temple of Chichén Itzá, the Castillo, is also traditionally attributed to Kukulcán, which may explain the fact that this structure is a particularly clear example of the symbolic structure of the Mexican pyramid. Its nine tiers and four stairways with a total of 364 steps (plus one extra step up to the sanctuary on the terminal platform) make it a stone symbol of the nine heavens of Mexican cosmology, and of the nine days in the year on which the sun enters them in turn. This symbolism also explains the fact that the stone balustrades of the four flights of steps represent feathered serpents, and that the wide doorway to the sanctuary is divided by pillars in the form of feathered serpents carrying the lintel on their tails; the feathered serpent was the Toltec sky symbol.

Tradition has it that Ce Ácatl himself, who had after all assumed the name of 'feathered serpent', built a temple with feathered-serpent pillars at Tula; this must be the Temple of the Morning Star, excavated in 1940, which was destroyed with particular thoroughness by his opponents in 1168.

Both the Castillo at Chichén Itzá and the Temple of the Morning Star at Tula follow the style of the Classic pyramid in that each of their tiers consists of a sloping batter and a slightly projecting upper panel. The tiers of the Temple of the Morning Star and the Temple of the Warriors of Chichén Itzá, like the tiers of the pyramids at Teotihuacán and Xochicalco, were covered with sculptural decorations.

Despite their links with the past, both these Toltec pyramids show one marked departure from Classic tradition. At the foot of the stairway in each case there is a large colonnaded hall. This is a clear sign of a radical change in the social and religious structure of Mesoamerican life which followed upon the arrival of the Toltecs in the Mesa Central. Theocracy had largely been superseded by what J. Eric S. Thompson calls 'aggressive militarism'.[22] The warriors had become the ruling class, and the priests no longer formed an indispensable link between god and man. Nor was the dark, narrow temple sanctuary any longer the only possible place of worship. At religious festivals warriors forgathered in large numbers and required light, open halls with their own altar platforms and sacrificial stones. The ball courts too, several of which have been found in both Toltec capitals, now took on an even greater importance than before; as symbolic representations of the firmament they were ideal centres of worship for the astral religion which became dominant in Postclassic times. The largest of the four ball courts at Chichén Itzá, 272 feet long from north to south, was probably reserved for ritual purposes; this would explain why it is lavishly ornamented with sculptures and frescoes. The interiors of two small temples which adjoin the ball court at either end are decorated with large reliefs depicting religious ceremonies. The Temple of the Jaguars, which stands on top of the east wall of the ball court, is decorated inside with frescoes. This is a highly characteristic example of Toltec architecture, and only the stone corbelled vault inside is derived from the Maya. All the Toltec temples at Chichén Itzá have vaults of this type instead of the flat slab ceilings found in Tula.

Between the ball court and the Temple of the Warriors are three massive stone platforms which are exact counterparts of those which once stood between the great temple and the ball court in the Aztec capital Tenochtitlán.[23] Reliefs on the sides of the three platforms at Chichén Itzá show that they served the same purpose as those in Tenochtitlán; one bore the stone basin which held the sacrificial blood, one carried the skull rack (*tzompantli*) and the third was the place where the 'gladiatorial sacrifice' took place.

The stone sculptures within and at the entrance to the Temple of the Warriors on top of its pyramid are of three types which originated at Tula and which still formed part of the necessary equipment of Aztec temples: squatting human figures which were used ceremonially as torch and banner bearers; a 'chacmool', a reclining figure, holding in its lap a bowl to contain offerings of liquor or blood, which is the *leit-fossil* or archaeological trade-mark of Toltec influence; and an altar slab supported by four small Atlantean figures known to the Aztecs as 'supporters of the sky' because of the feathered serpent (a sky symbol) carved on the sides of the slab.

The feathered-serpent pillars of the Temple of the Warriors are square in section (those of the Castillo and the Temple of the Jaguars are cylindrical) and on its façade images of the Toltec god of the morning star alternate with masks of the Maya rain god. The fusion of Toltec and Maya cultures is further illustrated by the great North Colonnade which adjoins and partly intersects the walls of the Warrior Temple. Its roof was supported not by four-sided pillars like those of the older galleries but by cylindrical undecorated pillars with rectangular capitals such as frequently appear in later Maya buildings.

This strange mixture of Toltec and Maya forms also appears in much of the representational art of Chichén Itzá. The Toltec pantheon and

Toltec ritual are preserved; Chichén Itzá contains many examples of the four basic religious motifs brought by the Toltecs from the Mesa Central: two of them in animal shape (the feathered serpent and the eagle–jaguar combination) and two in human shape (the sun god and the god of the morning star). The feathered serpent was a creation of the Classic period, but had changed its significance; from a water and vegetation symbol it had become a sky symbol. The eagle and the jaguar represented the earthly warrior caste whose duty it was to feed the sun and the morning star with the blood and the hearts of sacrificial victims. The sun and the morning star themselves were the heavenly warriors whose missiles were their rays. They were therefore always shown with spear and spear thrower: the sun god in profile, sitting in a circle of rays of light, and the morning star god seen full-face, gazing out from the jaws of a plumed being with the features of a jaguar and the forked tongue of a serpent.

These deities are represented in other guises as well, both in Tula and in Chichén Itzá. The 'sun-close-to-the-earth' (in Náhuatl, *tlalchi-tonatiuh*), i.e. the rising sun, was represented, as J. Eric S. Thompson has shown, by a recumbent human figure with the attributes of the rain god, carrying a torch.[24] According to Hugo Moedano, the four colossal stone Atlantean figures of warriors which support the roof of the Temple of the Morning Star at Tula represent the god of the morning star, as do the skeletons emerging from the jaws of snakes shown in the bas-relief frieze on the 'serpent wall' which runs parallel with the north side of this Temple.[25] These figures are reminders of the long journey through the underworld from which the morning star emerges when it rises in the sky. On their heads the Atlantean warriors of the Temple of the Morning Star wear the turquoise-encrusted diadem which became the sign of kingship among the Aztecs; each wears on his back a round ornamental disc with four symmetrically arranged turquoise serpents (a sun-symbol) and on his chest a flat ornament, shaped like a stylized butterfly, which was one of the attributes of the fire god.

This close connection between kingship and warriorhood on the one hand and fire, sun and morning star on the other is characteristic of Toltec and Aztec religion in general. In no other Mesoamerican city do warriors occupy so prominent and central a position in the life and religion of the state as they do in Chichén Itzá, where they can be seen standing in majestic poses on doorposts and pillars and, on temple friezes, marching in solemn processions or charging their enemies in the heat of battle.

On a rock relief near Tula, and in the little temple behind the Temple

34

of the Jaguars at Chichén Itzá, the priest-king himself, Ce Ácatl-Quetzalcoatl, appears accompanied by his *alter ego*, a feathered serpent which rears behind him in massive coils; the relief in the little temple at Chichén-Itzá, a ritual scene, does not, however, represent the priest-king himself but the wooden idol which the Toltecs erected after his death and which they adorned with a 'serpent mask' which seems to have been one of his attributes even before he left Tollan. This mask, originally made of turquoise mosaic, was replaced on the wooden idol by a mask built up of strips of beaten gold. In 1912 this mask was recovered from the mud of the Sacred Cenote, a natural waterhole to the north of Chichén Itzá into which the Maya used to throw costly votive offerings, as well as living human beings, to appease the angry rain god in times of drought.[26] The Toltecs continued this practice; any kind of human sacrifice fitted in with their conception of man's inescapable duty to place his life at the disposal of the gods.

Their own method of human sacrifice was taken up by the Aztecs and survived until the Spanish conquest. It consisted of holding the victim down on a low stone block, opening his chest with a stone knife, and tearing out the heart. This ritual appears on the Gulf Coast as early as the Classic Veracruz period. It is depicted very realistically in several places in Chichén Itzá.[27]

Another type of blood sacrifice was self-mutilation by piercing the tongue and ears with thorns; again, we have already come across this practice on the Gulf Coast. After use, the bloodstained thorns were placed on vessels or bundles of grass. In some Toltec reliefs warriors can be seen marching in procession to venerate these sacred objects.

In the relief mentioned above, in the small temple behind the Temple of the Jaguars, three files of Toltec and one of Maya warriors can be seen marching in procession to the wooden idol of Ce Ácatl, while a group of priests make offerings of feather mantles.

But these tributes were not always paid to an actual image of a god. The sun god, for instance, was often represented by his throne, a stone bench representing a jaguar. In a mural painting in the Temple of the Jaguars this throne can be seen, surrounded with flames, under a canopy in front of which a human sacrifice is being carried out. This very throne was discovered *in situ*, still painted a brilliant red and encrusted with round plates of apple-green jade, in the sanctuary of the original structure over which the Castillo was later erected. On the seat was a wooden disc, bearing the sun symbol of four symmetrically arranged turquoise serpents, on which some pious hand had laid pieces of jade as votive offerings.

35

Jaguar thrones are also to be seen on the reliefs of Palenque (Chiapas), the great Maya city on the south-eastern borders of Mexico. Perhaps the Toltecs first saw them during their long migration through the regions of the southern Gulf Coast, from which they also took the practice of self-mutilation of the genital organs, and the phallic idol, which appear in a relief in the northern temple of the great ball court of Chichén Itzá.

It almost goes without saying that Toltec religion included observation of the heavens and a body of calendar lore; Ce Ácatl had introduced both during his reign at Tollan, and was himself identified with the morning star.[28] The upper storey of the Caracol at Chichén Itzá served as a platform for observing the sunset at the solstices and the equinoxes; and a platform in front of the Temple of the Warriors bears a relief inscribed with hieroglyphs setting out the great discovery, made long before by Mesoamerican astronomer-priests, that eight solar years exactly equal five Venus cycles each of 584 days.[29]

The sober, factual narrative of the Maya chronicles (very unlike the mythical reinterpretations of history to be found in Aztec sources) shows that the Toltec followers of the priest-king Ce Ácatl were prepared to fight to bring their unruly Maya subjects to heel. Their blood sacrifices must have served the same purpose. A fresco in the Temple of the Warriors shows them overrunning a Maya village and carrying off their captives for sacrifice. As in Aztec art, the black and white stripes painted on the naked bodies of the captives show that they are destined for the sacrificial knife.

There are also gold discs, found in the waters of the Sacred Cenote, which probably date from the period shortly after Ce Ácatl-Quetzalcoatl-Kukulcán's return to Tollan and subsequent death, and which show bloody battles and a human sacrifice. Ce Ácatl's bloodless religion seems to have been forgotten as rapidly in Chichén-Itzá as in Tula, where the unpopularity of his reforms had originally led to his expulsion.

When the Cocom, an indigenous dynasty, came to power in Mayapán (near Mérida, the present state capital of Yucatán) about AD 1200, Chichén Itzá fell into decline. Although the Cocom attracted crowds of Mexican warriors to Mayapán, this city had nothing of the former brilliance of the Toltec art and religion of Chichén Itzá. It became a purely residential city, a sea of houses from which rose a few ill-constructed temples. The stone figures of the gods gave way to clay effigy vessels and primitive wooden images of ancestors, and human sacrifice, which among the Toltecs had at least had a higher ethical meaning, degenerated into mere butchery.

The latest traces of the Toltecs in Yucatán are to be found in the old cities of the east coast of the peninsula, and particularly at Tulúm, which was still inhabited as late as 1544. Its temples show many of the characteristic forms of Toltec art such as colonnaded halls, serpent pillars and 'chacmools,' but were dedicated to Maya deities. These are depicted in the mural paintings and in the relief carving of a descending winged being which appears above several of the temple portals.

3. THE MIXTECA—PUEBLA CULTURE
AND THE AZTECS

The assertion of the *Historia Tolteca-Chichimeca* that two separate peoples, the Tolteca-Chichimeca and the Nonohualca, once lived in Tollan, leads Mexican scholars to the conclusion that Toltec culture itself sprang from the mixing of two different elements. One, the more primitive, came, like all the Chichimecs, from north-western Mexico and spoke a Uto-Aztecan language related to the Náhuatl of the Aztecs. The other group, already highly civilized, was called Nonohualca ('the dumb people') because it originally spoke a foreign language. It has been identified with the Mixtecs (and other related civilized peoples) of the mountains of Oaxaca, to the south, who could trace the ancestry of their kings back to AD 692. The Mixtecs spread from their mountain homeland, La Mixteca, as far as both oceans and brought the Oaxaca valley, as well as the southern part of the Puebla plateau, under their sway. The city of Cholula, which had already been important in the Teotihuacán period, became a centre from which Mixtec influence spread into central and northern Veracruz, northern Puebla and the Valley of Mexico. Like Teotihuacán and Tula, Mixtec culture had distant outposts, which have been excavated in Sinaloa (north-western Mexico) and in Quintana Roo and British Honduras (both in the Yucatán peninsula). It is possible that they influenced the Toltecs as well; but as less Mixtec influence is apparent in Tula than in other areas, it would be better to bear in mind simply that the Aztecs, the most recent of civilized Mesoamerican peoples, were influenced by both Toltec and Mixteca Puebla cultures.

At one time most writers on the subject tended to regard Aztec religion as a relatively independent and unified entity. But the historical record itself offers evidence to the contrary.

The Aztecs (so called after their mythical homeland of Aztlán) or Mexica (so called after Mexitli, one of the names of their national god

Huitzilopochtli) migrated into the Valley of Mexico in the late twelfth century, by which time the region had long been inhabited by civilized peoples. They founded their capital city of Tenochtitlán around 1370,[30] and did not begin their political expansion until 1430. This alone suggests that their religion must have been a mixture of very ancient and very new, alien and native elements. In addition the most popular gods of the Aztec pantheon were closely linked with the ritual calendar, which in its final form was a creation of the Mixtecs; significantly, the purely Aztec god Huitzilopochtli was not one of the calendar gods. Many Aztec deities can be traced back into the pre-Aztec past, and their origin in foreign cultures can be irrefutably demonstrated; the same is true of many ceremonies and religious practices.

As a conquering people, the Aztecs, like the Romans, naturally brought strange gods and rituals back from their wars along with material booty and captives. In the process of incorporating the gods of a conquered people into the existing pantheon, the priests often identified a new god with an existing one; or they regarded him as a particular aspect of the existing god, or allotted him a narrower field of activity. In many cases the links between the new god and the old were purely superficial; Tepeyollotli, for example, a mountain and cavern god from the Isthmus of Tehuantepec, was regarded as a particular aspect of Tezcatlipoca.

The Danish scholar Arild Hvidtfeldt points out that the Náhuatl word *teotl* did not originally mean 'god' (as it does in Huehueteotl, 'the old god') but 'holy' (in the sense of 'potent'), and that in Aztec religious texts a god is frequently replaced by his 'image' or 'surrogate', his *ixiptlatli*, which was accepted as identical with him. Hvidtfeldt concludes that Aztec theology had not yet progressed far beyond the stage of 'dynamism', in which men believe in the *mana*, the 'power' or 'strength' possessed by a living creature, an object or a happening. The *ixiptlatli* might be a figure of the god moulded in dough and eaten by the participants in some ritual, or it might be a captive sacrificed as the image of the god, whose flesh and blood the worshippers consumed; in both cases *teoqualo*, 'god is eaten', and the eater receives some of the 'power' of the god.[31] For the same reason the skin of a victim who had represented the god was worn at certain festivals.

There is no doubt that magic, the simple endeavour to acquire supernatural power, played a major part in Aztec religion; nevertheless, the idea of personal gods was already present in pre-Aztec cultures, and it is impossible to believe that the Aztecs took everything they could over from these cultures while remaining on a lower level of development in religion alone. It must be remembered, however, that Aztec documents were mainly compiled by the priests and the nobility, and so we know relatively little of the beliefs and customs of the common people, except that a number of religious ideas of great antiquity survived among them, including the belief in the 'lord of beasts' which still survives today. Most of these beliefs belong to the sphere of animism.

As far as the individual soul is concerned, Josef Haekel tells us that the belief in the shadow as a soul and in the loss of the soul in sickness and death are both derived from an idea which was widespread in ancient America, that of the *alter ego* in animal shape, so closely linked with a human individual that it suffered all the ills which affected him or her.[32] Every god also had an *alter ego*, and these were a frequent subject in pre-Columbian art. In Nicaragua and southern Colombia there are colossal Preclassic and Classic stone figures of gods and men each with his animal *alter ego* clinging to his back. In Mexico the god or man often carries the head of his *alter ego* on his own head, or peers out through its mouth, or is wrapped in its skin. The Toltec representation of Ce Ácatl-Quetzalcoatl, with the coils of his eponymous *alter ego* the feathered serpent poised behind him like a monstrous shadow, is a version of the same idea. The Aztec kings awarded helmets and costumes representing eagles, jaguars and coyotes to warriors who had shown their prowess. These ornaments were intended not only to frighten the enemy but to endow the warrior himself with the strength of the animal in whose guise he appeared. However, although the word *nagual*, used by present-day Indians of southern Mexico to denote the animal *alter ego*, is derived from the Náhuatl word for mask or disguise, *nahualli*, these warrior ornaments do not represent the individual totem animal, the *alter ego*, but a group totem. Eagles, Jaguars and Coyotes were military orders which, like the 'earth and sky folk' among North American tribes, clearly point to ancient divisions within the tribe. Some of the heraldic devices which Aztec warriors wore on their backs were also group totems. On the other hand the turquoise serpent, the humming bird, the deer and the other symbols seen on the backs of Aztec gods do represent the *alter ego*.

Before dealing with the theology of Postclassic Mexican cultures, I must refer briefly to their cosmology. According to the most ancient version, the earth is a flat disc sandwiched between the bases of two immense step-pyramids; each step of the upper pyramid represents one hour of the day and one station of heaven, and each step of the nether pyramid represents one hour of the night and one station of hell. The stream which flows round the earth and round the bases of the two pyramids is called the Chicunauhapan, 'nine stream', because there are nine heavens and nine underworlds.

The Aztecs replaced this stepped universe with a layered one and increased the number of heavens to thirteen. In the step hypothesis the highest heaven and the deepest hell lie at the apex of each pyramid; in the horizontal layer hypothesis the two constitute the top and bottom layers. The older idea is the more logical; it fits in better with the idea that the sun climbs and descends a pyramid each day (and does the reverse every night), and it also coordinates spatial and temporal ideas better than does the idea of a layered universe.

The Aztecs regarded each of the thirteen upper layers as the seat of a particular deity or natural phenomenon, and each of the nine nether layers as a region in which a succession of terrors awaited the sun and the souls of the dead.

Ideas of the after-life, too, underwent a change. Originally there were only two after-worlds: Tamohuanchan in the highest heaven and Mictlán in the deepest underworld. Tamohuanchan ('the house from which one descends' – an Aztec corruption of a Maya word) was envisaged as being rather like the paradise of the great rain god of Teotihuacán, a well-watered grove full of flowers and fruit; the peasants of the barren uplands could imagine the beyond only as the ultimate in fruitfulness. The nomadic hunters and gatherers of northern Mexico, on the other hand, thought of the highest heaven as a thorny savannah rich in game. Aztec society was dominated by the warrior, and Aztec religion by the warlike sun god. So warriors who had fallen in battle or been sacrificed by enemy peoples; kings, as holders of an essentially military office; and merchant venturers, whose perilous lives demanded considerable energy and courage, were granted a specially privileged after-life. Their souls accompanied the sun as far as its zenith, where they handed it over to the souls of women who had died in childbirth. These women, who were honoured as 'female warriors', then escorted the sun until it set. At noon, when their spell of duty ended, the souls of the warriors flew down to earth in the shape of brilliantly coloured birds and butterflies; while the 'female warriors' changed at dusk (and at solar eclipses) into night-flying ghouls (*tzitzimime*). All pregnant women were in danger of turning into *tzitzimime*; so on the night before the beginning of each new 52-year Calendar Round, when evil spirits were particularly feared, they were placed in clay maize silos and guarded by warriors. Meanwhile the rest of the population hid indoors, wearing masks of agave paper to make themselves unidentifiable.[33]

Those who did not belong to the elect eked out a dismal posthumous existence either in Mictlán or on earth, where the general run of souls migrated to the bodies of weasels, skunks and dung beetles. A dim recollection that the rain god Tlaloc had once been the principal deity led the Aztecs to give him a special position; in his kingdom of Tlalocán he had custody of the souls of lepers and of those who had drowned or been struck by lightning. He dwelt on all the cloud-covered mountain-tops; so there were in fact many rain gods (Tlaloque).

According to the older (Mixtec) belief, the earth took its origin from a crocodile living in the primeval sea (hence the use of the crocodile as the earth symbol in the *Codex Borgia*);[34] or from a rock, raised from the waters by the Mixtec supreme deities, on which the sky rests supported by a copper axe.

The Aztecs believed that the earth was originally a monstrous toad, brought down from heaven by the gods Tezcatlipoca and Quetzalcoatl, who made the parts of its body into mountains and valleys, waters and the plants of the earth. This motif recurs in the Aztec myths which tell of the creation of the agave and other food plants.[35] Many Aztec stone vessels carry the toad as an earth symbol; receptacles were often regarded as symbolizing the world.

According to Mixtec and Aztec myth the earth has passed through a number of epochs, and has been destroyed and recreated several times; the number four, applied to the four ages of the prehistoric world, corresponds to the four cardinal points. When, at the end of the last age, the sky fell, Tezcatlipoca and Quetzalcoatl transformed themselves into two trees and put it up again with the aid of four subordinate deities. In gratitude for this the supreme being made Quetzalcoatl and Tezcatlipoca rulers of the firmament, and the four inferior gods became 'supporters of the sky', an idea which had received concrete expression in Atlantean figures of Toltec art.[36]

In the beginning, when there was no earth and no heavenly bodies, fire was created; then an 'inchoate sun', then (not surprisingly in the creation myth of a calendar-obsessed civilization!) the divisions of the year. Then sky, earth and underworld appeared in turn; and the time was ripe for the appearance of the heavenly bodies. Two despised subordinate gods leaped into a fire at Teotihuacán and rose in the sky as sun and moon.[37]

The stars, some of which are known in Aztec myth as Mimixcoa ('cloud serpents'), because they are all manifestations of Mixcoatl, the god of the Pole Star, must have existed before the sun, because they served as its food. This belief must have appeared only when votaries of an astral religion, seeking celestial parallels for the myths and rituals of this world, saw the stars as prototypes of human sacrificial victims. The moon, thought of as female, appears variously as the persecutress of the stars and their ally in the struggle against the rising sun.

Josef Haekel has shown that the creation of man and the discovery of food plants appear in Aztec myth not as cosmic events but as magical acts in which Quetzalcoatl plays the part of a wizard rather than that of an omnipotent creator.[38] Thus he appears in this myth in the company of his *alter ego* or familiar (*nahualli*). He steals the 'precious bone' (made up half of male and half of female bones) from the underworld, the ruler of which exerts all his cunning to prevent him from taking it. This bone is then ground down in Tamohuanchan (here a terrestrial cave, not a part of heaven) by the earth goddess. Quetzalcoatl mixes the resulting powder into a paste with blood from self-inflicted wounds on his penis, and moulds it into the shape of man. Then he transforms himself into an ant and seeks out the food plants where they lie in the heart of a mountain, which the lightning god then splits open so that the rain gods can extract them.

There is a local myth which fits better into the framework of the creation myths outlined above than does the Quetzalcoatl myth. In this version of the story the maize god, whose body is the source of all food plants, is the son of the sun god and the earth goddess, conceived in a cave. The 'cave of origin' is an essential feature of many myths; the Náhua tribes believed that their forbears had come from 'Chicomoztoc', the 'place of seven caves', in northern Mexico. According to the Mixtecs the first man and the first woman grew from two trees which grew on the bank of the Yutatnoho, 'river of origin', near Apoala in northern Oaxaca.

Many years ago Konrad Theodor Preuss established a broad distinction between tribal and nature gods in ancient Mexican religion. Haekel places the supreme being and his descendants in a third distinct category.[39] The great god of ancient Mexico shares many of the attributes possessed by the supreme being in other religions. The Aztecs regarded him as the only 'true god' (*nelli teotl*), omnipresent and intangible as 'night and wind' (*yohualli ehecatl*), while at the same time he was the supporter of life 'by whom we live' (*ipal nemohuani*). He was 'our mother and our father', who sent the seeds of children into their mother's womb from on high, who made human beings grow and who fed them: the 'lord of our flesh' (*tonacatecutli*). He was male and female at once, thus combining the functions of begetting and childbearing; hence his title of 'god of duality' (*ometeotl*).

The supreme being played no direct part in the Creation, but Quet-zalcoatl and Tezcatlipoca, to whom he delegated it, may be regarded as his manifestations, emanations, emissaries or sons; they even share some of his titles, including *ipal nemohuani*. However, these two gods, the most prominent figures in the Mexican pantheon, appear in so many different guises that it is impossible to define them from this or any other single point of view. Early students of Mexican religion, for example, made the mistake of interpreting them in terms of an astral religion which did not appear until a very late date. There is now no doubt that Quetzalcoatl and Tezcatlipoca were originally local deities. The cult of Quetzalcoatl originated among the Mixtecs and those Náhua tribes which stood under Mixtec influence, and was carried by them to places as far afield as Guatemala, El Salvador and Nicaragua. The cult of Tezcatlipoca arose among the Toltecs of Postclassic times and the older Náhua tribes of the Valley of Mexico and the Puebla Valley.[40] The wind god Ehecatl, who was identified with Quetzalcoatl, was a Huaxtec deity.

Apart from their basic role as joint Creators, Quetzalcoatl and Tezcatlipoca frequently appear as antitheses or adversaries of each other, as in their 'historical' conflict at Tollan, where Quetzalcoatl in the guise of the priest-king Ce Ácatl was expelled by Tezcatlipoca as representative of the warriors. While Quetzalcoatl personifies the god-head in its light-bearing, positive aspect, Tezcatlipoca personifies it in its dark, negative aspect. He is the lord of the north and of night and cold, the great magician who sees what is hidden, the incalculable one who rules as he pleases. Some of the attributes shown in representations of him – the severed foot and the 'smoking mirror', worn on the side of his head, from which he takes his name – may be ancient astral attri-butes which he possesses because he is identified with the 'one-legged' constellation known to us as the Great Bear. Tezcatlipoca's *alter ego* was the jaguar; that of Quetzalcoatl the feathered serpent. There have been attempts to find connections between these symbolic beasts and the stars; the jaguar, with his spotted coat, is thought to represent the starry sky as a whole (Seler); the feathered serpent the zodiac (Beyer).

Much closer to the old pattern of tribal deities are Mixcoatl, national god of the Chichimecs, and Huitzilopochtli, national god of the Aztecs. Mixcoatl ('cloud serpent'), known in the ancient Chichimec city of Tlaxcala as Camaxtli, dimly recalls the very ancient god known as the 'lord of beasts', still worshipped by the Cora and Tarahumara of north-western Mexico, modern descendants of the nomadic Chichimecs. The advanced Mexican cultures identified him with the Pole Star; the pictographic manuscripts consequently show him with the distinguishing mark of an astral deity, a black half-mask decorated with white circles. Nevertheless the Aztecs still associated him with hunting and the north; his *alter ego* (*nahualli*) was a deer, and in his honour they carried out ritual hunts in artificial miniature savannahs.

The name Huitzilopochtli means 'humming bird on the left'; the warm sun is brought from the left-hand (i.e. south) side of the sky by the humming bird (*huitzilin*) which is Huitzilopochtli's *alter ego*. One of the Sahagún texts says explicitly that Huitzilopochtli was once an 'ordinary human being'; and one of the early Aztec warrior chiefs was indeed called Huitzilopochtli. The Aztecs deified him and carried his sacred mummy bundle with them as an oracle on their migration to their home in the Valley of Mexico. Huitzilopochtli's later identification with the sun god stems not only from his connection with the humming bird but from his warlike nature; the sun is a warrior who, as one myth tells us, chases the moon and the stars from the sky with his weapon the turquoise serpent, the *xiuhcoatl*, a symbol of fire and light.[41] In the Aztec pictographs Huitzilopochtli appears as the light-bearing counterpart of the dark Tezcatlipoca, to whom he bears a close resemblance.

The remaining gods took no part in the work of creation; their powers were strictly limited, as they were subject, even within their own spheres of influence, to the play of natural forces. As patrons of human activities and personifications of natural phenomena, they were usually anthropomorphic. They were extremely numerous, largely because one function was often allotted to a number of gods differing only in nationality. Thus the very ancient fire god, and patron of kings and warriors, Xiuhtecuhtli ('turquoise lord'), also known as Huehueteotl ('old god'), had a number of female aspects or emanations who were worshipped in various parts of the Valley of Mexico. One of these was called Itzpapálotl ('obsidian butterfly') because a stylized butterly, a flame symbol, was worn by the fire god as a pectoral ornament. Another fire goddess, worshipped in the town of Xochimilco, bore the name of Chantico ('in the house'), and represented the warlike aspect shared by all fire and sun gods; her emblem, worn on her forehead, was a torrent of fire and water, the glyph for war. The ancient indigenous earth goddess of the Valley of Mexico, whose cult was localized at the old Toltec city of Colhuacán, was Cihuacóatl ('woman serpent'). Under the name of Ilamatecuhtli ('ancient lady') she was the female counterpart of the 'old god' of fire, Huehueteotl. As life-giving mother goddess she was represented by little clay idols showing her with a child in her arms. When the Aztecs came they brought with them another earth goddess, Coatlícue ('serpent skirt'), who represented the earth in its destructive aspect, swallowing up all living beings when they die and all heavenly bodies when they set. Two grotesque colossal stone figures of this goddess which once stood in her temple at Tenochtitlán, the House of Darkness (*tlillancalli*), show her with a skirt of serpents and upraised claws like those of a beast of prey.

Alongside these native earth goddesses the Aztecs worshipped a goddess called Tlazolteotl ('filth goddess') because she was believed to eat filth, i.e. sin. Her attributes and functions clearly point to the Gulf Coast as her place of origin: the cotton which she wore as an ornament on her forehead and ears was imported from the Huaxtecs of northern Veracruz, and the custom by which her priests heard the confessions of those taken in adultery originated among the historic Olmecs of southern Veracruz. The sexual significance common to many earth goddesses of the Old and New World appears also in the phallic dances performed at her festivals.

The attributes of the rain god Tlaloc had been clearly set out in the art of Teotihuacán. Aztec stone carvings still show his characteristic mask, but this has been misinterpreted so that its eye ornaments appear as two serpents. As I have said, with the end of the Classic period this god lost his status as the most important god in the pantheon and became a straightforward nature god. According to Sahagún's text and some of the pictographs in the *Codex Borgia*, he has four pitchers from which he pours rain on to the earth; and according to which pitcher he uses, the result is a good maize crop or a harvest spoilt by vermin and frost.[42] When Tlaloc becomes angry and breaks his pitchers, the result is thunder and lightning. His consort is Chalchiuhtlicue ('precious-jade skirt'), the goddess of springs and streams. In Mixteca–Puebla art she wears a serpent's head helmet-mask; in Aztec art she appears in the costume of a noble Aztec lady. She had originally had a much wider sphere of activity, as is shown by the fact that the older Náhua peoples of the eastern and southern parts of the Valley of Mexico identified her with Xochiquetzal ('flower plume'), the youthful goddess of sexual love and of all the arts proper to woman, and the mother of the maize god.

The Toltecs regarded the water and maize goddesses as one; the rock relief at Tula shows one figure bearing the attributes of both.[43] The Aztecs had another separate maize goddess, Chicomecoatl ('7 Serpent'), who seems to have been exceptionally popular. Numerous images have been found which show her wearing an immense four-sided headdress and carrying a twin maize cob, the Aztec name of which, *chicahuaztli* ('for giving strength'), shows that it was used in magical ceremonies intended to fructify the fields.

Most of the masculine vegetation gods of the Mesa Central originated among foreign tribes. Xipe Totec, for example ('our lord the flayed one'), came from the Pacific coast of Mexico where one small tribe had long practised the ritual flaying of human victims. He appears at Teotihuacán, and among the Toltecs and Mixtecs and is easily identified by the human skin he wears as a garment or by his mask of human skin. The Aztecs adopted his cult in the reign of their sixth king, Axayacatl (1470–81), and regarded him as a god of spring; his second skin symbolizes the new garment which the earth puts on every spring. Another vegetation god is Xochipilli ('flower prince'), originally a god of the Mixtecs of Oaxaca who worshipped him as the young sun god. The helmet-mask which covers his head originally represented the head of the coxcoxtli, a jungle fowl of the tropical regions of Mexico, whose voice is the first to be heard in the dawn chorus; but this mask, like that of Tlaloc, was misinterpreted by the Aztecs, who reproduced it as a bonnet with tufts of feathers.[44] They honoured Xochipilli primarily as the god of dancers, musicians and ball players. The sun god of the Aztecs themselves, Tonatiuh ('he goes to shine'), originated among the Toltecs. The Aztec moon god was less in evidence, but can be detected in manifold disguises, principally that of the gods of pulque (agave beer), whose name, Centzon Totochtin ('the four hundred rabbits') refers to the supposed shape of a rabbit seen in the moon. Their pied faces and half-moon shaped bone nasal ornaments also betray their lunar origin. Their nasal ornament and a rabbit together make up the glyph for 'moon'. The cult of the pulque gods was strongest in what is now the state of Morelos, where their temple stood on a rocky cliff above the township of Tepochtlán, and where the harvest was celebrated with drinking bouts and sexual orgies held in their honour.

The principal temple pyramid of the Aztec capital, Tenochtitlán, was built during the reign of Moctezuma I (1441–69) on the emplacement of an earlier structure which was as old as the city itself. The pyramid was subsequently enlarged more than once by the addition of a new layer of masonry. Along with the rest of Tenochtitlán, it was destroyed by the Spaniards, who built their own Mexico City on the ruins. Excavations have revealed nothing but a part of the base of the pyramid; and yet after its last rebuilding (1487) it measured 250 × 330 feet at the base and rose in four or five tiers to a height of 100 feet. Two wide stairways were built into the façade of the structure, and the terminal platform carried two temples, one for Tlaloc and one for Huit-

zilopochtli. The serpent balustrades, a fragment of which is still in place
at the foot of the lowest layer, are a sign of long-lasting Toltec influence,
and so was the colonnaded hall which probably once stood in front of
the pyramid, and which housed bas-relief friezes showing processions
of warriors, as well as a rectangular altar bearing similar reliefs.[45]

Other characteristic Toltec art forms ('chacmools', banner holders
and altars supported by Atlantean figures) were retained but underwent
a transformation. The elaborately ornamented 'serpent wall' which
surrounds the Temple of the Morning Star at Tula reappeared in
Tenochtitlán in the shape of a low rampart the top of which was
crowned with massively carved figures of serpents. A similar serpent
wall round the pyramid of Tenayuca (north of Mexico City) is still in
existence. The Mexican archaeologist Juan Palacios sees this 'ring of
serpents' as an allusion to the serpent skirt of the Aztec earth goddess
Coatlícue.[46] The great pyramid of Tenochtitlán took its name from
Coatépetl, 'serpent mountain', on which the earth goddess gave birth
to Huitzilopochtli, and like the Toltec pyramids it also represented the
arch of heaven which the sun god daily climbs. Like most Aztec pyramids, it was orientated to face the point at which the sun sets at the
summer solstice. The astral symbolism of the pyramids themselves
was continued in the small temples which surmounted them and
which were known to the Spaniards, because of their shape, as *torres*
('towers').

In front of the great temple of Tenochtitlán lay three stone platforms
and a ball court, just as in Toltec Chichén Itzá. Also within the rectangular walled temple precinct, into which ran the four causeways linking
Tenochtitlán with the mainland, stood eight or nine smaller pyramids
bearing temples of the sun god Tonatiuh, Tezcatlipoca, Xipe Totec and
others. Outside the precinct stood the temple of Coatlícue and a round
pyramid bearing the temple of the wind god, which we can reconstruct
on the analogy of a similar temple in Calixtlahuaca on the plateau of
Toluca west of Mexico City. It is significant that of all the Aztec temples
so far discovered only two have sculptured walls. The temple of the four
hundred pulque gods near Tepoztlán is one; and the other is a temple
hewn out of the living rock of a mountain near Malinalco, in the southern Mesa Central, in the early sixteenth century. The monstrous jaws
which frame its entrance suggest that it is modelled on the cave temples
of the god Tepeyollotli, while the vigorous carvings of eagles and
jaguars within point to its use by members of the Aztec military orders
of jaguar and eagle knights, whose patron deity was Tezcatlipoca,
Tepeyollotli's Aztec counterpart.[47]

In place of reliefs and other wall decorations, the Aztec temples were adorned with detached sculptures, many of which, excavated in Mexico City and elsewhere, show late Aztec art at its highest peak of development. Whereas Toltec and Teotihuacán statues always betray their origin in the rectangular stela which dominates the sculpture of the Classic period, Aztec sculptors progressively freed themselves from this stereotype. Their art culminated in a number of masterpieces, which include some figures of the 'flayed god' Xipe Totec which are frightening in their immediacy. There are of course other Aztec sculptures in which realism is sacrificed to religious symbolism, as in the figures of the goddess Coatlícue; and these are a reminder that these statues were not made in order to give aesthetic satisfaction: they were intended as expressions of the pitiless religion and the grimly earnest philosophy of a deeply religious warrior nation.

The supreme being of the Aztecs required of his worshippers only piety, humility and exemplary conduct; he was worshipped only in prayer. Many of these prayers have been preserved, and reveal profound religious sentiment. The nature gods, on the other hand, could be encouraged, helped, guided and even on occasion coerced by means of religious ceremonies which carried a strong element of magic. Few of these ceremonies had evolved into symbolic acts like the rituals of many advanced religions; but even the bloodiest Aztec rites had a definite ethical basis. Man, in the words of an Aztec hymn, must 'pay his debt'; he must make his contribution to the preservation of the world-order even if this entails the sacrifice of his own life.[48]

According to legend, the custom of preparing for an act of worship by ablutions, fasting and sexual continence was originated by the Toltec priest king Ce Ácatl-Quetzalcoatl. The rite sometimes referred to as 'baptism', which was carried out soon after the birth of a child, was thought of as a spiritual as well as a physical cleansing. The midwife prayed that the water might wash away all the evil which the child had inherited from its father and mother.[49] People frequently fasted for as many as twenty days; priests fasted even longer, sometimes up to eighty days. They either retired to a house set aside for the purpose, or signified their separateness from the rest of the community by wearing a cord of plaited reeds.

The actual process of influencing the gods began with prayers, which often took the form of incantations. Votive offerings consisted, as they had since the age of Teotihuacán, of symbols of the gifts which were desired from the gods. One specifically Aztec form was the votive paper (*tetehuitl*) coated with latex.

Incense was burned every morning to greet the sunrise, as well as accompanying most sacrifices and offerings. Sweet smelling copal resin, or wormwood leaves, were laid in the bowl of a clay spoon-shaped censer and heated over glowing charcoal in a brazier of a type which remained almost unchanged from the age of Teotihuacán to that of Tenochtitlán. The Mixtecs placed their incense on a wooden post set upon a masonry altar.

Blood sacrifice by self-mutilation, in which the worshipper pierced or scratched his tongue, ears, chest or legs with sharp bones, thorns and obsidian knives, was practised long before Aztec times. On the Gulf Coast and in Puebla it took even more drastic forms than it did in later times; so it is legitimate to assume that the Aztecs did not learn it until after their arrival in the Valley of Mexico. When gods scarify themselves in their friezes and in their myths, the occasion is always some especially important event. The blood was smeared on agave leaves, and placed on bundles of grass or in vessels, just as it was among the Toltecs. At the beginning of each ritual self-mutilation a few drops of blood were sprinkled upwards and towards the four cardinal points.

One of the most important points of difference between Classic and Postclassic periods in Mexico is the immense increase in the rate of human sacrifice which took place during Postclassic times, particularly among the Aztecs. At the most conservative estimate, twenty thousand people were sacrificed in four days on the occasion of the last rebuilding of the great temple at Tenochtitlán in 1487. The scale on which the Aztecs practised human sacrifice can be partly explained by the fact that their almost uninterrupted series of military expeditions had led to an immense concentration of prisoners of war in the Valley of Mexico, who would have become a danger to their captors unless steps were taken to reduce their numbers.

Human sacrifice most commonly took the form of heart sacrifice, a custom which the Aztecs probably learned from the Toltecs, in whose religion it played an important part. Among the Mixtecs it was rarer, and dogs were often sacrificed in place of human beings; the same was true of the Maya.

Political circumstances alone cannot have given rise to the hideous increase in the frequency of human sacrifice among the Aztecs. The basic reason was religious; these were primarily sacrifices to the sun god, as can be seen from the Aztec names for the human victim, his heart and the sacrificial stone vessels in which it was placed; all three incorporate the word *quauhtli* (eagle), the *alter ego* of the sun god Tonatiuh. In Aztec, Toltec and Mixtec representations of the human sacrifice, the sun god is to be seen devouring the hearts of the sacrificial victims.[50] The inside of every *quauhxicalli* ('eagle vessel') was ornamented with suns; and so are the huge stone discs which once lay in the temple precinct at Tenochtitlán and which played a central part in all ceremonies of human sacrifice. On the so-called Calendar Stone a sun symbol encircles the features of the god, the date '4 Motion', glyph *Nahui Ollin*, which represents the end of the present (fifth) 'sun' or age of the world, and those representing the four prehistoric ages of the world and a circle with the signs of the 20 day names. On the outside of the Stone of Tizoc appear representatives of all the cities and regions conquered by the Aztecs up to the reign of Tizoc, their seventh king (1482–6). These stones too are *quauhxicallis* and reflect the idea, implicit in the Toltec image of the enfeebled 'sun-close-to-the-earth', that the sun requires to be fed with human blood and human hearts if it is not to remain in the underworld or stop short in its passage through the heavens. Priestly tradition said that the end of the present (fifth) age of the world would come on the day 4 Motion and so this day, as well as the end of each 52–year Calendar Round, were occasions of special anxiety.

The sacrificial victims, who were destined to turn into stars, were costumed as star gods: their bodies were painted white or with red and white stripes, and they wore white garments, feathers in their hair and the black half-mask of Mixcoatl. White was the colour belonging to the twilight before sunrise.

It was not, therefore, an innate tendency to cruelty, but a fanatical belief in man's duty to keep the sun in the sky, that led to the practice of human sacrifice and to the belief that death on the altar was a glorious end. Thus the Aztec wars in which sacrificial victims were captured were regarded as a religious duty. As Alfonso Caso has shown, this conception of warfare explains the reliefs on a stone model of a temple pyramid, the 'Teocalli de la guerra sagrada', which was excavated in Mexico City in 1926. On it a number of gods are seen worshipping the sun; in front of the mouth of each figure, as if symbolizing a prayer or a hymn, appears the glyph 'fire and water', signifying war.[51]

The Aztecs also sacrificed male and female victims – usually flayed – to their earth and vegetation gods. To the dwarfish rain gods they sacrificed small children, who were drowned in springs, water-holes and special parts of Lake Texcoco. In these sacrifices the victims were not intended as food for the god but as a symbol of the god himself, his surrogate, *ixiplatli*. This kind of sacrifice was intended to rejuvenate or reinvigorate the god-victim, as in the ritual killing of kings in some Asian and African kingdoms. Such sacrifices probably originated during the Classic period, the flaying ritual being taken over from the peoples of the Gulf and Pacific Coasts along with the cults of Xipe Totec and Tlazolteotl, and the sacrifice by drowning from the Maya of Chichén Itzá. Two other types of sacrifice, the gladiatorial sacrifice in which the victim was fettered to a stone disc with a hole in the centre and made to fight against two warriors, and the arrow sacrifice in which he was tied to a ladder-like frame and killed with arrows, were unknown to the Aztecs before their arrival in the Valley of Mexico. As Sahagún refers to these acts as 'scratching [the earth]' and 'coupling with the earth', Seler has seen them as magical acts intended to prepare the earth for sowing.[52] They originated among the Mixtecs, but they also show interesting parallels with certain rites practised by the maize-growing tribes of North America.

The festivals of the Aztec calendar, which took place at the end of each of the eighteen 20-day 'months' of the solar year, had gradually taken on the form of religious dramas: the actors were priests, warriors and victims. They reflected the sequence of natural events during the year, and were intended to influence them in man's favour.[53]

The rites in honour of the rain gods were celebrated during the dry season, and were intended to ensure timely and abundant rains; children were sacrificed by drowning, and the priests bathed by night in Lake Texcoco, miming the behaviour of waterfowl.

The rites of the earth and vegetation deities Xipe and Tlazolteotl were celebrated in spring and autumn and culminated at harvest time in phallic dances and a ritual drama in which the conception and birth of the maize was enacted.

Another group of festivals, according to Konrad Theodor Preuss, referred, at least in part, to the victory and defeat of the sun in its battles with the moon and stars. At the *Toxcatl* festival in May, when the sun stood at the zenith over Tenochtitlán, a young captive, who had been accorded divine honours as the incarnation of Tezcatlipoca for a whole year, was sacrificed. After his death a dough idol was erected to represent Huitzilopochtli who, as the young sun, took Tezcatlipoca's place, and the young warriors and their female companions danced in its honour. Huitzilopochtli did not have a ceremony to himself until the festival of *Panquetzaliztli* in November; this was a dramatic representation of his birth on 'serpent mountain' and his defeat of his hostile brothers and sisters the moon and the stars.

51

In addition to the regular annual festivals there was an eight-yearly festival based on the curious idea that the different kinds of human food (carried by masked dancers) required periodic rest and renewal. There was also a ceremony on the ominous day 4 Motion, which recurred once or twice in every year, in which the sun was represented by a captive dressed as a traveller, who slowly climbed the steps of the pyramid of the sun; this was a piece of sympathetic magic intended to ensure the continuance of the sun's daily ascent of the heavens.

The Aztecs had no ancestor cult like that which existed in Peru, although at the funeral of a fallen warrior they set up a mummy bundle in the costume of the star god Mixcoatl, to which they offered sacrifices. When a king died they sacrificed before a wooden statue dressed as Quetzalcoatl. The souls of the common dead were feared rather than reverenced; funeral customs make it clear that the intention was not only to ease their journey to Mictlán but also to prevent their return. Apart from the drowned, lepers and those who had been struck by lightning, all of whom were the property of the rain god Tlaloc, the dead were cremated. The ashes of kings were enclosed, together with a green precious stone representing the heart, inside an elaborately carved lidded stone casket, and ceremonies in their honour were continued for four years, after which time they were assumed to have completed the arduous journey to Mictlán.

The relatively unimportant part played by the spirits of the dead in Aztec and Toltec religion accounts for the absence of elaborate burials among them. The Mixtecs, on the other hand, were still building passage and chamber tombs similar to those of Monte Albán in the early Postclassic period. A later tomb in Cholula, probably built under Mixtec influence, takes the form of a small temple platform inside which were buried the uncremated skeletons of a nobleman and his wife together with that of a dog (their escort on the journey to Mictlán), pottery and a bone rasp.[54] This last was a musical instrument used at funerals, when all resonant instruments were banned. It consisted of a human femur with a row of transverse notches across which a sea-shell or a deer's shoulder blade was scraped. At other ceremonies music was made with horns, reed pipes, gourd rattles, two-tongued wooden log drums (*teponaztli*) and skin-headed drums (*huehuetl*), which often had richly carved sides; the priests blew large spiral trumpets. Two games which also have mainly ritual origins, the ball game and a board game called *patolli*, both of them originally designed to influence the course of the sun, have survived in some remote parts of Mexico until the present day.

Although magicians played an important part in the everyday life of the Aztecs as diviners, conjurors, physicians and sorcerers, the public life of this wholly theocentric people was largely dominated by priests.

Sahagún lists no less than thirty-eight different grades within the priesthood.[55] First came the high priest, usually a member of the royal family; then two dignitaries who had charge of the ceremonies which took place in the temples of Tlaloc and Huitzilopochtli on the Great Pyramid; both bore the title of Quetzalcoatl. Other senior members of the priesthood were those who carried out human sacrifices (each of these had four assistants who also acted as butchers, flaying and dismembering the bodies for the cannibal ritual known as *teoqualo*), priests charged with the burning of incense, confessors, and auxiliary priestesses who served the earth goddess Tlazolteotl.

With their black body-paint, their matted hair and their ears lacerated by self-mutilation, the Aztec priests had an uncouth and sinister appearance. They carried little bags of incense ready for use on their arms, and slung on their backs were gourds containing quids of tobacco which they chewed in order to put themselves in a trance state. They were the scholars and scientists of the community; astronomy, astrology and the calendar were all priestly responsibilities, as was the composition of the pictographic manuscripts, which were largely concerned with divination.

In all these respects the Aztecs were the heirs and continuers of the civilized peoples who preceded them, in particular the Mixtecs and the Náhua of Puebla; this is clearly shown by a comparison between the *Codex Borgia*, a manuscript written in the Puebla area, and the manuscripts of the Aztecs.

The *Codex Borgia* deals with the principal divisions of the Mesoamerican calendar: the priestly 'almanac year' of 260 days, the solar year of 365 days and the Venus period of 584 days; with the terrestrial polarities of light and dark, rainy season and dry season, etc.; and with the four quarters of earth and heaven. As well as these purely enumerative sections it contains a sacred epic in pictographic form, which according to Seler deals with the fortunes of the planet Venus in the heavens and in the underworld. We are told that the calendar had been reformed in what is now the state of Morelos by the ancient calendar gods Oxomoco and Cipactonal; as far as the locality is concerned this may be true. Classic Mexican culture had left a monument commemorating a calendar reform which does indeed stand in Morelos: the temple on Mount Xochicalco.

53

3. ZAPOTECS, TOTONACS AND TARASCANS

After the close of the Classic period, as we have seen, it becomes possible for the first time to identify extinct cultures with present-day peoples; in Mexico outside the Mesa Central this applies to the Zapotecs of Oaxaca, the Totonacs of Veracruz and northern Puebla, and the Tarascans of Michoacán. In all these cases it is difficult to establish just which elements of their religious life were indigenous survivals from Classic times and which were the result of Mixtec and Náhua influence. There are traces of Toltec influence too, although not nearly so many as can be found among the Aztecs; the square-fronted round pyramid, a few examples of which have been found at Tula, becomes more common in the area of Cempoala on the east coast and reaches its highest point of development in the *yácatas* of the Tarascans in the west, five of which stand in a row on a great platform in the Tarascan metropolis of Tzintzuntzan near Pátzcuaro. The structure and external appearance of these marks them off from all other Mexican temple pyramids; the sides are steep and divided into numerous small steps, and the platform on the top is so small that there was room only for one small temple on the round rear section.[56]

The Toltec origin of these pyramids is not entirely beyond doubt. At Teayo, in northern Veracruz, stone figures of gods in a typical late Toltec style, in which the square form of the stela is clearly recognizable, stand round a step pyramid which is purely Aztec in form. These figures are contemporary with the *Lienzo de Jucutacato*, a pictographic manuscript which tells of the immigration of Toltec craftsmen into Michoacán, and with a coloured rock painting near Ixtapantongo on the borders of Michoacán, in which a figure imitated from one of the Atlanteans which supported the roof of the Temple of the Morning Star at Tula appears at the head of a group of eight gods.[57]

The Zapotecs show few signs of Toltec influence. Their political and religious institutions, on the other hand, show many features which date from the Classic period and which point to a cultural link with Teotihuacán for which there is also archaeological evidence.[58]

In the largest of the three palace complexes of Mitla dwelt the Zapotec high priest, the *Uija Tao* ('great seer'); who was a kind of priest-king like those of Teotihuacán. Temporal matters, with the exception of the judiciary, were in the hands of a temporal prince, who resided at Zaachila, and his lieutenant, who resided at Tehuantepec. When the Spaniards arrived these two offices were held by a father and son, Cocijo Eza and Cocijo Pij. Both temporal rulers treated the *Uija*

Tao with the utmost respect and obedience; he stood in a close and special relationship with the god, whose will he revealed to the people.

The example of the Zapotecs illustrates more clearly than that of any other nation in Postclassic times the distinction between Classic theocracy and the kind of warrior-kingship under which the high priest was considered as a subject of the king. Zapotec kings wore priestly ornaments, and their name (or title) was that of the supreme god; and the institution of the *Uija Tao* throws a fascinating light on the probable nature of Classic theocracy elsewhere in Mesoamerica. He lived in his palace, strictly cut off from the outside world, and begat his successor, in some wild orgy, on a noble maiden. This was the only way of protecting the sacred office of high priest from the invidious necessity of electing or appointing a successor. Thus the Aztec legend which relates that the normally celibate Toltec priest-king Ce Ácatl-Quetzalcoatl was banished because he copulated with a woman at a feast is based on a misunderstanding. Far from being an offence, this was in accordance with an ancient and hallowed tradition. The real cause of his downfall was probably his attempt to reestablish the traditional Classic theocracy in Tollan.

The cult of the god Cocijo Pitao ('great Cocijo') was also very ancient. This god appears in the effigy vessels of the Classic Monte Albán culture and was rain god as well as supreme god; as the Lord of the Year he had close ties with the priestly 'almanac year' of 260 days; he gave his name to the first day of each of the four sections into which this was divided. Similarly the agricultural calendar of the Classic period had attached much more importance to the weather god than to the astral deities who preside over the calendar of the Postclassic period.

Next to Cocijo Pitao in importance was the corn god Pitao Cozobi, who also appears on Monte Albán vessels. In the rites of his cult he was represented by the finest cob of the corn harvest, which was ornamented and kept as a fertility fetish in a shrine in the cornfields until the next sowing.

The Zapotec jaguar god can be traced to the La Venta culture. He is a close relative of the earth and cave god common to most southern Mexican peoples, from the Mixtecs of Puebla to the Tzental of Chiapas, under very similar names such as 'heart of the kingdom', 'heart of the place', etc. He appears in the Aztec pantheon as Tepeyollotli ('heart of the mountain'). He was an oracular god whose voice was the echo.

The Zapotecs believed in the same supreme being, thought of variously as a god or as a goddess, as the peoples of the Mixteca–Puebla cultures; but there was no Zapotec sun god. There is an idol at Teotitlán del Valle in the Oaxaca valley which according to Burgoa descended from the sky in the guise of a luminous bird; this legend clearly refers, however, to the Mixtec solar deity whom the Aztecs worshipped under the name of Xochipilli.

Zapotec religious observances did not differ essentially from those of the peoples of the Mesa Central; but they did not practise human sacrifice on anything like the same scale as did the Aztecs. The priest who carried out these human sacrifices was not an important dignitary, as he was among the Aztecs, but one of the minor subordinates of the *Uija Tao*. At solar eclipses the Zapotecs sacrificed dwarfs, as these were thought to be creatures of the sky. This practice, and that of castrating those chosen for the priesthood at an early age, may possibly be a remote echo of the stunted goblins of La Venta. Among the Zapotecs the practice of confession did not apply to sexual offences only, as it did among the Historic Olmecs; it was followed by an act of penance for all the sins of the individual in which the blood from self-inflicted wounds was allowed to drip on to a cord plaited from reeds (*tola*).

The Totonacs of the Gulf Coast originally lived in a unitary state under rulers whose names (many of which are simply dates) suggest Mixtec influences; but at the time when the Spaniards landed in Mexico the southern Totonacs lived in a loose confederation of city-states. Cempoala, north-west of the present-day port of Veracruz, is the only major Totonac site about which much is known. By comparison with the quantity of archaeological information we have about the religion of the Classic cultures of the state of Veracruz, and with the detailed Spanish accounts we possess of the religious life of the other historical peoples of Mexico, our information on Totonac religion is comparatively sketchy, and we are forced to rely more on observation of present-day customs than we do in the case of other Mexican peoples.[59]

Belief in the *alter ego* was still current in the Misantla district in recent times. The tutelary spirit of each child was identified from the tracks found in ashes strewn around the house during the night of its birth. The circumcision of children, which the early accounts mention as customary in the area of the Gulf Coast further south, clearly links up with the self-mutilation of the genital organs practised in the Tehuacán area of Puebla. On feast days adult Totonacs performed another rite of self-mutilation which consisted of drawing twenty-five blades of grass, threaded on a string, through a hole pierced in the tongue.

Every three years there was a sacrifice of child victims followed by a *teoqualo* rite in which men and women alike ate a paste of seeds and tree sap mixed with the blood of the victims. The Spaniards were told that these sacrifices were intended to protect the young crops against insect pests, hail, cloudbursts and drought, which indicates that these sacrifices were carried out in honour of the rain god, and that this deity was a prominent member of the Totonac pantheon. Spanish reports also speak of a Totonac trinity consisting of the sun god, the maize goddess and their son the culture hero; this may well be a Christian interpretation of the bisexual nature of the supreme being in many Mesoamerican religions, and the frequent appearance of a creator or culture hero as his/her emanation or incarnation.

Totonac agrarian rites also included a characteristic ceremony which survives as the *juego del Volador* (flier game) performed on religious feast days by the Totonacs of Papantla (Veracruz) and the neighbouring Otomi of Pahuatlán (Puebla). Dancers, sometimes dressed as birds, climb to the top of a tall 'maypole' and launch themselves into space holding on to long ropes attached to a revolving cross-piece at the top. Pictographic manuscripts from Mixtec territory show that the *Volador* ceremony was once coupled with the Mixtec 'arrow sacrifice', part of the great sacred drama of the conception and birth of the maize. The modern Huichol tribe of north-western Mexico perform a dance of the same type in which dancers representing fertility goddesses are accompanied by phallus bearers, and which is intended to aid the growth of the crops. The Pipil of El Salvador, a Náhua tribe, performed the same dance but interpreted it quite differently.

Apart from their six fully-fledged priests, the Totonacs had a number of subordinate functionaries who tended the eternal flames in the temples, as well as two scribes, the so-called 'monks', who prepared the pictographic manuscripts. Both these institutions suggest Mixtec influence, as does the *juego del Volador*. Circular braziers or fire altars of a type depicted in the Mixtec codices have been found in the ruins of Cempoala; and the extant Mixtec codices themselves are probably those found in the coastal area south of Cempoala, where we know the Spaniards saw their first pictographic manuscripts. There is no other record of pictographic manuscripts being found among the Totonacs.

Mixtec influence can also be seen in the temples of Cempoala. Their rectangular pyramids and layered terraces edged with stepped crenellations resemble Mixtec structures contemporary with the penultimate rebuilding of the great pyramid of Cholula. A temple on one of the Cempoala terraces has its inside walls painted with the characteristic Mixtec sun, moon and morning star symbols; and the excellent Totonac pottery found at the Cerro Montoso near Cempoala and on the Isla de

Sacrificios near the city of Veracruz shows unmistakable signs of Mixtec inspiration.

The Tarascans of Michoacán had much in common with the essentially Preclassic cultures which long survived in the states of Colima, Jalisco and Nayarit, to the north and west. The Tarascans differed from these largely in their exquisite craftsmanship; otherwise they remained an alien, barbarian people, almost untouched by Classic culture. It was not until a comparatively late date that they received a veneer of civilization from the Puebla–Mixteca culture and a tardy admixture of mainly theological influences from the Aztecs. These outside influences hardly affected their cultural individuality, as their temple architecture shows; and they were equally successful in defending their political independence against Aztec armies.

Many features of Tarascan culture are the result of their physical environment, which is totally unlike the eastern Mesa Central. Michoacán is a well-watered, thickly wooded, hilly area with large lakes. Fishing is as productive a source of food as agriculture, and wood a more important material than stone. Tarascan houses and temples were therefore built of wood, and stone carving remained at a primitive level while pottery and metalwork were comparatively highly developed.

The Tarascan king, ruler of a league of three cities, was also the spiritual leader of his people. The image of the great god of the Tarascans was in his keeping, and he frequently officiated in person at religious ceremonies. The high priest or 'annunciator' (*Petamutí*), like his Zapotec counterpart, acted as chief judge of the kingdom; but he did so only as a representative of the king.

Some information about Tarascan religion is to be found in the anonymous *Relación de la provincia de Mechuacán*, written in the mid-sixteenth century, which has been annotated by Seler and Nicolás León.[60] It clearly shows that the beliefs and practices of the Tarascans had been strongly influenced by those of the Aztecs, and had thus presumably lost many of their original characteristics. As in central Mexico, the rain and vegetation gods of the Classic period had been largely supplanted by astral gods. The principal figure in the Tarascan pantheon, the great god Curicáveri, a sun god in the shape of an eagle, who was the patron of kings and warriors, seems almost a carbon copy of Huitzilopochtli. The relationship between Curicáveri and another astral deity, whom he supplanted, Urendequa Vécara ('he who goes before'; the morning star), the national god of an ancient Tarascan city, parallels that between the Aztec Huitzilopochtli and the Chichimec Mixcoatl. The 'gods on the right hand and on the left' corresponded exactly to the Aztec star gods who were also divided into two categories, northern (right) and southern (left): the Mimixcoa and the Huitznahua. Another of the Tarascan deities, the goddess Xaratanga, resembles the Aztec earth goddess in that she embodies the earth and the fruits of the fields, as well as conception and birth. She was patron of the steam baths taken by pregnant women to promote an easy labour; and naturally she was closely associated with the moon. As goddess of agriculture she once turned two of her priests into serpents as a punishment for their presumption in drunkenly adorning themselves with her holy symbol, a garland of cultivated plants. Another Tarascan myth tells of a ball game between a solar hero and the Lord of the Night, in which the solar hero is defeated and later avenged by his son. This is one of the archetypal legends of the American Indian; it also appears among the Maya.

Appropriately enough for a people whose theology allotted a dominant role to the sun and the morning star, Tarascan religious observance centred on the use of fire. All this is natural enough in a country where there is continual volcanic activity, and where wood is in plentiful supply. The king and the high priest, whose assistant priests were called 'burners' (curiti-echa), had the same responsibility for lighting and fuelling sacred fires as any of their subjects. A ritual fire was lit at the beginning of every military campaign and to mark important events within the family, such as weddings.

Like the Aztecs, the Tarascans waged war with the primary object of capturing prisoners for sacrifice. Those captives who were chosen to be sacrificed to Curicáveri wore silver mitres on their heads and gold and silver discs on their chests; as surrogates for solar and lunar gods they corresponded to the victims in Aztec sacrifices who wore the costume of astral deities.

The only rain-making ceremony recorded among the Tarascans took place at a festival of the Creatress, Cueraváhperi. After two chiefs had performed dances in which they played the parts of clouds, the reeking hearts of the victims were thrown into sacred springs, so that the rising steam might turn into rain clouds.

Human sacrifice was also practised at the obsequies of Tarascan kings; recent excavations have confirmed everything the early written sources tell us on the subject.[61] After the body of the king had been cremated, the ashes were placed in an imitation mummy bundle which was buried in a large clay urn in a trench at the foot of the temple pyramid. Meanwhile the king's wives and servants were put to death and their uncremated bones buried behind the pyramid. Sometimes secondary burial was practised; some bones have been found to have been painted red, a practice which the Tarascans had in common with the Zapotecs. These Tarascan burial customs had remained unchanged for long ages; there is one grave in which the bones of the dead king's attendants are laid out radially round the urn containing his ashes, exactly as was done at Preclassic Cuicuilco. The grave goods buried with the attendants were the finest products of Tarascan craftsmanship. The graves at the foot of the main pyramid at Tzintzuntzan, containing five male and five female skeletons, have yielded superb examples of work in obsidian, copper, silver and gold.

II *Maya Territory*

There are far fewer historical and pictorial sources of information on the religion of the Maya than on that of the Aztecs. After the conquest of Mexico the Spaniards paid little attention to Maya territory for some time. Cortés and Alvarado led expeditions in 1524 and 1525, respectively; but Yucatán, where the last great monuments of Maya culture stood, was not finally conquered until 1546, by the younger Montejo. The only early Spanish author whose work can be compared with the post-conquest accounts of Mexico is Diego de Landa, who became the first bishop of Mérida in 1572. He is no Sahagún, but his work contains an abundance of important information on Maya civilization in its latter stages and has served as a point of departure for modern work on the decipherment of Maya writing. However, only three pre-conquest Maya manuscripts survive; the rest were burned, ironically enough, on the orders of Bishop Landa himself.

Of the three surviving Maya codices, now in Dresden, Paris and Madrid, the *Codex Dresdensis* is by far the earliest and the most valuable. None of them contains any historical information; they are compilations of astronomical, calendrical and liturgical lore and contain invaluable pictorial representations of Maya gods.

The *Book of Chilam Balam*, written in the Maya language of Yucatán after the conquest, is doubtless based on lost hieroglyphic codices; it contains a few scraps of historical information buried in a mass of prophecy, ritual lore and myth.

The problem of deciphering the Maya glyphs has engaged the attention of many scholars over the last hundred years. The earliest to attempt a solution were German (Förstemann, Seler, Schellhas, Beyer); subsequent workers in this field have mainly been American (Cyrus Thomas, Spinden, Morley) and English (Thompson), recently joined by a

Russian (Yu. V. Knorozov). We can now read about a third of the glyphs, including, most importantly, the numbers and the calendar signs; so we can accurately date the inscriptions on most of the early Maya monuments, and thus follow the development of Maya art over six centuries, from AD 300–900.[1]

Serious archaeological work began with the expeditions of the American traveller John Lloyd Stephens and his brilliant draughtsman Frederick Catherwood in 1841 and 1843. After a long pause research was resumed in 1881 by the English archaeologist Alfred Percival Maudslay, who worked intensively for four years photographing and surveying the principal Maya cities. Numerous other sites were excavated from 1888 onwards by workers from the Peabody Museum at Harvard and the Carnegie Institute of Washington. Much work in Maya territory has been carried out by archaeologists from the Instituto Naciónal de Antropología e Historia, Mexico City.

The first general survey of the archaeological evidence was compiled by Sylvanus Griswold Morley in 1947, followed in 1956 by J. Eric S. Thompson. The history of Maya art has been treated in detail by Herbert Spinden (1913) and Tatiana Proskouriakoff (1946 and 1950) New discoveries in this inexhaustible field are being made all the time. The latest which have a bearing on the history of religion are the frescoes of Bonampak in the jungles of the Mexican state of Chiapas (1946) and the richly ornamented royal burial found under a pyramid in the great ruined city of Palenque in 1952.

I. THE NORTHERN MAYA

Of the twenty Maya nations, all closely related linguistically, only the Huaxtecs of the northern Gulf Coast were in the mainstream of Mexican civilization. Long before the appearance of the typical Maya culture they had become isolated from the other Maya tribes, who still form a solid ethnic block in Guatemala, Yucatán, western Honduras and south-eastern Mexico, and whose cultural ties with the other civilized peoples of pre-Columbian Mesoamerica were comparatively loose. Thus, although clearly-marked Preclassic and Classic periods can be identified in the cultural development of the Maya, there is nothing corresponding to the clean break between Classic and Postclassic periods found among most Mexican peoples. This is because they kept more or less to themselves, had no interest, unlike the Náhua, in wars of aggression, and did not have their cultural development disturbed by invasion from without. In the face of overwhelming numerical odds, the Toltecs under Ce Ácatl-Quetzalcoatl never brought more than a small portion of the peninsula under their control, soon succumbed to Maya cultural influences, and were finally absorbed into the Maya population. When the Toltecs arrived Maya culture had already, without any detectable external stimulus, undergone a radical transformation: the transition from the 'Old Empire' to the 'New Empire' which began with the only major internal movement of population to have taken place within Maya territory, and was completed in a relatively short time.[2]

The cradle of Maya civilization lay in the midst of the huge belt of jungle and savannah which stretches from the Caribbean and the Río Motagua, in Honduras, by way of the Petén region of northern Guatemala, to the mouth of the Río Usumacinta in south-eastern Mexico. Climatic changes resulting in the spread of the jungle, and consequent economic difficulties no doubt contributed to the gradual abandonment of all the Maya cities of this belt; but social and religious conflicts must also have played their part. By AD 830 the Maya population of the area had moved to northern Yucatán, where a number of colonies were already in existence.

This mass exodus from the fertile southern jungle belt to the sparse and dry northern lands changed and to some extent impoverished the art and intellectual and religious life of the Maya; but the ancient religion remained unaltered in its essentials. The New Empire is therefore regarded today as a special form of the Classic culture of the Old Empire, owing its separate existence to environmental changes.

In the New Empire the strong religious bonds which had held the theocratic city states of the Old Empire together gradually loosened; and, after two and a half centuries of centralized despotic rule, the fall of the capital city of Mayapán in 1441 ushered in a period of decline and decadence, and a long period of civil wars brought about its final disintegration. The lowland Maya cannot therefore be said to have passed through a culturally distinct Postclassic period. The uplands of southern Guatemala, where Maya culture developed along different lines, are dealt with in a separate chapter.

The Maya Old Empire attained a higher level of development in architecture, visual art and intellectual life than any other pre-Columbian civilization. Morley regarded this as a completely independent and unaided achievement; but subsequent research has revealed that several important features of Maya civilization must have been taken over from the La Venta culture. The earliest known Maya religious edifice, a comparatively low, six-tiered earthen step pyramid with a stucco casing, which formerly carried a wooden temple, has no specifically Maya characteristics. The eighteen grotesque stucco masks on the balustrades of its four stairways strongly resemble the characteristic were-jaguar masks of the La Venta culture. This archaic pyramid, thought to have been built in the second century of our era, was found inside a later pyramid at Uaxactún in the Petén; this site also possesses the earliest known Maya hieroglyphic inscription, which bears a date corresponding to AD 328, and the earliest known Maya sculptures.

The subsequent development of true Maya architecture was rapid. South of Uaxactún is the next oldest known Maya city, Tikal, where one pyramid rises to a height of almost 230 feet. At Copán, in Honduras, there is a massive acropolis incorporating sunken courtyards, stepped pyramids and monumental stairways, profusely decorated with sculptures and inscriptions. In purely technical terms too, Maya architecture is more advanced than anything in pre-Columbian Mexico, as is shown by the corbelled vaults used instead of the flat slab ceilings of Mexican architecture. As well as the small two-roomed temples which were built on the tops of the pyramids, the Maya built long structures standing on low terraces and divided inside into two narrow compartmented galleries. In the New Empire in Yucatán, the temple pyramid lost much of its importance and these so-called 'palaces' (really storehouses or priests' quarters) appeared in ever larger complexes. In Uxmal they stand round huge plazas; in Zayil and Xlabpak they form massive three-storeyed structures in which the upper two floors were set back like the steps of a pyramid. Other architectural forms unknown in Mexico include the inner sanctuary or tabernacle built against the back wall of the temple to enclose the idol; the roof comb, a purely ornamental superstructure built on a temple roof; and (in one courtyard of the extensive Palace at Palenque) the tower.

The other arts too were dominated by religious themes. The easily-worked limestone which was available almost everywhere favoured the development of sculpture; and other materials were also used, such as sandstone (as at Quiriguá), volcanic ash (as at Copán), stucco (as at Palenque) or sapodilla wood (at Tikal). The stairways on Maya pyramids, as well as the façades, roof combs, door-posts and altar slabs of the temples, were covered with reliefs. In plazas and courtyards and on temple platforms, richly carved stelae, altars and 'zoomorphs' were erected; and yet, like the Classic peoples of Mexico and unlike the La Venta people, the Toltecs and the Aztecs, the Maya did not have true sculpture in the round. The stelae of Copán and nearby Quiriguá, the tallest of which is forty feet high, developed from rectangular pillars which were ornamented with reliefs first on one side, and later on two or four sides. They represent a frontal view of a human figure which gradually came to detach itself more and more clearly from the rectangular stone, but which never became a true statue. The smaller Maya stelae of the Petén, the Usumacinta Valley and Yucatán clung to simple bas relief to the very end; they show individual figures and groups of figures, almost invariably seen in profile.

About five hundred years after its archaic beginnings Maya sculpture reached its 'golden age', which lasted from AD 692 to AD 810. To this period belong a number of well-known sculptures of Maya gods. Two recurrent figures are the deities called by Spinden the 'god with the Roman nose' and the 'long-nosed god'.

The former was known to the later Maya as Itzamná; as a relief in Yaxchilán (a city on the Rió Usumacinta) clearly shows, he was a sky god. In this relief a head-and-shoulders representation of him can be seen between a sun symbol and a moon symbol against a background of astronomical hieroglyphs.[3] Sometimes his head looks out from one of the mouths of the double-headed sky serpent. In a courtyard in front of the main temple of Copán, which, as the sculptures on its façade show, was sacred to the sky god, his head appears in the centre of a stairway flanked by two half-erect jaguars. This attendant pair of jaguars is one of the most recurrent themes in the art of the advanced civilizations of ancient America; its significance in this case is the same as that of the two heads of the sky serpent. On monuments dating from the Old Empire the sky god is always depicted as an old man with a sharply aquiline nose, hollow cheeks and a single tooth, cut to a point, in his upper jaw; he often also has a little pointed beard.

The long-nosed god, on the other hand, shows decidedly non-human features. His nose droops like a trunk, and his lower jaw bears curved tusks or fangs like those of the serpent heads of Maya art. He was the rain and vegetation god, and the later Maya called him Chac.

Both these gods also possess alternative forms or aspects. Itzamná's counterpart is a god with thick rolls of flesh round his eyes which form an ornamental scroll on the bridge of his nose; the face of this god or aspect appears in a central position in a well-known altar-frieze at Palenque. He appears to be a solar deity and the temple concerned was therefore named the Temple of the Sun by its discoverers.[4] Chac's counterpart is a deity with a strangely shredded, upturned nose, who is either a wind god or a water god.

The maize god is represented as a handsome youth whose headdress consists of a cob of maize ringed with flower petals. Figures with his features (purely human like those of Itzamná) appear in the sculptured frieze of the main temple at Copán; on a stela at Piedras Negras (another site on the Río Usumacinta) he can be seen kneeling over a bust of the earth mother and strewing grains of maize on her head.[5]

The gods of the Maya are inseparably linked with a system of nature symbols which appear in Maya art as luxuriant sinuosities reminiscent of the jungle vegetation amid which Maya civilization was born. The most important of these symbols is the double-headed serpent, a monster with a living head at one end and a death's head at the other, both with gaping jaws. This reflects the ambivalent nature of the Maya gods, all of whom embody life and death simultaneously; but it may equally well be interpreted as a sky symbol, the living head representing the eastern gate of the heavens, from which the sun and the other heavenly bodies emerge, and the lifeless head the western gate into which they disappear. The body of the serpent represents the arch of the sky and is therefore often replaced by a 'sky strip'. In one form or the other, this double-headed serpent forms the canopy over the king's throne shown in a carved wooden relief at Tikal; the door-frame of temple portals at Copán and Palenque; and the frame of a niched stela at Piedras Negras which contains a seated figure of a king or priest.[6] Often the body of the serpent is shortened and compressed so that the two heads combine, rather like the two faces of Janus, and form the front and back of a monolithic altar known as a zoomorph. These altars are especially common at Quiriguá, where they are so overlaid with ornaments and inscriptions that the basic form of the double-headed serpent is almost unrecognizable; they were formerly thought to represent large tortoises. Inside the jaws of each zoomorph sits a human figure in very high relief; there is an analogy here with the jaguar altars of the La Venta culture. Serpent and jaguar are frequently associated in Maya art just as they are in La Venta art.

A smaller version of the double-headed serpent was the 'ceremonial bar', a symbol of authority delegated by the sky god, held by kings seen on many stelae at Copán and Toniná (a small site south of Palenque). The ceremonial bar is also a recurrent symbolic element in the religious art of La Venta and El Tajín.[7]

The ceremonial bar was later displaced as a symbol of kingship by the 'manikin sceptre', a staff surmounted by a grotesque figure with the features of the long-nosed god and ending in a serpent's tail.[8] The Maya had two other religious symbols connected with the sky: the ceiba tree, known as *yaxche* in Maya, 'first tree', and the 'serpent bird' which sits on the carved back of the double-headed serpent or on the top of the sacred ceiba tree. The religious significance of the two symbols is apparent from their attributes. The serpent bird combines the magnificent plumage of the quetzal of the Guatemalan jungles with the head of the long-nosed god Chac and a stylized serpent head on its wing; while the tree bears buds from which the head of the maize god emerges, its horizontal boughs end in reptilian jaws, and the top of its trunk has the features of the sky god. In this form the tree looks like a crucifix; hence the names of Temple of the Cross and Temple of the Foliated Cross which were given by eighteenth-century travellers to the two temples at Palenque in which it appears on the panels behind the altars. In a relief on the sarcophagus in the crypt under the Temple of the Inscriptions at Palenque the 'first tree' can be seen rising above or behind the corpse of a human sacrificial victim, which in turn rests on the head of an earth monster. On top of the tree sits the serpent bird, and round its trunk the double-headed sky serpent coils itself.

The art of the Old Empire incorporates many other religious motifs: I shall mention here only the jaguar and bat gods who reappear in the reliefs and clay vessels of the New Empire, and the death symbol, a skull and crossbones, which appears so often that one is temped to conclude that the Maya were as death-obsessed as the Aztecs.

The most prominent figures on Maya stelae and friezes are not, however, gods, but kings and priests. At Copán and Quiriguá, they are majestic and resplendent single figures oppressed by the weight of immense headdresses. In the cities of the Petén and the Usumacinta valley, and also at Palenque and in the Yucatán peninsula, the reliefs usually contain two or more figures and depict ceremonies of homage, battle scenes and triumphal processions. Jade carvings, almost as popular an art form among the Maya as they were in the La Venta culture, frequently deal with similar themes. So do the clay reliefs produced in the district known as Alta Verapaz, which nestles between the mountain chains of the south of Guatemala. The graceful and lifelike clay figurines found on the island of Jaina, off the west coast of the Yucatán peninsula, depict dignitaries, priests, warriors and great ladies, as well as the dwarfs, dancers and ball players in attendance at court; but no gods or mythological scenes are to be found among them, unless the very frequent groups showing an amorous old man with a young woman, or the figure of a noble lady with a dwarf or slave crouching at her feet wrapped in the folds of her robe (like the Gothic *Schutzmantelmadonna*) depict gods rather than human beings.

The temple friezes, and the polychrome paintings on clay vessels, also very seldom deal with religious themes as such. The great frescoes at Bonampak, which cover the walls and vaults of three rooms in one building, show a series of scenes: a performance at court, in which musicians and fantastically masked dancers or actors take part; the presentation of a royal child by a group of women; a great victory in a jungle battle; the torture and sacrifice of captives on a temple pyramid; and a victory celebration in which dancers with huge feather headdresses take part. The only concession to the supernatural is in the frieze of animal figures and rain-god masks which runs above the main mural; it is possible that the beasts represent constellations, and therefore the sky, as they do on many Mexican reliefs.

The consummately drawn polychrome paintings on pottery vessels, which are found in tombs at Uaxactún and in the Río Chixoy valley in Guatemala and which date from the last period of the Old Empire, mostly depict public events and ceremonials: the reception of ambassadors, the king carried in procession in a sedan chair, two dignitaries negotiating, each attended by his suite. Only one of the very last of the painted pots from Yucatán has a religious subject. On one side is a sacred deer wearing an ornamental saddle and flanked by warriors, one of whom blows on a large snail-shell shaped trumpet while the other grasps the antlers which the deer has just shed. On the other side of the pot there appears a tree with a trunk in the form of a human face, with a serpent coiled round it as on the sarcophagus relief from the Temple of the Inscriptions at Palenque.[9] The tree is flanked by two small figures of stags seated in the same way as men. The panels of hieroglyphs which appear between the figures are obviously a commentary on the action, but unfortunately they have not yet been deciphered.[10]

The plastic arts play a comparatively insignificant part in the history of Maya religion in the New Empire. Stelae and altars were no longer built, and architectural decoration had undergone a radical stylistic change. In the uniform landscape of Yucatán, Maya architecture became heavier and more massive and the decorations on the façades of buildings became rigid and inexpressive. Angular geometrical forms replaced the luxuriant stone and stucco reliefs of Old Empire architecture. The change sprang naturally from the practice of facing walls with a mosaic of carefully cut flat stone plates. The commonest motifs were criss-cross patterns, key or fret patterns, rows of false columns, and above all geometrically stylized heads of the rain god with his trunk-like nose highly prominent. Sculptures in the round also appear occasionally; they are mostly mediocre, but there is one fine head of a tattooed man inside the stylized jaws of a serpent. This head, now in the Museo Nacional in Mexico City, comes from Uxmal and is in the Chenes style

67

common in south-western Yucatán, in which the whole façade of a building is decorated with a single huge rain-god mask whose jaws form the entrance.[11]

Most of the Maya cities of northern Yucatán are built in the later Puuc style, in which small masks of the rain god are arranged one above the other on the corners of buildings and on the door-posts, rather in the manner of totem poles. The colossal full-face mask has its origins in Old Empire art—there is one framing the portal of the main temple at Copán[12]—but its strictly geometrical form is a product of the New Empire. The double-headed serpent too appears, in a geometrical form, as a straight beam with a stylized serpent head at each end. On two Puuc façades at Uxmal eight of these appear one above the other; with the addition of the earth's surface itself these represent the nine subterranean and celestial spheres of Maya cosmology.[13]

The temple colonnades of the Toltec city of Chichén Itzá contain other Maya religious symbols. On the base of each column appears the full-face mask of the earth monster, and on the capital there are profile views of the four Bacab or Atlanteans in the shape of little men wearing turtle carapaces, snail shells of two kinds, and spiders' webs. The moon god too is often represented, in vase paintings and in the codices, wearing a turtle carapace and with a snail shell on his back.

Near Mérida, the Spanish capital of Yucatán, there is a façade with two panels depicting animal spirits, executed in the style of the Old Empire; the upper panel shows denizens of the air, the lower denizens of the earth.

This comparatively sparse archaeological material is fortunately not our only source of information on the religion of the later Maya. Bishop Landa has left us a good deal of precious information on Maya religious practices, and the codices contain representations of many of the principal gods. These were studied in detail by Paul Schellhas at the end of the last century. The many points of agreement between the pantheons of the Old and New Empires bear witness to the continuity which Maya religion, in contrast to the other religions of Mesoamerica, maintained up to the time of the Conquest.

The Aztecs had a great number of gods because their religion was the product of a wide variety of national religious traditions; by contrast, the polytheism of the Maya was more apparent than real. Maya religion was basically dualist. Almost every deity had two aspects, one good and one evil. Each was both life-sustaining and life-destroying, and each therefore appeared in more than one aspect or guise, often even changing sex. This is a fundamental difference between the Maya and the other Mexican peoples from whom, at least in later years, they borrowed so many ideas.

It is hard to say whether Maya religion in its primitive state was itself partly the product of foreign influences. The Maya word *ku*, which, like the Aztec *teotl*, means not only 'god' but anything 'holy' or 'sacred', i.e. filled with supernatural force or power, was of great antiquity; so was the belief in a supreme being whose name, Hunab Ku ('only god') corresponds to the Aztec Nelli Teotl ('true god'). The Maya supreme being, like his Aztec counterpart Tonacatecutli, was not worshipped, and the little information we have on the Maya creation myth does not even mention his name.

On the other hand, the equally ancient Maya belief in a plurality of heavens and hells does seem to have been modified under the influence of the newer Náhua tribes; the New Empire Maya increased the number of their heavens from nine to thirteen. In the Old Empire nine gods (Bolon Ti Ku) were not only lords of the nine underworlds but played an important part in calendar lore. One of the nine day-names which they represented appears on every dated inscription from a very early date.[14] They also appear in several reliefs; whereas the gods of the thirteen heavens (Oxlahun Ti Ku) are represented in Old Empire monuments neither by images nor glyphs.

Rather like the Aztecs, the Maya postulated a number of previous ages of the world, each terminated by a deluge, and feared that the present age was destined to suffer the same fate. The last picture in the Maya *Codex Dresdensis* shows torrents of water coming from the mouth of the sky serpent and two hostile gods (Ixchel and Ek Chuah) joining in the work of destruction. The *Book of Chilam Balam*, too, contains an apocalyptic vision of the day (the last day of a Venus period) on which the 'crocodile of the house of drops' (the sky serpent), together with the god of death and the nine infernal gods, will destroy the known world (*petén*: 'the island'). The thirteen celestial gods will then be vanquished by the nine; sun and moon will fall down on their faces and heaven and earth be consumed by fire. To prevent this, the Creator has placed the four Bacab at the four cardinal points to support the heavens; similar Atlantean figures appear in Toltec and Aztec art.

The symbolic representation of the world in the *Codex Madrid* parallels that in the *Codex Fejérváry-Mayer*, a Mixteca–Puebla manuscript from Mexico, in every detail. The world is symbolized by a cross with the two great gods in the centre and the four cosmic trees in the arms of the cross.[15] Reciprocal influences have clearly been at work here.

I have already mentioned the two principal deities of the Maya,

69

Itzamná and Chac, in connection with Old Empire monuments. Itzamná means 'house of drops', i.e. Sky. He is the son of the supreme being and is identified with the sun god Kinich Ahau ('lord sunface'). The moon goddess Ixchel is his wife and also represents his 'negative', misanthropic aspect; she has his features and wears the serpent diadem of a goddess. In Tabasco, in the middle reaches of the Usumacinta, on the island of Cozumel, and elsewhere she was worshipped as the chief of the gods. Ixchel shares her functions as patroness of childbirth, and of such womanly tasks as basketwork and weaving, with the young moon goddess Ixchebelyax, just as the Aztec Tlazolteotl shares hers with Xochiquetzal. The cult of Tlazolteotl stems from the Huaxtecs (a Maya people); like Ixchel she presides over sexual rites and is closely linked with cotton weaving. It follows that the two are virtually one and the same deity, and that Ixchel, like Itzamná and Chac, represents one of the oldest of Maya religious concepts.

The stone phalluses that have been found in Uxmal and elsewhere in Yucatán testify to the existence of priapic rites among the northern Maya; however, Thompson considers that these objects were introduced from southern Veracruz by the Toltecs.[16]

Chac appears in the Maya codices more often than Itzamná, and in the New Empire he was certainly the most-worshipped god of all. Alone among the sky gods, he even survived the Spanish conquest. He is always associated with a serpent; in the Madrid codex he rides or stands on its back. The serpent symbolizes rain, and the water bottle which Chac always carries is in the form of a serpent. His other constant attributes are the torches which he carries in his hands, and which symbolize lightning.

The serpent on which Chac rides has the features of his twin or deputy, whom Seler considered to be a water god and Förstemann and others, more plausibly, a wind god (who 'sweeps the path before the rain god').

The youthful maize god (and god of agriculture in general) was widely venerated as Itzamná's deputy, but he was believed to be weaker than the spirit of destruction, Ah Uoh Puc, by whom he was continually assailed. Ah Uoh Puc's title as 'lord of the underworlds' was Uac Mitun Ahau ('lord of the seven hells'), under which name he was represented as a skeleton. Like Chac, he had an associate: the war god, together with whom he presided over human sacrifices. Among his other constant companions were the dog and the 'Moan bird', a mythical cloud spirit.

These deities were basically hostile to mankind. The black

scorpion-tailed Ek Chuah, on the other hand, who was a war god in one aspect, was the patron, in his other aspects, of itinerant merchants and rich cacao planters. This is another feature which may point to influence from Mexico; it will be remembered that warriors and traders enjoyed comparable status among the Aztecs.

In general the Maya gods are rather colourless; we have little detailed information on their functions. The Spanish chronicler Lizana tells us that the city of Izamal in northern Yucatán possessed five temple pyramids, dedicated severally to the sun god, the rain god, the war god and two separate manifestations of Itzamná. In the south temple Itzamná was honoured as a wise king of primeval times who had invented writing and who was consulted as an oracle;[17] the west temple, where he was venerated as the healer of the sick and the waker of the dead, was a place of pilgrimage. The sun god in the north temple was called Kinich Kak Mo ('sunface fire macaw') because he was visualized in the shape of a macaw swooping down out of the heavens at noon to kindle the sacrificial flame. This is also the probable interpretation of the image of a descending winged being found in the temples of Tulúm. The east temple was dedicated to Chac in his capacity as god of lightning and patron of the priests who lived in the temple itself. The temple of the war god Hun Pic Tok, who was named after the 'eight thousand stone knives' which formed the points of the spears of his countless warriors, lay in the middle of the town and was 'the most important of all'.

The later Maya, living in strong walled cities such as Mayapán and Tulúm, attached more importance in their religious life to the idea of war than to the cults which had dominated their religion before the Toltec invasion.

The Maya did not regard the Toltec Kukulcán (Quetzalcoatl) as one of their gods. But long after the end of the Toltec period there was a ceremony in his honour every November at Mani, the city which had replaced Uxmal, abandoned during the civil wars. This ceremony was attended by representatives from other parts of Yucatán who came bearing magnificent feather banners for the god; a similar ceremony appears in a Toltec relief in Chichén Itzá. This is just one example of the way in which ancient indigenous customs mingle with importations from Mexico in the religious life of the later Maya.

As in Mexico, every important religious ceremony had to be performed on an auspicious day, after the expulsion of evil spirits and a preliminary period of fasting and sexual continence; and, as in Mexico, prayer, votive offerings and the burning of incense were essential parts of the ritual itself.

71

Copal resin was burned in small clay bowls like those still used by the Lacandón (the only Maya people to have preserved their ancient way of life almost intact), when they sacrifice to the gods in the derelict temples of Yaxchilán. The outside of these incense-burners is decorated with a crudely modelled face; the vessels which were used for the same purpose in Mayapán at the end of the New Empire period, and which also served as idols, have a full-length effigy of a god made up of pieces of clay applied to the surface.

The clay vessels used as braziers in the Old Empire were also in the shape of a god: Itzamná's companion deity, the god with the strange loops round his eyes. They had holes for eyes and mouth through which the glow inside could be seen.

Blood sacrifice among the Maya commonly took the form of self-mutilation; as in Mexico this practice dates from the Classic period and persisted to the very end. A relief at Yaxchilán shows a priest pulling a cord with thorns attached to it through a hole in his tongue; and the Madrid Codex shows a man and a woman piercing their ear-lobes with obsidian blades. The people of the Alta Verapaz region went even further; in one of their caves Sapper found a little effigy vessel containing the bones of a little finger and the obsidian knife with which it had been severed.[18]

The animal most frequently sacrificed was the dog. Human heart sacrifice is shown in Old Empire reliefs at Piedras Negras, but was not practised on a large scale until the arrival of the Toltecs. It finally degenerated into mere butchery, as is shown by finds made at Mayapán and Spanish accounts of life in Tayasal on Lake Petén-Itzá, the last independent Maya city, which was conquered by Martin de Ursúa in 1697. Here as late as 1623 the Maya sacrificed the Franciscan missionary Delgado and a hundred men of his escort in the traditional way.

On the other hand, the human sacrifices made to the rain god in the Sacred Cenote of Chichén Itzá were an ancient local rite which the Toltecs did no more than continue. In the course of time they became a place of solemn pilgrimage for the whole Maya world. When the Sacred Cenote was dredged between 1905 and 1908 by archaeologists working for the Peabody Museum, Harvard University, objects were recovered from as far afield as central Mexico, Costa Rica and Panama.

The regular annual festivals of the Maya, like those of the Aztecs, occurred at the end of each of the eighteen 20-day 'months' (uinal) and in the five remaining days (uayeb) which made up the 365-day Vague year. At the time of the Conquest the Maya year began with the first uinal, Pop (August). However, the seventh uinal, Yaxkin ('green [new] sun') and the sixteenth *uinal*, Pax, at the end of the dry season, had both formerly begun the year, as can be seen from the ceremonies with which they were associated. It is even probable that the New Year was celebrated twice; the *Book of Chilam Balam* speaks of a 'greater' and a 'lesser' New Year. The end of each year was celebrated during the period known as the *uayeb*, the five intercalated days between the end of the last *uinal* of one year and the beginning of the first *uinal* of the next. The ceremonies followed a standard pattern except that the year god (the god of the first day of the year) changed from year to year, as did the *uayeb* god. The nature of the calendar means that only four of the twenty day names can begin the year or the *uayeb*. After the new year god had been ceremonially brought into the settlement, the *uayeb* idol was set up outside it, a different entrance being chosen each year according to the cardinal point with which the year god was associated. The purpose of this was to banish the threat of misfortune in the new year.[19] Among the ceremonies associated with these rites were a stilt dance, performed by the old women, and the sacrifice of a live dog (or a clay one with food strapped to its back), which was thrown down from the temple pyramid.

The first *uinal* of the new year was naturally the occasion for numerous renewal rites. In the seventh *uinal*, Yaxkin, formerly the first, all implements and door posts were reconsecrated by painting them blue, the sacred colour. In the eighth *uinal*, Mol, new wooden idols were made with every possible precaution against evil omens, in an isolated hut. In the ninth *uinal*, Chen, the temple was renovated, and in the tenth, Yax, the new clay idols were made. When the *uinal* Pop became the first of the year, these rites were transferred to it, and the Pop festivities were followed by the festivals of the various trades: the priests, physicians and magicians in the second and third *uinal*, the beekeepers in the fourth, fifth and eighth; and in the eleventh *uinal* the hunters made amends to the gods for the blood they had shed.

The most important annual festivals were those of the great gods. The feast of Kukulcán in the sixth *uinal*, Xul, has already been mentioned; I need add here only that clowns took part in it. The rich spectators threw them money which they distributed among the priests and dancers who took part in the festival. The feast of the war god Cit Chac Coh ('idol of the red puma') in the sixteenth *uinal*, Pax, like the feast of Kukulcán, began with a gathering of the notables and priests in the temple cities in honour of the war chief, who during the whole feast was honoured as the war god himself. He was carried in a litter to the temple of Cit Chac Coh, where warriors performed a dance, sacrificed a dog and placed its heart in a covered dish before the idol of the god.

In the thirteenth *uinal*, Mac, which included the vernal equinox, the deity honoured was Itzamná, principally in his capacity as sun god. A great fire was lit into which were thrown the hearts of all the animals caught in a ceremonial hunt; the fire was then extinguished with water. This ceremony was known as *Tup Kak*, 'putting out the fire', and has certain things in common with some Aztec rites: the hearts, for instance, were intended as food for the sun, the water was to bring rain to the sun-parched fields, and the 'sun-ladder', a specially built small blue pyramid, was there to help the sun to climb through the heavens.

The fifteenth *uinal*, Muan, sacred to the god Ek Chuah, was also claimed by the cocoa planters as their festival; the feast of Ek Chuah therefore ended with the sacrifice of a dog with cocoa-coloured markings. This was the only festival at which it was not permissible to get drunk; at all the other Maya festivals mead flowed like water. By contrast, the Aztecs drank their *pulque* (agave beer) in quantity only at fertility rites.

The Yucatán puberty rite shows some affinities with the ritual fasts of the Náhua: to keep hostile spirits at bay those present were encircled by a consecrated cord, and sexually mature boys had to attend a 'confessional'.[20]

The Maya, like the Aztecs, recognized more than one class among the dead. The privileged class consisted of warriors, women who had died in childbirth, priests, and also, curiously enough, those who had hanged themselves. In the Maya paradise, these fortunate ones sat under a ceiba, the sacred tree which rises through all the levels of the universe, in a state of eternal bliss. The rest of humanity vanished into Mitnal, the gloomy underworld.

It was generally believed for many years that Mesoamerican pyramids, unlike those of the Egyptians, were not built over tombs. The only pyramid known to contain a burial was at Holmul, a small site in British Honduras, where no less than ten burials were found inside a pyramid and in the temples (later rebuilt) on its terminal platform. The whole picture was changed by the discovery in 1952 of an elaborate crypt under the pyramid known as the Temple of the Inscriptions at Palenque. Sixty-seven steps in two flights, which were filled in after the burial, lead down from the terminal platform to a narrow vaulted tomb chamber, eighty feet below the top of the pyramid and six feet below ground level, almost filled by an enormous monolithic sarcophagus with a richly carved lid. Inside this, as in the burial at Uaxactún, lay the supine skeleton of a king or high priest, almost covered in costly jade ornament and with a greenstone mask over his face. Around the walls of the chamber were reliefs depicting the nine Bolon Ti Ku, the 'lords of the night', who were there to act as guardians of his rest. The six or seven sacrificed human beings whose skeletons lay on the floor of the chamber, plus two additional victims represented by realistic stucco heads, were clearly intended to act as his retinue on the journey into the other world. Alberto Ruz Lhuillier, the Mexican archaeologist who discovered this burial, considers that it took place in AD 633.[21]

In the New Empire and in the Toltec period, burials became much less elaborate. We do, however, hear of a number of strangely primitive-seeming burial customs which were practised even by the élite.[22] In northern Yucatán the ashes of a noble were placed in a hollow in the head of a wooden or clay statue and covered with a piece of his skin. The Cocom of Mayapán boiled the corpses of their kings to remove the flesh from the bones and made the front of the skull into a mask with the aid of plant-gum. These ancestral images and skull masks were placed with the family gods and honoured at each festival with incense and offerings. This form of ancestor worship was unknown elsewhere in Mesoamerica.

In the feudal aristocracy of the city-states of the Old Empire, every king (ahau) was also a high priest (ahau can, 'lord serpent'). Priest-kingship was hereditary and the monarch took part in only the higher religious duties. The subordinate priests (nacom), together with their assistants, old men called Chacs after the rain gods, carried out human sacrifices, smeared the idols with blood from self-inflicted wounds every new year, and officiated at puberty rites. Other priests healed the sick, transmitted oracles and foretold the future using a zaztun ('clear stone', i.e. rock crystal). Tozzer tells us that the zaztun must first be placed in a vessel of mead (balche) in order to awake it to consciousness.[23]

The most important category of priests was that of the hieroglyph and calendar specialists (ah kin, 'he from the sun'), an intellectual élite who expounded the sacred texts and included skilled mathematicians and astronomers. Their achievements in these fields show gifts of observation and computation which can be likened without exaggeration to those of the scholars of the ancient East and of classical antiquity. In great centres such as Uaxactún and Copán they employed the simplest of means (sightings taken of landmarks on the horizon) to determine the length of the solar year, the lunation and the Venus period, and predicted eclipses by dead reckoning, all with greater accuracy than their Old World contemporaries,[24] and used this information to create a calendar in which each date was fixed by so many co-ordinates that it recurred only once every 374,440 years. It is thought that the hiero-glyphs and the calendar first appeared in the third or fourth century BC. The zero point of Maya chronology is in 3113 BC; as in most ancient time-reckonings this zero point is situated in a purely mythical past.

2. THE SOUTHERN MAYA AND THEIR PACIFIC COAST NEIGHBOURS

The jungle belt which was the cradle of Maya civilization is bordered on the south by the Guatemala highlands, a plateau which rises to be-tween four and five thousand feet above sea level and encloses several beautiful mountain lakes (Lakes Atitlán, Amatitlán and Güija). Where the plateau borders the narrow Pacific coastal strip there is a chain of volcanoes, most of them still active. The highlands are inhabited by Maya peoples who fall into three main linguistic groups, the Mam, the Quiché-Cakchiquel and the Pokoman, and speak languages more closely related to each other than to those of the northern Maya peoples of the jungle belt and Yucatán.

Mexican tribes advanced along the Pacific coastal plains at an early date and settled in areas as far east as present-day Honduras and El Salvador. On linguistic evidence, the peoples of this coastal strip, the Xinca, the Lenca, the Xicaque and others, are believed to be related in varying degrees to the Mixe-Zoquean tribes of the Isthmus of Tehuan-tepec. They were later joined by Náhua tribes who penetrated as far as Nicaragua. Thus the Maya were driven back from large sections of the Pacific coast.

This influx of alien peoples from the west affected the highland Maya much more deeply than the Toltec invasion affected their kins-folk in Yucatán. Náhua influence in the Guatemala highlands has long been known from two sixteenth-century collections of Maya myths and chronicles which were discovered about a hundred years ago, the *Popol Vuh* ('book of the community') of the Quiché, and the *Annals* of the Cakchiquel. The work of a number of archaeologists, notably Samuel K. Lothrop (1923) and Alfred V. Kidder (1935), has proved addition-ally that, here as on the coast, Mexican influences took hold long before the Náhua reached Mesoamerica, and after the Maya had passed through a native Preclassic or Formative period which differed in many respects from the Preclassic of central Mexico.

The difference is apparent in Preclassic Maya pottery, and still more so in the very primitive but varied stone carvings which, as Lothrop has demonstrated, establish characteristic types which appear in the better-known sculptures of the later Mesoamerican civilizations.[25]

Preclassic art can be traced at least as far back in time in Maya territory as it can in the Mesa Central, and it lasted much longer. Some of the Preclassic stone figures just mentioned, which have been found at Copán, show that the Preclassic stage of cultural development overlapped with the Classic. In the great ruined city of Kaminaljuyú, excavated by Kidder in the suburbs of Guatemala City, artifacts belonging to the Preclassic Miraflores Phase appear in close proximity to others belonging to the Classic Esperanza Phase.

To everyone's great surprise it soon became apparent that the strongest cultural influence detectable at Kaminaljuyú was not the contemporary Classic Maya culture of the Old Empire, but the culture of Teotihuacán, 750 miles away. This influence was strongest at the time when the Teotihuacán culture had reached its apogee (Teotihuacán III) and the great age of the Maya Old Empire was beginning. According to Kidder this phenomenon cannot be explained by peaceful contacts between one people and another; as at Chichén Itzá, a full-scale invasion must have been mounted and carried out by a Mexican nation, in this case the otherwise unwarlike Teotihuacanos.[26]

The temples they built at Kaminaljuyú and the elaborate tripod vases, decorated with fresco paintings on an applied layer of stucco, which they buried in graves in the city, bear a detailed resemblance to the architecture and ceramics of Teotihuacán. These contacts seem to have worked both ways; certain forms of pottery developed at Kaminaljuyú, especially hour-glass shaped incense burners, turn up at Teotihuacán in a simplified and schematized form. At Kaminaljuyú the lower halves of these vessels bear whole appliqué figures; at Teotihuacán only full-face masks remain.[27]

Naturally Guatemala received more than architectural styles and richly decorated clay vessels from Teotihuacán: religious ideas, deities and rites came from the same source. The splendid fresco-painted clay vessels are among the most common grave goods in both areas; but the graves themselves and the modes of burial are different.

At Kaminaljuyú the graves are much bigger than at Teotihuacán, approximately rectangular trenches reaching a maximum length of 15 feet and a maximum depth of 13 feet. The corpse, wrapped in a shroud, sits upright in a wooden coffin in the middle of the grave, just as in an early post-conquest description from the adjoining territory of Alta Verapaz in the north. As well as clay vessels the graves contained jade ornaments in the la Venta style, and pyrites mirrors decorated on the back with scrollwork patterns which reveal their origin in the Classic Veracruz culture of El Tajín. As at Palenque, the dead man's servants were killed at his graveside to serve as his escorts into the other world, and each female servant was given a small *metate* (quern or grinding stone) so that she could provide her master with food during the journey. An elaborately ornamented human skull was found in one of the graves; this was probably a trophy won in battle. In another grave was the skeleton of a small dog whose function, as in the burials of many other Mesoamerican peoples, was to conduct its master safely over the river of the dead.

The tombs of Salcajá in the west and Acasaguastlán in the east of the Guatemala highlands are similar in their arrangement to those of Monte Albán; they consist of half-sunken chambers with an opening in the side, closed with a stone slab, and reached by a sloping passage which was filled in after the interment. At Acasaguastlán one of the tomb chambers has niches at the end and on both side walls, which enhance the resemblance between it and tombs of the Classic period in Oaxaca.[28] Just as Kaminaljuyú had links with the Teotihuacán culture at its highest point of development, Acasaguastlán was in contact with the finest flowering of Classic Monte Albán culture, and also with Classic Maya culture. A clay vessel found in one Acasaguastlán tomb bears ornate and fantastic relief decorations which make it one of the most famous examples of Classic Maya pottery.

In the Classic period Kaminaljuyú, in its wide, open valley, was a cultural centre comparable in importance with the great temple cities of the Petén. It was deserted by its inhabitants at the same time as the Old Empire cities. In Guatemala, as in Yucatán, the Maya now began to concentrate for safety's sake in smaller, more compact townships built on hills or on plateaux surrounded by deep *barrancas*; this was the period when the Náhua tribes who called themselves Pipil ('princes') began their incursions into southern Maya territory. They occupied large tracts of the Pacific coast and penetrated inland as far as the middle Motagua valley. Their language, an archaic Náhuatl dialect, and a 'chacmool' found in their territory in El Salvador, which for all its crudeness clearly resembles the 'chacmool' figures of Chichén Itzá, indicate that the Pipil originally came from the sphere of Toltec cultural influence on the Mesa Central. The strength of their influence on the Mam, the Quiché and the Cakchiquel of the Guatemala highlands is apparent in the temple architecture of Zaculeu, Utatlán and Iximché, the citadel-like capital cities of these three Maya peoples.[29]

Pipil influence also affected the legends and religious life of the highland Maya to such an extent that they almost forgot their Maya background and uncritically took over the origin and migration myths of the Náhua. For instance, they believed that they were themselves descendants of the Toltecs, and that they had arrived in their present territory by way of the Gulf Coast with the *yaqui vinak* ('emigrants', Náhuatl *yaque*) from Tollan. The creation myth in their *Popol Vuh* is an exact copy of the Mexican legend; Cucumatz (a literal Quiché translation of the name Quetzalcoatl) and Huracan ('one-leg', i.e. the lame god Tezcatlipoca) play exactly the same parts in it as their counterparts do in the Mexican myth. Cucumatz embodies the androgynous nature of the Aztec supreme being: Huracan, another universal god, who dwells in heaven, on earth and in the underworld, retains some of the attributes of the ancient mountain and cave god of southern Mexico. According to the *Popol Vuh* the earth rose from the primeval sea and reached its present form only after several incomplete creations. All civilization originated at Tulan (= Tollan), the common place of origin from which the whole human race dispersed towards the four cardinal points.

Mexican origins are apparent in numerous other mythical characters and episodes; we hear, for example, of 'four hundred boys' who have changed into stars and can thus be identified with the Centzon Mimixcoa ('four hundred cloud serpents') of Aztec mythology. But they are linked in the *Popol Vuh* with an extended narrative which has many fewer Mexican elements than the creation myth; it is in fact the only major survival of the older, popular Maya traditions, and thus makes up in part for the loss of almost all the myths and stories of the northern Maya. The central figures are two divine brothers with the calendar names Hun Hunahpu and Vucub Hunahpu, corresponding to the Aztec dates 1 Flower and 7 Flower. They are great ball-players and descend into the underworld in response to a challenge issued by the death-gods Hun Came (1 Death) and Vucub Came (7 Death). After passing through many treacherous trials the brothers are defeated and killed. Their sons Hunahpu and Xbalanque, who are conceived by magic and brought up by their grandmother, finally avenge their fathers after defeating in single combat a number of hostile nature spirits – a fire god in the shape of a macaw (Kinich Kak Mo), the volcano god Zipacna and the earthquake god Cabrakan. They win the ball game in the underworld, slay the infernal gods, restore their fathers to life and elevate them into the heavens as the sun and the moon. Some of the episodes in the legend, such as the trials in the underworld and the physical features bestowed on friendly or unfriendly animals as a reward or as a punishment, appear in many other Indian myths concerned with visits to heaven or hell.

Xbalanque ('she-jaguar'), who represents the lunar aspect of the younger pair of heroes, is referred to by the Spanish historian Fuentes y Guzmán as the principal deity of all the highland tribes of Guatemala in Postclassic times. In Classic times, however, the place of honour was occupied, as in Classic Mexico, by a rain and storm god.

On the Pacific coast of Guatemala the early movements of population which altered the way of life of the Maya, and drove many of them from their homes, are represented by the stone monuments of Izapa, on the border between Chiapas (Mexico) and Guatemala, and the stelae, detached sculptures and rock-friezes of Cozumalhuapa and El Bacíl in the department of Esciuntla (Guatemala). These last were long attributed to the Pipil although they show few affinities with the typical Nahua culture of these tribes.[30] Cozumalhuapa does, however, show clear links with the earlier Mexican cultures of La Venta, Teotihuacán, Monte Albán and El Tajín; and the stone 'yokes' and *hachas* which have been found in southern Guatemala tell the same story. The mere fact that stelae and altars are far more common than detached idols is enough in itself to suggest close contacts with the Classic cultures of Mexico; and many of the details in the reliefs show that they were carved by people whose religion differed from those of the Maya and Nahua. Most of the stelae of Cozumalhuapa carry reliefs showing gods floating in the clouds with votaries worshipping them. On one stela the god depicted is clearly a sun god stepping out of a monstrous pair of jaws (the heavens) surrounded by flames and with eagle talons on his hands. Another stela shows the morning star god, his head crowned with a three-pointed Venus symbol. The cloud-borne deities include goddesses: one of them wears the serpent diadem of Ixchel, another a large headdress entwined with flowers like that which was later to be an attribute of the Aztec maize goddess. The worshippers wear a stiff belt with the image of the double-headed serpent, as well as a leather guard on the hand which is upraised to salute the god; these are clear signs that they are ball players.

One stela depicts a human sacrifice by decapitation; the ethnic characteristics of the severed heads show that this is a celebration of victories over nations from all the points of the compass. There is also a large rock frieze at Cozumalhuapa which seems to interpret a historical event in terms of myth; a tall warrior defends himself in a sort of enchanted forest against two dwarfish enemies, clearly of a different racial type, who employ magical arts against him. It is probable that both these reliefs depict hostilities between the builders of the stelae and the indigenous Maya.[31]

According to the Spanish historian Torquemada the ancestors of the Pipil set out southward from what is now the state of Puebla in the eighth century of our era. It is more likely that this migration took place rather later, and that it was linked with the break-up of the Toltec empire. The true origins of the Pipil are probably indicated by the fact that their religious centre, like that of the Zapotecs of Oaxaca was called Mita (= Mitla), and was a place where Quetzalcóatl was worshipped both as Toltec priest-king and as a culture hero.

By the beginning of the fifteenth century the Pipil had begun to appear in Nicaragua and settle among the linguistically unrelated Chorotegans, who seem, on archaeological and ethnographic evidence, to have been closer to the Chibcha of southern Central America than to the civilized peoples of Mesoamerica. The Pipil of Nicaragua, the Nicarao, remained a typically Náhua people both in their social structure and in their religion.

The principal deity of the Pipil was Tamagastad (Aztec Tlamacazatl, 'the priest', a title of Quetzalcóatl). The ancient rain god was regarded as the son of the supreme deities Omayateite and Omeyacigoat (Aztec: Omeyotecuhtli and Omeyocihuatl, the 'lord and lady of duality'); but the national deity Quetzalcoatl took pride of place.

This people of traders and warriors turned Mixcoatl, the ancient Chichimec god of the chase and the stars, into a god of merchants. Human sacrifice, ritual cannibalism and self-mutilation played the same important part in religious life here as among the Aztecs, and with the same rationale: that the gods needed nourishment. The Nicarao paradise opened its gates only to warriors who had fallen in battle or been sacrificed. The Nicarao had brought the *juego del volador* from far-off northern Puebla, and had preserved all its religious significance. The protagonist, a dancer who placed himself on the top of a pillar, represented the sky god, and the four whirling 'flyers' represented the thunder, lightning, wind and rain which the sky god sends down on the earth. The Pipil also took the *juego del volador* with them to the highlands of Guatemala, where it has survived among the Quiché until the present day.[32]

The material collected twenty-five years ago by Leonhard Schultze Jena in the Pipil village of Izalco in El Salvador shows that many of the ancient beliefs, myths and rites of the Pipil have survived into our own time. They still believe in an androgynous supreme being whom, like the Aztecs, they call 'our father and our mother'; and they still believe in the 'old one in the mountain', an earth god and lord of beasts, and in the 'rain boys' who, like the dwarfish 'little rain gods' (the Tlaloque) of the Aztecs, live on the mountain tops, from which in the rainy season they pour water through coarse- or fine-meshed nets. Like the Aztec lightning god, they once split open a mountain in order to extract the seeds of the maize plant.

CHAPTER TWO

SOUTH CENTRAL AMERICA AND THE ANDEAN CIVILIZATIONS

Hermann Trimborn

I *South Central America and the Northern Andes*

The area from Lake Nicaragua to central Ecuador, between the advanced civilizations of Mesoamerica in the north and the Inca Empire in the south, was largely occupied by a group of peoples whose common language was Chibcha. Their original home was somewhere in the Cordilleras of Colombia, but we do not know where. In the course of their expansion north and south they took possession of the three Cordilleras into which the northern Andes are divided and of the Magdalena and Cauca valleys which lie between them. They superimposed themselves on an older population which, in eastern and northern Colombia, was of Arawakan origin and was linguistically and culturally related to the agricultural peoples of the Orinoco and Amazon lowlands. The Chibcha probably moved out in several successive waves; and the stimulus which carried them as far south as the Equator and as far north as Costa Rica may well have come from the expansion of another people: the Caribs, who thrust outwards from their native Guianas with astonishing energy, and who have left Carib-speaking enclaves even in the northern Cordilleras.

This patchwork of different peoples, to which must be added a number of isolated linguistic groups such as the Chocó, did not by any means have a common level of culture. At the time of the discovery of America only three areas could boast a civilization more developed than the common run of tropical agrarian cultures. These were: firstly the miniature Chibcha kingdoms in Costa Rica and Panama; secondly, the tribes of the middle and upper reaches of the Cauca valley; and thirdly, the highland Chibcha, or Muisca, of the Bogotá plateau. But even these were by no means all at the same level of development.

In the Colombian Andes primitive and advanced groups often existed

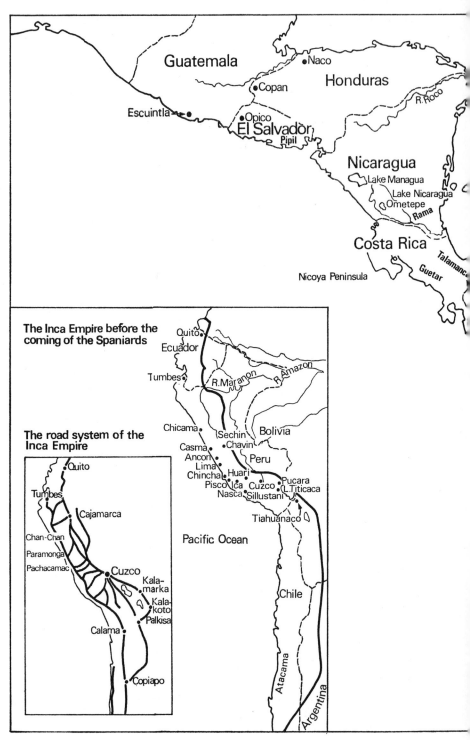

Map 2. South Central America and the Andes

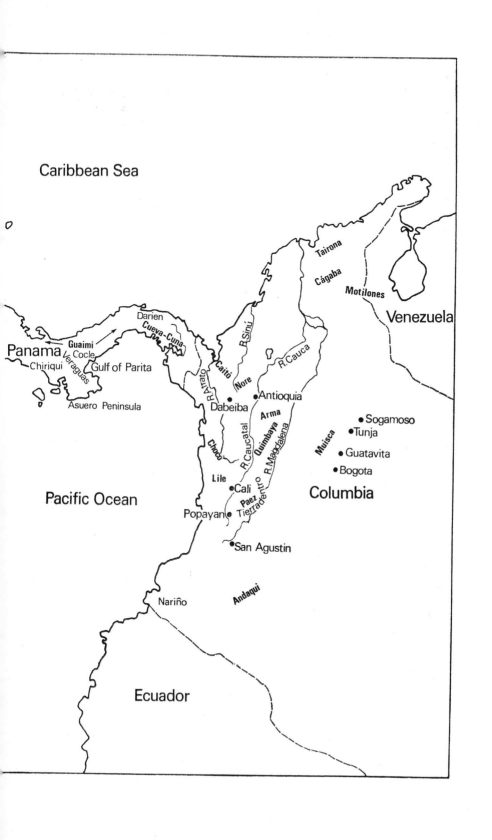

Caribbean Sea

Tairona

Cágaba

Motilones

Venezuela

Darien

Cueva-Cuna

R.Sinú

R.Cauca

Panama

Guaimi

Cocle

Veraguas

Caitó

Nore

Chiriqui

Gulf of Parita

Dabeiba

●Antioquia

Asuero Peninsula

R.Atrato

Arma

● Sogamoso

●Tunja

Muisca

R.Caucatal

Quimbaya

R.Magdalena

● Guatavita

Choco

● Bogota

Lile

Pacific Ocean

●Cali

Paez

Tierradentro

Columbia

Popayan●

●San Agustin

Andaqui

Nariño

Ecuador

side by side. The result was a multiplicity of regional cultural spheres, distinguished from each other by a combination of environmental, ethnic and linguistic affinities and external contacts. Quite apart from these tribal and local variations there was a general cultural ambivalence – no less important and no less confusing – within the individual communities themselves. Advanced and primitive social and religious attitudes existed side by side in a state of unresolved conflict.

In 1914 and 1915 Konrad Theodor Preuss studied a backward agrarian community in the Sierra Nevada de Santa Marta, in northern Colombia, whose religion served as a key to the ideas and attitudes of the vanished people who developed the advanced Muisca culture. This tribe, the Cágaba, like the Ica of the same mountain range whom Gustav Bolinder studied in 1914–15 and 1920, are a Chibcha-speaking people and were presumably once subject to the influence of the now extinct Tairona of the adjoining coastlands.

The Cágaba believe that the world was created by the great mother Gauteóvan who created the sun from her own menstrual blood, and who is also the origin of everything else in the world, including man's enemies the evil spirits who cause disease. Like the creator gods of many other religions, Gauteóvan was forced into the background as far as worship was concerned by the masterful sun god with his numerous attendant nature spirits.

Other offspring of Mother Gauteóvan were four primal priests, the ancestors of the four present-day lineages of priests. These four *Urpriester* are the culture-heroes of Cágaba myth, and the founders of morality and law. The myth also traces the descent of the present-day priests from their archetypes through innumerable generations. All of these must be learned by heart; the priests cannot write. The four primal priests made a pact with the spirits on behalf of mankind; the spirits 'took off their faces' and gave them to the priests to enable them to influence nature, the weather, the growth of crops, animals and diseases. This is a reference to the masks worn by the Cágaba priests in their ritual dances. These are very old carved wooden objects in an archaic style; the recent Cágaba do not do any decorative wood carving at all.

As the myth would lead us to expect, the tribe is very much under the sway of the priests, the *mama*, who live in the temples and are responsible not only for the preservation of the moral order but also for the continuance of the cycle of cosmic events. Religious life centres on the seasonal festivals; there is one in March intended to ward off the diseases attendant on the onset of the rainy season, and one in September to temper the dryness of the dry season. On these occasions the whole

86

community gathers round its circular temple. This was formerly known as the 'house of the sun'; now it is called the *cansamaria*, an obvious corruption of the Spanish *casa de María*.

Ultimate authority resides in the priests, and the sacred and secular aspects of society are consequently closely linked. This is a typical theocracy in the making. The office of priest is handed down from father to son. No outsider may become a priest unless his predecessor adopts him as his son to preserve the chain of succession. Future priests pass the nine years of their novitiate in seclusion in the temple, undergoing many mortifications. They may not marry until this novitiate is completed. Their converse with spirits, particularly those of departed priests, and their self-mutilations give them superior powers which they exercise in all spheres of human activity. Their authority, even on such matters as marital relations, is unlimited, and no important act in anyone's life can be accomplished without their participation. Quite apart from their proficiency as healers, based on a knowledge of the properties of all kinds of medicinal herbs, roots and infusions, their superior status is particularly apparent at the great annual festivals. On the eve of each feast-day the villagers make confession to their priests; this probably accounts for the fact that the settling of all disputes and the requiting of all misdeeds lie in their hands. They deal with breaches of the law by imposing penances such as that of spinning thread in a dark hut. The practices of confession and penance, which were widespread in pre-Columbian America, are definitely not the product of Christian influences; neither is the distinction between 'good' and 'evil' spirits, which is firmly based on utilitarian rather than on ethical criteria.

The supernatural powers of the priests are brought into play above all by the mask dances in which they wear the 'faces of the spirits' and enter a heightened state of consciousness in which they identify themselves with them. These dances are accompanied by chants which are memorized as a part of priestly lore, and by instrumental music played on *maracas*, drums, flutes and horns. In this way they seek to influence the spirits in order to avert sickness, ill-luck and death. They also set out to control the weather and direct the souls of the dead on their way. Each corpse is burned in a crouching position along with all his personal belongings; a cord attached to the septum of the nose serves as a guideline to lead the soul out into the open air.

All these beliefs and ideas reveal a dualistic attitude as well as a belief in a supernatural power residing both in nature and in human beings. This power is called *aluna* and can be reinforced in the individual by abstinence. It also resides in magical amulets and stones.

Another feature of Cágaba religion is number symbolism; the number 9 recurs with special frequency. The priestly novitiate lasts nine years; the dead must be mourned for nine days; the widow or widower can remarry only after a delay of nine months; after childbirth the mother must live apart from her family for nine days.

All these features reveal an attitude to the world which is clearly of great antiquity; in all its essentials it is the same as that which prevailed among the Chibcha in general at the time of their discovery by the Spaniards; and the study of the twentieth-century Cágaba also makes it easier to understand the intimate association between religious and secular power which existed among the ancient Muisca, the Chibcha of the Colombian Andes.

The powers of the Muisca kings were believed to be of supernatural origin, and were acquired only by passing through a six-year novitiate of self-mutilation, abstinence and fasting, during which the novice was forbidden to eat salt, pepper or meat or to see the sun. The superiority acquired in this way was linked, in a way characteristic of the religious attitudes of theocratic civilizations, with the idea that kings were incarnations of higher beings.

The *Cipa* (ruler) of Bogotá, for example, was looked upon as a terrestrial manifestation of the moon goddess. The sun god was incarnated in the person of the *Zaque* of Tunja, who therefore retained a sort of spiritual seniority even after the military defeat of his people by the subjects of the *Cipa*.

One logical consequence of sacred kingship was the assumption that no ordinary mortal could look upon the man-god without being destroyed by his overwhelming power; the ruler could be approached only with downcast eyes. Conversely, certain offenders were condemned by law to look the king in the eye, in the confident expectation that they would be annihilated.

The purest example of the union of priestly and secular authority among the Muisca was the *Suamoj*, the priest-king who ruled over Iraca at the time of the Spanish conquest. His temple was a holy place whose importance transcended political boundaries; even in time of war there was free access for all pilgrims, an example of an 'international law' based on shared religious assumptions. The same inter-tribal convention governed the right of asylum granted by the village of Suesca.

The Musca priests, known as *cheque* or *jeque*, were not only intermediaries between gods and men, but also practising magicians and healers. Their novitiate lasted twelve years. During this period they were subjected to numerous forms of dietary abstinence – they were rarely allowed to eat meat, and never pepper or salt – and strict sexual continence. They chewed coca leaves in order to put themselves in an ecstatic state. Both kingship and priesthood were passed on by matrilinear succession; the successor to a dead priest was usually his sister's son.

The supernatural powers which the priests acquired during the novitiate, and which they were expected to maintain by dint of vigils, silence and chastity, enabled them to converse with higher beings, and to impose their will on nature and on their fellow-men. We find them engaged in healing the sick, rainmaking (this was done by scattering ashes from a mountain-top) and divination. They also acted as oracles through which the gods answered the questions of their votaries. Even the earliest written sources tell us that there was a distinction between true *jeques* and *hechizueros*, whose functions were restricted to healing and divination.

The priests were of course in charge of the religious festivals. We learn of several agricultural ceremonies, including a harvest festival in September: all were fertility rituals and included mask dances whose origins lay in a more primitive level of development, horticultural rather than agricultural.

The Muisca did not practise cannibalism; this may be because they had not mixed with the so-called Carib tribes and were very much on the defensive against them. They did, however, take head trophies, a practice which has the same rationale as cannibalism, the acquisition of the strength of the defeated warrior.

Sacrifices consisted mainly of offerings of *chicha* (maize beer), garments (which were stored in the temples), incense, emeralds and gold. Offerings presented to the god and culture hero Bochica consisted of figurines (*tunjos*) cast by the *cire perdue* process, while the mother goddess Bachué was honoured with incense. Human sacrifice was mainly carried out in honour of the solar deities. As in Mexico, these gods were thought to require human flesh and blood to preserve and increase their strength. The victims were young boys; these were usually either captured in war or bought from travelling salesmen from the inland tribes, but sometimes they were voluntarily supplied by noble families. They were sacrificed at puberty by the Mexican method of cutting out the heart. In time of drought a boy might be sacrificed on a mountain top before dawn and his blood sprinkled over the rocks to eastward. Or the sacrifice might take place in front of an idol; at Guachetá (where the Spaniards first set foot on the Meseta), an overlifesize wooden idol stood on a bloodstained sacrificial stone on which a boy was sacrificed every week.

Another method of sacrifice resembled the Mexican arrow sacrifice. A slave was fastened in a basketwork cage on a raised platform and killed by spears from the spear throwers of the warriors; his blood was offered to the sun god.

The close connection between religious ideas and magic is illustrated by the Muisca custom of driving the main supporting piers of their palaces into the earth through the living bodies of young girls. The use of human flesh and blood was thought to ensure the solidity and safety of the structure. Slaves were sacrificed in the same way during the building of the 'Temple of the Sun' at Sogamoso (Suamoj), and the Colombian archaeologist Hernández de Alba has found human skeletal remains in the course of excavating a Muisca building at Tunja.

The Spaniard Pérez de Barradas lists the names of twenty-eight gods as members of the Muisca pantheon. In many cases the astral significance is clear; solar beings can be clearly distinguished from lunar beings (which, here as elsewhere, belong to an earlier stage of development). The moon goddess was called Chia, the sun god Sua. These two names combined are the origin of the portmanteau word *usachie* which the natives applied to the Spaniards under the impression that they were children of these two deities. Behind these two astral deities, it is possible to detect traces of an older belief in a Creator, Chiminigagua, who was no longer worshipped, having been eclipsed by younger deities and reduced to the level of a mythological figure.

Here as elsewhere the various gods were specialists. Chuchabiba (the rainbow) was the patron of pregnancy; Nencatacoa was worshipped by women; Huitaca was a goddess of dancing, drunkenness and sexual pleasure and thus an antagonist of the culture heroes who had brought order into human life by establishing custom and law.

Muisca mythology is by no means free of inner contradictions; there was no unified priestly caste as there was in Peru, and the mythical themes and the names of the characters were subject to much local variation.

The creation myth runs roughly as follows. After the Creation everything was in existence except the sun and moon, so that the earth lay in darkness. There were only two human beings, the kings of Sogamoso and Tunja or Ramiriquí. They created mankind, the men from yellow earth and the women from a plant. In order to obtain light, the king of Sogamoso instructed his nephew the king of Ramiriquí to climb up to the heavens and give light to the world; and the king of Ramiriquí became the sun. It soon became apparent that this was not enough to illuminate the nights as well; so the king of Sogamoso himself ascended into the sky and became the moon.

Social institutions, like natural phenomena, tended to be interpreted in terms of primordial mythical events. The custom whereby the *Zaque* of Tunja always married his sister is accounted for as follows: long ago a *Zaque* by the name of Hunsahua fell in love with his sister. When she became pregnant and was scolded and ill-treated by her mother, she fled with her brother in the direction given by a spear which he threw from his spear thrower. Her child was born in the territory of the *Cipa* of Bogotá, and turned to stone. The lovers travelled on to the falls of Tequendama where they tired of their wanderings and themselves changed into stones.

Similarly, the myth of the earth god Chibchachum has an aetiological or explanatory function. Chibchachum is also the god of cultivators, merchants and goldsmiths. One day he became angry with mankind and turned the whole valley of Bogotá into a lake. Then Bochica appeared on a rainbow, his hair and beard down to his waist, wearing a tunic and cloak but no shoes. (In other versions this culture hero is called Nebterequeteba [Neuterequeteua, Nemterequeteba] and Chimizagagua.) He hurled his golden staff at the rocks so that they opened at once and let the water run away; and this is how the falls of Tequendama came into being. Bochica then condemned Chibchachum to carry the earth on his shoulders for ever; previously it had rested on four wooden posts. Every time Chibchachum shifts the weight from one shoulder to the other there is an earthquake. This myth, told in various versions at Bogotá, Tunja and Sogamoso, reflects the conflict between solar and lunar deities, even though the sun and moon gods themselves are not introduced into the narrative but are represented by various other characters. Just as the vanquished earth god Chibchachum is a lunar figure, the victor Bochica is a solar hero. Some twenty human life-spans (1400 years) in the past he was believed to have passed through Muisca territory from east to west. The Muisca still pointed to his footprints on the rocks. He then vanished from sight at Sogamoso after bequeathing his power to Idacansas, the legendary ancestor of the rulers of Iraca. Bochica's journey was commemorated by a Muisca causeway which ran eastwards across the savannah from Sogamoso. This is an additional piece of evidence that roads must have been at least partly religious in origin; there are analogies in the paved roads in Tairona territory, the Maya processional way from Tulúm to Yaxuná, and similar sacred roads in the coastal belt of Peru. In his capacity as culture hero Bochica brought mankind agriculture and laws. He taught weaving by painting a picture of a loom on a rock; this is a case in which we can detect a direct link between the religious use of pictographs and a mythological theme. Bochica also bestowed on the rulers of legendary times the power to command diseases and the weather. In the same way the Cágaba priests receive similar powers from the mother goddess Gauteóvan.

The Muisca too worshipped a mother goddess of fertility who belonged to the earlier, lunar religious horizon. Simón assigns her origin to the Tunja district. When the light created by Chiminigagua fell on a lake in the neighbourhood of Tunja, there emerged from the waters Bachúe, also known as Furachogua ('good lady'). With her she brought a three-year-old boy whom, when he grew up, she married. She bore him five or six children at a time, and on their travels together she peopled the entire earth. In her old age she returned to her lake, admonished mankind to keep the commandments of religion, and turned herself and her consort into water serpents.

The sacred lakes of the country were all believed to be the dwelling-places of serpent gods, and all had links with the cult of Bachúe. At the lakes of Guatavita, Guasca, Siecha, Teusacá and Ubaqué, Bachúe received offerings of gold, emeralds and garments at ceremonies marked also by feasting and sacred games. She also had sacred springs, at which the only offerings made were of incense.

The lake of Guatavita, the best known of the sacred lakes of Muisca territory, lies 9520 feet above sea level. Here Humboldt and Bastian found the remains of a temple and some steps leading down to the water's edge. The sacrifices which took place here later gave rise to the legend of *El Dorado*, the 'gilded man'. On certain feast-days the ruler of Guatavita was anointed all over with gum, and gold dust was sprayed all over him through blow pipes. He was then rowed out into the lake on a raft, and stepped into the water, thus making an offering of the gold on his body.

A local legend accounts for these ritual offerings to a serpent deity in terms which show clear affinities with the Bachúe myth. The ruler of Guatavita once found out that his favourite wife was committing adultery with one of his vassals. The adulterer was impaled, after his genitals had previously been cut off and served to the king's wife at a banquet. When she found out what had happened she left the palace with her little daughter and threw herself and the child into the lake. The king ordered the magicians to bring her back. The mightiest of their number dived down and returned with the news that he had seen the king's wife alive in a castle, holding the serpent spirit in her lap, and that she refused to return home. From that time forward everyone brought votive offerings to the lake. The serpent spirit sometimes took on the shape of the king's wife and foretold such evils as drought, famine and disease.

Like the sacred lakes, rocks, mountains and caves were believed to be the homes of supernatural beings; it is possible that the numerous rock drawings in Muisca territory have some connection with their cult.

The gods were also worshipped in temples, but none of their idols of wood, cotton, wax, clay, copper or gold, which were hollowed out to receive the offerings of their votaries, still exists; they were sought out and destroyed after the Conquest by Spanish monks and priests.

Ancestor worship was another feature of Muisca religion. The soul (*fihizca*, 'breath') was believed to go on a perilous journey through chasms of black and yellow earth, crossing a river in a boat made of cobwebs (this was why spiders were never killed) to the centre of the earth, where the wicked find punishment and the righteous a pleasant after-life well-provided with drink, food and women. It must remain an open question how much our Spanish sources are influenced by Christian ideas when they say that the dead were judged on ethical criteria. The close resemblance between the after-life and life on earth explains the custom of interring with the dead not only food, drink, clay vessels and weapons but also wives and slaves who were drugged and buried alive. In the Muisca after-life the same social distinctions applied as in this world.

The disposal of the dead took place in lakes, caves, rectangular graves and circular shafts with and without a stone slab over the entrance. Evidence of secondary urn burial has also been found. The corpses of rulers were disembowelled and mummified by drying over a fire and stuffing with resin. The sources are not fully in agreement on this question of *élite* burial, which suggests that there were local variations. Royal corpses have been found in crouching postures on the floors of temples and on raised platforms; but we also read that the rulers were buried with their wives and attendants arranged in layers above them, and that the *Cipa* of Bogotá was lowered into a lake in a golden (i.e. probably gilded) sarcophagus. However the rulers were actually buried, it is clear that the practice of mummification was reserved for the *élite*. Here as elsewhere its purpose was to preserve the shape of the body as a guarantee of survival after death. In principle, the placing of grave goods with the corpse was common to all classes of burial, but *élite* graves are naturally better stocked than any others. The concept of the 'living corpse', implicit in all Muisca burial customs, explains why the mummies of dead kings were carried into battle so that they could give the warriors the benefit of their strength and wisdom. Incidentally, the existence of this practice shows that the custom of depositing the remains of the rulers in lakes can hardly have been general. The numerous graves that have been found since 1935 are rectangular and contain few grave goods.

The thoroughness of the compilers of our Spanish written sources has fortunately meant that we have a good deal of information on the thought of the ancient Muisca and their attitude to the world. One important aspect of this is their interest in numerology, the emphasis being on the number 6; this is instanced in the twice six years of the novitiate for the priesthood, the six-day celebration which took place when a girl reached sexual maturity, the six winners in the ritual footraces and so on.

The civilization of the Muisca was an isolated phenomenon in a sea of primitive agricultural peoples who had remained at a lower stage of social and political development. But as this simple farming culture is the soil from which advanced civilization springs, it would be surprising if the two cultural levels did not have certain attitudes in common, although the affinities are not so apparent as they are between the Muisca and the Chibcha-speaking Cágaba.

The Panche, south-western neighbours of the Muisca, show signs of an animistic lunar religion typical of many primitive agrarian cultures. The central position in their religion was taken up by the female moon, but the belief in spirits was also important and expressed itself in conjurations and propitiatory sacrifices. The Lache, on the other hand, whose territory bordered that of the Muisca on the north-east, had a markedly solar religion. Their temples, called 'houses of the sun', were placed on eastward-facing mountain slopes, and they believed the shadows cast by people and objects to be a divine gift of the sun. Like the Muisca, they had holy lakes in which they deposited offerings to the gods. The belief that gods and heroes had been changed to stone is a characteristic of many Andean cultures; among the Lache it took the form of a belief that the souls of the dead resided in stones, from which new human beings would one day emerge. As far as burial customs are concerned, the sources mention mummification (doubtless reserved for chiefs) and cremation; cylindrical shaft graves have also been found. Burial was in two stages: when the soft portions of the body had decayed the bones were exhumed and given a secondary burial in large clay urns, together with various grave goods.

Similar patterns of religious life can be traced as far afield as the Venezuelan Andes, where the supreme being, Ches, was thought of as living in the mountains, a typical solar trait. The antithesis between solar and lunar deities characteristic of the Muisca is echoed here in the tradition that the principal place of pilgrimage in pagan times was the temple of a female deity, Ecaque. Here too, priests mediated between gods and men; and the votive offerings of the faithful were stored up in the temples.

What I have said of the Cágaba also applied in part to the vanished civilization of the Tairona, whose former cultural and polical domination of the northern coastal area of Santa Marta has left its mark in the shape of numerous stone monuments. This may well have been a theocratic culture like the Old Empire of the Maya. The priests were also augurers who interpreted the flight of birds. Their gods were worshipped in temples; and there seems to have been one great ritual centre. 'Megalithic' graves made of stone slabs have been found underneath the foundations of their houses; but it was more usual for the bodies of the dead to receive a secondary burial accompanied by small quantities of grave goods, in urns buried in cemeteries.

In the valleys of the Cordillera Central, between the Muisca of the eastern Cordilleras and the Chibcha tribes of the Cauca valley, there were pockets of older-established tribes, such as the Patángoro of the western slopes of the Magdalena valley. Our written sources give contradictory accounts of their cosmology and religion. We hear of a nebulous, unworshipped deity called Am, of sun and moon deities and also of an 'evil' deity called Chusma (or Chanzan) whom some sources nevertheless refer to as a sky god well disposed towards mankind.

The world view seems to have been based on the dualism of matter and spirit; the after-life was visualized as the home of disembodied spirits 'like the wind'. This belief in a paradisaical other world was partly responsible for the frequency of suicide among the Patángoro and other Andean peoples. Members of many tribes preferred a voluntary death and eternal life in a carefree Elysium to survival under Spanish rule. There also seems to have been a belief in a long-lost earthly paradise, although it is impossible to establish to what extent this idea is a product of Christian influence. One's suspicions are aroused by the fact that the earthly paradise is thought of as having been brought to an end by the agency of a serpent. One myth that is purely Indian in origin is that of a deluge which is survived by one man, for whom a wife sprouts from a bamboo stalk.

Our material evidence of the religious beliefs of the Pijao of the southern Cordillera Central consists of a number of small idols made of wood,

95

stone and clay. The written sources tell us that when the Spaniards arrived the Pijao had large and imposing images of their gods, including a wooden figure of the god Eliani at Cacataima, an idol in the shape of one of the Pijao themselves at Otaima and a great stone image near Neiva which represented the triple god Lulumoy with three heads, six arms and six legs. Although the Pijao gods were thus represented in human shape, it is probable that they were thought of as immaterial beings; the Pijao, like the Patángoro, were dualists. They believed that the human soul left the body at death and went to reside in the body of an animal, usually a deer, for which reason deer were taboo animals. The dead were buried in lateral chambers at the bottom of shafts which were sometimes as much as ten feet deep. In most cases this was a secondary urn burial consisting either of skeletal remains alone or of the products of cremation.

Mediation between mankind and the supernatural world was the responsibility of priests and priestesses, whose duties included fasting. They were also augurers, reading the omens from the flight of birds, and magicians, seeking to influence events directly without recourse to gods or spirits. Feathers and animal hairs were believed to be sources of magic power; but the principal form of magic practised by the Pijao was cannibalism. Those eaten were usually enemy warriors. Pedro Simón vouchsafes the information that the bravest warriors of the tribe itself would sometimes voluntarily submit to being butchered so that their fellows might partake of their strength at a ritual feast.

The Paex, a tribe living in the Cordillera Central south-west of the Pijao, had holy places known as *itaqui-finó* ('places where the sun reveals his secret'), where they worshipped their sun god and also, according to Spanish sources, a culture hero called Guequiau, who was supplanted after the Conquest by a new hero whose myth reflects the reaction of the Paez to the arrival of Europeans. This is Juan Tama, the son of the stars, whose footprints on a rock near Bitoncó were the object of great religious awe. Juan Tama, a foundling brought up by the Paez, became the ruler and teacher of all the Indians in the area. He forbade them to have anything to do with the white men, and before his final disappearance into the waters of a lake he chose as his successor a certain Calambás whose heirs ruled thenceforward from Bitoncó.

The Paez world view is dualistic: it includes hostile nature spirits (such as the rainbow), and teaches that the disembodied spirits of the dead, whom the living must assiduously propitiate, are eventually reincarnated. In pre-Spanish times corpses were cremated and the ashes buried, the chiefs together with their wives and possessions. Since the coming of the Spaniards cremation has been replaced by interment, although the practice of burning the hut in which someone had died persisted for a long time. It has now given way to a ritual cleansing by the shamans. Shamans are spirit mediums, healers (who heal the sick by driving out evil spirits) and magicians and diviners. They are thought to possess psychic powers which in theory everyone can attain. Magical powers also reside in the lakes, and to conciliate the often hostile spirits which lurk on high slopes and mountain passes, travellers place a stone on a pile by the wayside, as they do all over the Central Andes.

Similar ideas of the destructive powers of spirits were current among the Andaque, the historical inhabitants of the San Agustín area where so much archaeological work has been done on the remains of an earlier period. Like many other peoples they were much concerned with ritual cleanness and uncleanness, and set aside special huts for use by menstruating women. Their defences against harmful supernatural influences included *couvade*, self-mutilation as a source of spiritual power, and ritual dances which included pantomimic representations of various animals. To this day the peoples of the remoter districts of Colombia preserve a strange mixture of pagan and Christian theology and ritual.

In what is now Ecuador and the southernmost extremity of Colombia, those pagan deities whose names are known to us were preponderantly astral. Thus, we learn from Garcilaso that the Cañari worshipped the moon, and from Cieza that the Manta of the central coastal region worshipped the sun, the moon and also the sea. The religion of the islanders of Puná in the Gulf of Guayaquil seems to have centred on a marine deity; we also hear of fish-shaped spirits and a cat god or goddess. The Coconuco of southern Colombia had a lunar and stellar religion, and we know that the people of Popayán in particular had wooden and metal idols in their houses.

Mountains as well as heavenly bodies were considered to be gods in themselves; and some of them were linked with the legendary origin of a particular tribe. The Panzaleo, for example, traced their descent from the volcano Tungurahua, the Puruhá from a union between the feminine Tungurahua and the masculine Chimborazo. The Cañari accounted for their origins in more than one way. According to one version they had emerged from a lake; according to the other, they were descended from the sole survivor of the deluge, who had mated with a hen parrot. The Cara placed great emphasis on the serpent, not only in their myths but in the superstititions of everyday life. A look from a snake might prove fatal; and its effects could only be countered by a period of purification by means of fasting. The Pasto, too, thought snakes to be creatures of ill-omen; they also used the sighting of certain birds as a basis for divination. The Puruhá, on the other hand, sought their omens in natural phenomena: lightning and the rainbow were thought to be particularly bad signs.

The existence of priests, individuals charged with speaking to the Gods on behalf of the community, is common to a wide variety of ethnic groups ranging from the Huancavilca and Manta of the coast of Ecuador and the Panzaleo of the Ecuadorian highlands to the peoples of Pasto and Popayán in the southern highlands of Colombia. The present-day Nariño of southern Colombia deal with diseases which are caused by such things as the 'evil eye' by sucking and by various other modes of treatment including breathing on the patient after the healer has chewed certain plants.

Human sacrifice is by no means unknown in this area between Peru and the Cauca valley. Its former existence has been confirmed among the Puruhá, and the Manta; the Huancavilca from a Peruvian province of that name practised heart sacrifice.

Religious festivals included the maize harvest rites of the Puruhá, and the three-day festivals of dancing and feasting which took place at Pasto and Popayán. The Huancavilca had a fertility rite which included sprinkling the fields with human blood.

The early sources speak of a strong homosexual element in the culture of the coastal peoples of Ecuador; this may well have involved a ritual expression of the Manta myth according to which the human race once consisted entirely of men.

In the whole of what is now Ecuador and southern Colombia there was a ritual pattern attached to the death of anyone, especially a member of the *élite*; and many customs which are certainly of great antiquity, such as the placing of food and drink in graves, have persisted into recent times. No Cara funeral procession ever came home by the route it had taken on the way to the burial place; and the hut in which someone had died was abandoned. There is a certain amount of further information gathered from archaeological evidence. The Cañari of the Ecuador highlands buried their chiefs in a sitting position in deep cylindrical graves, surrounded, by wives, attendants and all sorts of possessions. Men of rank among the Manta of the Ecuador coast were buried along with living wives, objects of value and food; maize beer was poured into their graves through a tube. In the Department of Nariño in southern

Colombia there are many shaft graves of varying depths, which fit into the general pattern of Colombian tomb-building; secondary burials in urns have also been found. The belief that the dead survived was general; at Popayán it was linked with a belief that the souls of the dead were reincarnated as children.

When the Spaniards arrived, the middle and upper reaches of the Río Cauca, along with the valleys of its tributaries, were the seat of an ancient dominant civilization which is famous for its copper-gilt work made by the *cire perdue* process and for its highly developed shaft and chamber tombs.

Despite this comparative wealth of purely archaeological material we have very little idea of the cosmology and theology of the peoples concerned. The Spaniards dismissed all the tribal deities as manifestations of the Devil, and their very names have mostly been lost. We know that the Carrapa tribe worshipped the sun, that in the Anserma area the sun and moon were worshipped as children of the supreme being Xixarama, and that the tribal deity of the Quimbaya, a nation of goldsmiths, was called Nabsacadas. We have no direct evidence from the middle Cauca valley of the existence of priests as intermediaries between god and man, except in the case of Anserma. But there is every reason to suppose that, here as in the upper reaches of the valley, each community had its own priest-magician-diviners, and that there was no overriding priestly caste.

The Anserma priests were also healers; they knew the virtues of medicinal plants, practised massage, and sucked their patients' bodies to remove the 'intrusive objects' which were believed to cause disease.

We read in early Spanish accounts that at Anserma the people prayed for rain to the twin idols of sun and moon. The god Xixarama had a temple on a rise in the ground, where two virgins were sent (when?) to have intercourse with him. We also have detailed descriptions of the wooden idols of the Pozo, the heads of which were human skulls with the fleshy parts restored in wax. The inhabitants of Arma also worshipped idols; they and their neighbours the Paucura placed their offerings on wooden platforms covered with mats. Our Spanish sources tell us that the Carrapa, like the peoples of the upper reaches of the Cauca valley, had no temples. We do, however, know that the Quimbaya, Caramanta, Cartama and Coré did have temples, and that there were partly gilded wooden idols and sacred dances.

We know little about the offerings made to the gods. The Carrapa sacrificed when someone was ill, and the Pozo before setting out on a military expedition. The Quimbaya made offerings of maize and cloth; the Arma burned incense before their idols.

Not unnaturally, human sacrifice is the best documented, because the most remarkable, of the religious customs described by early Spanish observers. We have a reasonably clear picture of the forms of human sacrifice practised in the region; they show clear resemblances with those found in Mesoamerica. Spanish sources tell us of human sacrifice among the Caramanta, the Cartama, the Cori, the Pozo, the Paucura, the Arma and also the Picara. But this does not exclude the possibility that it was also practised in other communities where the Spaniards failed to observe or to record it. We are told that the Arma sacrificed captives taken in war; and this probably applies to the other tribes as well. But although captive women and children were sacrificed as well as male prisoners, the demand for victims often outran the supply, a problem which was also common in Mexico. The Aztec solution was the 'Flowery War', waged by both sides with the sole purpose of acquiring captives; the peoples of the Cauca valley dealt with the situation by buying surplus stocks of captives from neighbouring tribes. This alliance between commerce and religion may seem strange to us; but at least these practitioners of human sacrifice did not engage in the common cannibal practice of feeding victims up like livestock.

We have a certain amount of information on the frequency of this practice and the number of victims. According to Robledo's companion Cieza, the Paucura and the Arma sacrificed two individuals every week; but Robledo himself says that the Paucura killed five victims a day. In Arma the sacrifices took place on the wooden platforms already mentioned; in Caramanta, Cartama and Cori they took place inside the temples. There is no record that the 'sacrificial stones' referred to by some archaeologists were ever used for this purpose. The Pozo had a unique form of sacrifice: the victims were stuck on high split poles and turned to face the sunrise, a feature which suggests that they were sacrificed in honour of solar deities. Other tribes seem to have offered the god only the heart of the victim, although the Arma at any rate are reported as having eaten the rest of the body as a corporate act of religious communion. The purpose of human sacrifice was to avert some general catastrophe, and it is clear that it was addressed to one of the solar deities who were worshipped in the shape of wooden idols and who were closely linked with the tribal rulers.

Although the position of ruler was not acquired by supernatural means such as fasting, and had no theoretical connection with priest-hood, the dynastic hereditary chiefs of the Cauca valley were considered to have powers denied to ordinary men and to have privileged access to religious truth. They received a specially large share of trophy heads; and they played a privileged part both in human sacrifices and in cannibal feasts. Their palaces incorporated 'chapels', and in them the Spaniards also sometimes came across a sort of gallery of ancestors. With these clear connections with religious life, it is not surprising that these rulers were thought of as beings of superhuman powers. This explains the fact that they were carried in litters and on the backs of their subjects, so that they would not lose strength through contact with the earth (this is called the 'earth taboo'). Their burials followed the 'living corpse' pattern, in which death is thought of as a transition to another world very similar to our own. In many places the bodies of rulers were mummified by drying; burial was usually in shaft and chamber tombs on mountain slopes. The shaft, which might be either round or rectangular in section, leads into a lateral oblong or oval burial chamber, which is sometimes lined with stucco or with stone slabs and painted. Among the grave goods found in these burials are maize beer, food, weapons, vessels and personal ornaments; and the ruler took with him into the grave his attendants and the best-loved and fairest of his wives. Although the dead rulers lived on, as it were, on a higher plane, they still concerned themselves with the fate of their peoples, stood by them in all their activities, and lent strength and counsel to them in battle.

An examination of the attitudes and ideas of the Cauca valley culture shows how close this relatively late civilization was to extremely primitive levels of cultural development. Drumheads of human skin, for instance, have been found in Peru, in many other parts of the Americas and elsewhere in the world; but no less than six hundred and eighty of these instruments were found in one Cauca village alone! Even more gruesome was the practice of human taxidermy, as reported by the soldier Cieza from the palace of the ruler of Lile (near Cali).

When we entered we saw above us a long platform, running the whole width of the room, on which stood rows of dead bodies – those who had been defeated and made captive in war and who had been cut open with flint knives and then flayed. After their flesh had been eaten, their skins were stuffed with ashes, their faces were moulded in wax on their own skulls, and they were placed on the platform so that they looked like living people. Some had spears, some lances and some clubs in their hands.[1]

Eckert has shown that these human trophies are a reflection of the idea of the 'living corpse'. The preservation of the bodies of defeated enemies as trophies kept them in the power of the victor and ensured that even after death they remained bound to his service as instruments of his greater glory.

The Nore country, between Antioquia and the mountain barrier of the Sierra de Abibe, is the northern outpost of cannibalism. Soon after the arrival of the Spaniards the Nore ruler Nabonuco appeared in their camp accompanied by several wives. Two were to lie on the ground and serve as his bed; a third, lying crosswise, was to be his pillow; and a fourth, together with her unborn child, was to be eaten if the occasion demanded . . .

Another ruler in this area, round the source of the Río Sucío, was Nutibara, in whose kingdom the Spanish conquerors tell us of a temple facing eastwards in which a jaguar deity was worshipped. Further south on the Río Sucío was the kingdom of Dabeiba, the subject of many myths, said once to have been *tierra fría*, a cold land, changed by a shaman's tobacco smoke into *tierra caliente*, a hot land. This may be a mythical reference to some real-life migration. The legend of the gold-covered temple of the chief Dabeiba and the solid gold idol of the storm goddess Dobeiba can only mean that some great ceremonial centre once stood near the Río Atrato. There can be no doubt that it existed; but all efforts to find it have so far failed.

Petrus Martyr knew of the worship in Dabeiba of a masculine sky god; but although this god plays the part of Creator in Dabeiba mythology, he was much less worshipped than the storm-goddess Dobeiba. 'It is she who in her anger sends lightning and thunder, and destroys the crops; for they imagine, like children, that Dobeiba flies into a rage when they neglect her sacrifices'.[2] This anthropomorphic attitude is also reflected in the custom of burning sacrificed slaves in front of the image of Dobeiba; 'for they imagine that the scent of these fires is pleasing to her, just as we believe that our saints love candlelight and incense'.[3] The storm goddess also played the part of culture heroine; she was thought of as a learned and beautiful woman who had advanced from the human world to the divine. Petrus Martyr also says, however, that the natives believed that Dobeiba was the mother of the Creator; perhaps this is a trace of the victory of a lunar religion over a solar religion.

Between gods and men stood priests, whose heightened powers were partly due to their periodic abstention from sexual intercourse. 'At these times they hold aloof not only from loose women but also from their own wives'.[4]

The oldest sources make a distinction between the temple of the sky god (which they call 'the rich hut of the devil') and the 'house of Dobeiba' which was guarded by a puma.[5] Later writers treated these two temples as one, and also embellished fact with fancy, so that the supposed 'temple of Dobeiba', blazing with gold and precious stones, was the object of many arduous and fruitless expeditions.

In pre-Columbian times the temple of Dobeiba was a place of pilgrimage for the inhabitants of the lower Atrato basin. The rulers seem – like those of the Cauca valley – to have had private 'chapels' of their own.

It seems to have been the normal practice to worship gods in the form of idols; but critical examination of the primary sources shows all the stories of pure gold idols to be embellishments of the truth. The only individual idol of which we know for certain is a figure of Dobeiba which, like the idols of the Cauca valley, was probably made of wood. There is some doubt whether the gold, clay and stone figurines found in graves in the Dabeiba region are figures of gods or portrait figures like those made by the coastal cultures of Peru.

We know that prayers and sacrifices were offered up to the gods, and that in Dabeiba the sacrifices included human ones. The victims (specially purchased slaves, and perhaps also prisoners of war and members of other tribes) were throttled and burned before the images of the gods. Vadillo asserts that a girl was offered to Dobeiba every month. This, together with the fasts (in which the whole people joined) at the time of the waning moon, suggests a desire to restore the failing powers of Dobeiba, the moon, by an infusion of human strength.

The people of this area thought of the after-life strictly in terms of this world; as Petrus Martyr ingenuously puts it, 'The natives are so simple-minded that they have no word for the soul and no idea of its power; and yet they affirm that everything in the world lasts beyond the span of its earthly existence'.[6] The disposal of the dead consequently exemplifies the 'living corpse' complex. Interment was the general rule; but burial mounds, often of imposing dimensions, were the prerogative of the élite, with whom all sorts of utensils and ornaments were buried. Food was deposited on these graves yearly. The two exceptions to this rule serve to underline the nature of the reasoning behind it. One exception, already referred to, was the practice of cremating sacrificial victims. Petrus Martyr accounts for this by saying that the smoke of these offerings was agreeable to the gods; but a truer explanation may lie in the idea that human beings offered to the goddess and consumed by her as smoke could never live after death in the same way as other people. The other exception was certainly the result of a desire to prevent the survival of the 'living corpse': unchaste priests, that is, those who had violated the prescribed period of abstinence, were burned to death.

The mountainous area between the lower Atrato basin and the western tributaries of the Cauca is inhabited by the Catío, a people who have retained much of their ancient religion to this day. We hear today of deities with the names of Antomía and Calagavi (or Caragabí); and early written sources tell of a 'good' god, Avira, and an 'evil' god, Cunicava. These may have been astral deities; we hear that the natives of this region once worshipped the stars. There do not seem to have been any temples. The Catío had a deluge myth; and they believed that the souls of the dead passed into animals. It remains uncertain to what extent the ideograms said to have adorned the garments of the Catío belonged to a scheme of cosmological symbolism.

The low-lying plain between the lower reaches of the Cauca and the Caribbean seaboard was the land of Cenúfana. This was subdivided into the three regions of Fincenú, Pancenú and Cenúfana proper, which shared a common tradition that the land was once ruled by three deities. First among the three was Cenúfana, who chose the richest land for his own province, leaving his sister to rule Fincenú. Such was his love for this sister that his own subjects and the people of Pancenú were made to pay her the same reverence as did her own people. With this in view he ordered that all chiefs should be buried in the country of his sister, round the great temple of Fincenú in the Sinú valley, the holy place of all the Cenú. This structure was still standing when the Spaniards arrived. It held a thousand worshippers and contained twenty-four gilded wooden idols. Next to each of these a hammock was slung to receive votive offerings.

In another area there was a temple with a nave and two side-aisles, built of wood, in which two male and two female 'caryatids' served to hold up a hammock, presumably that of the god. The gods appeared to their priests in the form of animals, including jaguars, and the priests passed on their words to the people.

Not surprisingly, the Sinú valley, where stood the sanctuary of Fincenú, was famous in the Conquest period for the rich booty contained in its burial mounds, which are described in detail by Pedro Simón and Antonio de Herrera. Their descriptions apply only to *élite* burials; the common people were interred in simple graves or else left in the open to rot. When a man of rank was buried, a trench was first dug deep enough to hold the corpse and the grave goods, which were placed on its left. The face of the corpse was turned to the east. The trench was filled in and surmounted by a mound, a feature peculiar to this area and those of the Dabeiba and Nore. These red earth-mounds, which the Spaniards called *mogotes*, were sometimes conical, sometimes pyramidal. They were already so old at the time of the Conquest that tall trees were growing on them. The natives hung little golden bells on the branches of these trees to distinguish them from others; and these bells served to attract the Spaniards to the richest sources of booty. In this way the first Spanish expedition alone, under Pedro de Heredia, collected treasure worth 150,000 ducats.

Within the area of the northern Andes, cultures like that of Cenúfana, which show advanced features such as the existence of an *élite*, lived side by side with remnants of a much older and more primitive agrarian culture. These primitive North Andean peoples are best considered together with the primitive cultures of eastern South America, who are discussed in the final section of this book; but for the sake of contrast I shall discuss one characteristic example here: the Chocó, of the jungle area on the Pacific coast of Ecuador which bears their name.

Chocó religion, like that of the Cuna, the Chibcha tribes of the Isthmus of Panama, includes a creation myth involving a world-tree. The Creator, who is also the culture hero, is a purely mythological figure without a cult. The dominant element in Chocó religion seems to have been animism: the belief in good and evil (i.e. benevolent and malevolent) nature spirits who are identified to a greater or lesser extent with the spirits of the dead. It was believed that each human being has two souls, a good and a bad, which after death meet with different fates: the good soul goes up to heaven and the bad soul remains behind. It is possible that Christian influence has been at work here, especially as the soul is referred to by the word 'animara'.

The evil souls of the dead, which remain on earth, take possession of the living, and cause diseases. The shaman's task is to drive them out with the aid of other spirits who also help him in many other ways. All this is done in miniature huts three feet or so high, built in the same pattern as dwelling huts.

The shaman goes through a sort of novitiate in the course of which his activities include making little wooden ships, containing figures representing spirits, which recall the sun and moon boats of the Cuna. Through the novitiate the medicine man acquires a guardian spirit or familiar of his own which resides in a stick. Basically, then, the Chocó have an animistic interpretation of the world, with some Christian and Chibcha influences.

An early observer, Pascual de Andagoya, says of the inhabitants of the Isthmus of Panama that they had neither idols nor religious worship. This was no doubt an attempt on his part to defend them against the charge of idolatry; his remark that the common people never spoke of such matters is probably closer to the truth. Pascual did in fact know of the existence of a kind of priest in this society, the *tequina*, who communed with 'their devil', the god Tuira. The place of worship was a tiny structure with no door and no roof, where the priest conversed with Tuira at dead of night, changing the pitch of his voice to simulate a conversation, and reported later on what answers Tuira had given to his questions. Apart from the official priests in the service of the ruler, who were probably also the custodians of the pictographic writings, there was a class of sorcerers and witches who used balms prepared from certain herbs, which they claimed to have received from Tuira himself, and which gave them their supernatural powers. To avoid frightening his human votaries, Tuira appeared to them in the guise of a beautiful child, taking care to conceal the three talons on each of his hands and feet. In this guise he accompanied the witches when they went to a house to carry out their nefarious purposes. Even Pascual de Andagoya is convinced that one of these witches was once seen simultaneously in a village and in a plantation a league and a half away.

Other sections of the community also often claimed special powers; among the Coclé of the Paris area, for instance, the warriors were distinguished from the rest of the population by their abstention from meat; they ate only fish and *leguan*.

Tuira was by far the most important of the Isthmian gods. We do, however, hear in Panama of another god called Chicume, and in Darién of a sky god, Chipiropa, who sends the rain and controls everything that appears in the sky. In the myths of the Cueva there was a beautiful lady who lives with her child in the sky: Andagoya detects an analogy with Christian ideas in this and in the deluge myth according to which an Indian Noah escaped with his wife and children in a boat.

Burial customs differed from one place to another. Only persons of rank were formally buried at all. On the Pacific coast of Darién deep trench graves have been found. On the Atlantic coast of the eastern part of the isthmus, on the other hand, there exist secondary burials in clay urns. In the Coclé area graves have been found in which the corpse of a ruler, mummified by drying over a fire, sits on a dais surrounded by the supine bodies of his wives and servants. Multiple burials have also been found, as well as all sorts of grave goods. In Veragua there are tombs in which an oblique cylindrical shaft three feet in diameter, and anything between ten and twenty-three feet long, ends in a sepulchral chamber; this type of burial, unknown elsewhere in Central America, closely resembles certain forms found in Colombia. In Chiriquí the dead were buried in rectangular or oval pits the sides of which were lined with undressed stones.

On the Pacific coast of Costa Rica, interment and cremation were practised side by side. The Costa Rica highlands, on the other hand, are characterized by rectangular stone cist-graves. Clay figurines of animals and human beings have been found in these burials.

At the time of the Conquest, the Chibcha of Panama were accustomed to dry the bodies of their dead chiefs over a fire and either bury them, sling them in hammocks or set them up in a kind of ancestral gallery. Gaspar de Espinosa was present at the burial of the ruler of Paris, whose corpse was mummified over a fire and buried amid all sorts of treasure (including 355 pounds weight of gold ornaments). His wives and servants either took poison or were drugged and buried alive.

Andagoya gives us an account of an *élite* burial among the Cueva, another tribe on the Isthmus of Panama: the funeral rites of the chief Pocorosa. When a ruler died, those of his wives or concubines who claimed to love him most were buried with him to serve him in the beyond; and even when they were unwilling, they had to die if it was the king's dying wish. The dead ruler himself was provided with his golden ceremonial weapons and wrapped in large numbers of his best garments; then his son and heir gathered together the whole royal household and all the nobles of the kingdom, and the dead king was suspended by ropes in a half-sitting position, charcoal braziers were lit around him to dry the body, and the fat was collected in two clay vessels. When he was completely mummified he was hung up in his own palace. While this was being done, twelve black-clad nobles stood guard some distance from the body, and all others were forbidden to approach. One of the twelve had a muffled drum which he struck from time to time before intoning a sort of canticle to which the others sang the responses. Two hours after midnight they all uttered loud cries so that Andagoya and his companions started up and grasped their weapons; then there was a sudden silence followed by more drumming, like a knell – and then suddenly everyone began to laugh and drink, except of course the twelve who stood guard over the corpse; they maintained their watch day and night. Whenever one of them had to excuse himself, they all accompanied him, still muffled in black. Andagoya discovered that the chanting of the twelve nobles was a recital of the deeds of the dead hero. Exactly one year later, there was a memorial ceremony. The dead ruler's favourite foods, his weapons and little models of his boats were taken, together with the mummy itself, to a specially cleared plot of ground where the 'grave goods' were burned to ashes so that their smoke should reach the soul of the dead man in heaven.

This is a very interesting example of the transition between the idea of physical or quasi-physical survival (the 'living corpse') and that of a soul separable from the body. The funeral offerings are destroyed in the same way as the body, so that the dead man's soul can use them.

The anniversaries of the deaths of past rulers were celebrated with feasting and drinking; and the memory of dead conquerors was commemorated in song.

Besides the pre-Columbian archaeological record and the reports of early Spanish adventurers, there is another and quite distinct category of information derived from study of the present-day inhabitants of the area. The Chibcha territory of southern Central America has provided two major contributions of this kind: a study of the Talamanca group and one of the present-day successors of the Cueva, the Cuna of Darién.

The tribes of the Talamanca group, including the Guaimi, formerly believed in a supreme being who ruled over a pantheon of benevolent and malevolent deities. The 'priests' found by the Spaniards were not solely engaged in worship of the gods: they healed the sick, foretold the future, and above all propitiated the evil spirits which brought disease and death. Among the Guetar there was an organized priesthood which carried out human sacrifices at regular monthly intervals as well as at funerals. We also learn that the concept of ritual 'uncleanness' and purification was familiar to the western Panamanian tribes.

The supreme being believed in by the Cuna was provided with a wife, and another deity, clearly an ancient fertility goddess, was responsible for shaping unborn children. The fact that the supreme being was thought of as omnipotent and omniscient does not necessarily indicate Christian influence. Gods, culture heroes and animal spirits all had their places in a repertoire of myths which included the destruction of the world ('800 years ago') by eclipse, fire and flood at God's command. The 'world tree' motif appears in the following form: every time the culture hero ordered a certain tree to be felled a giant frog came overnight and healed the wound in the bark. So the culture hero ordered his brother to kill the frog. Then the tree was felled; and there arose from the point of its stump the waters of the earth, green plants and all manner of beasts.

Like the Cueva, the Cuna had custodians of supernatural lore. These were not true priests but shamans, male and female. The shamans had mastered the magical chants, which were recorded in pictographic script charged with symbolism, and knew the remedies for disease, which was thought to be the work of destructive spirits who acted partly on their own account and partly as agents of divine justice. A few of the shamans were qualified to deal with epidemics affecting whole villages, and another small hereditary *élite* specialized in diagnosis and divination.

The earth was thought of as a disc with eight worlds above it and eight below, an obvious borrowing from Mesoamerican cosmology. The sky was also thought of as a hemisphere covering the earth; this may well be a remnant of an older cosmological system. The sun and moon ships sailed across the dome carrying menacing spirits.

Inanimate as well as animate natural objects were thought of as possessing souls; but the kind of 'soul' which leaves the human body at death to travel to a kingdom of the dead was clearly distinguished from the mere life force which resides in animate as distinct from inanimate bodies. Again, there was the concept of a life force which resides in different individuals to different degrees and which can be increased or diminished. The existence of these three separate concepts is an indication that Cuna religion is the product of a number of different outside influences and a number of different indigenous cultural horizons.

Life after death was visualized in a way which suggests Mesoamerican influence: where one spent one's after-life depended on the manner of one's death. The corpse of a dead man was suspended in a hammock for two days and then laid on two poles and buried in a trench grave. His personal belongings were buried with him and food was left on the grave.

The account I have just given of religious ideas and customs in the whole area occupied by Chibcha tribes refers to the state of affairs which was described by the Spanish conquerors of the first half of the sixteenth century, and which persisted in part into the Colonial period. Some of the information can be directly linked with archaeological evidence; but it is generally impossible to say whether the peoples and culture patterns involved can be identified with the bearers of older advanced cultures. There are, however, two unequivocal pieces of evidence which show continuity with older levels; they centre on the archaeological zones of San Agustín and Tierradentro.

San Agustín is not an isolated site but a wide area over which numerous finds in the same style have been made. It is significant that this site is not even mentioned in the accounts of the Spanish conquerors who first came to the area in 1537. The credit for the discovery of the site goes to the Spanish friar Juan de Santa Gertrudis, as early as 1757. Later workers in the area included the Colombians Francisco José de Caldas in 1797 and Carlos Cuervo Márquez in 1882, the Germans Alfons Stübel (1869) and K. Th. Stöpel (1912) and, best known of all, Konrad Theodor Preuss, who in 1913–14 described no less than 120 separate remains. Since then the work of the Colombian Gregorio Hernández de Alba, the Spaniard José Pérez de Barradas, the Americans Wendell Bennett and James A. Ford and the Germans Georg Burg and Horst Nachtigall has brought the total of known monuments to 328.

The simplest form of stone sculpture in the San Agustín culture is the carving of incised patterns; a more sophisticated technique is that of bas relief. A frieze at the Alto del Tablón site, described by Lunardi, shows human figures with upraised hands who seem to be engaged in worship. Walter Krickeberg has called it an 'eternal prayer in stone'. There are also stone columns with human facial features and arms lightly carved on their surface, which represent a transitional stage to the numerous huge monolithic statues which first attracted attention to this vanished culture. These anthropomorphic and zoomorphic figures often reach a height of 13 feet. They can be classified into two stylistic groups: one group stylized and forbidding in their intensity of religious feeling, the other marked by vivid realism and great technical mastery but bearing no sign of direct religious significance at all. It is possible that the differences between these sculptures mark a line of technical development in which the religious origins of the art were progressively lost from view. Traces of black, white, red and orange paint have been found on them. They did not all serve the same purpose by any means: some served to mark nearby graves; some were actually laid on graves as sepulchral slabs; some stood inside the temples as caryatids or Atlanteans; some were idols pure and simple.

Attempts have been made to deduce from these statues the nature of the gods that were worshipped at San Agustín; it is thought that moon and earth gods as well as sun gods, culture heroes and wind gods have been identified. Many of the gods are depicted with attributes of the stonemason's craft, the hammer and celt. Many carry a second figure on their heads or elsewhere, thought to be representations of the *alter ego*. Others wear masks on their faces or trophy heads round their necks. Many are characterized too by a wide mouth with feline fangs, a feature which appears in the wooden Cágaba masks described above, and which plays an important part also in the cultural history of Peru during the Formative and Classic periods. The conventional 'archaic' severity which characterizes these sculptures, their impersonality and boldness of outline, has always reminded observers of the works of the related Classic cultures of Teotihuacán (Mexico), Chavin de Huantar (Peru) and Tiahuanaco (Bolivia). This is an art concerned above all with giving form to inner visions.

Many of the San Agustín statues stand in a sort of stone chamber or cist open at the front and covered with earth so that from three sides it looks like a simple tumulus. Some of these mounds are 80 feet in diameter and contain more than one chamber. The chambers themselves sometimes measure 14 by 10 feet; and in these cases it is clearly possible to call them 'temples'. They are rectangular in plan, and their roofs are supported partly by the walls and partly by pillars and Atlantean figures. The walls are often painted with geometrical patterns, and the entrances sometimes flanked by Atlanteans. Like the statues, these structures may be described as megalithic, as they are not built of stones or bricks in courses but put together from huge single blocks of stone; many of them are recessed into hillsides, and it is tempting to suppose that these were sacred to earth gods or to ancestors.

San Agustín tombs are rectangular cists made of vertical slabs set into the ground and covered with single flat slabs. Some of them contain monolithic sarcophagi with carved lids.

Like Teotihuacán and Monte Albán in Mexico, and Tiahuanaco in Bolivia, San Agustín seems to have been the religious centre for an agricultural population settled over a wide area, and may indeed have been a place of pilgrimage for the inhabitants of a large part of what is today southern Colombia.

Finds belonging to the San Agustín style are scattered over a wide area, but must be carefully distinguished from those belonging to the localized culture of Tierradentro in the southern Central Cordillera between Neiva and Popayán. Tierradentro culture is characterized by the monumental sepulchral chambers investigated by the Colombian archaeologist Gregorio Hernández de Alba and the Spaniard José Pérez de Barradas. It is important to realize that these are quite independent of the San Agustín style remains found in the same area, and which, in their simplicity of execution and the absence of certain features such as the cat-fang motif, are basically a late 'provincial' (or 'epigonal') development of the San Agustín style. The characteristic Tierradentro remains, on the other hand, are quite different. They are subterranean chambers cut into the soft rock (granodiorite), either on artificially levelled terraces or on the high mountain slopes, and are circular or elliptical in ground plan. The roof of each chamber is either vaulted, or flat, or pitched one way, and is supported by rectangular 'pillars' of living rock. As the style evolved, the walls came to be hollowed out into alternating niches and pilasters, and this resulted in the appearance of lateral chambers. The wall decorations, mainly geometric patterns of parallel lines in black, white, red and orange but also including rhombuses, suns, and human faces and figures, were originally painted on the bare rock. Decorations in the later tombs are painted on a coat of lime plaster. Access to the chamber was through a diagonal shaft with accurately cut stone steps. Its entrance faced east; and after burial it was filled in completely and closed with a stone.

No art of sculpture accompanied this sepulchral architecture. It is noteworthy that no remains of places for people to live in have been found either. The variations in technique and ornamentation between one chamber and the next suggest the possibility of establishing some line of stylistic development; Pérez de Barradas has attempted to do this, postulating an evolution from an intense and severe early style to a more decorative 'baroque' manner.

No direct cultural relationship or filiation between San Agustín and Tierradentro has been established. There are crucial differences between the burial practices of the two cultures, Tierradentro favouring a sophisticated form of the western Colombian shaft grave and San Agustín making use of the monolithic sarcophagus.

Whoever the peoples may have been who created these two cultures, it seems clear that the Andaquí and the Paez, who inhabited San Agustín and Tierradentro respectively at the time of the Conquest, and who knew nothing of the nature or even the existence of the remains, were the destroyers rather than the heirs of the cultures they replaced.

It is now considered certain that San Agustín is the earlier of the two cultures and that it is one of the 'Classic' and theocratic cultures of ancient America. The Tierradentro horizon is located somewhere between the end of the theocratic phase and the arrival of the Spaniards.

The region between Lake Nicaragua and Ecuador is characterized by sharp local differences between tiny ethnic groups. The Chibcha, in particular, the dominant group, are remarkable for their 'balkanization'. There are several reasons for this cultural diversity. First there was no central power like that of the Inca empire to the south which might have had a unifying effect by acting as a dominant cultural influence. Another contributory factor was the ethnic diversity, which results from the history of population movements in the area.

Linguistically completely isolated groups, such as the Esmeralda, the Manca and Huancavilca, the Puruhá and Cañari, frequently live alongside groups related to the Chibcha such as the Cara of Ecuador. In Colombia Chocó-speaking peoples form isolated groups in close proximity to the Motilones, who are Caribans; and the Pasto, members of the Tucanoan group of eastern South America, live alongside members of the dominant Chibcha group. The close juxtaposition of different ethnic groups, with its attendant trade and marriage connections and its tiny local subdivisions, is not the only aspect of this diversity. A rich cultural variety does not exclude certain generally shared features; but these are of a very elementary nature and are of much less significance than the ethnographic distinguishing marks which contribute to the task of establishing a sequence of cultural horizons.

Most obvious of the common cultural characteristics is the belief in personal deities, usually anthropomorphic but often wholly or partly zoomorphic. Peoples unused to abstract thought tend to see a basic distinction not between man and beast, or man and spirit, but between animate and inanimate. The haziness of the distinction between man, beast and god leads to the idea of metamorphosis which in its turn gives rise to the series of cultural phenomena known as 'totemism'. The not uncommon idea of an 'inactive god', *deus otiosus*, with theoretical supreme status but no cult, is the result of the relegation of a historically superseded deity to the status of a myth.

Divine intervention in human affairs has as its corollary human attempts to influence the gods through religious ceremonies. The custom of making offerings appears again and again, and so does the concept of ritual 'purity' and 'impurity'. The belief that heightened powers (generally labelled 'magical') reside in certain things and especially in certain human beings, and that these powers may be acquired through abstinence and fasting, was almost universal. Survival after death was universally believed in; as far as our incomplete information goes, it is clear that no distinction was made between 'body' and 'soul' and that life after death was thought of as resembling life on earth. There is no universally valid answer to the question whether the individual was thought to pass to a 'numinous' plane after death; and it is not known to what extent there was a cult of the dead. Nevertheless, there is a certain amount of significant evidence on this question. One only has to think of the interpenetration of secular and priestly authority among the Muisca, based on concepts which we can still study among the living Cágaba. It is a totally different question whether royal power has its origin in priestly power or *vice versa*; it is most likely that the two had separate origins, and that an aristocratic caste usurped the functions, and misused the authority, of the priests for political ends; this was probably the origin of the theocracies of the Classic period.

In Cágaba and Muisca cosmology man is under an obligation to play his part in a cosmic drama through self-denial and self-mutilation, ritual dances, prayer and votive offerings. It is too easily forgotten that the Cauca valley in western Colombia and the Meseta of Bogotá both witnessed true human sacrifice (as distinct from cannibal feasts and the burial of wives and servants with their lord as grave offerings) in forms (such as heart-sacrifice) which show close affinities with Mexican customs. The priests are the custodians of the cosmic and terrestrial world-order which depends on divine intervention and cannot be disturbed without harm to all; its psychological correlative is the consciousness of sin.

One is struck by the affinities of style and subject between the religious sculpture of the early Classic period of San Agustín and its counterparts in Central America and the Andes. Its bold, severe, impersonal style deliberately eschews realism because its function is to externalize mythological images and inner visions. Their idols, which seem so alien to us, so unlike our visual image of what a human being is like, are in fact a way of giving concrete expression to what we know as the concept of transcendence or metaphysical reality.

II   *The Central Andes*

Our sources of information on the ancient cultures of the archaeological region known as the Central Andes – Peru, Bolivia and parts of northern Argentina and Chile – are of two kinds. Archaeological sources include architectural remains, pottery, and textiles; and literary sources are the accounts of indigenous society before, during and after the Conquest compiled by Spanish chroniclers and based on their own investigations 'in the field' and on what they had learned from Indian informants. The most valuable of these written sources are undoubtedly those written by authors who, as sons of Spanish fathers and Indian mothers, possessed a knowledge of native languages, and particularly Quechua, which gave them direct access to native culture. Francisco de Avila was among many who wrote not in Spanish but in an Indian language; Felipe Guaman Poma de Ayala and Juan Santa Cruz Pachacuti Yamqui Salcamayhua wrote in bad Spanish mingled with Quechua. It is true that systematic academic study of Peruvian antiquities made its appearance comparatively late. Baltasar Jaime Martinez Compañon, bishop of Trujillo, did some valuable work in the 1780s; but modern techniques of excavation did not reach the area until the end of the nineteenth century, with the arrival on the scene of the 'father of Peruvian archaeology', Max Uhle. The activities of the treasure-seekers or *guaqueros*, who have been active since early Colonial times, have also brought to light a great deal of material. Their name comes from '*huaco*', otherwise spelt '*guaco*', the term used for the ceramic grave goods that have been found in immense quantities in these areas. It is applied to the persons of the gods; to the constellations associated with them, with their influence on human life; to the holy springs where the water gods resided; to holy rocks and mountains which were heroes petrified; to holy caves which were entrances to the realm of the earth mother and of the dead; to the dead themselves, their remains and their burial places; and to all temples and sanctuaries.

Any description of the ancient religions of the Central Andean region must both move, as it were, in two dimensions: spatial and temporal. There have several times been 'Pan-Peruvian' cultures and religions; but some religious and cultural features have always been purely local; while historical changes, both cultural and religious, have always been partly offset by certain elements of continuity.

One of these constant elements is polytheism. Deities often appear in antithetical pairs; often too as a fruitful man–wife combination. The size of the pantheon was partly a result of the process of empire-building, in which local deities were assimilated and developed into 'specialist' gods, patrons of one particular aspect of life. In the Imperialist period, that of the Inca empire, this process led to a functional hierarchy of gods and a priesthood organized on the pattern of the civil service. Luis Valcárcel sees the bewildering multiplicity of Inca gods as an array of 'facets' of one god, of whom the others are mere symbols; but this is probably an over-simplification. The gods of the Central Andes do, however, have a certain number of shared characteristics; many of them for instance are also culture heroes. Typical too is the linking of gods with natural (and especially astral) phenomena and the existence of plural deities with several (usually three or five) aspects.

The tendency to think in terms of myth is of course another universal trait; as Werner Müller has pointed out, one myth in particular, that of the deluge, is of the utmost antiquity in all parts of the Americas.

Andean religion always has an ethical content: certain behaviour is enjoined upon man by the gods. As a corollary, there is also a consciousness of sin.

Another universal factor in ancient Peruvian religion is the ancestor cult. It is frequently hard to distinguish in individual cases where simple respect for the dead ends and worship begins. Without reference to any consistent distinction between body and soul, the dead are visualized as 'living corpses'. Simple grave goods appear even in the pre-ceramic horticultural period. In the course of development towards an advanced society, after the disappearance of the primitive egalitarian social structure, graves became more and more lavish. At the top of the social scale the 'grave goods' included the bodies of servants and wives. A form of mummification in which the guts were replaced by grass, and the corpse wrapped in textiles and left for the dry climate to complete the process, was common though not prevalent.

Parareligious ideas and practices – the idea that supernatural powers could be possessed or acquired by the individual – were current over a wide area. In many cases which are often simply labelled 'magic' by modern writers, there was originally believed to be a genuine causal relationship: as for instance in the belief that tempests, thunder, hail and eclipses could be averted by making a noise. But there are also signs of a belief in supernatural effects; these include woven amulets, figurines of alpacas buried in the pastures as fertility charms, and the *apachita*, roadside cairns erected in such places as the tops of mountain passes. The skull trophies, of which examples have been found in Nasca and elsewhere, are also magical objects; they stem from a belief that a relic of a vanquished opponent is capable of imparting some of his strength; the same idea underlies the drum-heads of human skin commonly used in western Colombia. In the Central Andean cultures cannibalism, on the other hand, was either non-existent or raised to the divine plane in the form of human sacrifice. Not all the parareligious or magical practices that have been recorded have been interpreted; we do not, for instance, know the reason for the periodic prevalence of trepanning.

The question of totemism is difficult. There can be no doubt that local units were grouped according to their (often animal) 'origins'. But the frequent use of animal names to refer to people does not necessarily imply the existence of clan totems. It is often no more than a survival (like the cult of zoomorphic deities) of a primitive state of mind which distinguished between animate and inanimate objects rather than between human and animal.

Against the background of these general features I shall first give an outline of what is known from archaeological evidence of the beliefs and religious customs of the prehistoric cultures, and then discuss what is known of religion at the time of the Conquest and of its partial survival up to the present day. For this period written sources will of course be of the first importance.

After an early period during which man settled down in villages on the coast, living mainly from the sea supplemented by a limited amount of civilization the story of civilization in the Central Andes begins as far as we know with the Chavín horizon of the northern Peruvian highlands. Here for the first time several tribes seem to have shared a common vision of the world, and a common artistic outlook; Chavín is the first of the Pan-Peruvian styles. It was probably imposed by a conquering aristocracy. This style, which is characteristic of the 'Formative' stage of Andean cultural development, dates mainly from the first half of the first millennium BC. The central motif in the Chavín style is the 'Feline God', who takes on the shape of a jaguar or puma and whose attendants are serpents and condors.

The site from which the style takes its name, Chavín de Huántar, lies in the valley of a tributary of the Río Marañón. Here in 1873 Raimondi found a stela with a bas relief representing an upright feline monster holding sceptres in its claws and crowned with a superstructure of gaping carnivore jaws with serpents emerging from them. The chief structure at Chavín is a massive platform-like temple. Together with other rectangular structures this encloses a sunken courtyard. In the interior of this so-called 'Castillo' (which is not a 'castle' at all) underground steps and galleries have been found. The outside walls are faced with smooth stone slabs, with massive wrinkled human heads, sometimes with cat fangs, tenoned into them, and the remains of a carved frieze. There can be no doubt that this was a place of worship and perhaps of pilgrimage. But no signs of settlement on any scale have been found. Similar sites have since been found in other parts of the northern Cordillera, such as the three-stepped temple platform at Kunturwasi at the head of the Jequetepeque valley.

The Chavín style spread far beyond the north highlands and had an especially strong influence on the valley oases of the north and central coasts, where Larco Hoyle has named it the Cupisnique style after the

Cupisnique valley. Most of the material here comes from cemeteries. The dead were buried in flexed positions, resting on their backs or sides, in graves that were sometimes lined with stone slabs. The abundant grave goods of the *élite* include a very large quantity of pottery, commonly decorated with effigies of felines or parts of feline bodies. A number of architectural remains from the coastal area are also ascribed to the Chavín horizon; these include a temple site in the Virú valley with remains of sacrificed llamas, a platform with a stairway in the Nepeña valley, terraced step pyramids in the Casma valley and terraced platforms (with the earliest known representations of trophy heads) in the Sechín valley.

The Peruvian archaeologist Julio C. Tello seeks to place the origins of the Chavín style in the plains of eastern South America. Robert von Heine-Geldern, on the other hand, refers to influences from south-east Asia.

In the next (Classic) age there seems to have been a falling-off of religious activity; this is certainly true of the dominant Feline God cult at least. The unique, certainly religious stone carvings of Huaraz and Recuay, in the north highlands, for instance, are massive stylized representations of warriors and women. This, however, belongs to the Classic phase of highland culture, and takes us rather ahead of our narrative; for there was another Formative culture, on the Paracas peninsula on the southern coastline of Peru, which overlapped chronologically with the Chavín horizon itself and was influenced by it.

The burials in Paracas were first excavated by Julio C. Tello in 1925. The earlier ones are known as the Cavernas from the fact that they are cut deep into the hard rock. Perpendicular shafts with steps lead down to circular chambers up to twenty-five feet below the surface, in which anything up to fifty-five individuals are buried together in a flexed position and wrapped in shrouds. Their skulls have often been trepanned. Grave goods include quantities of pottery with patterns including carnivore motifs which suggest Chavín influence.

A later group of burials is called the Necropolis. It is famous for Tello's find of 429 mummies in rectangular graves filled with sand. These corpses too are in a flexed position. Since these finds were made the French archaeologist Frédéric Engel has made the long-awaited discovery of traces of settlement. The Paracas culture lasted from about 700 BC to AD 100.

Later excavations have shown that the Paracas culture was succeeded in the south coast area by cultural elements traces of which have also been found in the Pisco and Ica valleys, but which seem to have originated in the valley round Nasca and appear to have developed out of the Paracas culture. Thanks to excavations carried out by Duncan Strong we now know that there was also a sizeable settlement, with temple platforms and pyramids, at Cahuachi. Nasca culture is characterized by shaft graves with round sepulchral chambers containing flexed corpses in winding sheets. The grave goods, both textiles and pottery, suggest that the cult of the dead must have absorbed all the energies of the people.

The motifs in Nasca art are mainly mythological and supernatural. The dominant forms are complex daemons whose attributes frequently include trophy heads. The majority of these are zoomorphic: cats, carnivorous fish, millipedes and birds. They are not to be understood as reproductions of nature but as parts of a whole mythical world view expressed by a strict iconographical canon. The Nasca style remained dominant in the south coast area for very many years: carbon 14 datings show that it lasted from about AD 100 to 800, when it disappeared for ever under the impact of another world view and another formal language, that of Postclassic Tiahuanaco.

In the north coast area the Classic stage is represented by the culture of the Mochica, which spread from its point of origin, probably in the Chicama valley, to all the oases between Jequetepeque and Casma. Earlier localized phases (Salinar and Gallinazo) were followed by the appearance of Mochica culture proper at some time not very long before the birth of Christ. This is the period in which two large pyramids, the Huaca del Sol and the Huaca de la Luna, were built in the Moche Valley after which the Mochica style is named. The Huaca del Sol consists of a low substructure and an oblong terrace sixty feet high, surmounted by a smaller terrace seventy-five feet high on which stood temple buildings since demolished by the religious zeal of the Spaniards. In the central coast area, the pyramids of Maranga (now within the city limits of Lima) and the large buildings at Pachacámac, an important religious centre in the Lurin valley, are probably contemporary with the Moche valley pyramids.

The archaeological remains of the Mochica culture consist of these adobe pyramids together with an incredible profusion of graves and grave goods. Interment normally took place in rectangular pits in which the corpse was placed in an extended posture, often wrapped in a bundle of canes. Hollow canes have also been found which lead from the grave into the open. We do not know for certain why this was done; it has been suggested that the reeds served to allow food and drink to be passed to the 'living corpse', or alternatively that they served as an exit for the soul when it came to leave the body. These two interpretations, one 'pre-animistic' and one 'animistic' or 'dualistic', contradict one another only in theory; in practice they may very well have coexisted quite happily.

The extreme dryness of the soil in the Peruvian coastal strip, and the incredible variety of objects, even including work baskets, which were placed in graves, have made it possible for us to have an extremely vivid picture of life in the Mochica culture. Did the dead need all the objects they had used in life because the after-life was just like this life? Or was it simply that the objects were there by right of possession? We do know that pottery and textiles were made specially for use as grave goods, and the fact that the pottery includes a fair proportion of effigy vessels suggests many questions. Some of the effigies, for instance, show illness and deformity; was this perhaps intended to draw off these evils from the dead man himself on to the image? The vessels depict all aspects of life in this world and the beyond. They reflect the authority wielded by the priests, who often appear in masks; priests or gods with cat fangs may well be an echo of the Chavín culture. The mythical beings depicted frequently appear with animal or bird attributes (thus, there are winged messenger-figures in hummingbird masks). There is an abundance of grotesque spirits and mythological creatures, fish, bats and birds. Beans appear as warriors, and ears of maize sometimes have human heads. This pattern of imagery survived for a very long time, and we shall have occasion to refer to it again.

While these coastal cultures were at their height, the Chavín Feline God lived on in the south highlands in the Classic culture of Tiahuanaco, which probably arose shortly after the birth of Christ and ended in a decadent Postclassic phase, about a thousand years later. The condor and the puma are conspicuous *leitmotive* in Tiahuanaco art; and it is also thought that the bearers of this culture worshipped a god called Huiracocha. This very important deity was almost certainly native to the south highlands; he was believed by later peoples to have created the sun and moon on Lake Titicaca, and is identified with the central figure on the so-called Gate of the Sun, a monolithic doorway at Tiahuanaco itself. The origin of the name Huiracocha has not yet been established with any certainty. It seems to have been taken over from some vanished language. (The word *Viracocha* is still used as an honorific by Andean Indians when they address 'Europeans'.) In any case it is clear that Huiracocha was an extremely ancient creator god, who maintained his position throughout the whole religious history of the Central Andes and still played an important part in the late Inca pantheon.

No significant traces of settlement have been found at Tiahuanaco; this seems, like Chavín and Pachácamac, to have been a centre of worship and a place of pilgrimage. Its most important remains include the fifty-foot high Akapana, which now looks like a small hill but which was once a temple pyramid; it is possible that this in its turn was originally produced by cutting away a natural hillock. On the terminal platform foundations of buildings as well as a cistern have been found. At the foot of the Akapana is the complex known as the Kalasasaya, a slightly raised, walled-in area about 445 by 425 feet. It once had a sunken courtyard in the middle surrounded by terraces reached by six monolithic steps. Some of the large blocks which make up the containing wall are still in place; the rest, especially the smaller ones, have been used as building material in the surrounding villages. Within the complex stands the best-known structure on the site, the 'Gateway of the Sun', carved from a single block of andesite 12 feet 6 inches by 10 feet and weighing 7 tons. The most noteworthy thing about this monolith is the central figure above the opening, thought to be Huiracocha himself. From his head issue eighteen rays, six of which end in puma heads. In each hand he holds a sceptre topped by the head of a condor.

The largest survivor of the many carved monoliths which once stood at Tiahuanaco is over twenty feet high. The severe, hieratic stylization of these sculptures suggests that the artists were not quite ready to break away from the form of the column or stela and make them into true statues. The temples were probably built, under priestly direction, by crowds of pilgrims who saw their work as pleasing to the gods, and the stylistic and thematic discipline imposed on the sculptors, here as in all the Classic theocracies of ancient America, gives their work its great emotional intensity.

The exact relationship between Tiahuanaco and the Pucára culture, which flourished in the area between the north-western end of Lake Titicaca and the site of Pucára itself, is still a matter for conjecture.

This culture has a number of artistic themes in common with Tiahuanaco, including the jaguar and puma motifs. At Pucára itself there is a temple with horseshoe-shaped inner and outer walls of red sandstone enclosing a terrace bounded with white sandstone slabs and a sunken court, seven feet below the terrace, reached by a stairway. The Pucára style of sculpture is much livelier than that of Tiahuanaco.

Another northern highland site which may well date from the period of expansion of the Tiahuanaco culture is the temple of Wilkawain, with its three storeys each divided into seven rooms provided with separate ventilation shafts.

The Postclassic period which was ushered in by the spread of Tia-huanaco influence to the coast can be studied in a series of major finds from the Peruvian coastal belt. These include grave goods from ceme-teries at Pachacámac and Ancón. These textiles and ceramics display an accomplished technique, but their decoration has less religious con-tent than in earlier periods. All over the coastal area the dead were buried in a flexed position in mummy bundles.

In the Urbanist or City Builder phase of the Postclassic, from about AD 1300 onwards, there appeared a belated successor of the Mochica culture in the shape of the north coast empire of the Chimú, which at the time of its absorption into the Inca empire about 1450, extended from Túmbez in the north almost to Lima in the south. Apart from a few post-conquest written sources, our main source of information on the culture of the Chimú lies as always in their grave goods, whether golden ornaments, cups and dishes, copper implements, pottery, or textiles. The Chimú believed that mankind had been created in four separate castes, by four different heavenly bodies. As a people accus-tomed to wresting their arable land from the stubborn desert, they gave pride of place among these four astral deities not to the parching sun but to the rain-bringing moon, the source of fertility, who was wor-shipped in Pacasmayu and elsewhere in the Si An, the 'house of the moon'.

Like the Chimú empire, the state of Cuismancu to the south, which included the area round Lima, and that of Chincha still further south in former Paracas and Nasca territory, have left remains of terraces and pyramids built for religious purposes.

The first Postclassic religious centre of the central highlands seems to have been Huari (in the Mantaro basin near the present-day town of Ayacucho) which archaeological evidence shows to represent a cultural compromise between the Postclassic coast cultures and the Decadent Tiahuanaco culture.

In the area of Tiahuacano itself there arose in Late Postclassic (City Builder) times the so-called Chullpa culture of the Aymara. *Chullpas*, which are turret-like tombs built of a mixture of dressed and undressed stones and clay, form long rows or 'streets' which often make up whole cities of the dead. Sometimes (as at Sillustani) they are round, some-times square; all have false vaults. Grave goods are few. Most *chullpas* contain a sepulchral chamber, but some (early?) examples are built over an underground chamber lined with split stones.

As I have said, and as the foregoing outline of 'prehistoric' development shows, any account of ancient Peruvian religion must move in two dimensions: variations are both geographical and chronological. The historians of the Conquest period were well aware of the richness of contrast that marked religious life in Peru in the last 'historic' phase of the Postclassic, that of the Inca empire. The illustrated chronicle of the half-Indian, half Spaniard Felipe Guaman Poma de Ayala, for example, sees this rich diversity, on which the Inca empire imposed a measure of unity, as follows. The inhabitants of Anti-Suyu (the north-east quarter of the empire) worshipped gods who appeared in the form of a coca-bush, a jaguar and the serpent Capac Apu Amaru. The people of Colla Suyu (in the south-east) made offerings of children, llamas, pottery, fish, shellfish, *chuño* (dehydrated potatoes) and maize beer. Their principal holy places were on the islands in Lake Titicaca. There they made offerings of gold and silver figurines, as well as twenty children a year. The inhabitants of Cunti-Suyu (in the south-west) worshipped mountain gods and the sea god, and offered up to them children, llamas, coca leaves and shellfish. The inhabitants of Chincha-Suyu (the north-west) worshipped the mountain-peaks. Burial customs too, according to Guaman Poma, varied in the four quarters of the empire. In Anti-Suyu he says that the dead were eaten and their bones kept in trees. In Cunti-Suyu the dead were buried in sepulchral chambers called *ayap llactan* ('villages of the dead') along with gifts of cloth, and with coca leaves, silver and gold in their mouths. Interment was the custom in Chincha-Suyu too, where ceremonies lasted for five days after death, and another funeral feast took place five days later still. As to the Aymara (Colla) of Colla-Suyu, we learn from Guaman Poma that their grave goods mainly consisted of foodstuffs.

I shall use information from both archaeological and written sources in attempting a survey of the beliefs of the north and central coastal peoples, and of the highlanders who founded the Inca empire.

A notable hypothesis to emerge from the recent work on the religion of the coastal peoples, carried out by the Peruvian archaeologist Rebeca Carrión Cachot de Girard, is that the most important features of religious life remained essentially unchanged over a period of 2000 years.

The religious ideas of the coastal peoples are mainly apparent in the shape and decoration of their ceramics; but thousands of small representations and textile designs tell the same story.

The most important gods are those associated with astral and meteorological phenomena; sun god and moon goddess are the central figures, with a retinue of feline and condor figures which probably reached the coast as a consequence of Chavín expansion. The sun-moon pair represents both the powers of the cosmos and those of terrestrial fertility; above them stands a supreme being who is not, however, always clearly distinguished from the various inferior deities. The idea of a *deus otiosus*, like some of the remote and ineffectual deities encountered in the earlier part of this section, does not seem to have suited the genius of the coastal peoples of Peru. On the contrary, there were close reciprocal links between gods and men; men 'responded' to the actions of the gods by acts of their own and most notably by sacrifices. Their religion has especially close links with their dominant practical preoccupation agriculture. The food plants, especially maize, take on an important religious significance of their own.

Sun and moon worship was not of course restricted to the coastal peoples of Peru: it was common to all the Andean peoples. The two deities were thought of as a primeval pair created by the supreme being, and represented in Peruvian coastal art either as twin human figures or in the form of the earth fertilized by the sun. The supreme being, often represented separately, the sun god (dominant in highland religion), the moon goddess (dominant in coastal religion) along with gods of the morning and evening stars, were all constant elements in the Peruvian pantheon; but the central theme everywhere was the sexual union between sun god and moon goddess. From this point of view the recurrent motifs of ancient Peruvian art can easily be accounted for. The sun often appears in the guise of lightning, which is represented by a (usually two-headed) serpent, which in turn is the symbol of rain; or it may take on the form of the rainbow, the 'sling of the gods'.

Both sun and moon mostly appear as beings in human shape emitting rays which end in serpent heads. Their union is consummated in a holy place surrounded by crenellated walls. In attendance on them are certain plants and animals which are either fertility symbols or actually conducive to fertility; among these the carob and the lucuma constantly recur. Feline figures are also in attendance; so are monkeys, which are thought of as an embodiment of fertility. The gods also appear in the forms of birds, or with ornithomorphic attributes: in a myth from Huarochirí, near Lima, the deity Pariacaca is born from an egg. Among sacrificial beasts llamas – chosen according to colour and markings – played a special part. The frequent depiction of disembodied llama heads may be more than a schematized rendering (the part for the whole); but it may in fact signify that the llamas were sacrificed by decapitation. The blood of the victim was sprinkled over the fields and smeared on the walls of the temple and on the faces of those present, who also consumed a mixture of sacrificial blood and maize flour, known as *sancu*. In the grave goods we can trace the process by which animal victims came to be replaced by wooden, cloth and pottery models.

One of the most charming things in Peruvian mythology is the belief that the gods carry out their beneficent work for men with the help of certain animals. The evidence of the decorated pottery is here most revealingly complemented by the written record: as in the episode in the myths of Huarochirí in which pumas, foxes, snakes and all kinds of birds help Pariacaca to build an irrigation channel in fulfilment of a vow made to the local fertility goddess Chokesuso. In many cases the symbols are chosen in a way which reflects an understanding of real causal relationships: thus the birds, which provide guano, are linked with fertility. Other relationships are either purely symbolic (the connection between cats and rain) or based on a misinterpreted causal connection (the toad as a bringer of rain).

I have already mentioned the process by which basically different deities sometimes merge into one composite god. One example is the assumption of the attributes of a fertility god by another god; possibly the sun god. In Mochica pottery the god is often shown sowing seed against the background of his mountain home. This basically anthropomorphic deity often also acquires feline characteristics. One important attribute of this god is his sceptre, which sometimes appears as a maize plant, sometimes as a digging-stick, sometimes as a cudgel and sometimes as a serpent.

The plant most commonly depicted is maize, although beans, groundnuts and manioc also appear. The frequent use of the maize motif reflects its liturgical significance (as a constituent of the *sancu*, the ceremonial meal of maize-flour and sacrificial blood). Maize for sacrificial use was prepared at times of fasting and abstinence by the virgins. There were also idols made of maize, both local *huaca*, objects of general worship, and household gods known as *conopa*. Pablo José de Arriaga, one of the clerics employed in extirpating 'idolatry' and therefore an expert on ancient Peruvian religion, writes as follows on the subject of these *saramamas* ('maize-mothers'):

One kind of *saramama* is a doll made of maize stalks and dressed in a skirt, a shawl and silver shawl pins, and they believe that she can conceive and give birth to plentiful maize. Others are made of stone, and are shaped like ears of maize with the grains individually carved; these are used in great numbers as household gods or *conobas*. Others consist of specially productive maize plants which have yielded many large cobs or a pair of twinned cobs. These then are the principal *saramamas*, which are worshipped as mothers of the maize.[7]

The union of the sun god (partly identified with the supreme being), the patron of water, irrigation channels and terraced fields, with the moon and earth goddess, promoter and protectress of the growth of plants, is usually depicted as taking place on high mountain slopes. In the written records we learn that they turned to stone after mating; while Francisco de Avila recounts the myth in poetic form in his tales of the goddess Chokesuso and the well god Anchicara.

Another frequent fertility symbol is the rainbow, depicted as a double-headed serpent; while the maize god himself appears especially frequently on the late black ware of the Chimú, as a feminine figure (a *saramama*) or as a masculine figure, or even as 'man and wife'. When a deity appears with both male and female characteristics this does not mean that he is androgynous but symbolizes the sexual union of god and goddess. A myth peculiar to the north coast cultures is that of twin gods one of whom must be slain that the food crops may spring from the several parts of his body.

The gods provide the fruits of the earth; but not without the active participation of their votaries. This participation most commonly takes the form of sacrifice; and where fertility is desired the most favoured sacrificial offering is blood. There are numerous representations of animal acolytes carrying out the sacrifice, which is often not depicted but symbolized by a sacrificial knife or a severed llama head. The acolytes are frequently shown as a triad of mythical birds.

Plant fertility was obviously the central preoccupation in the religion of the peoples of the central coast. In their art we see the gods sowing seed or standing in the middle of a field of maize; or with rays issuing from them which end in cobs of maize. Sceptres and other attributes were also frequently shown as cobs of maize. Again, the fertility goddess is often shown in a granary watching over the harvest. It is true that these iconographic features, almost without exception, are known only from finds in the coastal region; but the written evidence, which deals mainly with the highland cultures, tells very much the same story. The maize cult must be regarded as a Pan-Peruvian phenomenon.

The illustrated chronicle of Guaman Poma tells us of the 'guardians of the fields', whose functions Tschudi describes as follows:

This office . . . was not purely concerned with policing the fields; it had a religious element as well. During their whole term of duty the guardians had to fast, i.e. abstain from salt and peppers, and have no intercourse with their wives.[8]

In maize fields – and on all other cultivated fields – a stone was erected to promote the growth of the crops.

Chichic or *huanca*, writes Arriaga, is the name they give to long stones which they set up in the fields, and which they also call *chacrayoc*, that is 'lord of the field'. They believe that each field belongs to its own *huaca*, whose office it is to promote the growth of the crops, and as the 'lord of the field' they worship it and bring offerings to it, above all at sowing-time.[9]

The agricultural bias of Peruvian religion is further illustrated by the way in which religious festivals were closely linked with the vegetation cycle. Four major festivals took place at the equinoxes and solstices. On 22 June, the winter solstice, there was *Inti Raymi* (or *Onkoy Mita*), which coincided with the appearance of the *siete cabrillas* (the 'seven kids', the Pleiades, which were also objects of worship) and was the occasion for the nuptials of the Virgins of the Sun. This festival continued in Spanish times but was moved for obvious reasons to the Christian feast day of Corpus Christi. On 22 December there was *Capac Raymi*, a festival which coincided with the initiation of the young men, the *Huarichicuy* or putting on of the breeches. The festival held on 22 September was called *Situa*; on 22 March there was the feast of *Ayrihuay*.

In the sixth month, which is called *Hatun Cuzqui Aymoray* and corresponds to our May, a hundred llamas of different colours were sacrificed. The Indians still have a feast called *Aymoray* or Aymoraña which takes place at the time of the maize harvest. The people used to go in procession from the fields to their own houses singing songs in which they prayed for long life for the maize. Each in his own house would then make a maize *huaca*, which was called a *mamasara* and which was made by placing the best maize from the field in a little trough to the accompaniment of prescribed ceremonial and a three-night vigil. The little trough, which was called a *pirua*, was wrapped in the richest blanket the household possessed and thus adorned was the subject of much worship. They believe that this is the mother of the maize in the field and that the whole crop will benefit from the reverential treatment accorded to the *mamasara*. In the same month a special sacrifice is made in its honour. The wizards ask it if it has strength for the coming year, and if it answers 'no' it is taken back to the field, with all possible ceremony, and burned. Then they make another *pirua* with the same ceremonies, saying that they are renewing it to prevent the crops from spoiling. If the answer to their question is that it has strength enough to live on, it is kept until the next year. This superstition still persists to this day.[10]

On most of the offshore islands remains of places of sacrifice and traces of offerings have been found under the guano. The belief here was that the moon goddess was ruler of the sea and of the guano. Representations of human and animal heads are very frequent; do these perhaps stand for the sacrificial victim from whose scattered members the food crops grow?

The written sources are of course more reliable as sources for late pre-conquest times than for earlier times; and these sources concentrate on the highland culture of the Inca, both because of its political dominance and because the Spaniards found its centralized structure and the ideas of its ruling class comparatively easy to grasp. This heavy bias in the source material makes it necessary to make a special effort not to neglect the regional variations which existed within the Central Andean area.

Both the Aymara and the Inca had as their central deity the creator god Huiracocha. Huiracocha was represented in human shape. He had existed from the beginning of time, was immortal, and dwelt on high. He was not only the creator but also the active maintainer of the world and its life. He delegated his various functions to inferior deities whom he created himself, notably the sun and the other heavenly bodies. This delegation of authority was surely first attributed to Huiracocha by some speculative theologian seeking an explanation for the eclipse of the Huiracocha cult by those of a multitude of gods linked with aspects of everyday life. Huiracocha's role as Creator leads naturally to his appearance in explanatory myths in the guise of culture hero. He thus never suffered a complete eclipse; and his cult survived alongside those of the numerous rival deities, admittedly as a part of official rather than popular religion. At Cuzco, the capital, he was worshipped in the guise of a solid gold figure the size of a ten-year-old boy with right arm up-raised in a commanding gesture and right hand (except the thumb and index finger) flexed downwards. This figure and others like it were not the only centres of the cult of Huiracocha; but we know that he did have certain temples set aside for him, notably at Cuzco and at a place called Cacha, where he was said to have appeared once to an emperor who later assumed his name.

The tribal god of the Inca ruling dynasty was Inti, the sun god, also called Punchau ('light of day'). He was thought of as human in shape, but frequently depicted as a golden disc with a face. The cult of the sun god may have existed among the Diaguita of Argentina before they were absorbed by the Inca empire; but we know that it was introduced into Colla-Suyu, the south highland territory of the Aymara (or Colla), by the Quechua-speaking Inca *élite*. As in the lowlands, the sun cult was intimately connected with fertility; and it had closer ties than any other cult with the dominant 'state religion'. It is, however, an oversimplification to speak, as do the Spanish chroniclers, of the 'lands of the sun' and of 'Virgins of the Sun'; both institutions served wider religious ends than those of the sun cult. Unlike the masculine but sexually inactive Huiracocha, Inti had taken a wife, Mama Quilla, the moon mother, who presided over the basically lunar calendar and the religious festivals associated with it.

Like the principal deities of so many other early civilizations, Huiracocha and his lieutenant Inti presided over an impressive array of subordinate deities, some of them taken over from conquered tribes, some of them native to the Inca pantheon. These latter, who were probably held in common by all the peoples of Peru, include Pachamama, a subterranean earth mother invoked in daily rites by both Inca and Aymara. Another important deity, worshipped by the Diaguita as well, was Illapa (known to the Aymara as Thunupa), who was both dreaded as a storm god and adored as a bringer of rain. It is characteristic of the essentially anthropocentric world view of the ancient Peruvians that the storm god was thought of as a man with a club and a sling, who draws the rain from a stream (the Milky Way) which runs through the heavens, using pitchers which are then kept by his sister until he breaks them with his thunder club, discharging bolts of lightning from his sling all the while.

In addition there were hundreds or even thousands of anthropomorphic and zoomorphic deities – *huaca* – whose cults were local or regional. For instance, the Huanca of the Jauja area in the Mantaro valley worshipped a god called Huallallo to whom they sacrificed dogs. The Aymara believed in large numbers of supernatural beings divided into two categories, benevolent (*achachila*) and hostile (*auca*). The Spanish chroniclers even speak of a personified evil principle called *supai* in Quechua (the Inca language) and *supaya* in Aymara; but it is hard to tell how much Christian missionary influence may have been at work here.

Alongside from these *huaca* worshipped by whole 'clans', villages or tribes, there were household gods (like the Roman *lares et penates*) which were called *conopa* in Quechua and *huihuiri* in Aymara. They were less powerful than the gods mentioned so far, but they could be helpful in such matters as preventing the loss or theft of property. One of these domestic guardian spirits is known to the present-day Aymara as Ekeko. He is probably an ancient fertility god who has declined to his present menial status over a long period of time. He takes the form of a male figurine which on a given day is hung with miniature replicas of the possessions which the household desires to acquire or to preserve. The *conopa* tended to reside in some material object which was then regarded as the agent of their power, so that they often became mere amulets rather than independent deities.

Among the religious elements which were familiar to the Andean tribes long before the advent of the Inca empire is the idea that certain heavenly bodies and constellations play a part in shaping human destinies. As we shall see, the morning star plays a part in myth if not in theology; and the Pleiades were honoured everywhere in ancient Peru as important arbiters of human destiny. Several other constellations were thought of as wild beasts; and the constellation *Lyra* was the heavenly llama which governed the supply of llama wool.

As I have said, the multiplicity of gods was partly due to the adoption of the gods of conquered peoples which is characteristic of polytheistic imperialist cultures. In the Inca empire this process was symbolized by the building in Cuzco of a Pantheon, the *Corichanca*, where the *huaca* of all the nations under Inca rule were kept and brought out on the appropriate feast-days.

The most important example of this process of god-adoption was Pachacámac who, in spite of his Quechua name (which means 'world-maker'), cannot be identified with the Inca creator god Huiracocha. He was an ancient and renowned deity of the central coastal regions, where his eponymous sanctuary in the Lurin valley was a place of pilgrimage. Another god taken over from the coastal tribes was the ancient goddess of the fishermen, who was incorporated into the highland Inca pantheon under the Quechua name of Mamacocha ('sea mother').

One of the principal elements in the religious life of the ancient Peruvians (unlike that of the Mexican peoples) was a deep-rooted ancestor cult, remnants of which persist to this day; they were preoccupied with the question of survival after death.

In the area round Cuzco (Chanapata) Rowe has unearthed pre-Inca burials in round or oval chamber graves containing a flexed corpse but no grave goods.

It would be appropriate in this context to deal with the cultures of the southern periphery, which are known to us almost exclusively from the contents of their graves. In the territory of the Atacameños the mummified dead were grouped round tables in the centre of subterranean chambers where offerings were brought to them every year. Among the Chilean Diaguita there seems to have been more than one mode of burial: on the coastal strip individual cist graves are found in association with raised burial mounds, also containing cists, and circular graves containing multiple burials which suggest that men of rank were buried together with their wives and servants. In the Quebrada de Humahuaca the dead seem to have been buried in cist graves under the floors of their own houses; while on the high plateau (the Puña de Atacama) natural caves were enlarged to form burial vaults. In both areas individual burials appear alongside collective ones.

In apparent contradiction to the widespread belief that the dead intervene directly in the affairs of the living, they were thought by the Incas to reside in kingdoms of the dead. It is uncertain to what extent the survival myth recounted by our Spanish sources (in which the fate of the individual soul is determined by ethical criteria) is a product of Christian influence. According to this interpretation the righteous go to a solar paradise in the sky, the 'upper world', Hanac Pacha, and the unrighteous to the underworld, Ukhu Pacha, in the bowels of the earth, there to suffer torments of cold and hunger, with nothing to eat but stones. The use of specific native terms for the upper and nether world suggests that these are indigenous concepts; but it may well be that the division was originally made on the basis of status rather than virtue. Support for this supposition is provided by an alternative – and clearly older – version in which the aristocracy passes automatically into the upper world, the kingdom of the sun god, while the common people live on in the depths of the earth, the kingdom of the earth mother Pachamama.

This last idea – the association of Pachamama with the cult of the dead – is no doubt connected in some way with the veneration accorded to natural caves (chincana) which have often been fitted out with altars and with shallow internal niches which formed 'doors and windows' through which ancestral spirits might pass; they differ from real windows and doors just as the essence of the ancestral spirit differs from that of ordinary living people. The relationship between man and the spirits (whether ancestral or nature spirits) lies at the root of a number of other religious ceremonies. One has only to think of the reverence accorded to boundary stones and the stones which acted as guardians (huanca) of the fields; or again the apachita, the cairns placed on mountain passes and summits all over the Central Andean region, and which are still looked on today as a protection against misfortune. Each passer-by adds one stone to the apachita, and coca leaves and other offerings are also placed upon it.

I have already referred to the portable guardian spirits thought to reside in certain amulets which although made in a shape (human, animal or vegetable) which recalls the individual spirit within, form a transition to the parareligious belief in the intrinsic magical properties of objects such as the bezoar stones called *illa*. Any strangely shaped natural object was considered to be a token of good or bad luck; hence the precautionary rites with which men encountered any kind of freak or deformity.

Ancient Peruvian theology in general was dominated by benevolent gods (benevolent, that is, as long as their cult was not neglected) to whom mankind stood in a kind of parent-child relationship. Malevolent beings (*supay, supaya*) which the Aymara visualized in the shape of a floating severed human head or a three-headed aquatic monster, belonged to an earlier cultural horizon and had been relegated to a subordinate status in the spirit world. Another feature of Aymara religion was the belief that the crops must be respected as the property of the guardian spirits of the fields, who shared their proprietary rights over domestic animals with the spirit of the high savannahs, Huasa-Mallcu.

To judge from the way in which different 'strata' of myth seem to overlie each other in the mythology of the highland peoples of Peru, the idea of multiple gods seems to date from the earliest phases of advanced civilization. One example is the triple god Tanga-Tanga who was worshipped at Chuquisaca; but in earlier times it is clear that fivefold deities were more common than three-fold ones.

One recurrent mythical element is the metamorphosis of deified mythical figures into personified rocks and mountains. One example among many in the myths of Huarochirí is that of the snow-capped mountain Pariacaca. In the Inca origin myth, as we shall see, one of two brothers became the holy mountain Huanacauri and the other a great boulder which lay in Cuzco; and there can be no doubt that some similar belief was attached to the strangely-shaped rock which stands on the ritual site known as the Kenko, high above Cuzco.

A characteristic of polytheism in advanced civilizations is the emergence of 'specialist' gods, the patrons of fertility, rain, divination and other human concerns. This process goes hand in hand with the adoption of the local and regional gods of subject peoples. While these two processes were going on within Inca civilization the secular and religious *élite* was engaged in spreading its own sun cult as a means to a political end, that of securing a measure of imperial unity.

Myth is basically an attempt to express transcendental ideas in an assimilable form by clothing them in the forms of the world of appearances. It also provides an explanation of the origins and causes of natural and cultural phenomena. This function is filled in Inca mythology by the creation myth of Huiracocha.

Huiracocha created heaven and earth, but they still lay in darkness. Then he created men of gigantic stature and breathed life into them. But they did not please him, and so he destroyed them by turning some into the huge stone statues which are still to be seen at Tiahuananco and by drowning the others in a universal deluge. Then he caused the sun and moon to rise from the islands in Lake Titicaca, and at Tiahuanaco he fashioned normal-sized men out of clay and drew on their bodies the outlines of the clothes they were to wear. He then taught them their various languages, ways of life and moral codes and sent them below ground to the places where they were to emerge and live. When all this was accomplished Huiracocha set off into the north. Many men failed to recognize and honour him, because he went in the guise of a beggar leaning on a staff. In Cacha they were even about to stone him, when Huiracocha caused fire to fall from the heavens, which burned the rocks all around. When mankind prayed to be spared he was merciful. He went on his way to Cuzco, and on across the Andes as far as Manta, on the coast of Ecuador, where he walked out westward on the waves of the sea.

This is a summary of a myth which is preserved, with an abundance of embellishment, in the Spanish chronicles. It shows that Huiracocha combined the roles of Creator and culture hero. Several parts of the myth are explanations of observed facts; the mysterious huge monolithic statues at Tiahuanaco are ascribed to an early and imperfect creation by Huiracocha, and the ashes and lava which issued from the volcano Tinta are interpreted as a reminder to the inhabitants of Cacaha of the fire which once fell from the heavens. But the core of the myth is in its setting, the ancient homeland of the Aymara round Tiahuanaco and Lake Titicaca. The Inca undoubtedly took this creation myth over from their conquered southern neighbours the Aymara and adapted it to suit their own theology and cosmology; among the Aymara themselves Huiracocha was confounded and partly identified with Thunupa, a bearded white-skinned culture hero from the north. Another explanatory element in the Inca creation myth is the attempt to reconcile the idea of a single act of creation at Tiahuanaco with the belief that each individual ethnic group had sprung from its own local soil. The apparent contradiction is dealt with by saying that Huiracocha sent his creatures into the earth with orders to emerge at the places ordained for them.

According to the courtly tradition of the Inca, the tribal ancestor and culture hero, identified with the dynast Manco Capac, emerged from within a hill some eighteen miles from Cuzco. The myth runs as follows: in this hill there are three caves. From the middle one there emerged in far distant times four brothers and four sisters, who all wandered off together in search of a place to settle. One of the brothers was imprisoned by the others in a cave in the mountain Huanacauri, another turned to stone on the same mountain, and the third turned to stone when they reached the site of the future city of Cuzco. The choice of the site was made by the golden staff of the last surviving brother, Manco; where it sank into the ground he and his sisters laid the first stone of the city. He left the subsequent destinies of the tribe in the hands of his son Sinchi Roca, from whom the lineage of the royal house could be traced in unbroken succession for ten generations until the arrival of the Spaniards. From a historical point of view this thus indicates that Inca rule in the immediate surroundings of Cuzco dates back at least as far as the thirteenth century. From a mythological point of view it is interesting to see how this Inca national myth, as recorded by the half-Inca writer Garcilaso de la Vega in the eighteenth century, fits in with the Huiracocha creation myth. According to Garcilaso de la Vega, Manco Capac was a culture hero sent by the sun god from his Isla del Sol in Lake Titicaca; clearly the Titicaca myth was present in the Inca national consciousness alongside their own tribal origin myth.

The most important of the personified celestial phenomena which play so prominent a part in Inca mythology is of course the sun, Inti, the mythical 'father' of the dynasty. The fact that the ruler was thus considered to be the Son of the Sun (*Intip Churin*) gave rise to a theory of Divine Right according to which the dynasty was entrusted with a hereditary mission to rule the terrestrial sphere. The divine ancestry and divine vocation of the emperor led naturally to his being paid divine honours, at least posthumously. When he died his corpse was ceremonially mummified to ensure his survival as a 'living corpse'; it was for this reason that Atahuallpa, captured and condemned to death by the Spaniards, elected to be converted to Christianity so that he could be strangled rather than burned. As the Son of the Sun, the Inca lived on for ever surrounded by the wives and servants who had been buried with him, and amid all the splendour of his royal household. This concept of divine kingship, with its strange combination of the practical and the metaphysical, is peculiar to Inca culture.

The familiar motif of a series of 'antediluvian' ages of the world containing partial or imperfect creations, which we have already encountered in the Huiracocha myth, appears in another form in the illustrated chronicle of Guaman Poma de Ayala. According to this myth the earth was inhabited in the first age by the fabulous *hapiñunu*, and the Huari-Huiracocha-Runa, human beings who worshipped Huiracocha. A second age brought the Huari-Runa (the Quechua word *huari* denoted the possession of supernatural powers). The third age was that of the Purun Runa ('wild ones'), and the fourth that of the Auca Runa, who could turn into animals at will. This is a clear example of a composite tradition incorporating elements of disparate origins.

The organization of the late Inca empire, as seen by European observers, included a priestly hierarchy organized in much the same way as the governmental machine: a typical feature of advanced civilizations. But there is a widespread tendency to overestimate the degree of centralization within the Inca empire in religion as in other things; outside this organized body of priests stood thousands of shamans, local mediums and healers who, at least in the remoter provinces, were quite independent of central control. The Diaguita seem also to have had their own priests who officiated at sacrifices as well as concerning themselves with all kinds of magical practices and with healing.

The priestly caste of the Inca empire was headed by a high priest who was a brother or other near relative of the emperor, and who wielded considerable influence in affairs of state. The most likely interpretation of the various names for him that have come down to us is that he was known as Huillac Uma (speaking chief). Under him were a number of categories of priests, differing both in status and in function; but our sources give no clear and unified picture of their titles and grades. We do know that there were special priests for divination, sacrifice, temple service and the confessional; and we also know that even under the Inca empire there were still magicians for all purposes including healing. We also have some recent evidence which enables us to deduce something of the sacerdotal organization of the ancient Aymara. We know that they made a distinction between *pako* and *laika*, the practitioners of white and black magic respectively. These magicians cannot strictly be called shamans, as they did not claim to be possessed by spirits. The Aymara diviners were called *yatiri*, and were said to be 'called' to their profession by being struck by lightning. The healers were known as *collasiri*.

A word must be said concerning the Inca institution of the *Aclla Cuna*, the 'Virgins of the Sun' or Chosen Women. Specially appointed officials visited all parts of the empire and selected ten-year-old girls to be taken to convent-like institutions, the Aclla-Huasi, in Cuzco and other principal cities. There they came under the authority of mothers superior

135

(*mama-cuna*) chosen from their own number, and were vowed to chastity. Their duties and functions were of various kinds. Some devoted themselves to service in the temples, where they brewed the maize beer (*chicha*) used in religious festivals; others were kept for use as sacrificial victims, and others served the Inca himself as weavers, became his secondary wives or were given in marriage to nobles who had deserved well of the state. This remarkable institution was governed by a high priestess, the *Coya Pacsa*, of very high birth, who was regarded as the earthly consort of the sun god just as the moon goddess was his heavenly consort.

In the Inca empire, as elsewhere, the priests were obliged to preserve their supernatural powers by a wide variety of abstinences and self-denials; but in return they and the Virgins of the Sun were provided for by the State. All lands and flocks were divided into three portions: one for the peasants, one for the gods, and one for the emperor. In addition to this religious expenditure, each individual community set aside a portion of its remaining land for the service of the local *huaca*. Each of these local shrines had its own custodian, who might be an old man or an old woman of the village.

I shall deal in one moment with the forms of public worship in which the Inca priests were engaged; but first it must be stressed that not all religious experience, and not all 'human response' to the actions of the gods, was the monopoly of the priestly caste.

Individual piety was expressed mainly in abstinence; an individual might decide to abstain from pepper and salt, from meat or *chicha*, or from sexual intercourse. Among both the Inca and the Aymara sacrifices were offered up by individuals as well as by priests; one form of sacrifice which has survived to this day is libation.

Prayer too was an intensely personal activity, consisting as it did in a direct plea to the deity for favour or forgiveness. In the myths of the Huarochirí district, inland from Lima, as handed down to us in the Quechua language by the priest Francisco de Avila, there are some spoken formulas such as the following: 'Huiracocha, creator of mankind, creator of the earth, whatsoever may exist is Thine. Thine are the fields, and it is for Thee that Thy men exist'.[11] Recourse was had in times of sickness to the goddesses Llacsahuato and Mirahuato, whose local cult was looked after by a woman: 'You are creatresses of men and know of my sin; make known to me what I am sick of and what is the sin which makes me suffer'.[12] There were similar formulas for use on occasion such as passing a spring or crossing a river, each of them addressed to the appropriate deity. There was a special posture for repeating these prayers: the upper part of the body was bent forward, the arms stretched out in front with the palms of the hands outwards, and the fingertips often raised to the lips in a gesture rather like blowing a kiss; this procedure bore the name of *muchay*. The Aymara knelt on one knee to pray. Their prayer formulas were similar to those of the Inca; one noteworthy Aymara custom was to ask each other at certain festivals for forgiveness for past ill-will.

Prayer was more than a private thing; it formed one of the public duties of the priesthood, whose intercession was thought to add weight to the requests of the individual. On certain public occasions there were also collective 'congregational' prayers, some of which have survived and are poems of considerable literary merit. The area about which we are best informed in this respect, Huarochirí, has a collective prayer to be used in time of general sickness, a parallel to the personal prayer quoted above. The congregation cries out to a god called Macahuisa: 'Help us and preserve our village and heal us of all manner of ills!'[13] Naturally enough the prayer for rain is also a collective one: 'Let there be rain upon the earth! For if no water flows from this lake we men are in great need. Rain, we beseech Thee, for this we come!'[14] 'Thine is the lake and thine the water; give us water in plenty!'[15]

The second important function of the priesthood was sacrifice. Where the major deities were concerned, at least in the greater centres of population, there were special priests who devoted themselves exclusively to this task. The principal objects of sacrifice were food and healing, and the offerings were chosen according to the preferences of the god, as revealed by the omens. Among the objects offered up by individuals or by the community were all kinds of food, luxuries like coca or *chicha* (which recur in the myths of Huarochirí as the food of the gods), wool, complete garments (which, like the coca leaves, were burned), miniature garments, and gold and silver figurines. And when the common man had nothing else to give, he sacrificed his own eyebrows. The victims most agreeable to the gods were domesticated animals, guinea-pigs and llamas, rather than wild animals. The llama in particular was used for sacrifice in a number of different and precisely regulated ways. It was always killed in the same way, by cutting its throat; but the victims were selected for their colour and other distinguishing marks according to the deity involved and the reason for the sacrifice. We are told that Huiracocha was offered brown animals, the sun god white ones and the storm god dappled ones. At public sacrifices the expense was borne out of the 'gods' share' of the crops; if an individual engaged a priest to offer up a sacrifice on his behalf, the priest took his share of the offering.

In Cuzco there was a sacrifice to the sun god every day, and we can gain some idea of the number of llamas consumed from the fact that a hundred beasts were sacrificed every lunar month, an average of three or four a day.

What we know of the sacrifices offered up by the Aymara agrees more or less with what we know of the Inca. The offerings included coca, *chicha*, salt, *aji* (pepper), all kinds of food, flowers, gold and silver, llama foetuses and male llamas. The Diaguita liked to offer the sun god the head of a deer – or better still that of a defeated enemy.

A question which must be treated separately is that of human sacrifice. There can be no doubt, in spite of all that has been said to the contrary, that human sacrifice did take place. It is true that it was never practised on the same immense scale as in Mexico; it has been suggested that this was because the llama was available as an alternative source of blood. Human sacrifice was in fact reserved for the very greatest of the gods and confined to the most momentous occasions, such as famine, pestilence, defeat in war, or the accession of a new monarch. This last was marked by the sacrifice of no less than two hundred children. The Aymara sacrificed children by strangling, and we may assume that the Diaguita of the Argentine did the same; the bodies of strangled children have been found in urns. The Inca had the custom, when they subdued a province, of choosing a number of the best child 'specimens' and bringing them to Cuzco for sacrifice to the sun god. Normally, however, they sacrificed only flawless children and virgins voluntarily given up by their families or collected by itinerant tribute-gatherers (cf. the account of the recruitment of the Virgins of the Sun, above). Boys were sacrificed at about ten years old, girls between ten and fifteen. Some victims had their hearts cut out; some were strangled and had their throats cut. Their blood was sprinkled on the face or body of the idol.

Although religious life was by no means confined to temples, religious centres of one kind and another did play an important part in the communal life of the Inca, and their upkeep was among the principal tasks of the priests and the Virgins of the Sun. Temple complexes included living quarters for the priests as well as storehouses for offerings. The principal Inca temple, the so-called Temple of the Sun at Cuzco, was a large walled precinct with interior courts ringed by chambers decorated with tapestries or even with plates of gold. The right of entry to the temples was restricted to the priests and officials.

Illustrations of the most important of the symbolic representations of the gods, as they appeared in the 'Pantheon' or Coricancha (Temple of the Sun), in Cuzco, appear in a manuscript by Juan Santa Cruz

Pachacuti Yamqui Salcamayhua which has been described by Robert Lehmann-Nitsche.

Feast days and ceremonies formed a very important part of religious life. There were ceremonies for special occasions such as droughts, epidemics, earthquakes, lost battles, and for the accession, sickness or death of the monarch; but most religious festivals followed a regular seasonal pattern which was fitted into a lunar calendar. In Cuzco ceremonies took place in the great open space known as the Aukay Pata (now the Plaza de Armas) to which all the gods in the Coricancha, including the mummies of former emperors, were brought for the occasion.

The twelve lunar months (*quilla*) were:

Capac Raymy, which included the initiation ceremony for the youths of the nobility, the *Huarachicuy* or 'putting on of the breeches', and their ritual foot race to the mountain Huaracauri (the *Huarachicuy* was a solar festival and included the summer solstice on 22 December);

Camay, which corresponds more or less to January;

Hatun Pocoy, the festival of the ripening maize;

Pacapucuy or *Paucar Huaray*;

Ayrihua;

Aymoray, the month of the maize harvest;

Inti Raimy or *Ancay Cuzqui*, the seventh month, which included the winter solstice (21 June), at which sacrifices were offered up to the sun god;

Chahuahuarquis, the month devoted to the *chacracunacuy*, the reallocation of the fields in readiness for the new agricultural year;

Yapaquis, the month in which the fields were made ready for *chacrayapuy*, the sowing;

Situa or *Coya Raimy*, the tenth month, originally a lunar festival, when purification rites by water and fire were carried out as a protection against disease, and all the provincial *huacas* were brought to Cuzco for a ceremony of tribute;

Umaraimy or *Cantaray*, when prayers were offered up for rain to nourish the seedling crops; and

Ayamarca, the twelfth month, which saw the preparations for the puberty rites or *Huarachicuy*.

It is worth repeating that none of the many attempts that have been made to express the Inca calendar in terms of our own has been or can be successful. All the Inca months are lunar months, so that no exact equivalence is possible.

Our information on Aymara festivals dates from more recent times but most probably more or less reflects what happened in pre-Columbian times.

When the harvest was completed there was the *Choquela*, a festival designed to ensure a good harvest for the next year. Interestingly enough, however, the central feature of this agricultural festival was a ritual vicuña hunt in which the victim was sacrificed and 'brought back to life'; clearly an ancient hunting rite. To make the fields fertile there were rainmaking ceremonies which took place on the mountain Atoja near Chucuito. In the course of time the fertility god Ekeko became a god of good fortune in general, whose miniature idols, hung with tiny models of things desired, are still to be found in Aymara houses to this day.

Divination in various forms entered into every aspect of life in ancient Peru. Every important decision and medical diagnosis, the question of honesty in the confessional, the whereabouts of lost or stolen property, the detection of a hostile magician at work, the choice of an heir or of an acceptable sacrificial offering, and even problems of military tactics, were referred to the priest-augurer known as the *umu* in Quechua. Each enquiry was accompanied by a sacrifice proportional to the importance of the information required. When a god was consulted in person (the most important of these oracular deities were Pachacámac and Apurimac, the 'old speakers'), the priest spoke both questions and answers, using different voices. The future was also foretold from the movements of snakes and spiders, and especially from the lungs of sacrificed llamas. The priest-augurer would blow into a vein and interpret the patterns which formed in the surface of the lung. People noticed and interpreted every possible kind of omen, just as the Aymara do today; their *yatiri* read the future in coca quids. The priest would chew a few leaves and spit them into his hand. If the saliva ran evenly down the outstretched fingers this was a good omen; if not, not.

Both Quechua and Aymara placed great emphasis on the significance of dreams. There was a vast dream-lore. To dream of fire, for instance, betokened sickness; to dream of a shooting star or a comet meant the death of the emperor. Other evil omens were the rainbow and certain animals such as foxes, spiders and snakes.

Another important source of the power and prestige of the priesthood was the confessional, based on a consciousness of sin which the priests were at pains to keep alive. Bolivian school-children still repeat to this day a moral formula which dates from Inca times: '*ama sua, ama llulla, ama kella*' ('thou shalt not steal, thou shalt not lie, thou shalt not be idle'), a fair sample of the ethical system which underlay the 'state socialism' of the huge Inca empire. Apart from such precepts there were naturally a whole series of religious prohibitions such as those on killing, especially by magical means, and adultery. In the popular mind sin and all unlawful conduct harmed both the individual and the community; so the evildoer must be brought to account and made to perform penances to avert the consequences of his deeds. In the myths of Huarochirí we hear for instance of the wife of the rich man of Anchicocha: 'Her husband knows her adultery now; for since her sin a serpent has dwelt upon his fine house and consumed his substance.'[16] The idea of the consequences of sin is contained in the little prayer in time of sickness from the village of Checa, already quoted: 'O Llacsahuato, Mirahuato, you are creatresses of mankind and know of my sin. Tell me what ails me, tell me what sin makes me sick!'[17]

Sins were normally confessed directly to a priest, a custom which may well have been of Aymara origin; the word for father confessor, *ichuri*, is an Aymara word. The *ichuri* was sworn to silence, the penitent sworn to tell the truth. His veracity was tested by reference to the oracles, and he might be struck on the back with a stone to induce him to make a true confession. The monarch himself confessed his transgressions only to the sun god. In times of national emergency, as for instance when the emperor was sick, the whole people might engage in a collective act of confession.

The absolution of the penitent took place in one of two closely related ways. Either he bathed in running water which carried his uncleanness away, or he held a handful of straw which the priest spat on and threw into a river. Both customs indicate that the confession itself took place beside running water. (Ritual ablution was also practised by the Aymara as a purification rite on occasions such as bereavement.) The imposition of penances such as prayers, abstinence and fasting was an integral part of the confessional system.

Finally, the priestly caste also had charge of the initiation ceremonies, the *Huarachicuy*, which took place in the month of the summer solstice, *Capac Raymi*. In these rites the young nobles submitted to a number of ordeals designed to increase their strength, the principal of which was the foot race to the summit of the holy mountain Huanacauri which plays a part in the Inca origin myth. Francisco de Avila and Diego Dávila Briceño speak of analogous foot races to the snow-covered sacred mountain Pariacaca as a re-enactment of some happening in mythical antiquity.

In addition to the priests with their socially benevolent activity there was an obscure and inferior class of evil sorcerers. A sorcerer convicted of murder was punished by the extirpation of his whole 'clan'. These men sometimes employed poison, sometimes 'anti-amulets' or bad-luck charms, sometimes actual scraps of tissue belonging to the body of the intended victims; or they destroyed him in effigy. They also dealt in 'love magic'. The Aymara too had their *laika*, black magicians, as well as their lightning-struck *pako* or white magicians, who could tell the origin of sicknesses, detect thieves, influence the spirits and act as oracles.

Under the name of *hamauta*, the priests were the custodians of the learning and 'science' of the civilizations of ancient Peru. The predominance of solar elements in Inca religion corresponds with a heliocentric cosmology in which there were only two 'cardinal points', east and west. There were no Quechua words for north and south, and although the empire, Tahuantinsuyu, the 'four lands', was divided into four quarters, these were based on natural physical divisions, rather than on direction. Chinchasuyu (north-west) was the north coastal valleys, Antisuyu (north-east) the forests of the Montaña, to the east of the Andes, Cuntisuyu (south-west) the Peruvian Andes proper, and Collasuyu (south-east), the Altiplano, the Aymara highlands, and the remote southern provinces.

More important than the east-west orientation seems to have been another and older system of 'orientation': the division of all social and territorial units into *hanan* and *hurin*, 'upper and lower', upstream and downstream.

The Aymara on the other hand had a seven-point, three-dimensional 'compass': north, south, east, west, zenith, nadir and 'middle' (the standpoint of the observer). The east is the sacred direction for the Aymara; sacrificial victims were always made to face eastwards, and the vast majority of their turret tombs or *chullpas* have entrances facing east.

I have already mentioned that the great agricultural festivals were based on a lunar calendar; but sowing times were determined by observing the rising and setting of the sun from the middle of the great square at Cuzco, in relation to towers built on the horizon to the east and west. Eclipses of the sun and moon were much feared; it was thought that a serpent or a puma threatened to eat the moon and attempts were made to scare the beast away by raising a din by means which included beating dogs to make them howl. We have no evidence that there was a system of calendar notation; if there was, it was certainly the responsibility of the priesthood. Those who claim that the Inca did have a form of writing point to the pictographic system still in use in certain remote areas of the Andes for recording prayers, and the fact that the Quechua language has a native word for 'to write' (*kellka*), which must have had some objective correlative. One thing is certain: that the famous knotted cords (*quipu*) used by the Inca were strictly a system of recording numbers. They are still used in counting flocks.

In all this we must bear in mind that the life and thought of the ancient peoples of ancient Peru were very much less rational than we might assume. Everything to do with number was deeply imbued with symbolism. The same was true of colour, which was far more than a matter of decoration. I have already mentioned the lost system of colour symbolism according to which llamas were selected for sacrifice to particular deities. This sort of complexity was lost on the old chroniclers; but Francisco de Avila, as always, is a mine of information. To take only one example: when the gods are angry with mankind they send 'yellow and red rain'. The same source leaves no room for doubt that in pre-Inca times the number five played a dominant part not only in practical but also in religious life, as in the five-day religious festivals and the frequent appearance of quintuple deities. Trinities also seem to have been a comparatively ancient feature of the native pantheons.

In the Inca empire the quinquenary system of counting had given place to a vigesimal system (using all the fingers and toes) and to a decimal system. Naturally enough our Spanish sources tend to concentrate on the decimal system, which greatly impressed them by its consistency and its patent superiority to the chaotic state of European units of measurement at the time.

For administrative purposes (as in counting the number of households in a given village) numerical units were often used notionally, rather as we use 'dozen' and 'hundred' to denote approximate quantities.

The learning of which the priests were the guardians was handed down in an academy known as the *Yachahuasi* ('house of knowledge'), an institution corresponding to the Aztec *calmecatl*, with exclusive responsibility for the instruction of future priests and the other youths of the ruling *élite*.

Epic poetry and drama were also religious activities and as such came within the province of the priests. We hear of two forms of dramatic performance: the *huanca*, a kind of dramatized epic, and a kind of genre drama or comedy called *aranhuay*. The literary tradition has of course been broken; but even today prayers, poems and even plays appear containing material which must date from pre-Columbian times.

As we have seen, disease was believed to be a punishment for sin, a consequence of hostile magic or the work of evil spirits; so medicine was another priestly function. The priest-physician, who was engaged and paid by his patients, had at his disposal a large repertoire of medicinal herbs as well as such things as maize, flour, guinea-pig lard and amulets. He frequently prescribed bathing at the confluence of two rivers. Diagnosis was supported by divination and treatment was invariably preceded by a sacrifice – much faith was placed in the effectiveness of sucking pathogenic 'intrusive bodies' out of the system; and the belief that sickness might be the consequence of divine wrath led in some cases to the sacrifice of the patient's own child as a surrogate. As well as priest-physicians there were midwives who also engaged in the forbidden practice of procuring abortion by massage.

We know from the evidence of skeletal remains that trepanning was a very widespread practice. In some instances it is thought to have been done on therapeutic grounds; but we have no means of knowing for certain.

Much of ancient Andean medicine still makes sense from a purely therapeutic point of view; but all that concerns us here is to indicate its intimate links with a deeply religious, animistic and symbolic view of life. Thus, when there was an epidemic among the Aymara, they draped a black llama with the clothes of a sick man and drove it out of the village in the hope that it would carry the sickness with it.

All ritual, all festivals, all dancing, music and poetry in ancient Peru were predominantly religious in content and function. This is why native culture as a whole was so energetically suppressed by the Spaniards; but some compensation for the consequent gaps in our knowledge lies in the fact that some of the old ways of thought and some of the old customs have nevertheless survived four hundred years of European domination. The 'conversion' of the Indians did not go forward rapidly, or without resistance, or without leaving considerable remains of the old religion behind. The mass baptisms without previous instruction which took place during the Conquest period led to pretended conversions which left the old beliefs basically intact. The *encomienda* system, under which Spanish landowners were responsible for the religious welfare of the natives under their control, resulted in the use of the Christian priesthood as mere tools of the planters who paid their stipends; many landowners employed priests as stewards. We still possess examples of the not unfriendly criticism levelled by the natives at the spiritual and moral shortcomings of the priests and monks in the early Colonial period. At the beginning of the seventeenth century the order went out from Lima for a systematic campaign of *extirpación de las idolatrías* which led to the destruction of countless thousands of idols and other objects connected with worship, but which incidentally provided us with a number of valuable written sources of information on native religion.

The cult of the heavenly bodies and of other *huacas* continued in colonial times under so ingenious a Christian disguise that people eventually came to believe that the gods of the two religions were identical. Thus the Virgin Mary was identified with Pachamama, and the weather god Illapa with St James (Santiago). Similarly, as in Europe, pagan festivals coalesced with Christian ones. The summer solstice festival, at which men prayed to Illapa for rain, was identified with Christmas; the feast of *Inti Raymi*, at which prayers were offered up against frost and drought, became Corpus Christi. The Uru, a primitive Andean tribe, shifted their great spring festival from 23 September to 14 September, the Christian festival of the *Exaltación*.

The Peruvian writer Luis Valcáreel lists the *numina* worshipped in Colonial times as follows, in descending order of importance: Pachamama, the mountains (*apu*), and the dead (*machu*). The belief in apparitions of the dead is still widespread, as is the practice of placing offerings (*potajes*) on their graves on All Souls' Day. Sun, moon, lightning and stars have disappeared from the popular religious consciousness; but springs, rivers and lakes are still regarded as places of origin and the dwelling-places of supernatural beings.

The belief that illness is caused by spirits dies particularly hard. The Aymara believe to this day that many diseases are caused by evil spirits and the evil eye; although obvious natural causes are recognized as such. One common syndrome is the '*chullpa* sickness', supposed to be caused by fragments of bone from prehistoric graves which have somehow found their way into the system and must be removed; not, however, by the method of sucking.

Each individual knows and uses a large variety of remedies, and a specialist is only called in when self-medication fails. Diagnosis is commonly attempted by divinatory means, such as augury from the entrails of a guinea pig. The remedies themselves are more often made from vegetable than animal or mineral ingredients. Mercury is used as a treatment for syphilis. The *collahuaya*, itinerant physicians, news carriers and storytellers, travelling freely across ethnic and political frontiers, were formerly famous for the extent of their medical knowledge, both genuine and otherwise.

After the suppression of the old priesthood and its public worship, many of the private and domestic observances of the old religion survived and are still practised today. There is still a shadowy class of 'magicians' who practise divination and healing (often for people of European stock as well as Indians) and intersperse their rites with Christian signs and formulas. As manifestations of individual piety, sacrificial offerings, more or less surreptitious, are still made. They most often consist of food, and especially drink, or of small coins. The expensive llama sacrifices of former days have given place to less extravagant sacrifices of guinea pigs. A feature of the votive offerings is the use of tiny metal models of all the possessions of the individual peasant.

Three ritual survivals of pre-Columbian religion are apparent to the traveller in the Andes: the burning of incense, the pouring of libations (of *chicha* or sometimes even lemonade) to and for the earth, and the *apachita* (cairns) which are to be found on mountain passes and peaks, and which every wayfarer augments with one stone. Some of these are now surmounted by crosses. Just as in Europe, the popular mind still believes in occult forces. Love magic is still attempted, as is 'black magic'. Divination is still practised from the flight of birds; ill-omens are still believed in and so are prophetic dreams.

A traveller on a fleeting visit to Peru might nevertheless come away with the impression that not much of the old religion survived. The attentive observer will know better. On 26 June 1960 the Oruro newspaper *La Patria* reported that a twelve-month-old child had been sacrificed in the mining district of Huanuni, and on 2 July 1960 *El Diario* (La Paz) carried a story of cannibalism resulting from fighting between two groups of peasants at Escoma on Lake Titicaca.

CHAPTER THREE

NORTH AMERICA

Werner Müller

To deal with the religions of the primitive peoples of a huge continent in a short space is an almost insoluble methodological problem. The aboriginal population of North America was almost incredibly sparse – about a million in 1600 including Eskimos – and split linguistically and ethnically in a way which has no parallel anywhere in the world. Hand in hand with this goes a multiplicity of religious forms which makes logical arrangement extremely difficult.

I have therefore based my account on the customary large cultural areas of North America, and chosen individual tribes within these larger units as examples of religious life. It is not possible to sum up the entire religious life of each people; so I have emphasized a different theme in each section with the object of bringing all the major distinguishing features of North American religious life into focus in turn: shamanism, the after-life, the dream, the supreme being, reincarnation and so on. Even so, it has been impossible entirely to avoid overlapping.

I have excluded the last cultural area to develop, that of the prairie Indians, which did not really come into being until well into post-Columbian times, in the seventh century. I can do no better than refer the reader to the two books (*Black Elk Speaks* and *The Sacred Pipe*) in which Black Elk gives us an impressive testimony to the spiritual life of these tribes.

In general I have restricted myself to describing what *is* (or was) and left theory on one side. There is no lack of hypotheses already; what is needed is an accurate description of the true nature of North American tribal religion. A glance into any general work on ethnography or the history of religion will make this only too clear.

One of my main endeavours has been to bring to light the nature of the alien consciousness which underlies the forms of religious belief which I discuss. The reader may recall the fallacies and platitudes which greeted the publication of material from Lévi-Bruhl's diaries, to the effect that primitive people think just as we do, have the same basic forms of mental and spiritual life, and so on. Of course five and five still make ten even if one lives in a 'state of nature'; but this sort of factor is comparatively insignificant beside the basic fact that primitive man

Map 3. North America

lives in a state of intense involvement in the sense phenomena which surround him. The discursive intellect, which resolves the world into formulas, is quite different from the soul which converses with trees, mountains and houses. If the following pages make the reader more aware of this distinction between two modes of consciousness, it will help his understanding of the world in which he lives.

148

I *North America in 1600*

About the year 1600 a line drawn from the mouth of the Kennebec river in New England roughly along the 44th parallel, across the Appalachians, along the northern edge of the Great Lakes and over the plains to the Rockies separated two great cultural regions. North of the line, in what is now New England and Canada, lived peoples of the kind known to the ethnographer as hunters and gatherers. These are people without agriculture of any kind, and without any knowledge of the advanced arts of weaving and pottery: they take from the countryside only what offers itself for the taking. With their few poor implements they wander from place to place, dressed in skins or furs, living in smoky hide tents or shelters, without any idea of storing food for the morrow, scattered in small bands over immense areas, exposed to all the horrors of the long sub-Arctic winter, and barely scraping a precarious livelihood by wandering from forest to waterside and back again.

South of this world of poverty, of which the earliest chroniclers give such a melancholy picture, the continent presents a very different aspect. Even in pre-Columbian times a native farming culture had reached as far north as the 44th parallel. Maize, beans, squash, tobacco and sunflowers were cultivated; and the cultural pattern was consequently very different from that of the Indians of the north. Permanent houses were built, with load-supporting beams; either rectangular, with gabled or barrel-shaped roofs, or in the shape of beehives covered with grass or earth. Palissaded villages and wide maize fields formed great clearings in the virgin forest which would have made it clear even to a distant observer that nature was no longer in undisputed control.

Life had become settled and predictable; food-storage in granaries had put an end to the annual recurrence of the hungry season; hunting and fishing had become secondary pursuits, and the unpredictability of their results was no longer a real threat to the livelihood of the tribe. Weaving and pottery added to the material amenities of life and formed the basis of artistic activities. A complex social framework involved the individual in a tribe and the tribe in a larger federation ruled either by an absolutist paramount chief or by a representative council. The mode of life thus lacked comparatively few of the elements required for what we would call civilization.

This general picture of life in central and eastern North America contrasts with what we find on the other side of the Rockies, on the comparatively narrow coastal belt between the mountains and the Pacific. Taking the mouth of the Columbia river as the dividing mark, the position is neatly reversed, with primitive hunters and gatherers living south of the line in California and in the great inland basins, and more advanced peoples inhabiting the British Columbian coast and as far north as Alaska.

If it does nothing else, this division into primitive and advanced cultures will make it clear that human life in North America was influenced by historical as well as environmental factors. The fact that sunny California, the Garden of God, was still inhabited, when the Europeans came, by primitive peoples who harvested acorns and grazed in the fields of flowering clover like so many cattle, is a consequence of the natural isolation of this farthest edge of the continent. Sheltered by a mountain barrier from the influence of more advanced peoples, it was an undisturbed refuge for the remnants of ancient and backward tribes. On the other hand the fact that the rugged storm-lashed fjords of British Columbia became the home of the unique culture of the Pacific fishing tribes must surely be the result of outside cultural influences; Patagonia, which occupies a similar geographical position in South America, has remained to this day on the same primitive cultural level as pre-Columbian California.

The midwestern and eastern regions of North America must also be seen in a historical perspective. The forest area between the Mississippi and the Atlantic, originally peopled by a single culturally homogeneous layer of hunters and gatherers, was transformed culturally by the spread of agricultural techniques from the Gulf Coast area into an agricultural area. Even the last indigenous cultural growth to appear, the equestrian nomadic culture of the prairies, which appeared after about 1680, conformed basically to the same pattern. The prairie Indians lived in permanent villages near the rivers, where they grew maize and other crops. Their buffalo-hunting expeditions across the prairie were confined almost entirely to the period between sowing-time and harvest.

On closer inspection this vast area of farming culture does of course prove to be divided into a number of ethnographic regions. Thus besides the prairie Indians there were the Algonquin round the Great Lakes, gatherers of wild rice who form a kind of transition between pre-farming and farming culture. Further east were the Huron-Iroquois tribes, advanced intensive maize-growers. On the Atlantic coast there lived peoples whose way of life showed an incomplete assimilation of cultivation techniques. The south-eastern coast as far as Florida was the home of old-established maize-growers, as were the sunny deserts of Arizona and New Mexico. All these cultural units, however, in spite of their cultural differences, had one clear thing in common: the cultivation of maize or Indian corn.

The border between hunters and gatherers to the north and farmers to the south was not a rigid line following the 44th parallel; it was a wide transitional zone in which, as one moved southward, northern elements gradually disappeared and hesitant signs of agriculture began to appear, but in which no fully-fledged farming culture could appear.

Even the very first outside observers were aware not only of the total dissimilarity of the two basic cultural patterns found in North America but also of the gradualness of the transition between the two. In the winter of 1604–5, Samuel de Champlain remarked on the emptiness of the countryside round the French fort at Sainte-Croix in the mouth of the Sainte-Croix river (now called Dochet Island). For 25 leagues up the Penobscot (Maine) he saw nothing but two empty bark tents. He doubted whether hunting in winter would produce much game – the Cervidae can be chased in snowshoes only if the snow is deep enough – and he witnessed frightful scenes in which the starving Indians ate even putrefying carrion. 'Their way of life', Champlain concludes, 'struck me as wholly miserable.'[1]

In summer 1605 he set out southwards to chart the coast. At the mouth of the Saco in southern Maine (altitude 43° 20' N) he was astonished to see maize fields. He noted the neatness of the fields, the cultivation of beans, squash and tobacco, and the permanent palissaded villages. These Indians were no longer nomads.

As he went further the same picture renewed itself again and again. The sketches with which Champlain illustrated his report show a dense population. Five Indian villages stood on the site of present-day Plymouth, Mass., alone. The further south he went, the more advanced the maize-farming culture became. Near Cape Ann, 60 miles south of the Saco, the birch-bark canoe of the northern tribes gave place to the heavy dugout of the southern coast Indians. Further south still, Champlain was struck by signs of crop rotation, thatched long houses, clay cooking pots, wooden mortars for pounding maize, and the use of bark-lined pits as granaries. Champlain was keenly conscious that he was in a different land with different people, worlds removed from the north country with its simple hunters and gatherers. Later exploration showed that the same basic division between north and south, hunter and maize-grower, primitive and advanced society, runs for thousands of miles, three-quarters of the way across the whole vast continent.

The division applied to religious experience as well as to material culture. To the north of the 44th parallel religion was a matter for the individual, impoverished in its external manifestations; to the south there were complex rites, communal worship, and a priesthood: religion existed in and for the community as a whole, theatrical, emotional and essentially outward-looking. This great cultural divide is a basic factor in the religious life of all the disparate regional cultures of North America.

II *The Lonely Drum: The Canadian Algonquin and Athapascans*

Canada from Labrador to the Mackenzie River is inhabited by two linguistic groups, the Algonquin and the Athapascans. The Algonquin are the indigenous inhabitants of northern New England, Labrador, the Hudson's Bay area and as far west as Lake Winnipeg. Their boundaries are fluid, for since the last remaining Algonquin tribe, the Cree, has been equipped with guns, it has been spreading further north. The same expansionist impulse drove Algonquin tribes from their original centre on the Winnipeg River as far as the Atlantic coast; in pre-Columbian times a chain of Algonquin-speaking groups occupied the eastern coastline as far south as Carolina. A second group moved south across the Great Lakes and through the forests of the Mid-West as far as the Ohio. In the course of their migration from Canadian hunting country into the maize-growing southern half of the continent the Algonquin found new cultural resources: in the territory south of the 44th parallel we find complex religious patterns such as would have been impossible in the poverty-stricken north. The Algonquin tribes which still live in Canada lead the same lives as all the other hunters and gatherers of the north, bearers of a nebulous, feebly defined culture; more complex religious and social forms are rendered impossible by the sheer hardness of the life.

Behind the Algonquin looms an even more shadowy group, the Athapascans, whose territory covers the whole of northern Canada as far as the Eskimo territory which borders on the Arctic Ocean. They are said to have expanded southward from the direction of Alaska at some early date, driving the Algonquin before them. This supposition seems improbable; the cultural structure of the Athapascans is so vague and ill-defined that it at once succumbs when brought into contact with any more advanced culture, however narrow the distinction. It is probable that the Athapascan tribes arrived in Canada to find large tracts of land empty, and filtered slowly from lake system to lake system until they reached Lake Winnipeg and the firm boundary of Algonquin territory.

The culture of these hunting tribes is basically the same from Alaska to Nova Scotia. What George Keith wrote of the Indians of Great Bear Lake at the beginning of the nineteenth century was still true of the Micmac of New Brunswick a hundred years later.[2] Through the endless and convenient network of waterways the light birch bark canoes of the Indians could cover great distances; this is a great asset to any community obliged to keep up a constant seasonal migration.

The Canadian hunting tribes spend the spring and summer by a river or lake – nowadays in the vicinity of a trading post – and the autumn and winter in the forest, where each family possesses its own hunting grounds. The families live far apart in total isolation, and only for a short time each summer do they coalesce into a larger social unit. During these few weeks at the trading post they learn who has survived the hard months and who has been lost in the forest, injured, starved or frozen to death.

Big game such as moose and caribou can only be hunted on snowshoes. The wide frames of the snowshoes keep the hunter on the crust of the snow and enable him to run down his quarry, which can only flounder through the drifts. This method of hunting becomes impossible when there is a thaw; and then real hunger sets in. From the very first, European observers have told tales of frenzies of hunger, of cannibalism, and of whole bands of Indians succumbing fatalistically to starvation.

By contrast with the well-adapted culture of the Eskimos, the equipment and hunting technique of the Canadian Indians gives an impression of imperfection and incompleteness. In Spring, for instance, no advantage is taken of the return of great flocks of ducks from the south.[3] The central fact of life in this culture remains the isolation and defencelessness of man.

The scanty material culture is matched by a rudimentary religious structure; but even among the Canadian Indians religion is not by any means merely a mirror of everyday needs and desires. The hopes and desires of these people, like those of mankind everywhere, are concerned with factors which go far beyond practical everyday life.

Missionary activity started very early – in eastern Canada in the seventeenth century, in north-western Canada from 1860 onwards – and there exists today an amalgam of paganism and Catholicism in which native religious ideas are only dimly detectable.

Practical difficulties have always stood in the way of collective religious experience. But it does seem that the summer gatherings at the trading-posts have led to the appearance of something like tribal gatherings. St Anne's Day (26 July) is celebrated as a national holiday by the Micmac of New Brunswick with canoe races, foot races, dancing, wedding ceremonies, christenings and feasting. This festival is certainly derived from an earlier tribal assembly; the only question is how important a role religious feeling played in it in pagan times.[4] Petitot describes a spring festival among the Great Slave Lake Indians on the Mackenzie; and the Beaver Indians have twice-yearly feasts at which food is thrown into the fire, prayers are offered up for food and good tracking snow, and there is dancing round the flames.[5] This is all we know of the ceremonial calendar.

Priesthoods and religious communities were conspicuous by their absence, as were the religious institutions which only they could have organized. Religious experience was an individual concern, symbolized by the figure of the shaman or medicine man.

To some extent, however, every hunter was his own shaman. Speck emphasizes the intimate connection among the Labrador tribes between work (hunting, fishing, trapping) and 'operating *mentu*' (which may be approximately translated as 'medicine making'). *Mentu* consists in all those supernatural aids, such as the conjuring of helpful spirits, the interpretation of dreams, the observance of taboos, without which all physical work is useless. To the Canadian forest Indian his work is a religious act. The beasts of the chase are sacred, and so is their flesh, which is thought to have its own value as medicine. The meat of domestic animals introduced from Europe is believed to be positively dangerous.[6]

The foundation of the psychic powers indispensable to every hunter lies in his guardian spirit, whom he apparently acquires through the process known as dream-fasting. Our information varies on this point. Dream-fasting does not seem to exist among the Labrador Indians, but among the central Athapascans round Great Bear Lake it is done even by five-year-old children.[7] The children are left without food at a specially designated spot outside the camp. Their growing weakness leads to partial loss of consciousness, and finally to hallucinations; and the first hallucinatory image they see, whether an animal or a natural phenomenon, becomes the dreamer's guardian spirit for the rest of his life.

If the guardian spirit is an animal or bird, some physical relic such as a claw or a scrap of skin is carried on the person; if it is a force of nature such as wind or water or something immaterial such as a ghost, a symbol drawn on birch bark is carried instead.

In emergency a man calls upon his guardian spirit by drumming and singing; it appears in his dreams and is consulted on how to catch pole-cat and caribou. Without his guardian spirit or 'medicine animal' the Indian hunter is lost; to have no guardian means certain death.

The nature of this metaphysical guardianship varies from one case to another; and there is a definite hierarchy of persons with more and more potent (and numerous) guardian spirits until we reach the apex of the religious and social pyramid, the shaman.

Certain observers divide the shamans themselves into classes. There are some shamans who concentrate on foretelling the future, and some of these adopt a categorical tone worthy of an Old Testament prophet. Old Kean, a Kaska shaman who looked forward to the complete de-struction of the white man by the Second World War, later changed his mind and prophesied a universal deluge which would spare only the paleface.[8] Other specially gifted individuals engage in various hair-raising practices such as knife-swallowing, bullet-catching and lycan-thropy. Others work as physicians, using techniques such as wound-sucking, ash-blowing and the application of medicinal roots and herbs. These groups are not really separate classes; they are specialists within one shaman class whose senior members have all-embracing powers.

Like the hunters, the shamans are initiated into their adult career by means of a subjective experience, transmitted to the most potent among them not through a vision but by inheritance.[9] Unlike the priest, whose office largely depends on his knowledge of ritual, the shaman is inde-pendent of all extra-personal factors. He depends on himself alone; the office and the man are identical.[10] The reputation of great shamans spreads over the whole countryside. Their drumming and chanting are listened to with great reverence. It is believed that their souls leave their bodies almost every night, make lengthy visits to heaven and learn there all that they desire to know. When the spirit of such a shaman returns from one of his journeys, the drums on the walls begin to sound without being touched. His medicine song is heard far and wide, and his body dances six inches above the ground.[11]

These men with their unconquerable 'medicine' are believed to be immortal. They are consulted on individual as well as collective prob-lems. They can drum up favourable winds, snow, frost, success in the hunting field and protection against enemies. They are the focus of all religious activity; to the forest Indian the shamans are the only element of security in a hostile environment. Their supernatural 'medicine' is the bulwark of a forlorn and precarious existence.

The shaman's most important accessory is his drum. For some reason there is little reference to the drum in the literature,[12] but there can be

155

no doubt of the essential part it plays in the art of the shaman. The drum is a skin-covered wooden hoop[13] painted with figures and symbols. A bowstring (an animal tendon) with pieces of bone twisted into it is stretched across the drum head and ends in a loop. Another 'snare' is stretched across the underside of the drum, again with a loop at the end. The two loops are used as handles. When the drum is beaten with a wooden stick the bone fragments 'sing'.

Speck says of the Labrador shamans that they think of their drums as living entities able to speak and understand what is said to them.[14] The close association of drum and drummer is illustrated also by the Penobscot name for a shaman, which is *medeolinu*, 'drum sound man'. In every case the buzzing sound of the drum and the song which accompanies its use are part of the technique of inducing the trance state, in which the shaman leaves his body to visit the Beyond and establish contact between the spirit world and the world of sense.

The few drumming songs that have been preserved contain the idea of commanding the spirits.

> I sit and beat my drum and through its voice I call the beasts from the mountains. The great storms also harken to my drum.
>
> I sit and beat my drum and storm and thunder answer its voice. The great whirlwind ceases his roaring to harken to the sound of my drum.
>
> I sit and beat my drum and the spirit of the night air comes and harkens to the sound of my drum. The great wind bird holds his wings silent to harken to its voice.
>
> I sit and beat my drum and the water spirit rises to the surface and harkens to its voice. The forest spirit ceases his woodcutting and harkens to its sound.
>
> I sit and beat my drum and the black man from the water rises up to harken to its sound. Lightning, thunder, storms, winds, forest spirit, water spirit and spirit of the night air are gathered together and harken to the sound of my drum.[15]

It would be a mistake to regard the shamans' stories of journeys to heaven and other supernatural experiences as fraudulent. The image sequences which form the core of these 'astral projection' stories patently come from the same source as the tribal myths. The difference is that mythology places in a firm textual framework what appears in the shamanistic trance as a chaotic stream of images.

Unfortunately we know little of the nature of what was communicated in these ecstatic states. We do know that it was probably very similar to the trance-messages of Siberian and Eskimo shamans, which were conditioned by the system of ideas generally accepted in the tribe to which the shaman belonged. Shamans see in their trance only what they know.

There once lived among the central Athapascans (the Yellow Knife and the Hare) a powerful wizard by the name of Nayeweri, 'he who was created by thought'. One autumn when he saw the birds flying off towards the warmer countries of the south, he followed them and soon came to the foot of the sky, where there was a huge cave from which a river flowed. This was the winter home of the shades of the dead. In the summer they roam the earth, but in autumn they fly south-westwards with the migratory birds and come to this cave. Nayeweri looked in, but he saw the spirits only as far as the knee. Some were casting nets, others paddling their canoes, others dancing. In front of the cave there stood a tree with the help of which Nayeweri climbed into heaven. For two days his body lay lifeless on the earth, and on the third day he returned from his journey and rose to his feet.[16]

The things seen and learned by the dreamer in this story are based on a belief common to all Canadian Indians, the idea of the south-west, 'the other country', as the home of the dead, and the place of origin of humanity and life in general. The Micmac believed the origin of their race to lie in the south-west, and Roger Williams notes that his Narragansett – a maize-belt tribe living in Rhode Island – constantly spoke of the south-west as the dwelling-place of the souls of their ancestors, the place where they themselves expected to go after death, and the source of their maize and their beans.[17]

The frequency of trance states is partly a consequence of the psychological instability of all sub-Arctic tribes. Petitot was the first to remark on this characteristic among the central Athapascans, and the occasional panic terrors to which it leads. He speaks of nervous overexcitability, hallucinations and monomania, and a morbid and extremely contagious vividness of imagination.

The heathen women are especially prone to these states. In some cases the hallucinations of one or two visionaries gain hold of a whole tribe and lead to the strangest actions. Every spring there is an epidemic of totally irrational panic fear during which people live in a continuous trance, oppressed by the fear of an imaginary enemy who pursues them ceaselessly, and whom they think they see everywhere, even when nothing is visible far and wide.[18]

This morbid and spirit-ridden state of mind is a concomitant of the featurelessness of the world of spirit. 'There are no gods, only Medicine', say the Athapascans of the Mackenzie Basin,[19] and consequently there are hardly any sacrifices or prayers; supernatural beings of all kinds are lost in nebulous daemonology. No one willingly leaves his encampment after dark; everyone starts at the slightest noise; for in the darkness prowl the *sekani*, 'Bad Indians' with enormous boots, who steal children, and who are human in that their tracks can be seen, and non-human in that they possess supernatural powers.[20]

The Algonquin tell of man-eating ogres of various kinds, some tall as a tree, some the size of a man; benevolent dwarfs; water spirits in springs; and narrow-faced, hirsute creatures who live shadowy lives in the sub-Arctic scrub and forest.[21]

Only one category of supernatural being emerges with any clarity, one of paramount importance to the hunter: the 'boss spirit'.[22] The Canadian Indian believes that every species of animal (the three most important being caribou, moose and beaver) has its own ruler. The bosses of the various species dwell in some remote and inaccessible place and control all their animal subjects. Without their consent no hunter can make a kill; and if anyone is foolhardy enough to maltreat his quarry by, for instance, throwing the bones to the dogs instead of burning them or throwing them into the water, the appropriate boss spirit will simply take the game away from his hunting-grounds, leaving the hunter to reflect at leisure, during long weeks of hunger, on the nature of sin as it seems to Indian eyes. The soul of the maltreated animal – every animal has a soul – complains to its master and he then keeps it by him instead of sending it forth to become a new caribou or moose.

Only the bear has no boss spirit; the bears are a family in which every individual is his own master. This may well be connected with the special awe in which the bear is held by all sub-Arctic hunters in America and elsewhere, and which is expressed in the ritual which accompanies every detail of the hunting, killing and eating of the animal. When a cave is found in which a bear is hibernating, it is politely invited to come out:

'Come, grandfather, the sun shines warmly enough,' or:
'Come grandfather, I want to light your pipe,' or:
'Come, grandfather, show your head.'

As soon as the bear has been killed tobacco is placed in its lair and between its open jaws; the victim smokes with the hunters. The carcass is honoured with a special feast to which everyone within easy reach is invited, and which is designed to ensure that the bear is completely consumed. The head is eaten first, without knives, by the men alone. The bones are burned at once, and the dogs are strictly kept away.

After the feast everyone dances round the bear's skull, which is painted red and given a place of honour on a pole outside the encampment. The only names for the bear which are allowed to be used are 'short tail', 'black beast', 'great food' and above all 'grandfather'.[23]

Our information suggests that this sort of bear feast is restricted to the Canadian Algonquin and unknown among the Athapascans.[24] There are no grounds on which to base an explanation of the meaning of the custom as practised in Canada, but reports of somewhat similar festivals among the southern, maize-growing Algonquin do suggest a specific purpose, namely the glorification of the supreme being, the Great Spirit.[25]

The whole question of the presence or absence of the belief in a supreme being among the Canadian hunters has been a controversial one for a long time. But we must suppose that there was such a belief: there is very early evidence in support of this supposition, and what we know of Indian beliefs leaves a place vacant which must have been filled by some kind of supreme being: if each kind of animal has its own archetypal boss spirit, then the human race needs to have one too. The northern Ojibwa, whose territories lie firmly within the hunting zone, draw an analogy between this supreme boss spirit and the captain of a steamboat or the Federal Government in Ottawa. All lesser bosses stand under his direction.[26] The Penobscot call him Ktahandowit ('great spirit'), Ketci Niweskwe ('great being'), Debelmelek ('our owner') or Giziulitolek ('our creator'). The last two titles at least must date from pre-Mission days, as they also appear among the St Francis-Abenaki and the Wawenock. The corresponding titles in Micmac are Nesulk ('he creates us') and Nishkam ('our forebear').[27] The Naskapi of today apply their title of Tcementu ('great spirit') to the Christian God; but they also refer separately to 'our creator' and 'our great owner'.[28] In the case of the central Athapascans too, ethnographers tend nowadays to regard this concept as existing independently of mission influence.[29] But one wonders whether this conception of the supreme being as an owner or boss spirit of mankind is not too narrow. There are signs that the supreme being was regarded not as an owner of men but rather as a 'boss' of the whole universe. 'He is in the sun, moon, stars, clouds of heaven, mountains, and even the trees of the earth,' says the Penobscot; and the Naskapi state something similar. 'He', they say, 'is a spirit like the sun, moon and stars.'[30] This incidentally goes to show how unsatisfactory our word 'spirit' is as a translation of the Indian *mentu* or *manito*. *Mentu* refers to palpable rather than impalpable realities. Light is one natural phenomenon which apparently might

159

seem to be entirely the province of the supreme god. The Athapascan name for this god, Yakista, contains an element which recurs in the word for sky (*ya*) and the word for the northern lights (*yakkrey*).

In the seventeenth century the French missionary priests Biard and Le Clerc heard the Micmac greeting the sunrise with the thrice-repeated *hohoho* which is one of the very few instances of actual prayer reported in the whole literature.[31]

The link between supreme being, light and sunrise must be pre-Christian, as it also appears among the southern Algonquin, along with the characteristic cry of '*ho*'. The same is true of another feature which must admittedly have been reinforced by European influence: the use of the title 'owner of the world and of men'.

The creation of the world plays no part in Canadian Indian myth. When the supreme being is referred to as the Creator, the reference is only to the creation of mankind; the world has always been there. It has undergone changes, but it was never created. There have been three successive epochs in the history of the world. In the beginning the animals were the masters, with mankind in a nebulous dream-state on the periphery. This epoch ended with the birth of the 'transformer' or culture hero, who rid the world of its primeval monsters and cleared the way for human life. All methods of hunting and fishing, the domestication of the dog and the building of canoes, can be traced back to him; it was through him that man became truly man. After his departure there began the third epoch, which still continues, and in which men and beasts can no longer communicate with each other, and only the shamans maintain the link between the human and extra-human spheres. One day the culture hero will return and then the earth will dissolve in flames.[32]

Thin and bare though it may seem in this brief outline, the mythical lore of the forest Indians is packed with matter. The art of storytelling is an outlet for all the spiritual aspirations which are frustrated by a life of monotonous and desperate poverty. The world of myth is a world transfigured. Poverty and privation are forgotten in the blaze of the creative fancy. The art of the forest Indians is the art of the spoken word. Only in the most fleeting and impermanent medium of all can the creative fancy find an outlet; their environment makes any more solid kind of art impracticable.

The extensive mythologies have not in the main been systematized in cycles, but all of them fit into the framework of the three ages of the world. Each story begins with a clear indication of the age in which the story is set: 'This story belongs to the time when the world was placed in order', or: 'They tell this story of the time when the world began', or: 'This story belongs to the time when the world ends'.

The genuine cycles of myths are basically concerned with the culture hero, his birth, his deeds and his disappearance from the earth. The Algonquin of New England in particular have a number of extended cycles of this kind. Their whole literature revolves around their culture hero, Gluskabe, 'the deceiver', so called because he always does the exact opposite of what he says. The central Athapascans have quantities of myths dealing with the 'first brother'. The deeds of these heroes can still be read from the natural features of the landscape, for it was the culture hero, the 'transformer', who formed the world as it now is. He is the greatest shaman who has ever lived; his prowess is the ever-present unattainable ideal which haunts every Indian hunter. Just as the Indian of this age seeks to catch beavers and elks, the mythical hero hunted huge monsters, giant beavers and giant elks; and this vision of the heroic past casts a feeble glow even into the miserable birch-bark wigwam of the present-day forest Indian. Only such a colourful imaginary world could possibly explain how even this most primitive of cultures has a mental horizon which extends beyond the day-to-day business of survival. It is this that enables one to guess where the sub-Arctic peoples draw the strength to endure, and even to desire, the life they lead. Improbable as it may seem, the Canadian hunters have a firm belief in the reincarnation not only of animals but of human beings. The physical features of a newborn child are always referred to those of some dead forebear; every child is thus a reincarnation. There are vague indications which suggest that the soul is believed to return after death to the 'owner', who after a certain time returns it to earth to begin a new life.[33] So even the inhabitants of these inhospitable wastes do not regard death as the end but associate it with a new beginning. Life even to them is not a burden but a thing of value.

III *Supreme Being and Big House: The Delaware and Algonquin of the Atlantic Seaboard*

In spite of their limited cultural repertoire, both of the great Canadian linguistic groups had outposts in the agricultural south. Sections of the Athapascans reached as far as New Mexico where they came wholly under the influence of the Pueblo. The Algonquin advanced in two separate directions, first across the Great Lakes and then along the Atlantic seaboard as far south as Georgia. This last tribal migration came into conflict with the Europeans in the sixteenth and seventeenth centuries. Officers operating in the hinterland of Pamlico Sound on orders from Raleigh in 1584–8; Captain John Smith and his companions, exploring the James Valley and Chesapeake Bay from 1607 onwards; Hudson sailing in the Hudson river estuary in 1609; the Pilgrim Fathers on the site of what was to be Plymouth, Mass., in 1622; all these encountered Algonquin groups. When the European invasion began and drove the Indians westwards, the Algonquin were the people who had the closest contact with the invaders.

In this long chain of tribes along the East Coast one ethnic group stands out, not only in the European written sources but also in the judgment of the Indians themselves. This remarkable group was the Delaware, called in their own language the Lenape. They had a special status in the eyes of many other Indian peoples; they were reverenced as the 'grandfathers', representatives, after a fashion, of authority and legality. In our written sources they are most often mentioned as the practitioners of a unique communal religious act: the new year festival of the Big House.

The signs are that the Big House was once widespread along the Atlantic coast, but our only reliable sources are the accounts given by observers of the Big House cult among the Delaware. This ceremony must have been particularly impressive: the European observers deal with it to the exclusion of all the other religious practices of the Delaware.

The ritual shows obvious signs of the assimilation of hunting Indian elements into the religious attitudes of a farming society. And yet both cultural elements are so closely joined that one might almost believe that they had always existed side by side. We have detailed accounts of the ritual patterns observed in two sections of the tribe which are now separated by thousands of miles: the Oklahoma Delaware in the West and the Ontario Delaware in Canada. The ceremony was discontinued by the Canadian group in the middle of the last century and by the Oklahoma group about sixty years later, shortly before the outbreak of the First World War; but the recollections of old people provided sufficient material to enable ethnographers to make a tolerable reconstruction.[1] We begin with the Oklahoma ceremony.

The Big House takes place in October as soon as the harvest is in; the whole tribe takes part. The duty of making all the prior arrangements falls on one person, who also acts as master of ceremonies. The three totem groups, wolf, turtle and turkey, assist the organizer by turns.

As soon as a messenger has announced the date, people repair to the scene of the ceremony, a clearing in the forest. There stands the Big House itself, a rectangular hut with a gabled roof built of wooden beams and orientated according to the cardinal points. There is a door in each gable, and in the middle stands a massive wooden pillar which supports the ridge of the roof. Inside the windowless structure, twelve sculptured faces can be glimpsed in the half-light, two on the centre post facing east and west, six on the vertical supports of the long walls, and four on the doorposts. All the faces are painted in two colours, red on the right-hand side and black on the left.

The structure as a whole, and each part of it, has a symbolic significance. The two large faces on the centre post represent the countenance of Gicelemukaong, the Creator, who lives in the highest heaven. The post on which his face appears represents him in his aspect as centre post of the universe, the supporter of the whole structure of creation.[2] Similarly the floor of the structure represents the earth, the roof the sky, and the four walls the four sides of the horizon, where the ten lesser spirits sit round their Creator. The Big House thus represents the cosmos, and this endows the events which take place there with a high symbolic significance.

The ceremony itself is based on the idea of beginning a new year and a new world; this idea of 'beginning' is repeatedly impressed on the worshippers. The newly refurbished Big House inaugurates a new world and a new cycle. Six attendants, three men and three women, sweep the floor, carry out running repairs to the walls, set up a cooking hearth in front of the east door, collect firewood, and on the evening of the first day use the ancient fire-drill – matches and even flints are strictly banned – to light two 'pure' fires, one east and one west of the centre post.

When the rising flames illuminate the interior of the Big House the members of the community sit down round the walls dressed in their best clothes. Before a silent audience the orator – not the same person as the master of ceremonies – rises to speak. His speech is really an urgent prayer to the Creator. Something of the powerful simplicity of its language can be judged from this abbreviated sample.

We are thankful that so many of us are alive to meet together here once more, and that we are ready to hold our ceremonies in good faith. Now we shall meet here twelve nights in succession to pray to Gicelemukaong, who had directed us to worship in this way. And these twelve Mising faces (carved on the posts of the house) are here to watch and to carry our prayers to Gicelemukaong in the highest heaven. The reason why we dance at this time is to raise our prayers to him . . .

When we come into this house of ours we are glad, and thankful that we are well, and for everything that makes us feel good which the Creator has placed here for our use. We come here to pray Him to have mercy on us for the year to come and to give us everything to make us happy; may we have good crops and no dangerous storms, floods or earthquakes. We all realize what He has put before us all through life, and that He has given us a way to pray to Him and thank Him. We are thankful to the East because everyone feels good in the morning when they wake, and see the bright light coming from the East, and when the Sun goes down in the West we feel good and glad we are well; then we are thankful to the West. And we are thankful to the North, because when the cold winds come we are glad to have lived to see the leaves fall again; and to the South, for when the South winds blows and everything is coming up in the Spring, we are glad to live to see the grass growing and everything green again. We thank the Thunderers, for they are the *manitowuk* that bring the rain, which the Creator has given them power to rule over. And we thank our mother, the Earth, whom we claim as mother because the Earth carries us and everything we need. When we eat and drink and look around, we know it is Gicelemukaong, that makes us feel good that way. He gives us the purest thoughts that can be had. We should pray to Him every morning.[3]

Again and again the orator comes back to the theme of the Creator, whose face gazes down on the assembly from the centre-post, and who resides in the twelfth heaven, where he listens to the prayers of his votaries. Each of the twelve levels of heaven is inhabited by a *manito*, and the petitions of mankind are passed from one to the next until they come to the ear of the Creator. The close analogy between this idea and the architectural symbolism of the Big House excludes any possibility of Christian theological influence; the Delaware Creator Gicelemukaong is the centre of the Big House as he is of the world. His very un-European nature, profoundly linked with an image of the earth, is a subject to which I shall return.

After the introductory prayer the dream dance begins. Any of those present who feels the urge to dance takes up a tortoise-shell rattle and circles the centre post with a shuffling gait, reciting instalments of the vision in which he first saw the shape of his guardian spirit. A group of singers repeat his recital, beating all the while on a folded deerskin blanket. At the end the twofold prayer-call is heard, addressed to the two faces of the Creator, and the proceedings end with all those present uttering the same call, a long drawn out 'ho-o-o' repeated twelve times. A Delaware tribesman explains this as follows:

Did you ever hear that noise out in the woods, in the fall of the year? '*Ho-o-o*', it says. What is it? It is the noise of the wind blowing in the trees. When the Delawares pray in the Big House they raise their voices and cry '*Ho-o-o*' to God, and the Mising hears it and understands, for he is of the same nature as a tree, and there are twelve Mising carved in the Big House who will carry the prayers to the twelfth heaven.[4]

The cry of '*ho-o-o*' reminds us of the prayer call of the Canadian Micmac tribe: and there is another feature here which recalls a hunting and gathering society even more strongly: the stag hunt.

Recitals and orations continue much as described above for the first nine nights of the festival. During daylight on the third to sixth days there is a ritual hunt. A group of men under a leader set out into the forest, and their departure is blessed by Misinghalikun, the boss spirit of the deer, who lives in the Rocky Mountains and – himself mounted on a stag – watches over the beasts whom the Creator has entrusted to his care. When the hunting party sets out, Misinghalikun ('living firm face') appears in person, dressed in a bear skin and wearing a great oval wooden mask painted red on the right-hand side and black on the left. He accompanies the hunters a little way into the forest, while the orator throws six quids of tobacco into each of the two fires and begs the Mising to start game for the hunters and assist their aim; the whole custom is an intact survival from pre-agricultural days.

As soon as the men return the quarry is butchered prayerfully and gibbeted on the deer post, a tree with lopped branches which stands in front of the east door of the Big House; this tree is crowned with a complete set of antlers. The meat serves for the ceremonial meal which closes each night session. This meat, from wild beasts which – unlike domestic animals – are still living as they did when the Creator made them, is considered 'pure'. The same epithet is applied to everything which is still close to its origins in the first days of the world: fire made with a fire-drill, the meat of wild animals, the juice of wild strawberries drunk at the Strawberry Dance in June. This again is a clear survival of an idea originating in hunting and gathering communities; we have already encountered it among the Naskapi.

On the ninth night the established routine is broken: the fires are put out and re-kindled, the drummers have new sticks, and the members of the community are given prayer sticks, some smooth, some decorated with a spiral pattern, which they raise in salute to the central post with every shout of '*ho-o-o*'. A large band of tortoise-shell rattles now accompanies the recitation of the sacred dreams, and six men are deputed to go outside in turn and utter their twelvefold '*ho-o-o*' in the dark outside the Big House.

The twelfth and last night is reserved for the women and their own dream songs. At midday on the thirteenth day the festival ends. All the participants leave the temple, stand side by side in a long row facing east, and utter the ritual shout twelve times, six times standing with the right hand raised, six times kneeling with the left hand raised. As with the Micmac, the ancient cry of '*ho-o-o*' is associated with the east, the light and the godhead.

There are few variations in the pattern of the Big House ceremony among different groups of the Oklahoma Delaware. Even in details one is constantly aware of the dualistic symbolic structure of the whole ritual. Thus, when men and women work together as temple attendants, the men sweep the floor from west to east, the women from east to west. The prayer sticks too are divided into six smooth and six spiral sticks, The prayer shout consists of six '*ho*'s' and six '*ha*'s', the '*ho*'s' corresponding to the decorated sticks, the '*ha*'s' to the plain ones.

In short, the regular rhythm of the ritual actions reflects the polarity of the two doors, the two fires and the two faces in the centre post. This dualistic structure is characteristic of the farming cultures of the maize belt, as we shall see when we come to deal with the Iroquois.

A very different picture is presented by the Big House ceremony among the Canadian Delaware of Hagersville, Ontario. The ceremony at Hagersville is called the bear sacrifice; a bear takes the place of the stag. The festival takes place on a day which has an astronomical rather than an agricultural significance: the first full moon in January. A hibernating bear is driven from its cave and brought, still dazed, to the Big House where it is killed with a blow from an axe under the centre post. Its pelt is attached to the eastern side of the post, its flesh consumed in a ritual meal, and its spirit rises to Patamawas ('to whom prayers are offered'), bearing with it the prayers of mankind.

Astral symbolism plays a part in this ceremony: the ritual functionaries stand in the pattern of the stars of *Ursa major*;[5] and this constellation signifies, as it does to us, a celestial bear.

The same peoples have a myth which tells of the flight of the birds in pursuit of the Great Bear as he swings round the Pole Star. This is the bear who lays down his life at the foot of the centre post of the world, under the two faces of the Creator, who clothes the pillar with his pelt, and who renews his sacrifice every year.

This annual rhythm helps to explain the meaning of the ceremony. As the Delaware themselves explain, its purpose is to ensure that the ordinary sequence of events shall be maintained and that the world shall never depart from its accustomed ways. This purpose is served by a symbolic re-creation of the world at every Big House ceremony. The first ceremony, in the distant past, followed upon a catastrophic earth tremor. The annual renewal of the rite has served to prevent a repetition of the disaster. This also accounts for the fact that the Delaware call their supreme being the Creator although their myths make no mention of an initial creation of the world; a very old account tells of a Delaware supreme god called Kickeron who creates all things anew every day;[6] creation for the Delaware is inseparable from eternal renewal.

The Hagersville ritual is a clear example of the juxtaposition of northern hunting culture and southern farming culture. The part played by the bear belongs to the universal heritage of sub-Arctic peoples; but the dualism characteristic of North American maize-growing tribes is also evident. The worshippers are divided not according to totem categories, as they are in Oklahoma, but according to sex. On the first night of the ceremony a ritual tug o' war takes place between the women on the eastern side and the men on the western side of the Big House. The deerskin drum is half white, half bright red, and the drumsticks are divided longitudinally into the same two colours.

The Hagersville Delaware have also provided us with a tolerably complete festal calendar, which reveals at first glance how completely maize culture took possession of former hunting peoples.[8] The year begins with the twelve-day bear sacrifice in January. In March there is the maple dance (also in the Big House), the object of which is to obtain a good syrup harvest. Immediately after it the trees are tapped and the rising sap boiled to make syrup. In May there is a seed-sowing ceremony, in June the strawberry dance, at which strawberry juice is drunk, and in September there is the green corn ceremony, a harvest festival in the widest sense of the word in which thanks are offered up for maize, beans and squash together. This rite too takes place in the Big House and lasts two days and nights with performances by the maize mask fraternity, orations, processions round the centre post and various dances which probably stem from the ritual life of the neighbouring Iroquois.

Naturally the Delaware festal calendar, besides such annual feasts as the Big House and green corn ceremonies, includes a number of lesser ceremonies such as the mask dance carried out by the French family in honour of the Mising mask. This family has charge of this precious ritual object and honours it with feasting and dancing to keep its temper sweet.[9]

Another important family ritual, the doll dance, is in honour of the maize mother. Some childish abuse of the maize once provoked her wrath, and she sent down a terrible sickness. Since that time she has been propitiated by a nocturnal ceremony in which the maize mother herself, in the form of a corn doll, is fed with flesh and hominy and honoured in twelve dances, one for each month. At sunrise, twelve attendants form a line facing east, holding dishes of food in their left hands, in readiness to hand them to the participants in the ceremony. The men on the north and south ends of the row carry large figures baked from maize flour; the northern figure represents the maize mother in woman's shape, the southern one a bear. At a word of command these effigy loaves are cast crosswise among the participants, who take the fragments and go home content.[10]

There are other rites which take place as a response to a given situation: these include the rainmaking ceremony in which the man deputed as rainmaker calls upon the 'grandfathers who thunder' for their help. Other rites are repeated over long periods, such as the football game which begins in spring and is played until the summer solstice in order to promote the growth of fruit and express the joy of mankind at the return of the warm season.[11]

The basic religious attitude which underlies all these rituals is the consciousness of living in a world (or a 'world house') full of living things. To the individual Algonquin nothing is inanimate; he sees life in all the things that surround him and impress themselves on his senses as real. There are the grandfathers of the four cardinal points, who send wind and cold weather; there are the 'elder brothers', the sun and moon. The thunderbirds in the clouds carry on their everlasting battle with the horned serpents who live in rivers, lakes and springs; earth mother, maize mother, mask spirit, snow boy, plants and stones, are all alive, all hear and speak.

All *manitos* pray, because we hear them sometimes, our grandfathers the trees, joining in earnest prayer when the wind blows through them.[12]

Another sentient, active being is also the Creator himself. He sits in the twelfth heaven; his hand rests upon the point of the centre post; prayer calls reach his ear; he himself founded the Big House ceremony. When he ascended to the zenith the prayer sticks could be seen flashing in his hands, and the doors of heaven shut behind him with a clap of thunder.

The idea that all phenomena, even the mightiest, are living, acting beings, lies at the heart of Indian religious thought. The central experience of the individual's life is the childhood vision which is re-enacted in the course of the Big House ceremony. The fast in which the guardian spirit is found takes place among the Delaware in about the twelfth year of life.[13] The parents take the child, boy or girl, to a prearranged place in the forest and leave it there to its own devices. Strictly forbidden to eat, the child remains alone with the silence of the daytime and the voices of the night. The idea is that it will implore the spirits to take pity. The sight of the pale helpless creature, its head smeared with mud and its arms raised, begging to be granted a vision, is calculated to arouse the pity of sentient powers. Growing weakness – to be at its most effective the fast should last twelve days – and partial loss of consciousness finally so touches the hearts of the spirits that they put an end to the child's suffering by vouchsafing a vision. The parents or other relatives who visit the child from time to time during its ordeal are at hand to carry it home after the vision has come; the child has been blessed by a higher power. The whole family remains profoundly happy for a long period.

The visions themselves take an infinite variety of forms. The apparition may be Misinghalikun riding on his stag; or it may be a black and white duck, or the thunderbird, or the sun. In each case the fasting child has the feeling of being 'blessed', having a guardian spirit as a prop and stay in its adult life. This vision is the central experience in the life of the individual; and the nature of what has been seen remains a jealously-guarded secret, for fear of losing the protection of the guardian spirit. Thus the fact that recitals of these visions take place on all twelve nights of the Big House ceremony testifies to the deep religious significance held by this ritual. The emotion aroused in the participants breaks down the inhibitions which normally apply to vision memories, although it is significant that during the dance, with its cadential turnings to face the two faces on the centre post, the dancer addresses the Creator rather than his fellow-men. The conversation is with Gicelemukaong, the song of the vision is for him, and he is the only intended recipient of a secret which has so long been held close. The sacrifice of this secret is the greatest sacrifice of all; indeed, true sacrifice consists only in this.

One wonders, and European observers have always wondered, where there is room in this world of living phenomena for a principle of evil. The answer – an astonishing one to a European mind – is that in the spirit world of the Delaware there is no such thing as an evil power or a domain of evil. The soul, *tsitsang* ('picture' or 'mirror image' or 'visible manifestation of a material substance') resides in the heart.[14] There is also a second psychic element which resides in the blood, and which enables the dead person to rove the earth as a ghost, while his *tsitsang* departs on the twelfth day after death for a happy 'land of pictures' in the south-west, divided from the land of the living by a river. There is another version according to which the soul flies up to the twelfth heaven of the Creator, where shines a brighter light than the sun, where care and sickness are unknown and where there is no more death and no more parting.

This paradise is only for the righteous; as for the wicked, all that is known of their fate is that they are shut out of paradise and must roam about outside.[15] The criterion for dividing good from bad is social behaviour. Those who lie, steal, quarrel with their neighbours, are unfriendly to their friends, and especially to their aged parents, in a word those who are a plague upon humanity (as a wise and venerable Delaware explained to the missionary Brainerd in 1744), are to be condemned. Brainerd quite correctly comments that the Delaware had only the haziest notions of reward and punishment in the hereafter, and that the fate of the individual soul depended, for them, entirely on his observance of the precepts contained in the second table of the Law (Commandments 6–10 of the Decalogue) and not on his acts of worship or his proper reverence for the gods.[16] This is true of all North American Indians: ethical criteria and standards of social behaviour are identical.

All this illustrates how poorly developed the idea of evil is among these Indians, and how utterly different their moral ideas are from those of Europeans. They regard as bad only those animals and powers which are hostile to man; for an unknown mythological reason these forces are symbolized by horned water snakes and by water in general. Practical ethics consists in keeping these hostile powers at bay by whatever means are necessary.

There was once a man who had a bad dream, probably sent by the water spirits, in which he was told to kill seven people. In a state of post-hypnotic suggestion he actually began to commit murder after murder. Nothing could be proved against him, as he concealed his traces with a somnambulist's cunning; but he remained under suspicion because someone had found out about his dream.

One day, as he sat brooding under a tree, he was killed from behind by an axe-blow from an unknown hand. No one tried to find the killer. The whole community was unanimous in the conviction that the person who had rid them of a bad man had done the right thing.[17] No hint of punishment in the hereafter; the North American Indian fears neither hell nor devil. Where a personified evil principle does appear in the early written sources, this is merely a misinterpretation of the Algonquin word *manito* and related words. *Manito* applies to *all* spirits, 'good' and 'bad' – or rather, friendly and unfriendly. It was the Europeans who brought with them purely ethical criteria of judgment. In Harrington's bitter words, 'the Devil (along with whisky and other blessings) was introduced by the whites'.[18]

IV   *Dream, Vision and Tradition: The Algonquin of the Great Lakes*

The Canadian Algonquin spread southward as well as eastward. The Algonquin of the Great Lakes area were still moving when Europeans came into contact with them in the mid-seventeenth century, pressing against the Sioux in the west and the Maskoki and Yuchi in the south.

The sturdiest and numerically the strongest of these tribes were the Ojibwa of Lake Superior; to the south, between the Mississippi headwaters and Lake Michigan, lived the Menomini, the Fox, the Sauk, the Kickapoo, the Potawatomi, the Miami, the Kaskaskia and the Shawnee, all tribes which played an important part in the history of the discovery of the area by Europeans and the wars of the end of the eighteenth and the beginning of the nineteenth century.

In the summer of 1855 some fortunate chance led the Bremen librarian and traveller Georg Kohl to visit the Ojibwa. He travelled along the south shore of Lake Superior, visited the various mission stations and Indian villages, and captured a last glimmer of the moribund Indian culture. Kohl, who seems to have had a particularly attractive personality, and to have found it easy to gain people's confidence, was possessed of a fresh and natural narrative gift, a warm understanding of alien ideas and a sure eye for what was essential. His two-volume work *Kitschi-Gami oder Erzählungen vom Oberen See*[1] stands head and shoulders above all later ethnological works; the professional ethnologist, confined by his training to rigid theoretical categories of enquiry, has usually seen much less than the Saxon librarian equipped with nothing but his two eyes and a notebook.

Unwittingly Kohl also provides an answer to the problem of what lies behind the survival of tradition among the North American Indians. Each tribe lives in a rounded and enclosed cosmos and cosmology of its own, and it is natural to wonder whether mere dogmatic statement is enough to ensure the survival of this cosmology from generation to generation. Is it enough to hammer ritual observances and mythological texts into the young, or do they feel the need for personal experience? The answer, of course, is that they do; and that all over North America this personal religious experience occurs in dreams. The dream is an unequivocal message from the beyond. Dreams are at the root of all religious institutions; the offices of priest and shaman are held by virtue of dreams; dreams give the orders for military and hunting expeditions, orders to kill and orders to lend a helping hand; only dreams can penetrate the darkness of ultimate reality. Finally, and importantly, dreams set the seal on tradition, legality and authority. Whether the vision emerges in a trance, in half-sleep or in sleep, it always uses the accepted images of religion and myth. Visions bring the traditions to life; and the traditions provide the raw material of the visions.

It was not long before Kohl realized the paramount importance of the dream in Indian life. Whatever the subject into which he enquired, the ultimate explanation always lay in some dream experience;[2] and it was not long before he grasped the significance of the puberty dream in the life of each individual.

The rapid decline of aboriginal culture came to his aid and removed the last obstacles. In the summer of 1855, when he was living in a wigwam in an Indian settlement, he succeeded in persuading two old men to recount their life-dreams. Both were Christian converts, but both were very reluctant at first to tell him. Sensing that these visions were central to Indian religious life, Kohl persisted; and he was rewarded with the following tales.

Little Raven, his first informant, had seen a black figure which bore him in three gigantic paces to 'deer mountain'. The mountain split open and through a long cleft the sunlight poured forth. After crossing the cleft the dreamer came to the house of the sun. As soon as he had accustomed his eyes to the glare, the sun got him to look down upon the earth, far below, its trees and forest, the mountains, Lake Superior and the whole curve of the world. Then he was able to look upwards, and through an opening in the roof he saw the arch of heaven, its constellations so near that he might have touched them. Then the sun showed him his future life and gave him eagle and bear as symbols to remember. Finally the sun dismissed him and with his spirit escort he climbed down an immeasurably tall fir tree, at the foot of which his sisters found him in the morning. They took him home and it was a long time before he recovered his strength.

The second informant, Cloud Head, was also carried on high in his dream. He saw the earth, with its four points, far beneath him, and the shining dome of the sky, which was filled with an immense quantity of game. This spectacle so enraptured him that the spirits had to remind him when it was time to descend.[3]

These dreams preserved by Kohl are remarkable for their cosmic scope. They are not just apparitions of one animal or object, as are the life-dreams of other tribes; the dreamer is caught up in a whole world of fantasy and symbol. A third Ojibwa life-dream, that of George Copway (Kah-Ge-Ga-Gah-Bowh), a nineteenth-century chief from Lake Rice in Ontario, confirms this peculiarity of the Ojibwa life-dream.

I saw, in my dream, a person coming from the east; he approached, walking on the air; he looked down on me, and said, 'Is this where you are?' I said, 'Yes.' 'Do you see this pine?' 'Yes, I see it.' 'It is a great and high tree.' I observed that the tree was lofty, reaching towards the heavens – its branches extended over land and water, and its roots were very deep. 'Look on it while I sing; yes, gaze upon the tree.' He sang, and pointed to the tree; it commenced waving its top; the earth about its roots was heaved up, and the waters roared and tossed from one side of their beds to the other. As soon as he stopped singing, and let fall his hands, everything became perfectly still and quiet. 'Now,' said he, 'sing the words which I have sung.' I commenced as follows:

> 'It is I who travel in the winds,
> It is I who whisper in the breeze;
> I shake the trees,
> I shake the earth,
> I trouble the waters on every hand.'

While singing, I heard the winds whistle, saw the tree waving its top, the earth heaving, heard the waters roaring, because they were all troubled and agitated. Then said he, 'I am from the rising of the sun; I will come and see you again. You will not see me often: but you will hear me speak.' Thus spoke the spirit, and then turned away towards the road from which he had come.[4]

These cosmic visions are peculiar to the central Algonquin. They appear in an attenuated form among the Algonquin and the Sioux of the prairies; but the Iroquois have visions only of individual guardian spirits in shapes such as dwarf, old man, eagle, bear and ant. The religious imagery of the central Algonquin in general shows the same cosmic scale of ideas; the same psychological traits mark not only individual spiritual experience but also the ritual and myth of the tribe.

This is immediately apparent in the dominant features of Ojibwa ceremonial life: the medicine society and the 'medicine hut'. Like the Big House of the Delaware, the medicine hut is charged with cosmic symbolism. But the environmental differences between the two tribes are reflected in the significance given to their religious buildings. The timing of the hut ritual depends not on astronomical data, nor on the divisions of the agricultural year, but on immediate need. The medicine society forgathers when there are candidates for admission, or when sick people seek initiation in order to enjoy the healing power of the ritual; unlike the Big House, the medicine society is thus a matter not for the whole tribe but for a select group of initiates. Others may witness the ritual, but have only an incomplete and inadequate understanding of what it means. Only the candidate for membership is granted detailed instruction. Thus Kohl, who was present at a ceremony at La Pointe, was unable to arrive at an adequate interpretation of it. It was not until the 1880s, when W. J. Hoffmann actually became a member of a medicine society, that a solution to the puzzle was published.[5]

Medicine society and Big House differ in their purposes. The Big House is intended to serve humanity as a whole by maintaining the accustomed sequence of events in the cosmos; while the medicine society is concerned only with the individual and his needs. All its rites, as well as all its herbal lore, are dedicated to this one goal. The Big House may be universalistic; the medicine society is individualistic. It is based on the religious attitude of the sub-Arctic hunter: total concentration on the self.

The society itself consists of an undefined number of men and women who as *mide* (or what are popularly termed 'medicine men') are greatly respected. They are the repositories of the sacred lore of the tribe; they know the myths in their sacred context, they know songs, healing plants and ethical laws.

If anyone wishes to join the fraternity, he must first take a course of instruction lasting several years with a particularly respected *mide*. Only then does he reach the first grade of membership; further training enables him to rise through the four grades to the highest of all.

His reception into each grade takes place in public; in spite of its esoteric character the medicine society plays a central part in the life of the tribe. The Minnesota Ojibwa build for each ceremony an oblong house-shaped framework of branches with a barrel-shaped roof. The interior of the hut is clearly visible, as the sides are covered only with a few cloths or pieces of bark as protection against the heat of the sun. On the short sides of the structure, which is oriented east–west, there are two doorways; at highest-grade initiations there are also two doors facing north and south in the middle of the long sides.

Along the east–west axis of the structure stand one, two, three or four coloured posts, according to the grade to which the candidate is to be admitted. The first three grades have round red and green poles, while the fourth-grade medicine hut – very seldom seen, as it is rare for a medicine society member to rise so high – is provided with a cross. The stem of this cross has a four-cornered base; and if it is made of round poles, which can be the case, a four-sided post stands immediately next to it.

The quadruple rhythm of the four doors, the four arms of the cross, the four sides of the square post, is unmistakably pointed out by the colour-scheme. The sides of the square post are painted in the four cardinal-point colours: white for the east, green for the south, red for the west and black for the north. In view of this symbolism it can hardly be in doubt that the medicine hut, like the Big House of the Delaware, symbolizes the world.

Significantly enough, the ritual adornment of the hut is connected with the worship of the supreme being Kitci Manito. The introductory dog sacrifices, in which the victim must be consumed entirely, are in his honour; the candidate is commended to him as a 'seeker after life'; the recitation is addressed to him; his voice is heard in the roll of the water drum; he sits on the curved roof of the hut, which of course represents the dome of heaven. The appearance of quadruple symbolism is confined to the fourth grade, of which Kitci Manito is the patron; the other grades have other presiding deities. The supreme being is thus expressly linked with the image of a quadripartite world.

The Algonquin symbol for the supreme being is a squared circle or a ring with four points:[6] the same symbol that is used for the earth. However different the two ideas may seem to the European mind, to the Algonquin the Great Spirit and the earth are identical. This cosmic theology is also found among the Delaware; as a Delaware shaman explained to the Rev. David Brainerd in 1745, the earth and all its mountains, lakes and seas are spread out on the belly of the great man. The shaman knew this because he had seen it when his soul travelled up to heaven.[7]

The penchant of the Algonquin for cosmic imagery, with its roots deep in the lore of dreams, is surely a legacy of the northern hunting and gathering culture, in which crosses, quadrifoils and four-dot patterns appear in almost all the decorative patterns on dishes, rattles and drums. Members of one sub-Arctic Algonquin tribe, the Naskapi of Labrador, told Speck expressly that these patterns represented Tcementu, the supreme being.[8] The close link between the earth-number four and the supreme being is thus present in Algonquin thought at the stage of sub-Arctic culture; but only in the southern maize-growing zone, with its greater technical resources and its stronger social cohesion, does the idea crystallize into a solid architectonic symbol, such as the Big House and the medicine hut. The structural and symbolic links between the two institutions in themselves indicate the antiquity of the underlying theological idea. Only the earth-symbolism of the great spirit Kitci Manito gives meaning to the medicine hut; he must therefore have been present from the very beginning, long before any European appeared on the shores of the Great Lakes.

The ritual itself, concentrated as it is on the individual, reflects the individual nature of sub-Arctic religious life. The candidate stands in the middle of the hut, and the four most senior *mide* 'shoot' a white shell, the emblem of life, into his body from their medicine bags. He has been born again and is in a position to live once more to a ripe old age. The very sick are initiated into the society when all other means fail, the idea being that death and rebirth turn a hopeless case into a new man who has left all sickness behind him.

Alongside this great-spirit ritual, which is practised only by the Minnesota Ojibwa, there is another type of medicine hut ceremony further south in Wisconsin. This is the medicine society of the culture hero Mänäbusch, 'Big Rabbit'. Like the tribes of the sub-Arctic regions the Mid-West Algonquin have endless cycles of stories about this myth-ical figure, comic and serious by turns. In Kohl's wigwam many an evening passed in the telling of tales of Big Rabbit, who once appeared on earth in the guise of a hare and made it possible for his uncles and aunts, i.e. mankind, to lead the lives they lead today. All handicrafts stem from him; he fought the monsters of the deep; he re-created the earth after a deluge, and on his departure he left it as it is today.[9]

The cosmic war between Big Rabbit and the water monsters, which thus ended in a catastrophe affecting the whole earth, began with a murder. The water beasts drowned Big Rabbit's little brother Wolf and thus brought death into the world. The victim returned to life on the fourth day after his death, but Big Rabbit was compelled to let him depart towards the sunset. There Wolf rules over the dead, and ever since then his aunts and uncles have had to travel the same road. His kingdom is a happy land, which the wicked may not enter; they fall from the shaky bridge made of a beam as soon as they attempt to cross the rushing river of the dead.

This episode brought the conflict between good and evil powers to a head. According to popular tradition Big Rabbit slew a number of the water beasts, and although his adversaries caused a deluge, and followed it with a fearful winter, they still could not injure him. According to the esoteric *mide* tradition, on the other hand, known only to the members of the medicine society, the two sides made peace; the water monsters bestowed the medicine hut upon Big Rabbit to console him for the loss of his brother.

This form of the medicine hut tradition, in which the hut is derived from the culture hero, differs from the Minnesota tradition which centres on the supreme being. The Wisconsin medicine hut has no coloured posts, has two grades instead of four, the ritual functionaries are divided into two groups, and the ritual itself is twofold; after the 'shooting' of the shell the candidate must eat the 'pearl', a grain of seed-corn with two sides.

The ceremony of admission is a re-enactment of mythical events. The candidate represents Big Rabbit himself, and two groups of functionaries represent the upper and nether powers which initiated the culture hero into the very first medicine hut. No mention whatever is made of the supreme being.

This second tradition is based on different patterns from those revealed in the Kitci Manito medicine hut ritual of Minnesota. The ritual is dominated by the number two, characteristic of southern cultures, rather than the number four which dominates in the north. The appearance of these two typologies reveals a historical sequence. And in spite of all the differences the Minnesota pattern has obvious affinities with the southern Big House ritual. In both cases the rectangular ritual structure is orientated according to the four cardinal points, and in both cases it symbolizes both the cosmos and the body of the supreme being. As the prairie Algonquin have analogous ritual structures, which they use in their sun dance and which carry the same symbolic significance, this kind of symbolic architecture must be of immense antiquity, at least within the Algonquin linguistic group. Any ritual pattern which is present over an area from the Atlantic to the Rockies must have a single prehistoric source. It is not without justification that the Delaware regard the Big House as the highest form of religious expression anywhere in North America and say that all other Indian forms of worship are branches of this one creed.[10] The Wisconsin medicine hut ceremony, on the other hand, with its dual symbolism and its concentration on the culture hero, is a late form of the northern Algonquin rite which gradually took shape under the influence of southern dualism.

It will now be understood why it is important that the Delaware, unlike all other North American tribes, have no culture hero, and consequently no culture-hero myth or ritual.[11] This is another indication that Delaware religious forms are of great antiquity: the Big House and the Minnesota medicine hut sacred to the supreme being Kitci Manito are representative features of the oldest level of religious development to be found in eastern North America. The next level is represented by the medicine hut of the Wisconsin culture hero.

The subtle inconsistencies from which the European investigator draws his conclusions are invisible to the Indian eye. The Indian regards this shifting world of images as the only framework of reality in terms of which he can think, and all new experiences are fitted into it. In 1911, when the first aeroplane flew over the Ojibwa reservation at Red Lake, Minnesota, the Indians knew at once what it was. The flying monster was of course the adversary of the mythical serpents, the thunderbird, whose eyes flash with lightning and whose wing-beat makes the thunder. Everyone hastened down to the shores of the lake to make offerings of tobacco to the monster.[12] The North American Indian, the 'son of the soil', dwells in the shelter of his structure of myths as in a fortified house.

There are other esoteric societies among the Great Lakes Algonquin besides the *mide* club; and just as among the forest Indians of the north the various classes of shamans are extremely hard to distinguish, it is impossible to tell whether the categories of 'medicine men' among the southern hunting tribes constitute separate 'professions' or whether they are merely groups of 'specialists' who all perform essentially the same function.

One of these categories is that of the *wabeno*, the 'east men' or 'men of the morning twilight'.[13] They do not constitute a society or club; each works alone on his hunting spells, love potions and healing medicines. The *wabeno* are thus closely concerned with everyday needs and problems. Confidence in them is unbounded and they themselves lose no opportunity to display their powers, by playing with glowing coals, putting their hands in boiling water, or swallowing knives. Superstition has it that they fly around at night as fireballs or sparks, and that they are to be heard in the distant howling of wolves.

The individual *wabeno* may well himself be a member of the medicine hut society; but the *jossakid* holds aloof from it. His main preoccupation is with foretelling the future with the aid of his guardian spirits. To this end he uses his characteristic 'shaking tent', which consists of between four and eight thick posts ten feet long driven into the ground to form a ring about a yard across. This framework is then covered with birch bark so that it takes on the appearance of a wide tube open at the top. At the beginning of each séance the *jossakid* crawls in at the bottom of the tube and begins to sing. Those present accompany his conjurations with their drums. Soon the whole very solid structure begins to shake violently from side to side, a sign that the spirits are hastening to obey the call of their master. The bells and deer hoofs attached to the structure jingle and rattle, thumps can be heard as the spirits land inside the tent, and voices can be heard, some high and clear, some deep and muffled. Then the *jossakid* himself begins to call out to his audience the answers given by the spirits to the questions asked by those who seek their help.

The *jossakid*'s tent is a typical piece of equipment among the Labrador hunters. Its appearance by the Great Lakes is another sign of the fidelity with which the Algonquin of the area have preserved their ancient heritage and how slowly they have absorbed southern cultural elements. The very existence of various categories of shaman demonstrates the vitality of sub-Arctic traditions: shamanism is inseparable from the eerie and nebulous daemonology characteristic of northern peoples.

The Ojibwa are haunted by visions of a hostile and uncanny environment. In the endless forests live ogres, whose footfall breaks the largest trees; there too are dwarfs who shake the posts of the wigwam, throw stones on to the roof, hide implements and play a thousand other tricks. There can be heard the heavy galloping feet of the ghost *manido*, who drives human souls down the path of the dead; woe betide those whose soul he catches abroad; their souls cannot return to their bodies but are driven westward to the kingdom of Brother Wolf in the west. Only the shade of the dead man remains behind by the grave; and the life of a shade is no life at all.[14] These spirits outside the community are joined by hostile powers within, witches and sorcerers above all.

Protection against all these threatening forces was once provided by the *jossakid*; since their disappearance the Ojibwa have had recourse to amulets. Significantly, belief in witchcraft has become much more prevalent in the last few decades. Once it was possible for a *jossakid* to summon his guardian spirits to his tent and cause them to destroy the souls of witches and warlocks, thus killing the individuals themselves. Now the Indian feels defenceless; his amulets are far less potent than the arts of the 'secret-men' of old.[15]

Belief in survival after death has persisted into our own day. In an Ojibwa cemetery, among the wooden box tombs which look rather like elongated slanting-topped dog kennels, there are posts carrying pennants, little piles of tobacco, little dishes of food and mirrors, all gifts for the shades which linger here and who maintain their links with the living. The soul of a dead man can return from its dwelling-place in the far west and unite with the shade to produce a new human being. Such reincarnated persons sometimes dream of episodes from their former life. 'My uncle,' declared one informant, 'lived four or five times, about five hundred years in all.'[16]

In the autumn, when the trout season causes the larders to overflow with supplies, every Ojibwa community builds a long wigwam and celebrates the festival of the dead. Choice foods are prepared in large cauldrons, and as soon as the participants have assembled, a few mouthfuls are thrown into the fire for the shades, and feasting and dancing go on until morning. The recollection of this festival, the most joyful day of the year, casts a glow over the ensuing hardships of winter.[17]

V *Twin Gods and a Dual World: The Iroquois of Lake Ontario*

The Algonquin of the Atlantic coast and the Great Lakes form southern outposts of sub-Arctic hunting cultures; the Iroquois on the other hand are pure and genuine representatives of the culture of the maize-farming belt. From whichever viewpoint one sees the way of life of the Iroquois, its most conspicuous characteristic is its inexhaustible plenitude and exuberance. The culture of the hunters and gatherers is thin and under-nourished; that of the Iroquois bursts out at the seams. This is true of the world of ideas as it is of material culture; every idea is pursued and exploited as far as it will go.

This cultural richness begins with the external forms. The southern outposts of the Algonquin toil over their miserable plots of corn, sown as a mere adjunct to the produce of the hunting field; but the Iroquois on the southern shore of Lake Ontario, with their broad acres and their three-crop farming – maize, beans and squash – give evidence of an ancient and successful agricultural tradition. In 1779, when Major-General Sullivan laid their territory waste and broke the power of the Iroquois League, he estimated the stocks of grain destroyed in the fields and in the granaries at 116,000 cwt, to which must be added huge quantities of beans and other greenstuffs.

The advanced form of agriculture was matched by a complicated social organization. No longer was language the only unifying factor for loosely connected groups of tribes; a new kind of organization, even a kind of national consciousness, made the Iroquois into a powerful body politic which stood out from the surrounding mass of isolated tribes. About the year 1570 five tribes, the Seneca, the Cayuga, the Onondaga, the Oneida and the Mohawk, joined in a confederation. Each tribe was divided, on the basis of existing tribal subdivisions, into two moieties each consisting of four clans named after animals and birds:

(1) Wolf, Bear, Beaver, Turtle;
(2) Deer, Snipe, Heron, Hawk.

Members of these moieties, which had no names of their own, regarded themselves as brothers. The clans were not allowed to intermarry, either within their own tribe or within the league as a whole. This clan organization covering five distinct tribes meant that all Wolves, from the Seneca to the Mohawk, were brothers, and the same was true of the Bears, Beavers, Turtles, Deer, Snipe, Herons and Hawks. The Seneca

Wolf felt himself to be closer to a Wolf from the Cayuga, Onondaga, Oneida or Mohawk tribes than to a member of the other clans of his own tribe; and this feeling of affinity welded the League into an indissoluble union.[1]

Political power lay in the hands of a council of about fifty senior chiefs or *sachems*, who took decisions on all important matters affecting the confederation as a whole. The Iroquois name for their league, Hodenosaunee, 'people of the long house', appealed to the pictorial imagination of its members, who saw it as a house sheltering five tribes, from the Seneca in the West to the Mohawk in the east, under a single roof, just like one of the large Iroquois family units in its gabled long house.

This solid social and political unit was a considerable problem both to its Indian neighbours and later to the European colonists. Full-scale armies with artillery had to take the field before the menace of the Iroquois was finally destroyed at the end of the eighteenth century.

For a long time attention was concentrated on the bloody history of the Iroquois at the expense of their mythology. It is only in our own time that Iroquois cosmology in its original form has been properly investigated,[2] and the pattern that emerges is one that had previously been known only as a feature of the civilization of Iran. The world is seen as the battlefield of two hostile powers, light and dark, good and evil, high and low. The dualism which is absent from the thought of the peoples of the north of Canada is here present in its most perfect form, developed with a mystical profundity of which by no means all the agricultural societies further south have proved themselves capable.

The Iroquois believe that terrestrial phenomena possess archetypes or 'elder brothers'. These archetypes (*ongwe*) have always existed and are immortal. They live on the side of the dome of heaven which we cannot see: Deer, Roe-deer, Dappled Fawn, Bear, Beaver, Wind Who Moves About from Place to Place, Daylight, Night, Thick Night, Star, Water of Springs, Maize, Bean, Squash, Sunflower, Fire Dragon with a Body of Pure White Colour, Rattle, Red Meteor, Spring Wind, Great Turtle, Otter, Wolf, Duck, Fresh Water, Yellowhammer, Medicine and Aurora Borealis. The houses of the *ongwe* are in general long, and the sleeping mats lie at the ends. In the morning the archetypes go hunting, in the evening they return.[3]

In the celestial village there once lived a couple whose daughter Awenhai ('fruitful earth') offered her hand in marriage to the celestial chief. The hut of this chief, the most exalted member of the exalted community of *ongwe*, stood in a wide field under the tree Onodja. The blossoms of this tree gave forth the celestial light; in that world above the sky there was no sun.

The chief accepted the maiden's offer and married her. But before he and Awenhai had ever slept together, he made her pregnant with his breath. No one had any idea that this could have happened, and the chief became so jealous of Aurora and the Fire Dragon with the Body of Pure White Colour that he determined to change the nature of the *ongwe*. He caused the tree of light, Onodja, to be uprooted, thus leaving a gaping hole in the canopy of heaven through which he hurled his wife together with Maize, Bean, Sunflower, Tobacco, Deer, Wolf, Bear and Beaver, and all their relations. There then appeared the terrestrial forms known to us, but the immortal 'elder brothers' or archetypes nevertheless continue to exist in heaven. Then the tree Onodja was set up again and the hole closed. Thus ends the first act of the cosmic drama.

Meanwhile Awenhai fell towards a light blue speck which she soon realized was an endless sea with many sea birds on it. No earth was anywhere to be seen. The animals saw her fall and set out to provide a firm footing for her to land on. Great Turtle was deputed to carry her, and the other animals were set to bring earth up from the ocean bed. Muskrat finally succeeded in doing this. The mud was spread out on the shell of the turtle, and the result was an island. At the same time the birds flew upwards in great flocks, caught the falling Awenhai, and set her down gently on the turtle's back.

The earth grew rapidly; bushes, grass and other plants shot up, and after two nights Awenhai found a deer carcass and a little fire, so that she could prepare a meal. Eventually she gave birth to a girl child.

Awenhai's daughter grew astonishingly quickly, and in no time there appeared all manner of suitors, but the girl took her mother's advice and rejected them all. One day there came one who wore fringes on his legs and arms. 'This,' said the mother, 'is the man you must marry.' The young man then came to the girl at night, but he did nothing but lay an arrow down next to her and depart.

Awenhai's daughter thereupon became pregnant. When her labour pains began, she heard twin voices quarrelling within her womb; one wanted to move downwards, the other to go towards the side, where the light shone through. So the elder of the two children was born in the natural way, but the younger forced his way out through his mother's armpit and killed her.

This second twin brother was a remarkable figure; his body consisted entirely of flint, and over his scalp ran a razor-sharp flint crest. For this

reason he was called Tawiskaron, which means 'flint'. The elder
brother was exactly like a human being. Awenhai angrily demanded
who had killed her daughter. Both children proclaimed their innocence,
but Awenhai finally decided to believe Tawiskaron and threw her
other grandson out of her hut. He did not die, but grew rapidly even
without the care which his grandmother lavished on Tawiskaron.

Awenhai suspended the body of her dead daughter on a tree near her
hut, and it became the sun. The head she placed elsewhere, and it became the moon. Both luminaries were fixed in their places; they must
give light to no one but her and Tawiskaron.

Meanwhile, the other grandson, the one shaped like a human being,
tumbled into a lake one day and sank to the bottom, where he found
himself before the entrance to a hut. He looked in and saw a man sitting
inside. It was his father, Great Turtle. From him the youth received a
bow and two ears of maize, one ripe and the other unripe, one for sowing
and the other for roasting.

After his return from the lake bed, he often went along the shore and
proclaimed: 'the earth shall grow yet farther, and men shall call me
Wata Oterongtongnia, "young maple sapling".' And the earth grew
wherever he walked, until it reached its present size. Then he created
the various animals and set them to grow fat in a pool of oil, so that
they should be as useful as possible. Tawiskaron sought to emulate his
brother, but when he tried to make a bird it fluttered erratically to and
fro; it was a bat.

The animals created by Oterongtongnia soon disappeared from view.
Awenhai and Tawiskaron had rounded them up and shut them in a
cave. Oterongtongnia went to liberate his creatures, but before they
could all escape Tawiskaron and Awenhai rolled the stone back in front
of the opening of the cave. So we now know only those animals which
succeeded in getting away.

Tawiskaron continued to interfere with his brother's work. Once he
built a bridge of ice across the lake in order to allow fearful monsters
from the land opposite to come across, but Oterongtongnia chased them
off and the bridge melted. Oterongtongnia's maize, which positively
oozed oil, was spoiled by his grandmother, who sprinkled ashes over
the cobs.

One day the sun disappeared. Oterongtongnia followed its faint
glimmer and finally discovered it in a tree on a wooded island. An
obliging beaver felled the tree, and the hare, who had also been taking
part in the search, raced down to the beach with it, and they all got
away safely in a canoe before their irate pursuers could catch them.

Oterongtongnia threw the sun and moon up into the sky, and since that time they have remained in the service of all the creatures on this earth.

Oterongtongnia then shaped human beings and brought them to life. When his brother Tawiskaron saw him doing this one day, he tried to imitate him but could produce only pathetic, feeble, gangling creatures with human heads and monstrous bodies.

Tawiskaron spoiled many things that his brother had done. For example, Oterongtongnia had arranged it so that the rivers had two currents, one upstream and one downstream, so that no one would need to paddle. Tawiskaron put an end to this arrangement; and he also created mountains and rocky cliffs to frighten mankind. But one day the end of his career was at hand.

The twins lived on opposite sides of the same hut. One day Oterong-tongnia heated the fire to such a temperature that little fragments of flint started to fly off Tawiskaron's body. Tawiskaron finally fled, pursued by his brother, who battered him to death with antlers and flints. The high mountains on the western edge of the world (the Rockies) are the remains of Tawiskaron.

Since that time the world has looked as it does now, and as it will until the end of time.

Superficially this summary of cosmic history resembles the creation myths of the sub-Arctic hunters; in both cases one epoch follows on another. But closer study reveals fundamental differences. Iroquois mythology almost overflows with images. It incorporates the idea of a pre-existence of the world, a cosmogony of sorts, and a cosmic drama involving two antithetical forces. The nature of Iroquois mythology is the best possible confirmation of my suggestion that dualism is a characteristic of southern cultures; this is a world of myth entirely based on polarities.

As the myth is not esoteric but is known in a more or less complete form to every member of the tribe, it is natural to enquire as to the practical value of the world view enshrined in it. Are these myths essentially products of the creative fancy, which despite their religious content are handed on merely as part of the traditions of the tribe, or is myth closely linked with religious practice? To put the question in Iroquois terms, are the twins still alive, and do they still influence the things that happen now?

The question will answer itself if we pay a visit to one of the Iroquois villages which still exist on the upper Alleghany, near Buffalo, near Syracuse, and in south-western Ontario, a day's journey from megalo-politan New York. The clan houses of former times have disappeared;

1 Funerary mask in green onyx. Culture of Teotihuacan.

2 Mexico, Hidalgo. Huge stone
statues, which surmount the
pyramid B at Tula. Toltec
culture, first Postclassic period.

3 Back view of a sculpture of
Quetzalcoatl, found at
Tamuin (San Luis Potosí,
Mexico). Sandstone. Huaxtec
culture.

10 Wood and fur mask
(masked medicine
society). Iroquois tribe.

11 Large mask with moving
eyes and jaws. British
Columbia (Mass river).

12 Lintel from house at the ancient
Maya ceremonial centre at
Menché (Yaxchilan),
Guatemala, showing a penitent
knèeling before a priest and
mutilating his tongue by passing
a rope of thorns through it.

13 Doll of painted clay. Central
Brazil (Rio Araguaya).

each family lives by itself. In the middle of the village of scattered huts there rises a large structure with a gabled roof, built of massive beams. This is the long house, the temple of the village, the scene of communal religious life. Christianity has made no headway among the Iroquois to this day.[4]

The four walls of the Long House are orientated according to the cardinal points, and there are doors in the north-eastern and south-western corners. The interior, lit by a number of windows, is a single large room, rather like the Delaware Big House except that the centre post is missing. At each end stands a stove; along the walls are a few benches.

An invisible line divides the structure into an eastern and a western half. The women enter by the north-east door and sit on the east, the men enter by the south-west door and sit on the west. This arrangement is common to all Long Houses except the two long houses of the Cayuga, which are divided not according to sex but according to the two moieties: Wolf, Bear, Beaver, Turtle on one side, Deer, Snipe, Heron, Hawk on the other.

The Cayuga arrangement has logic on its side; the clan-groups form the basis of the whole ritual. All ritual functionaries, led by the so-called 'faith-preservers' and including heralds, orators, singers, cooks and food distributors, work in pairs, one from each moiety. Each functionary thus has an opposite number in the other half-tribe with whom he works.

Ritual too is based on a set of polarities. The festal calendar falls into two halves, winter and summer. The winter half includes the harvest thanksgiving or bread dance (September) and the new year (February, 'when the Pleiades shine through the smoke hole'), and the summer half the maple thanksgiving (late March), the prayers for the young (early May), the prayers for the berry harvest (late May) and the prayers to the staple crops, maize, squash and beans (late July) and green corn (late August). Each half-cycle lasts six months, and the two pivots of the year are the new year and the green corn festival.[5]

The winter ceremonies, performed by the men, are thanksgivings. The summer ceremonies, performed by the women, are intercessions for a good harvest of maple syrup, for rain for the seedling crops, for wild fruit, for the cultivated crops in general, and for the successful ripening of the green corn.

The dualistic structure extends to all the details of the ceremonies. Two heralds march through the village, the deer and wolf moieties play each other at dice; and there are also two kinds of dance, those in honour of the Great Spirit and those that are purely 'social'.

Any attempt to investigate the origins and significance of this dualistic festal calendar and the dualistic arrangement of the long house must take into account a complicating factor which is almost unique in the history of North American native religions. At the beginning of the nineteenth century there appeared among the Iroquois a religious reformer and prophet: a Seneca by the name of Handsome Lake.[6] Thanks to this one man the disintegration of Iroquois culture was arrested, and thanks to him the Iroquois nation has so successfully resisted alien cultural pressures that there are still long houses standing to this day. It is not without reason that the pagan Iroquois of today call themselves 'followers of Handsome Lake'.

Until the fifty-fifth year of his life Handsome Lake was a devotee of the bottle and led just as dissolute and hopeless a life as most of his compatriots. In the year 1799 he became very ill, and was expected to die, when he was vouchsafed a vision. Three emissaries of the Great Spirit – as Handsome Lake later intimated – came to his bedside, restored him to health and announced to him that it was God's will that he should reform the life and religion of the Indians.

Cured of his sickness, Handsome Lake at once set out from village to village preaching the 'old way'; and not unexpectedly the recital of his miraculous vision made a deep impression on his hearers. Handsome Lake continued his work for fifteen years, and in this time he succeeded in so shoring up the vanishing pagan faith of the Iroquois that it has held firm to this day. This Iroquois St Paul did not take over the tradition uncritically; he made considerable changes, and did not hesitate to suppress what seemed to him too archaic. In short, his teaching is to the original tradition rather as the New Testament is to the Old.

The first result of his religious reform was a massive emphasis on the worship of the supreme being. The fact that the thoughts and prayers of present-day pagan Iroquois communities are directed exclusively towards Haweniyo, 'great voice', is a direct result of Handsome Lake's teaching, although the name itself originated in the eighteenth century, or even in an older period of pagan-Catholic syncretism. Handsome Lake at first intended to change this name, on the grounds that the conduct of mankind had become so abominable that the devil answered when one called upon God; but the power of tradition was too strong for him. To this day God is called Haweniyo and the devil Haninseono, 'he dwells on the earth'.

This comparatively modern dualistic theology conceals a surprising fact: Haweniyo and Haninseono are nothing but stylized versions of the divine twins Oterongtongnia and Tawiskaron.[7] Old people still living in our century remembered that the new year sacrifice of a white dog had formerly been addressed not to Haweniyo but to the good twin Oterongtongnia. This offering of a spotless white animal, which was first strangled and then painted with red spots and burned on a pyre, has recently been discontinued, obviously because of embarrassment in the presence of Europeans. This sacrifice was nevertheless the climax of the whole new year festival; the dog hastened to heaven as a messenger bearing the petitions of mankind.[8]

The key and dice game played between the two moieties is another expression of the ancient polarity. It symbolized the struggle between the two brothers; and the Wolf and Deer moieties took it in turns to represent each.

The most important element in Iroquois religious practices is the dance, and here again there was a clear polarity: the ritual dances, of which the great feather dance was the most important, were dedicated to the good brother and the first half of the day, when the sun climbs the heavens; and the so-called social dances, including the war dance, were dedicated to the evil brother and to the declining half of the day.

The whole ritual life of the Iroquois was thus divided into two, a division based on the duality of the central figures in tribal mythology. The present-day version of these ceremonies, with its emphasis on the supreme being, is of course the work of Handsome Lake, who either simply banned the rites of the 'evil' god or reduced them to the level of harmless recreation (the 'social dances'). Why he did this hardly needs an explanation: the European accusation of 'devil-worship' came far too close to the mark for Handsome Lake to be able to escape its logical consequence. The same external influence carried the concept of the good brother irresistibly closer to that of the supreme being. There was no place for such a being in the original Iroquois religion, any more than there is a place for the massive centre post of the Delaware Big House in the entirely dualistic symbolism of the Iroquois long house.

Even more than Iroquois myth, Iroquois ritual reveals the necessity of a dark as well as a light side to the world. The civilized idea of 'evil' has no place here: Iroquois religion is founded on the existence, which is taken for granted, of two halves of the universe which fit together like night and day, summer and winter, seed-time and harvest and keep the mechanism of the cosmos in motion.

Just what emotions underlie Iroquois worship can be seen from a glance at the principal rituals themselves, once dedicated to the good brother Oterongtongnia and now transferred to the 'Great Spirit'.[9] The feather dance is performed by about fifty men in costume. In a long

187

crocodile they enter the Long House through the west door and stop for a moment at the end of the room until the orator calls upon them to begin the thanksgiving ritual. They then form an oval ring between the musicians in the centre of the room and the spectators round the walls, and move round one behind the other kicking up their heels in time with the music of the rattles and drums. A ghostly syllabic chant, '*ha-ho, ha-ho, way-ha-ah, ha-i, ha-i*', emphasizes the rhythm still further. The gentle wave-like motion which runs continuously through the line of dancers, and the smooth, agile movements of their bodies, carry a strong feeling of joy and good humour. Suddenly the men switch to a much slower pace, and the orator intones thanksgiving in a loud voice:

> We who are assembled here thank the Great Spirit
> That we are here to praise him!

Hardly has the sound of his last word faded into silence when the dancers revert to their quick-time movement, which gives way to a slower pace whenever the orator intones a new thanksgiving formula. The alternation of quick dance and thanksgiving can continue indefinitely, as the orator gives thanks for almost everything in the world. He thanks the Great Spirit for fruit and water, for the beasts and the trees, for shadows and thunderstorms, for sun and vines, darkness and the moon, the stars and the life-supporters (maize, beans and squash), an unending 'music of the Great Spirit' as the Iroquois themselves call their feather dance.

All the while the bells on the knees of the dancers jingle, the rattles and drums keep up their din, and the shouts of excited onlookers encourage the dancers to renewed efforts. Towards the end all those present join in the act of thanksgiving; and if the sun, perhaps breaking through mist, floods the landscape and the window with light, then all those present are silently aware that Haweniyo has accepted their 'praying with their feet'.

The impressiveness of Iroquois religious festivals stems very largely from the speeches of the orator, which are delivered with an extraordinary intensity of feeling. This, for instance, is the prayer offered up at the maple festival, when tobacco is burned at the foot of a maple tree:

> O partake of this incense,
> You, the forests!
> We implore you
> To continue as before,
> The flowing waters of the maple.
> It is the will of the Creator
> That a certain tree

Should flow such water.[10]
Now may no accidents occur
To children roaming in the forests.
Now day is yours
May you enjoy it, – this day.[10]

Such examples as this demonstrate how strongly present-day Iroquois religion is dominated by the idea of the Great Spirit. This religious pattern seems to have begun to displace the worship of the twins some two centuries ago under the impulse of civilized thought; in any case the Creator Haweniyo appears in the memoirs of Colonel James Smith soon after the middle of the eighteenth century.

In May 1755, just after the defeat of Braddock on the Monongahela, the young James Smith became a captive of the red men and was adopted by a group of Ottawa, Wyandot and Iroquois who lived a nomadic life in what is now the state of Ohio. This was then a refuge for many tribes which were breaking up under the mounting pressure of European settlement. It was also in the process of being colonized by the Seneca and the Cayuga.

In Smith's extremely valuable journal there is an episode which captures the religious attitude of the Indian pure and almost certainly uncontaminated by European influences.

It was the spring of the year 1758. James Smith spent the winter with an adopted Iroquois brother, a much older man by the name of Tecaughretanego, and his son Nunganey, by the Ollentangy River, a tributary of the Scioto. It was a difficult time; Tecaughretanego, crippled with rheumatism, could not walk, and Smith had to take over the hunting himself. All the stocks of vegetable food had been taken by other members of the family when they went off to their hunting grounds.

But good fortune and Tecaughretanego's fortitude carried them through the worst of their tribulations. Smith refers to his blood-brother as a truly great man, a Socrates among the heathen, even though the light of revelation was not vouchsafed to him. In April 1758 Tecaughretanego could walk again. They paddled down the Ollen-tangy, but the river was so shallow that their boat was in danger of breaking up on the rocks. They landed, and Tecaughretanego made ready to pray for rain. He built a sweat house, rolled glowing hot stones into it, poured water on to the stones, and stayed in the rising steam for about fifteen minutes before addressing the supreme being.

He began each petition with *oh, ho, ho, ho*, which is a kind of aspiration, and

signifies an ardent wish. I observed that all his petitions were only for immediate or present temporal blessings. He began his address by thanksgiving,
in the following manner:

'O great being! I thank thee that I have obtained the use of my legs again
– that I am now able to walk about and kill turkeys, etc., without feeling
exquisite pain and misery: I know that thou art a hearer and a helper, and
therefore I will call upon thee.

'*Oh, ho, ho, ho,*

'Grant that my knees and ankles may be right well and that I may be able,
not only to walk, but to run, and to jump logs, as I did last fall.

'*Oh, ho, ho, ho,*

'Grant that on this voyage we may frequently kill bears, as they may be
crossing the Sciota and Sandusky.

'*Oh, ho, ho, ho,*

'Grant that we may kill plenty of Turkeys along the banks, to stew with
our fat bear meat.

'*Oh, ho, ho, ho,*

'Grant that rain may come to raise the Ollentangy about two or three feet,
that we may cross in safety down to Sciota, without danger of our canoe
being wrecked on the rocks; – and now, O great being! thou knowest how
matters stand – thou knowest that I am a great lover of tobacco, and though
I know not when I may get any more, I now make a present of the last I have
unto thee, as a free burnt-offering; therefore I expect thou wilt hear and
grant these requests, and I thy servant will return thee thanks, and love thee
for thy gifts.'

During the whole of this scene I sat by Tecaughretanego, and as he went
through it with the greatest solemnity, I was seriously affected with his
prayers. I remained duly composed until he came to the burning of the
tobacco; and as I knew that he was a great lover of it, and saw him cast the
last of it into the fire, it excited in me a kind of merriment, and I insensibly
smiled. Tecaughretanego observed me laughing, which displeased him, and
occasioned him to address me in the following manner.

'*Brother,*

'I have somewhat to say to you, and I hope you will not be offended when
I tell you of your faults. You know that when you were reading your books
in the village, I would not let the boys or anyone disturb you; but now, when
I was praying, I saw you laughing. I do not think that you look upon praying
as a foolish thing; – I believe you pray yourself. But perhaps you may think
my mode, or manner of prayer, foolish; if so, you ought in a friendly manner
to instruct me, and not make sport of sacred things.'

I acknowledged my error, and on this he handed me his pipe to smoke, in
token of friendship and reconciliation; though at that time he had nothing
to smoke, but red willow bark. I told him something of the method of reconciliation with an offended God, as revealed in my Bible, which I had then in

possession. He said that he liked my story better than that of the French priests, but he thought he was now too old to begin to learn a new religion, therefore he should continue to worship God in the way that he had been taught, and that if salvation or future happiness was to be had in his way of worship, he expected he would obtain it, and if it was inconsistent with the honour of the Great Spirit to accept of him in his own way of worship, he hoped that Owaneeyo would accept of him in the way I had mentioned, or in some other way, though he might now be ignorant of the channel through which favor or mercy might be conveyed. He said that he believed that Owaneeyo would hear and help everyone that sincerely waited upon him.[11]

A few days later the rain came and they passed in safety down to the Scioto.

Perhaps one detail or another of this report may smack of Christian turns of thought; but Tecaughretanego's religious attitude is undoubtedly essentially Indian. The Iroquois of 1600 must have addressed Oterongtongnia in very similar terms.

One last ritual pattern can also be traced back to the role of the twin gods as pivots of Iroquois religious life: the masked medicine societies. In spring and autumn the villages witness extraordinary carnival scenes. Young men are to be seen racing about in ancient rattling Fords, wearing horrific wooden masks and carrying brooms and twigs. They burst into the houses and set to work – joyfully welcomed by the occupants – to sweep diseases from every nook and cranny so that the people may remain healthy. These men in wooden masks are the so-called 'false faces', members of one of the two masked societies which appear in public: the other is the society of 'maize straw faces' who appear at ceremonies held in the long house, sprinkle 'medicine water' on those present and strew ashes, again with the purpose of averting disease.[12]

Although they are sometimes seen in public, these two societies belong to the wider confederation of secret societies, esoteric groups each with its own officials, rites and myths. All these societies concern themselves with the prevention and cure of physical and psychic ills, sometimes even employing antisepsis. Thus the water medicine society deals with broken bones, and the singers for the dead seek to bring peace to the shades of the departed; the darkness dance is directed at ensuring that dwarfs do not bring disease into the community; and so on.

With the exception of the mask rituals, secret society ceremonies all take place at night; and, significantly, Handsome Lake prohibited all the secret societies. The fact that these societies performed their rituals at night signified that they belonged to the 'evil' twin Tawiskaron and could not be fitted into a religion centred on the 'good' twin

Oterongtongnia. Handsome Lake's ordinance was in vain; the societies still thrive.

Their healing function is a clear indication of just how little the European idea of 'evil' has to do with the Iroquois adversary god. Iroquois mythology ascribes the origin of disease and the other ills of life to Big Hump, a double of Tawiskaron. In remote antiquity he fought a battle with the Creator but was defeated and compelled to take up the task of healing and helping mankind. He still dwells on the rocky rim of the world, where fever, consumption and headache take their origin. Among his followers are the 'false faces', gangling creatures with large heads and distorted faces, who like their master rush round in the wilderness far from the haunts of men. In mythical terms they are the results of Tawiskaron's abortive attempt to create human beings; in ritual terms they are represented by the masked men who drive sickness from the village every spring and autumn.

This division of the earth into an inner world, containing human beings and their villages and fields, and an outer wilderness full of stones, swamps and 'false faces' is still present in Iroquois thought. Even the facts of civilized life have been fitted into the system. Home and fields and security are all to be found within the reservation, where the 'good' brother rules; but outside is the kingdom of the 'evil' one, with his sinister adherents the white men, a wilderness of factories, tenements and asphalt roads.[13]

Iroquois dualism has thus survived to this day as an interpretation of a continually changing world. The cliché that a primitive mythology must necessarily disappear before the realities of the machine age is thus revealed as untrue; in this one place at least a mythical image of the world has triumphed, and succeeds in investing a lifeless and mechanistic civilization with an aura of myth.

The dual world reappears in the religious ideas of almost all the shadowy, little-known peoples of the south-eastern United States and also among the tribes of the comparatively recent prairie culture. Again and again we find the place of worship symbolizing the world: in the tent ring of the Sioux just as in the sacred square of the Yuchi, the Creek and the Natchez. Closely bound to this symbolic world-house are pairs of opposites, earth and sky, white and red, peace and war, which appear in a sociological rather than mythological form.

The origin of this dual image of the world seems to lie at least partly in the actual mode of life of maize-growing tribes, with its division of human life into two halves, female (agriculture) and male (hunting). But this is certainly not the whole story. This transition to a new mode of existence must certainly have caused great changes in religious life; but the seeds of dualistic thought had always been there in the Indian mind. This at least is suggested by the cosmogonies of the California tribes, which show distinctly dualistic features although they stem from a pure hunting and gathering culture.

But before discussing these tribes we must turn to another aspect of the same basically dualistic philosophy of life: that represented by the Pueblo of New Mexico and Arizona.

VI *The Kingdom of the Gods in the Middle: The Zuñi of New Mexico*

Pueblo religion is a difficult subject. Unlike the Iroquois, the Pueblo place great emphasis on ritual and very little on sacred myth; and the strong tendency among southern tribes towards prolixity and profusion leads to such hypertrophied forms that the observer comes away with the impression of a vast and chaotic mass of unrelated acts of worship. The mental confusion attendant on the study of even one Pueblo religion is a direct consequence of the nature of the material; if at the end of this section the reader is left with an impression of impenetrable chaos his impression will not be far from the truth.

In view of this it would be well to start by mentioning a few essential facts, which will serve as a guide through the labyrinth. These are all the more necessary because there are limits to the amount of simplification and systematization that can be done; the desire to master the subject intellectually must obviously not lead to falsification of reality.

Within the religious world of the Zuñi of New Mexico five dominant elements can be distinguished:

1 the sun father;
2 the Uwanami, the rainmakers, on the rim of the world;
3 the Wemawe, animal gods, north, west, south, east, above and below, as patrons of medicine;
4 the Koko, mask gods from the village of Kotluwalawa in Lake Whispering Water;
5 the Ahayuta, the war gods, the twin sons of the sun father.

These five divisions of the divine world are served by five priests or groups of priests:

1 the *pekwin* for the sun father;
2 the fifteen *Ashiwanni* societies for the rainmakers;
3 the twelve medicine societies for the animal gods;

4 the six dance groups of the *Koko* societies for the masked gods;
5 the bow priests for the two war gods.

These five elements are the central stem of Zuñi religion. They reappear again and again; but they are naturally attended by a variety of other forms, and do not always appear in the same order.

In the far north of the state of New Mexico there stands one of the southernmost peaks of the Rockies, Mount Tsikomo, nearly twelve thousand feet high and the highest mountain for many miles around. The view from its summit is overwhelming: to the north, west and south roll the great waves of the Jemez mountains, and in the east a plateau falls gently away to the canyon of the Río Grande del Norte. A thick forest of spruce, pine, cypress and elder trees covers the lower slopes and merges imperceptibly into stunted bush and tall grass until this too disappears and the bare rocky ground rears up towards heaven.

The surrounding mountains were a centre round which Indian settlements gathered. Just as the waters disperse in all directions and flow west to the Río Grande and the Gulf of Mexico and south-east to the Great Colorado and the Pacific, the dwellings of the natives are dispersed around the outer slopes of the gigantic plateau. In the east a chain of villages follows the Río Grande valley between Taos and Sia; in the south are Laguna, Acoma and Zuñi; in the west the Hopi live on three flat-topped mountains, each of which has more than one inhabited site.

In the exact centre of the summit of Mount Tsikomo there is a mound or cairn of loose stones, eleven feet in diameter and five feet high, from which rises a long barkless spruce trunk. For the Indians of the Río Grande valley, and for the Navaho to the west, this mound is the centre of the world, the middle point between the four cardinal points and between zenith and nadir.[1]

To the south, a little below the summit, is another holy place, the 'shrine of the middle'. From an oval ring of unhewn fragments of rock, eighteen feet along its major axis and thirteen feet along its minor axis, there emerge like the fingers of a hand a number of short stone-bordered paths, the 'rain paths'. Each of these truncated paths leads in the direction of one of the village-tribes, the *pueblos* that own and use this shrine: Taos, San Juan, Santa Clara, San Ildefonso, Jemez, Cochiti and Navaho.

A pool inside the ring of stones holds the water of the world. A clay vase behind this pool, filled from time to time from the holy spring below the summit, and a number of feathered 'prayer sticks', planted in the ground, testify to the fact that this is still a holy place. From here, the centre of the world, comes the water which is so essential for life in the low-lying plains. Away from the rivers and streams these southern expanses are more or less desert; outside the short rainy season they support only cactus and agave.[2]

It might be supposed that the poverty of the soil would force man to take up a nomadic life; but this is not so. As in the prairies further north, human settlements cluster round running water, and have done the same for thousands of years. Countless prehistoric dwelling sites lie along the north and western edges of the Jemez mountains, and even today the Río Grande valley contains no less than fourteen villages, or *pueblos*, to use the Spanish word which expresses their nature as permanent settlements with an ethnically constant population.

These permanent settlements form the solid core of the Indian population of Arizona and New Mexico; they are the dwelling-places of farmers who live mainly by cultivating their maize, beans and squash. Between the *pueblos* drift nomadic tribes, the Apache with their numerous tribal subdivisions, the Navaho, the Pima, the Papago and others, most of whom are migrants from elsewhere who have absorbed many elements of the Pueblo religion over the centuries. The villagers are the true aboriginal inhabitants; the seventeenth-century *conquistadores* encountered the same way of life as is seen here today.

After the Spanish invasion, and especially after the Indian rising of 1680, some settlements were moved to more easily defensible sites on the mesas, isolated steep-sided plateaux or table mountains. This was what the Hopi and the inhabitants of San Ildefonso and Cochiti did, while other tribes banded together into alliances such as the Seven Cities of Cibola, who grouped themselves round what is now the town of Zuñi. Zuñi will serve as an example through which to approach the complex religious world of the Pueblo Indians.

The need for security against attack had one irksome consequence: the fields, which had of necessity to be near water, were often miles away from the new dwelling-places. In the nineteenth century, when the danger not only from the half-forgotten Spaniards but also from the marauding Apache had subsided and the forts of the US Army guaranteed peace, the population began to return to the open countryside. Men built houses near their fields to spare themselves the long march to and from their work, and agricultural summer villages sprang up. Zuñi alone has three of these, Pescado, Nutria and Ojo Caliente, which by now have almost risen to the status of permanent settlements.

Zuñi itself has remained the centre of authority and religious life.

As soon as the last fruit is gathered in, everyone sets off for Zuñi, the middle of the world, the only place where the gods appear in person.

Like the other *pueblos*, Zuñi consists of dwelling complexes structured rather like a honeycomb, with the walls built of layers of stones and the ceilings of wooden beams; the cells are built in layers, each storey being set back from the one beneath and reached by a ladder. The whole forms an artificial hill containing numerous apartments each of which belongs to one family and has its own kitchen and storehouse. The number of rooms in the apartment varies according to circumstances; the ideal family consists of mother, father, daughters, sons-in-law and the unmarried or widowed brothers of the lady of the house. The family structure is thus matrilineal. Zuñi has 1900 inhabitants in all, who live in six or seven great complexes of dwellings, four plazas and a number of dwellings on the roads which lead out of the township.[3]

Zuñi shows no sign of having been laid out according to a plan, and yet to its inhabitants the settlement is divided up according to a fixed pattern. The informants who spoke to the ethnologist Cushing in the 1880s divided the *pueblo* into seven parts corresponding to the *seven* cardinal points.[4] There was a part of the village which had a conceptual link with the north, another with the west and others with south, east, zenith, nadir and middle. Zenith and nadir, impossible to localize, were placed just east or west of middle. This conceptual division of the village transformed it into a symbol of the cosmos; the same ideas must once have applied in the 'seven cities of Cibola', which together made up what is now Zuñi.

According to Cushing this sevenfold division set its seal on all the cosmology and sociology of Zuñi. Not only were places of worship thought of as divided according to the seven points of the ritual 'compass'; the clans too were divided into seven groups: Crane, Grouse and Evergreen Oak for the north; Bear, Coyote, Spring Herb for the west and so on. The seventh 'cardinal point', 'middle', belongs to the Parrot clan, the mother clan of the tribe.[5]

Kroeber has attempted to investigate the topographical basis of this cosmic social structure. His village plans reveal, however, that the clans were not all in the expected positions. Parrots lived on the north-western and southern edges of the village, Bears as expected in the west, Coyotes unexpectedly in the north, east and south; Spring Herb in the north-east. The other clans were similarly out of place. If the clans were once 'localized', perhaps when Zuñi was founded in 1683, Kroeber concludes that the pattern must very soon have been altered by such factors as some women deciding to live with their mothers-in-law rather than their mothers. This sort of breach of custom happens all the time. Kroeber consequently inclines to the opinion that the religious social divisions have no real significance at all; but here he goes too far. Such an institution may very well exist in people's minds and far transcend real life.

Colours too are divided according to the 'sacred compass': north = yellow, west = blue, south = red, east = white, zenith = many-hued 'like the light on the clouds', nadir = black, middle = all these colours. The seasons of the year, elements and human activities are similarly classified:

north: winter, wind and war;
west: spring, water and hunting;
south: summer, fire and medicine;
east: autumn, earth and religion.[7]

As Cushing rather helplessly says, the three other 'cardinal points', zenith, nadir and middle, are also fitted into this system.

The native name for the *pueblo* of Zuñi has its own cosmic significance: it is Itiwana, 'middle'. Zuñi stands in the centre of the world and marks the end of a period of wandering which had continued ever since the tribe first arose from its fourfold cavern within the earth.[8]

The name Itiwana has still another application; it means the solstices, the pivots of time, 'when the sun has reached the middle'.[9] These play a major part in Zuñi life. The calendar is divided into two parts at the solstices; and the summer half of the year merely repeats the month names of the winter half without any regard for appropriateness. Thus July has the same name as January, *Taiämchu*, 'limbs of trees broken by snow'.[10]

As the name for December and June ('turn round' or 'look back') suggests, the calendar, like the festal year, pivots on the solstices; and this brings us close to the solar and dualistic ritualism of Zuñi religion. The observation of the solstices is the responsibility of the *pekwin*, the 'place of speech'.[11] He is the holiest man in all Zuñi, the head of a large hierarchy. His power is derived directly from the 'sun father'; the word 'father' here is a sign of respect and veneration rather than an indication of a genealogical link.

The *pekwin* has nothing to do with worldly matters, which are dealt with for him by a number of functionaries appointed by the council of priests. But the *pekwin* is nevertheless of paramount importance to the community; he bears entire responsibility for the welfare of the tribe. Shortly before 1900, when a number of harvests failed, the *shiwanokia*, an important priestess of the rain fraternities, denounced the incumbent *pekwin* on the grounds that the droughts were caused by the impurity of his heart. The council of priests assembled and the accused man was removed from office. In its perplexity – suitable people for this high office were hard to find – the council selected a young man of the Dogwood clan.

The mother, who was present, wept bitterly and begged her son not to accept the position, saying to the elder brother bow priest: 'He is so young, and he might make some mistake, and then perhaps he would be condemned as a sorcerer.' The mother's grief touched the heart of the son, and he declined the honour which he most earnestly desired to attain.[12]

Another of the tasks of the *pekwin* is the maintenance of the calendar. On December mornings he watches from a petrified tree-stump east of the village as the sunrise gradually shifts towards the south-eastern corner of a mesa called 'maize mountain'. About 11 or 12 December he goes to the top of the dwelling-complex where he lives and makes the following proclamation: 'In ten days everyone must plant prayer sticks.' The solstice period itself, 'when the sun father reaches the middle', begins when the rising sun touches the edge of the mesa. The summar solstice is announced in the same way, except that the sunset instead of the sunrise is plotted against certain landmarks.[13]

The 'prayer sticks' which the Zuñi plant on the first day of the winter solstice ceremony are made in a bewildering variety of forms. They vary according to the groups of gods to which they are offered up, the status and importance of the worshipper who plants them and also according to the occasion. They range in size from the length of a finger to that of a whole forearm; and their decoration may be black, yellow or blue. The bright tuft of feathers on the end of each stick also varies; turkey breast feathers summon the ancestors and masked gods, turkey tail-feathers call the rainmakers; while eagle feathers address themselves to the sun, the moon and the animal gods.[14]

The making of these objects is an important part of every ritual, and especially in the 'advent' period between 11 and 21 December. Then clouds of feathers lie in the ritual chambers, together with masses of shavings and scraps of bark. The individual may also offer prayer sticks on other occasions, when he has some special desire. The priestly clubs plant prayer sticks at each full moon for their patron deities. But the whole *pueblo* does so at the solstices in honour of the ancestors, the sun and the moon. The prayer sticks are placed upright in the maize fields, in the river mud or at certain 'shrines' or holy spots such as springs or mountain tops. The pliant sticks with their nodding tufts of feathers waft the prayers of mankind to the gods.

A lesser but still significant form of offering is the throwing of a mouthful of food into the fire before every meal. No less characteristic of Zuñi is the practice of strewing flour as an offering. Every morning, when the people come out of their houses, they address the rising sun in certain fixed formulas and let flour trickle to the ground from both hands.[15]

To whom are these rituals addressed? The recurrent use of the plural word 'gods' indicates that ethnographic observers have gained the impression that there was a pantheon, a hierarchy of superhuman beings with clear personal characteristics. But the situation is not so simple as this. The earlier writers, Matilda Stevenson and Cushing above all, refer to a Zuñi genesis myth involving Awonawilona, also known as 'he-she' or 'container of the universe', the spring of life, manifested in the blue arch of heaven, the light, the air and the clouds. From Awonawilona's body sprang twin worlds: the 'all-covering sky father' and the 'fourfold-container-earth mother', from whose embrace were born the manifold forms of existence.[16]

This half-Polynesian myth has not been encountered by more recent workers. Ruth Bunzel reports that by her time the idea had completely disappeared, and that she met with little interest in the beginnings of the world. Awonawilona, literally 'those who guard our paths', represents, according to her, a group of palpable entities such as sun, moon, earth, maize, animals, war gods.[17]

If one remembers that the prayer formulas refer to every supernatural being as Awonawilona,[18] this idea is not as distant as it seems from Cushing's concept of the 'container of the universe'. For what could this all-containing entity be but the union of all sense phenomena? This is a new version of the formula 'god = earth', but one which has moved too far from its point of origin to be considered under the heading of the 'supreme being'. Like the Iroquois, the Zuñi have no real supreme god. This particular concept seems to exist much more positively among those tribes of New Mexico who are nomads, most of them migrants from Athapascan Canada: the Navaho have their supreme Holy Wind, the White Mountain Apaches their Ruler of Life, and the Pima their Earth Doctor.[19]

In Pueblo mythology the shadowy supreme being delegates the office of Creator, and thus his own essential characteristic, to paired creator deities; thus the Acoma god Uchtsiti delegates the task of creation to the sisters Jatiki ('brings to life') and Nautsiti ('more of everything in the basket'); the spider Sussistinnako of the Sia entrusts it to the mothers Utset ('east') and Nowutset ('west').[20] The general outlines of the Pueblo creation myth thus agree with Stevenson's and Cushing's Awonawilona myth; this does seem to represent a true Pueblo model.

The Zuñi may lack a true supreme god, but they share in the attitude, common to all Indians, that the world is an animate organism: wind, trees, night, clouds, houses, pots and garments are all *hoi*, living persons.[21] From this mass of living beings a few stand out as dominant realities, such as the sun father and the moon mother (not thought of as a sexual couple), earth and maize, sky and light. At the edge of the ocean which surrounds the world, in four villages disposed according to the cardinal points, live the rainmakers, the Uwanami. Cumulus clouds are their bodies, strips of mist their breath, rain channels their footprints.

Under the surface of the earth there is a system of watercourses which come to the surface at springs and lakes. There below lives Kolowsi, the horned serpent. The depths contain four caves, the 'four bellies of the earth mother'. In the fourth and lowest layer, the 'world of utmost darkness', the 'world as black as soot', the Zuñi were born. The sun father created the Ahayuta, the twin war gods,[22] and sent them to the lowest place of all to bring the human beings up. Led by them the Zuñi climbed through the bog world, mud world and wing world to our earth. A pool marks the sacred spot where they rose into the light, which is still symbolized by a dip in the floor of every *kiva* (ritual chamber). From there, still under the leadership of their two war gods, the Zuñi migrated by many stages to the 'middle', the township of Zuñi. It is clear that the idea of the middle of the cosmos dominates even the origin myths of the tribe.

In the course of this migration there appeared another group of gods, the Koko, known to the Hopi by the better-known name of Katcina; these are the mask gods, the ancestors and shades of the dead.[23] Their cult incorporates the picturesque mask dances so characteristic of the Pueblo. Some of these mask gods were born of the union of a brother and sister, others are children drowned while crossing the Zuñi river. They all gathered in the depths of Lake Whispering Water, some 86 miles east of Zuñi near St John, Arizona. There on the bed of the lake stands the village of Kotluwalawa, and in the middle of this Indian Vineta stands the four-windowed dance house of the mask gods. From there the gods come to Zuñi in splendid masks, seeking contact with the living. Kotluwalawa is the place where members of the *Koko* mask fraternities go when they die. 'To go to sleep and wake up as a little child in Kotluwalawa' is the prayer of all those for whom Whispering Water is the place of the dead.[24]

The twin war gods created one last category of superhuman beings: the Wemawe, the animal gods, who are the leaders of the medicine societies. The first Wemawe to appear, with the culture hero Poshäi-yanki, were medicine men. Now they live east of Zuñi in Shipapolima, the place where all members of the medicine societies go when they die.[25] And the deceased members of the rain club likewise go to the four villages of the rainmakers on the rim of the world.[26] The dead are thus classified according to their ritual fraternity, and the separate groups of gods are continually reinforced by the dead; the consequence, at least at Zuñi, is that the ancestors and the gods tend to be identified.

Ancestor worship has very deep roots at Zuñi. The ancestors are honoured with sacrifices of food; black-painted prayer sticks are set aside for them, and they, and not only the Uwanami, are the source of the blessed rain. Significantly enough the Spanish missions made their only impact on Zuñi religious life at this point; the Catholic festival of All Souls' Day has won a firm place in the Zuñi calendar and is cele-brated there as it is everywhere in the Catholic world.[27]

Into this framework of gods and natural objects or entities Man must fit himself. He has no prescriptive right to exploit the earth, the water and the forest; he is on a level with the rabbit, the deer and the maize. He must behave himself properly and treat even the animals he hunts as honoured guests according to precise rules. This feeling is the basis of the Pueblo way of life, with its theme of almost absolute harmony; wicked, unsociable or cantankerous human beings are not helped by the gods. This guiding line has been followed by the Pueblo in their ex-ternal affairs as well as in private life; only in the most desperate cir-cumstances have they ever taken up arms, and they still live on terms of good neighbourliness with the white Americans. There is no higher praise in Zuñi than to say: 'such and such a man is a nice polite man. No one ever hears anything from him. He never gets into trouble . . . He always dances in the summer dances'.[28]

As my outline of the pantheon shows, the Zuñi do not believe in a devil, and myths of a Promethean nature are unknown. Their relation-ship with the gods is innocent of such complexities. One last point: suicide is such an alien idea to the Zuñi that a question about it was greeted with shouts of laughter.

If one considers this extensive religious cosmos, and the fact that each category of gods has a number of priestly cults attached to it, it will come as no surprise that ritual life is extremely complex and varied.

There is no trace of the simplification carried out by the Hopi, who have merged the clans and ritual fraternities; in Zuñi the two types of social unit exist together. The overlapping of the two categories affects only the individual; such and such a ritual act can be performed only by a member of say the Bear or Deer clan, but the whole clan as such never joins in a common ritual.[29]

The resulting complexity of religious life makes it difficult to bring any order into the subject at all. Almost every adult belongs to one of the priests' clubs or one of the dance societies, and many have responsibilities to two or three such groups at once.

However, a few guiding lines are visible in this seemingly impenetrable tangle. Two ritual complexes face each other: the cult of the rainmakers, who live in the four oceans which surround the earth, in the springs and rivers, in the waters under the earth, in the cumulus clouds and in the fog, and the cult of the animal gods, whose sphere ot influence includes longevity, medicine and healing rituals. The rainmaker ceremonies begin directly after the summer solstice, on 1 July, and are firmly linked with the summer; while the animal gods are honoured only in the winter, with particularly large-scale rites at the winter solstice. Both cults are served by numerous fraternities.

The rainmakers are served by the fifteen priest clubs of the *Ashiwanni*, 'those who sing [for rain]'. Each of these has four to six members (in 1918 there were forty-nine rain priests), and each has its own ceremonial apartments, altars and fetishes. The division of the *Ashiwanni* is according to the sacred 'compass'; there is the *shiwanni* of the north, the east,[30] the south, the west, the zenith, the nadir and the middle, and there are also minor rain societies, the 'priests of darkness'. These rain priests have their own place in the hierarchy of holy men. Everything profane is kept away from them just as it is from the *pekwin*. Their only task is to provide moisture for the thirsty sprouting plants.

The most respected is the *shiwanni* of the north (not the one in the middle), with its assistants, of whom the *Shiwakanoia*, 'priestess of fertility', holds an especially important position. Its rites, like those of the other *Ashiwanni*, take place in dark chambers to which very few outsiders have ever been admitted.[31] The cult chamber of the *shiwanni* of the north is said to contain an altar which incorporates two little pillars of crystal and turquoise, and a heart-shaped stone, the 'heart of the world'. Veins from the stone are supposed to extend to the four cardinal points, and the altar represents the exact middle of the world.

Complete withdrawal from community life is an important element of the priestly vocation, emphasized by regular 'retreats' which last from one to eight days and are observed not only by the *shiwanni* but also by the other priestly clubs, who gather in their own ritual chambers and spend the time praying and chanting. In the summer half of the year one society of rain priests after another goes into retreat, eight days each for the four important cardinal point clubs and four days each for the smaller societies. In winter, when the rainmakers are inactive, the retreats last only a day.

During their conclaves the priests build an altar over a complex figurative pattern made with meal strewn on the floor. The appropriate *shiwanni* also lays on the altar, among other things, the *ettone*, highly sacred symbols which are kept in deepest secrecy: the *kia-ettone*, a bundle of four finger-sized tubes filled with water, and the *chu-ettone*, a similar bundle of eight tubes filled with seeds. For the Zuñi these fetishes have cosmic significance, revealed by the use of the numbers four and eight, and also associations with the distant past: these objects came from the underworld with the earliest ancestors of mankind.[32] Shivers of awe run through those present when these sacred symbols are drawn from the clay vases in which they are kept. Here is a sample of the prayer formulas which accompany this ritual:

> Rain-makers, come out from all roads that great rivers may cover the earth;
> That stones may be moved by the torrents; that trees may be uprooted and moved by the torrents.
> Great rainmakers, come out from all roads, carry the sand of our earth mother of the place.
> Cover the earth with her heart, that all seeds may develop,
> That my children may have all things to eat and be happy,
> That the people of the outlying villages may all laugh and be happy;
> That the growing children may have all things to eat and be happy.
> This way our great father *kiaettone* wishes you to come.
> This way our great mother *chuettone* wishes you to come;
> That we may have all kinds of seeds and all things good;
> That we may inhale the sacred breath of life;
> That our fathers *kiaettowe* and our mothers *chuettowe* may bring us happy days.[33]

The rainmakers are worshipped in the summer; but the ceremonies in honour of the animal gods, the Wemawe, are performed by the twelve medicine societies during the winter, with a particular concentration around the winter solstice.[34] Not only healing plants and healing rites but also witchcraft and black magic belong to the realm of the animal gods, who thus hold the keys of good and evil. They too take up positions in accordance with the sacred 'compass': mountain lion in the north, bear in the west, badger in the south, wolf in the east, knifewing or eagle above, vulture below. Each of the twelve medicine societies specializes in one ailment: one cures bad throats, another epilepsy, a third bullet wounds, and so on.

Admission to such a medicine society takes place, as it almost always does in North America, when the candidate is suffering from a serious illness. The power of the initiation overcomes the sickness, the patient receives a new heart and is henceforth under the protection of the animal gods. The extremely complex and detailed rites take place in the rooms set aside for each medicine society in the houses of assembly.

Almost nothing is heard of these groups during the summer; their drums must not even be touched. In November they begin to gather in their ritual rooms, to build altars and to repeat their chants. From this time onwards the animal gods are supposed to be present in Zuñi. Their principal festival coincides with the winter solstice celebrations; the members of the twelve medicine societies all go into retreat in their ceremonial chambers, which only members are allowed to enter. By day they make prayer wands, costumes and other regalia, in the evening they tell stories and give instruction in ritual, and at night songs are sung in honour of the animal gods. Only on the last night of the retreat is the full ritual performed. The members of the medicine societies dance themselves into a frenzy to the sound of singing, rattles and drums. On this night the priests are able to see hidden diseases in a crystal, and to draw pebbles, scraps of calico, feathers and pieces of fur from the mouths, noses and ears of those present. As the night wears on the frenzy grows; individual dancers rush out into the December air, barefoot and half naked, to visit other medicine conventicles. At sunrise it all stops suddenly, the altar is demolished, and everyone goes home.

The other practices of the medicine societies, their actual healing activities, take place when need arises. These too are secret.

Quite unlike the esoteric cults of the rainmakers and the medicine animal gods, the cult of the mask gods, the Koko or Katcina, is entirely public.[35]

One day the mask gods appear out of the wide open spaces of the New Mexican landscape, make a tumultuous entry into Zuñi, and dance on all the plazas in groups which are sometimes as many as seventy strong. This spectacle attracts visitors from far and wide. Rooftops and terraces are crowded with strangers, including whole busloads of tourists. Cameras click on all sides, but nothing disturbs the concentration of the dancers, singers and drummers; for them the immediate surroundings have disappeared and the godhead is near.

The difference between medicine societies and *Koko* groups extends to their social context. Each of the medicine societies consists of a very few priests; but the *Koko* groups include all the male inhabitants of Zuñi from the age of twelve upwards, divided into the usual six subdivisions. Each group has its own ritual apartments, the famous *kivas*, which are of course arranged (at least in theory) north, south, east, west, above and below.[36] The *kivas* of the Zuñi are four-sided rooms which can be entered only by climbing through a hatch in the roof and down a ladder. In these chambers the winter dances of the *Koko* take place; the summer dances are in the open. The calendar dualism reflected in the division between summer rain rites and winter medicine rites also appears in the *Koko* ceremonies. The winter ceremonies are marked by uninhibited gaiety, the summer ceremonies by solemnity and reverence.

The popularity of the *Koko* figures exceeds all imagination. They are the dead and the ancestors at once, and come across the Whispering Water from the village of Kotluwalawa to bring blessing and good fortune. In 1881, when Mr and Mrs Stevenson of Washington, DC, asked to see the holy lake, their Indian guide, who had at first no idea of what these white people wanted, could be induced to take the right path only with the greatest difficulty. The Zuñi believe that anyone who sees the Whispering Water must die within four days. Finally, however, he said that he was willing to act as guide. When they arrived the Stevensons rode round the lake. When they returned they found the old man by the water's edge, deep in prayer, his right hand extended towards the setting sun. He did not move until his prayer was finished. Then he turned round, smiling, and with his usual bright eyes, said:

I am very happy, and yet I know I must die. I shall be contented to die, for I have looked upon the waters of the house of my departed fathers.[37]

Such pieces of evidence suggest that there is a strong element of ancestor worship in the *Koko* cult; but true gods appear among them as well. There are the ten Koyemci, sacred clowns who make lewd jokes; the Shakalo, gigantic supermen; the Sayatlia, the exorcists; the chief of the mask gods, Pautiva; his messenger Käklo; and many others.[38] All these figures are recognized by their great pot-like helmet masks, the lower edge of which is usually edged with a fringe of fresh cedar twigs, and which carry the multicoloured emblems of the appropriate deity. From their earliest childhood Zuñi children learn from carefully made and coloured dolls to distinguish between the individual mask gods; from the first awakening of consciousness the divine world becomes familiar and alive to them in their play.

The mask gods appear eight days after the summer solstice and dance their rain dances until November. During this period they are continuously present in Zuñi; then they return to Kotluwalawa. In winter their visits are sporadic and attract little attention, just as the rain gods are largely ignored at this season. The harvest is past, and there is no need of moisture, which would only cause harm to the sheep. Snow is desired instead, so that an abundant springtime thaw may soak the fields.

Prayers for snow are addressed to the Ahayuta, the twin war gods.[39] Around Christmas their votaries, the bow priests, come into their own, together with the custodian of the great shell, the scalp chief and other less important groups.

At this point, rather than go into further detail about the ritual organization, I shall give an account of one part of the ritual calendar, namely the important winter solstice festivals. This will help to avoid giving the impression that the festal year is a random conglomeration of essentially unrelated ancient cults, synchronized into an annual cycle.[40] In reality the calendar is a refined and meaningful apparatus based on the same central themes as the ritual. Any analysis which did not take this into account would rob them of all meaning.

The winter solstice festival is divided into two periods of ten days each.[41] The first period covers the time from the *pekwin's* proclamation that prayer sticks may be planted to the solstice itself. During this time the whole village is busily engaged in making prayer sticks, wood is gathered for the new year fire, and two men from the Bear and Deer clans carve new images of the twin war gods, the Ahayuta. At nightfall ovens can be seen glowing everywhere. The women are baking busily in order to have a store; during the second ten-day period no light may be shown out of doors.

The tenth day, the solstice itself, is the day of the offering up of the prayer sticks. From morning to evening, people set out across the snow in their most colourful clothes to plant their wands at distant shrines or in their fields: blue for the sun father, yellow for the moon mother, black for the ancestors. Each individual reverently smears holy meal on his lips and prays for health, long life, clouds, rain and food. Even the smallest children understand exactly what they have to do.

As darkness falls celebrations begin in the principal *kiva*, that of the north. There the *pekwin* comes together with the servants of the twin war gods, namely the two brother bow priests, the priest of the great shell, the scalp chief and others. The new year fire is kindled on the altar of the *kiva*. 'Spiral songs' are sung and 'spiral dances' danced. At the same time the medicine societies begin their retreats; 'they go in', into their own ritual chambers.

On the next morning the population in general participates again. The images of the two war gods, carved from wooden boards, are carried to their shrines on high mountains, and smoke signals from these signify the beginning of the great curfew. For ten days no light may be shown out of doors, not even a cigarette or a match; and it is forbidden to clear out ashes. Only the most boorish and ill-bred would begin any task during this ten-day period. Fires are carefully covered; only the holy flame in the *kiva* of the north still burns, fed with cedar wood.

On the afternoon of the fourteenth day, after the medicine societies emerge from their retreats, everyone plants prayer wands for the mask gods, the animal gods and the ancestors. Water is brought from holy springs, and everything is then ready for the retreat of the rain priests on the sixteenth night. Pregnant women make pilgrimages to the shrines on the west side of the maize mountain, where they scrape a little dust from the rocks and swallow it to procure an easy childbirth and a healthy child.

On the nineteenth night of the solstice festival it is the turn of the mask gods and their votaries to make their contribution to the proceedings. Just before sundown two masked figures enter the village from the east, one in a white mask and dressed mainly in white, the other in a black helmet mask and dressed almost entirely in dark colours. They 'bring the new year from the east'. Both gods hasten to the *kiva* of the north, where the *pekwin*, the bow priest and the four masked Sayatlia (exorcists) await their coming, together with Pautiva, the chief of all the mask gods. The benches are crowded with spectators. The masked figures dance all night long to the singing of the great fire society, which is involved here because of the part played in the ceremony by the new year flame. Meanwhile the four Sayatlia run to all the other *kivas* and drive the old year out with horrendous shouts of '*puhu*'.

At first light the leader of the fire society makes a new flame with his fire drill, torches are lit from it, and gods and priests depart together, strewing meal, whirling bullroarers, bearing their prayer sticks and torches, to a place to the east of the village where the new fire is placed and the prayer sticks planted.

This procession, with its whirring bullroarers and its clattering rattles, brings the village to life again; the curfew is at an end, and light may be shown once more. Ashes and refuse are carried out into the fields together with glowing coals, and hundreds of little fires are soon to be seen glowing in the half-light, while the morning star glitters in the slowly lightening sky. The ensuing day – the twentieth of the festival – is full of rejoicing and good cheer; the mask gods rush round the streets and throw little gifts down to the crowd from the roof of the *kiva* of the north.

Towards noon the chief of the mask gods, Pautiva, disappears, soon to reappear, travel around the *pueblo* in a fourfold spiral, and make for a particular house on the south side, which has in its wall a niche with four little dolls, 'Pautiva's children'. He takes off the slab which covers the niche, and looks in; if the dolls have fallen over, the prospects for the coming year are bad. He repeats the process with other niches in the west, north and south. When the omens are bad, he always cloaks them in cautious words, such as:

The babies were lying down wherever I went. That is bad, but let us hope that it may not be true. We must all pray that it may not come true.[42]

On the evening of the twentieth day there appears Tciakwenaokä, a mask goddess who protects women in labour and brings fruitfulness. Great fires are to be seen everywhere, and there is dancing in the *kivas*. About midnight a group of mask gods appear and bring baskets of seeds into the *kivas* – running the gauntlet of a bombardment of glowing coals on the way – and distribute them among those present. Then these mask gods too go back to Kotluwalawa, and the new year festival is over.

Clearly, all these rites are dominated by the idea of a new beginning. The concentration at the turning point of the solar year, the curfew and the lighting of the fires, the retreats which seek health, life and rain, the blessing of pregnant women, the distribution of seed; all this concerns renewal, birth and new growth. The same symbolic complex also somehow includes the worship of the twin gods, the colour duality of the black and white masks, and other pieces of imagery whose content is not so immediately apparent, such as the spiral motif which appears in the 'great shell' and in Pautiva's spiral run.

The more closely one examines Zuñi religion, the better one understands what drives these people from their summer farm villages to Zuñi as soon as the harvest is in. The summer prayers of the *Ashiwanni*, the rainmaker fraternities, are seen by no one; but in winter the gods appear to everyone as a proof that Zuñi is the heart of the world. To this day no external influence has damaged this bastion of faith; the Pueblo Indians have unhesitatingly fitted alien realities into their own view of the cosmos.

In 1879 a Zuñi woman stayed with Mr and Mrs Stevenson in Washington. When she left to return home a member of the Congress, one Representative Landers, 'desiring to aid in Christianizing and civilizing the Zuñis', presented her with a canteen of cutlery. Two months later, when Mrs Stevenson visited the *pueblo* and enquired as to what had happened to the cutlery, she was told that the knives had been given to the rain priests and the medicine societies to make prayer sticks; the big silver spoons were being used to scoop the holy popcorn water from the medicine dishes; and the forks were playthings for the children in the streets. The gifts from Washington had been put to the best use; and everyone continued to eat with his fingers as his fathers had done.[43]

This is still the way things are today. The Zuñi and the Pueblo Indians in general still turn their backs on the civilized world. The rain-makers behind the mesas, the animal gods on the rim of the world, the mask gods beneath the sacred lake, are still the only realities. Even the mushroom clouds from the atomic explosions which take place in their deserts have not caused them to waver; they still know where the middle of the world is.

The immense variety of North American maize-growing cultures is apparent from even the most perfunctory comparison between the Zuñi and the Iroquois. Both religions reveal clearly defined dualistic structures, but with what a difference! In one case a rigid edifice of ideas, with text and ritual firmly grouped around the twin gods; in the other an almost complete neglect of twin patterns – the twin war gods, the Ahayuta, are relatively insignificant – and a dualistic calendar, with its summer rain gods and its winter medicine gods, its solemn hot-weather mask gods and its joyous and uninhibited cold-weather mask gods.

This is not merely a matter of the very different skies under which the two peoples live; their whole psychology is different. The tension between the hostile twins suits the warlike Iroquois; while the peaceful Zuñi are happy with the constant rhythm of their festal year, on which they concentrate to the exclusion of all active interest in the outside world.

VII *Death and Rebirth: The Kwakiutl of British Columbia*

One has only to think of the immensity of the territory east of the Rocky Mountains and south of the 44th Parallel to realize that the picture of its religious life I have been able to give is pale and inadequate. Between the Iroquois and the Zuñi there were in the seventeenth century a multitude of other maize-growing tribes, from the Erie, Neutrals and Conestoga in the north, members of the same linguistic family as the

Iroquois, to the Timukua in the south-east by way of the tribes of the Mississippi basin; all of these vanished at an early stage, and with the exception of the Natchez we know very little about them. A sympathetic study of their religion and thought was far beyond the capacity of the European mind at the time.

But the few examples we have been able to discuss will serve to give an idea of the spiritual values and the yet-unborn religious visions that were destroyed with the maize-growing tribes of the southern United States. Primitive cultures tend towards individualization, not generalization. With the growth of settled life the basic patterns become more and more complex, both from a linguistic and a religious point of view, so that even such firmly defined units as the Iroquois and the Pueblo begin to break up, one village set apart from the next by widening cultural differences. This tendency to split, which gives primitive cultures their immense richness and complexity, was brutally cut short by the European invasion of North America.

The extent to which this process can be carried, and the degree of personal identity that can attach to even the smallest unit, is illustrated by the example of the Pacific Coast fishing tribes, which inhabit a narrow coastal strip which lies on the side of the continent furthest from Europe and which continued its evolution relatively undisturbed into the nineteenth century.

On the western side of the continent the division between more advanced and less advanced peoples is the exact reverse of that in the east; here the primitives live in the south and the advanced tribes in the north. What is more, agriculture offers no reliable criterion; the cultural standard attained by the peoples of British Columbia – which is at least as high as that of the Pueblo Indians, if not higher – is based not on farming but on fishing.

The fjord coastline between Vancouver and Alaska, with its thousands of islands, brings the sea far inland. Food is there for the taking; there are fish and seals all the year round. With even the most rudimentary equipment, terrible and degrading winter hunger like that experienced by the tribes of inland Canada is impossible in British Columbia. The constant torrential rains produce thick stands of firs and cedars which are as inexhaustible as the fish of the ocean. Between the waters of the innumerable inlets and the steep, dark green wooden slopes lie the villages of the inhabitants, as remote as can be imagined from the conventional idea of 'Red Indian' dwellings. Approaching from the direction of the fjord – there are no other communication routes – one sees, raised a little above the beach a street of large low gabled wooden houses. From some of the seaward gables rise massive, elaborately carved poles carved from single tree trunks. On the beach below are brightly painted dugout canoes; with the gaily coloured poles and house gables they give the whole scene an extraordinarily exotic air under the eternally grey skies.[1]

Each house is like a massive wooden citadel. The posts, beams and planks are of gigantic dimensions, and the impression of excessive size is enhanced by the fact that these structures, approximately thirty feet square, might easily have been constructed quite solidly with much less expenditure of material. The framing inside the gable ends, which are the main supports of the structure, consists of pairs of posts so thick that two men can hardly reach round them. On these rest two immense beams which support only a comparatively light shingle roof. The walls, which consist of planks a handspan thick, are more suitable for a fortress than a mere dwelling. This is the kind of building that a megalithic culture might build if reduced to using wood instead of outsize stone blocks: no longer megalithic but megaxylic.

Round the inside of the walls runs a bank of earth and a row of bunks. Chests, spoons, dishes and legless sofa-like seats make up the rest of the furnishings, with the addition of all sorts of hunting and fishing tackle. In each of the four corners of the square house lives one family with its cooking fire; all in all a tolerably comfortable existence if one overlooks the oily smell of fish which hangs over the house and the whole village like a cloud.

The Pacific Coast culture, so massively embodied in the timber block-houses of its villages, is found all along the coast from Alaska to the mouth of the Columbia river. In the north it gradually gives place to Eskimo culture, and in the south to that of the Californian tribes; but the unity which encompasses all the disparate and fragmentary ethnic groups in the coastal area is remarkable.

The origins of the Pacific tribes are apparent from their languages. There are Athapascan tribes from the Canadian interior such as the Tlingit, Tshimshian and Haida; Old Salishan tribes such as the Kwakuitl and the Nootka, also from east of the Rockies; and New Salishan tribes such as the Bella Coola, who are the newest arrivals. The Pacific Coast culture crystallized in its purest form among the southern Kwakuitl on Vancouver Island and the adjacent regions of the mainland, and this group, studied over so many years by Franz Boas, will serve as a paradigm of the whole culture.

Here, if anywhere at all, is a primitive culture completely impregnated with religious ideas. Whether one approaches such a community from the standpoint of sociology, economics or intellectual life, one has to deal with an ever-present religious control and motivation. The 'civilized' division into 'Sunday' and 'everyday' is completely unknown in undisturbed primitive groups.

The existence of these Pacific fishermen is governed by the rhythm of a bipartite year. In the summer they leave their houses and go to the river estuaries and the entrances to the fjords to catch salmon, or to the forest to gather berries. They live in improvised bark huts and there is little social contact. Only occasional minor festivals interrupt the isolated and contemplative existence of each clan and each family.

In November all this changes. The coast is lashed by south-westerly gales, and the Indians return to their villages. Religious life suddenly comes into its own, and one festival follows close upon another. Pipes are played, bullroarers whirled, the roar of the drums is heard from the festal houses, and on the tall carved poles float garlands of fir twigs tied with bast, signifying that the god is present.

Unlike the Pueblo festal calendar, in which some kind of ritual activity is always going on throughout the year,[2] the Pacific Coast year swings from an inactive to an active phase, summer and winter, near to the gods and far from them. The tribe we have chosen as a model, the Kwakiutl, aptly describe the two periods as *bachus*, 'profane' and *tsetsaequa*, 'full of secrets'.

The social structure too is based on this rhythm; its basic units, the clans and the fraternities, do not exist simultaneously as in Zuñi, but apply to different times of the year. In summer the village community is divided into clans or super-families; in winter, into fraternities or religious societies. But of course the two types of classification apply to exactly the same individuals; and this fact too illustrates the difference between the basic impulses of this culture and those of the Pueblo, whose existence is governed not by the alternation of tension and repose but by a constant flow of events.

The clans of the Kwakiutl are not based on blood relationships but have a mythical origin. Each clan, which occupies a group of adjacent houses, is considered to stem from a single common ancestor, who descended from the sky or emerged from the underworld or from the ocean, bringing with him the patrimony of the clan: the emblems, masks, dances and names which are peculiar to it.[3]

The clan legend, an extremely important feature of the verbal lore of the Pacific Coast culture, deals in detail with the circumstances in which the clan ancestor or 'first one' received these things as gifts from one of the gods. Family history thus constitutes a sort of title deed.[4] This heritage is represented on the carved poles before the doors of the houses and in the paintings on the gables, from which it is possible to read the name, origin and hereditary possessions of the families concerned. It will be seen that in the course of time the evolution of clan tradition must necessarily have resulted in an immense variety of myths and modes of worship.

Among the goods which make up the heritage of each clan is an immense variety of fantastic masks which represent the finest achievements of the Indian wood carver's art. Some are hinged so that the face opens like a double door and reveals a second face beneath. Others have movable jaws or even revolving discs on top of the head. Considering that the other 'hereditary possessions' of the clan consist of dances, emblems and names, the inheritance system can hardly be said to be based on practical considerations. It is true that each clan also has tangible assets such as its own fishing, hunting and berry-gathering preserves, but the principal emphasis is definitely on the religious values which were gifts of the gods. A sharper contrast can hardly be imagined between Indian and urban culture, between the world of painted masks and the world of share-portfolios, than the difference between the two conceptions of 'hereditary possessions'.

The winter half of the year is dominated by the ritual fraternities, the members of which have to be specifically initiated. As with the Zuñi, the fraternities are linked with the gods. But the pantheon itself is very different. The Zuñi rainmakers and animal gods are schematic and impersonal, and only the mask gods are individualized to any extent in their emblems and functions. But the transcendental beings believed in by the Kwakiutl can with perfect justification be referred to as personal gods. They are individuals with their own distinct functions. This is a rare phenomenon anywhere in North America; neither the Iroquois twins nor the chaotic throng of gods at Zuñi can be said to constitute a true pantheon. The Kwakiutl pantheon is a genuine divine hierarchy, not arranged in accordance with a patriarchal family structure but based on the four quarters of the horizon.

It would only be confusing to attempt to enumerate all the fabulous lands on the rim of the cosmos in which the Kwakiutl gods have their homes; but one deity deserves special treatment. This is Baxbakwala-nuxsiwae, 'the cannibal at the north end of the world'.[5] This god, who appears in the form of a man, embodies an institution characteristic of the tribe. He feeds upon human beings. His other names refer to the same subject: 'he has eaten someone', 'he devours skulls on earth'. The cry 'hap, hap', 'eat, eat!' signals the presence of the god.

Baxbakwalanuxsiwae dwells in the exact north of the world with his family and his retinue. From the openings in the roof of his house there rises red smoke. His wife and his maidservant both catch people for their lord and master to eat. At the door there sits a raven who pecks out the eyes of the corpses as they come in. Also present are the fabulous bird Hochhoku, who cracks the brain pans with his long beak, and a man-eating grizzly bear.

This cannibal god is by no means a remote figure. He dwells at the north end of the world in the summer; but when the autumn storms buffet the houses he comes southward with his retinue towards the dwellings of men. He then lives in the festal house, appears in person behind a grotesque mask, and dances before the assembled villagers.

The arrival of the god is the signal for the transformation of the social structure. The clans are disbanded and the villagers re-group in fraternities and degrees. Each individual deity has his own adherents: there is a society of votaries of Baxbakwalanuxsiwae, called the *hamatsa*, 'devourers'; the wife of the god, the raven, Hochhoku and the grizzly all have their own fraternities. Membership of these groups is hereditary; each family has the right to introduce its children into its 'own' club. The fraternities have a fixed order of precedence, the *hamatsa* naturally being the senior society. It is reserved for heads of clans.

As well as this divine world there is also an origin myth – not a creation myth, in which the Kwakiutl are not interested – but the story of the origins of ritual life.

Originally there were only animals on earth. They lived on 'Crooked Beach' in two villages; one had Raven and the Otter as its chiefs, and the other had Head Wolf as its chief.[6] The two villages hated each other bitterly. The wolves had the winter ritual, i.e. the initiation ceremonies of the *hamatsa*, to themselves. When they celebrated it for the first time they were surprised by Raven and the Otter and killed. Since then the ritual has been the lawful property of the victors, and all the rites performed today are re-enactments of those primordial festivities on Crooked Beach.

After the victory of Raven and Otter there began the second age of the world, in which Raven and Otter acted as 'transformers', providing sunlight, filling the rivers with salmon, and regulating the tides and the wind; in short, like the Algonquin and Athapascan culture heroes, Raven and Otter gave mankind the wherewithal to live. Some of the animals now laid aside their animal shape and became human beings, while others remained as they were. On their travels these first human beings, the clan ancestors, received the clan patrimonies as gifts from the gods. The earth gradually took on the appearance that it has today.

There is a detectable relationship here with the tripartite cosmic history of the Canadian Algonquin and Athapascans.

The cosmos, like the origin myth, is divided with three levels, with the earth in the middle.[7] On the 'other side', above the 'upper rim of the clouds', dwell the sun, the dawn, the thunderbird and many other beings. The underworld is the realm of the dead. A mighty copper pole passes through all three layers and supports the earth and the sky. This cosmic house is the dwelling of gods and men.

The rites, like those of the Zuñi, concentrate on personal deities; the great difference lies in the purpose behind the rites. Whereas the Pueblo gods are servants of life and bring clouds, rain, snow, happiness and fruitfulness, for the Kwakiutl life is the servant of the gods. In the winter half of the year, one ritual follows hard upon another; but the purpose is not to beg the supernatural beings for fish, whales and seals, but to swell the ranks of their votaries by initiating new members into the various fraternities.

In Zuñi the life of the whole world is at stake, even that of squirrels and trees; but Pacific Coast ceremonialism is concerned only with man. The distinction is the same as that between the Delaware Big House and the central Algonquin medicine hut; in the Big House prayers are offered up for the welfare of the whole world, while the medicine hut concerns itself with the individual novice who is being initiated. This sharp contrast between universalist and individualist forms of worship has a historical origin. The central Algonquin, with their partial conversion to agriculture, are clearly among the newest elements of the Canadian hunting and gathering population; and the linguistic evidence shows the Pacific Coast fishing tribes to have the same origins. As will be recalled, the religious patterns of the Canadian forest Indians centre on the individual; and ethnographically speaking the Pacific Coast tribes of British Columbia are merely their most advanced representatives. Pacific Coast ceremonialism therefore is confined to individual rites; there is no festal calendar relating to such events as the beginning of a new year or the opening of the salmon season.

To clarify the nature of Kwakiutl religious thought, I shall give an outline of the ceremony of initiation into the fraternity of *hamatsa*, 'devourers', the votaries of the great god Baxbakwalanuxsiwae, the 'cannibal at the north end of the world'.[8] Naturally there are numerous other initiation rites, some of them actually fitted into the *hamatsa* rite itself, but the admission of a new member to the fraternity of 'devourers' is the most important of all Kwakiutl ceremonies.

The father of the candidate makes application to the chiefs of the tribe for his son to be admitted to the *hamatsa*. First the applicant's means are carefully investigated; initiation is an expensive business, as the whole tribe will expect to feast night and day at the candidate's expense. If the chiefs are satisfied that he is able to bear the cost, they give permission to proceed.

Some eight days later the opening ceremony of the initiation takes place. The presiding chiefs give notice of their intention to hold a winter dance, the candidate being such and such a man, son of such and such a man, and that from henceforth everyone is to take a purificatory bath every morning and rub himself with the tips of fir twigs. While the chiefs are still speaking, long-drawn piping sounds are heard from the forest north of the village. Oration and response are silenced, the whistling sound draws rapidly nearer, until it can be heard on the roof and round about the house. The candidate then suddenly disappears from the midst of the assembly, and a few minutes later the unmistakable cry of the cannibal god is heard: '*hap, hap*', 'eat, eat!'.

A little while later one of the chiefs enquires whether those present understand the significance of what is happening. One of them answers that Baxbakwalanuxsiwae has taken the candidate into his house in order to show him his secrets. The pipe is the clay pipe of the god, which announces his coming, and the candidate has been carried off by him into the forest.

After this opening session the preparations begin. First a special building is prepared for the ceremony, the 'place which holds the winter dance', the 'place of well-being', the 'time of happiness'. A garland of fir branches round the door-frame, sprinkled with white eagle down, is a sign of the purpose to which the dance house is to be put. Round its walls lie heavy planks to be used as drums, and each participant in the ceremony is given a pine stick with which to beat on them. In the middle of the room is a blazing fir which serves both as a source of light and as a point of orientation for the dancers, who dance anticlockwise round it.

Days pass, marked by ritual morning baths, until the ceremony of 'bringing back' the candidate from the house of the god, or rather from the remote corner of the forest where he has been undergoing the same purification rites as the rest of the villagers, in order to rid himself of his 'human smell'. He has also been cutting down his intake of food, and his growing physical weakness leads to a semi-conscious delirium in which he sees and experiences those things which the Kwakiutl call the 'secrets of Baxbakwalanuxsiwae'.

During this period he learns for the first time – obviously from the

elder *hamatsa* – the full text of the clan legend. This describes the wanderings of the mythical ancestor of his clan in ancient times, his experiences at the dwelling of the 'cannibal at the north end of the world' or
another god, and the gifts that the clan ancestor then received. In his
trance state the candidate relives the experiences and actions of the clan
ancestor; the clan legend he has learned by heart unconsciously affects
his mystical experience. This form of initiation is of course derived from
the technique of the dream fast, as practised by the Canadian forest
Indians, with the difference that here the experience is closely tied to a
specific legend; each individual follows the path once trodden by his
ancestor.

The trance experience in the forest is the central element in the
initiation rite. The dreamer is transported to the house of the god, where
he sees the mythical patrimony of his clan, the dance masks, carved
poles, dishes and other objects, which were once bestowed upon the clan
ancestor. The visionary trance is described in the many native accounts
of the initiation as 'dying'. Sometimes it is said of a man simply that
'he fell down dead and then awoke to a new life', but more frequently
there is a detailed description of what happens; the god swallows the
candidate, spits him out and restores him to his former shape. The texts
sometimes express this process in the crudest terms; but its true significance is apparent: this is a straightforward interpretation of the *unio
mystica*, the absorption into the godhead by a process of death and
rebirth.

Union with the god divests the candidate of his humanity; and this
has been prepared for by the rubbing with fir twigs which removes his
human smell. The metamorphosis is complete when the novice becomes
'wild', 'goes out of his mind', 'raves', 'goes into convulsions', all
Kwakiutl expressions for the fact that the human being who has passed
into the body of the god is no longer human but *the god himself*.

A number of aspects of the ritual make this clear. In his forest retreat
he provides himself with a corpse as provender for his return journey;
he takes a coffin from a tree (the Kwakiutl place their dead in trees) and
prepares the body by removing the corruptible parts and smoke-drying
it. For among the attributes of the god is his appetite for human flesh:
he bites everyone he can catch. In this state of exaltation the candidate
returns to his village. The winter ritual has the purpose of turning the
divinely possessed *hamatsa* back into a man, or, as the formula has it,
'healing' him.

On the evening after the first stages of the 'bringing back' ceremony
the worshippers return to the dance house. All through the night the

minor fraternities, inferior in rank to the *hamatsa*, perform all manner of ritual dances in order to lure the candidate back from the forest. But all these are in vain; the candidate fails to return.

At first light the situation changes abruptly with the arrival of the ghost dancer. Hardly have the people raised up their voices in the dance-of-death song when the old *hamatsa*, the full members of the cannibal fraternity, enter an ecstatic state provoked by the symbols of the dead corpses, skulls and worms; and the ghost dancer, who represents the whole world of the dead, naturally provokes the greatest excitement of all.

With loud cries of '*hap, hap*' the dancers circle the fire. Out in the forest the novice hears their voices; and suddenly he can be heard on the roof of the dance house. He tears the shingles loose and leaps down into the house. His head, neck, and arm and leg joints are ringed with garlands of pine branches, his face is gleaming black, and both his cheeks are streaked with blood since Baxbakwalanuxsiwae rubbed them with twigs. Four ceremonial functionaries, the 'healers', rush at him swinging their rattles and try to hold him fast. But the new *hamatsa* wrenches himself free and vanishes through the door. After this unsuccessful attempt to 'heal' the candidate the master of ceremonies sends the dancers home with a request to return about midday.

In the meantime two important changes take place: the *hamspeq* and the *mawitl* are set up at one end of the dance house. The *hamspeq* is a very long pole. The greater part of its length rises through an opening in the roof. At the top hangs a large fir garland bound with red bast. The prayers used at the erection of a *hamspeq* show that the fir wreath represents the cannibal god himself; it is cross-shaped with protuberances suggesting arms, legs and head. The *mawitl* is a free-standing wall or screen of boards, supported from behind and painted with the face of the cannibal Baxbakwalanuxsiwae himself, his raven or the bird Hochhoku. The space behind the *mawitl* is the dwelling of the god, and here the candidate places himself. He is not allowed to go round the right or left end of the *mawitl*, but must pass through a hole some five feet above the floor, which represents the mouth of the painted face of the god or the beak of Hochhoku or the raven. Thus when he emerges the candidate crawls through the mouth of the god, and when he enters he is apparently eaten; another concrete symbol for union with the godhead.

Hardly are the preparations complete when the candidate comes into the dance house. He climbs up the *hamspeq*, climbs down from the roof of the house and comes back in through the door. Before him paces a woman attendant holding in her arms the corpse which has served as provender for his journey. Once more the healers run to meet the candidate and this time they succeed in holding him fast by his heavy neck-ring so that he cannot bite anyone. Under their escort he circles the fire four times, half crouching and half upright. During this dance the elder *hamatsa* burst into the dance house, snatch the corpse from the attendant and go through a pantomime routine of eating it. The candidate also takes part in this mimic cannibal feast, thus confirming to the assembled company that he embodies the cannibal god in person. As soon as the corpse has been torn to pieces and the fire has been circled four times, the still-possessed candidate disappears through the mouth hole in the *mawitl*. The old *hamatsa* and the rest of the assembly remain behind. The 'healers' first calm the *hamatsa*, who are still in a state of frenzy, by taking them down to the beach and dipping them in the water. After this bath the *hamatsa* return peacefully to the dance house; their ecstasy has vanished. Throughout the Kwakiutl winter ceremonial, water is the great pacifier, the unfailing antidote to the madness of those possessed by the god.

Meanwhile the novice remains behind his *mawitl*. Everything is done to cure his madness; the spirit pipes are blown, the women dance, and the eagle down is strewn in thicker and thicker layers. In the evening comes the last appearance of the new *hamatsa*. He crawls out through the *mawitl* and dances with Hochhoku, the raven, and Baxbakwala-nuxsiwae himself in turns, the god being now personated by another person. The constant alternation between the candidate and the divine beings is another sign of the basic identity of all the figures who emerge from the *mawitl*.

After the last dance the new *hamatsa* sits down on a mat and is finally healed. First water is poured over him, and then he crawls four times through a wreath of cedar bast, which is run over his body from head to feet. This ring, with its projections representing head, arms and legs, is exactly like the great wreath at the top of the *hamspeq*, the symbol of the cannibal Baxbakwalanuxsiwae; and we may suppose that the passing of the wreath over the body of the candidate represents a final progress through the body of the god.

The ritual healing of the candidate is now at an end. For some time yet he will occasionally relapse into his cannibal trance state and bite someone; but this becomes more and more infrequent. He long remains subject to a number of special rules, and behaves like one who has forgotten the ways of men and needs to learn everything anew like a newborn child.

The rite ends with the burning of the pine 'drumsticks' as torches to light the way home, and they make a charming sight as they pass along the dark village street, flickering on the houses on one side and the boats on the other.

Taken all in all, the Kwakiutl winter dance ceremony is a surprising and fascinating phenomenon. Behind the apparent confusion of names, masks and rites, it embodies a religious philosophy which is among the profoundest creations of native American thought. The forms – repellent though they may be to a European mind – serve to enhance an impression of extreme antiquity.

The theoretical basis of this rite, the idea of death and rebirth, re-appears elsewhere in the Pacific Coast culture. The so-called *potlatch*, for instance, is certainly based on this idea. These are feasts at which one clan acts as host and actually gives away its entire patrimony, dishes, spoons, blankets, boats, canisters of oil and other things. Custom dictates that all these gifts be returned in duplicate within one year; the property of the clan is disposed of, liquidated, 'killed', only to be 'reborn' bigger and better than before.

The religion of the Pacific Coast Indians has been, not unjustifiably, referred to as 'Dionysiac'. The sacred frenzy, the tearing to pieces of the corpse and the metamorphosis of the votary into his god are reminiscent of the cult of Dionysus, the classic example of ecstatic religion.

The Indians too are aware of some of the wider implications and affinities of their religion. The rites are now illegal in British Columbia, largely on account of their 'cannibalistic' tendencies. The possibility of replacing the mummified corpse with an effigy loaf or cake did not occur to the intolerant Puritans who framed the law. As Kathrene Gedney Pinkerton puts it in her amiable travel book about the northern Pacific shore, *Three's a Crew*:

> The more intelligent Indians felt a quite justified resentment of the white people's misunderstanding of the so-called cannibal dance in which the dancers pretend to eat the flesh of a chief. 'They don't really bite him,' a mission-trained Indian explained. 'They just want to become like him. You know,' he added quickly, 'it's the same thing as the sacrament in Church.'

VIII   *The Creator and his Adversary: The Central Californians*

California is the place of refuge *par excellence* for the aboriginal inhabitants of North America. Here, behind the immense barrier of the Rocky Mountains, there gathered a multitude of ethnic splinter groups who became completely isolated from cultural developments to the east.

Their geographical position inclined them to look westward, across the Pacific, rather than eastward, across the Rockies; and yet they neither navigated the ocean nor underwent trans-Pacific influences as did the British Columbians to the north. Historical accident and a certain native conservatism and complacency led to the preservation here of an amazingly low cultural level which varied only in the few zones where outside contact was possible.[1]

In the north of the Californian cultural province, in the hinterland of Humboldt Bay, when Athapascan (Hupa, Mattoal, Wailaki) and Algonquin (Yurok and Wiyot) tribes settled, affinities with the Pacific Coast Indians of British Columbia are apparent. In the south, among the so-called Mission Indians (Salinas, Serraño, Gabrielino, Luiseño), unmistakable Pueblo elements appear. Between these two transitional areas, and around the Sacramento and San Joaquin rivers, there is a core of tribes who have been free from outside influence: the central Californians. The most important of these are the Kato, Yuki, Wintun, Maidu, Pomo, Wappo, Patwin and Miwok. These tribes are extremely valuable sources of information for the student of cultural development; not only are they physically and economically isolated on all sides, but with the exception of the Pomo and Yuki they form a linguistic group entirely peculiar to California, the Penutian.

Like the Canadian forest Indians, the central Californians are hunters and gatherers; they possess no trace of systematic farming. But whereas the Canadian tribes incline more towards hunting, the central Californians have specialized in gathering. The staple of their diet was acorns, which they crushed, washed repeatedly to remove the bitter taste and cooked into soup or baked into cakes. The economy was advanced enough to incorporate provision for the future; great stocks of acorns, fish, berries and seeds were kept in baskets against the coming winter.

The multiplicity of ethnic groups in California is illustrated by the great variety of house forms, which is certainly not a product of climate or landscape alone. The northern Californian gabled wooden house is an import from the north-west coast; in central California there are bark huts with conical roofs, and also sunken 'earth houses' with a shallow domed roof resting directly on the surface of the earth, entered by climbing through a hatch and down a notched beam. Dance houses and sweat houses for religious use are larger and more elaborate versions of the dwelling type. These pit dwellings give the Californian culture something of an Arctic aspect, particularly as there are sometimes even external tunnel entrances in the Eskimo style.

In central California these huts are grouped in villages; a dozen or so together make up a settlement under the rule of a 'captain'. The social organization does not rise above the natural unit of the family. There are neither clans nor sibs, and the village captain is more a counsellor than a chief. Unlike the tribes east of the Rockies, who all suffer from wanderlust in varying degrees, the central Californians hardly ever travel further from home than the two or three nearest villages. The countryside within a few hours' walk of their own hearths is their world; outside this limit all is darkness.[2] The individual groups usually live together in peace; the very narrowness of their horizons precludes any violent movement or conflict. In spite of a number of remarkable if isolated achievements in the craft of basket work and the organization of a gathering economy, this is basically a community at a very primitive cultural level.

This archaism is also apparent in the quest for religious expression.[3] Ritual life is not highly developed; emphasis is on the sung or spoken word. The dominance of myth parallels the situation among the Canadian forest Indians. Taken together with the importance of shamanism, the importance of finding a guardian spirit, and the dug-out dwellings, this reinforces the impression that the central Californians are southern representatives of sub-Arctic modes of thought and behaviour. Only one feature marks these tribes off clearly from their sub-Arctic kinsmen; the subject matter of their mythology. Creation myths and the concept of a creator, largely absent among the Canadian tribes and indeed everywhere else in North America, have played an important role.

As a result of this unusual emphasis on verbal tradition, investigators have all too often concentrated their attention on the unique mythical texts and completely overlooked the religious practices. But wherever the daily life of these Indians has received attention from ethnologists, we are vouchsafed some astonishing glimpses of the soul of the people. Jaime de Angulo has written an informative study of the psychology of the Californian Indians based on his work among the Achomavi, a tribe who live on the upper reaches of the Sacramento. Despite a certain amount of north-west coast influence, they belong culturally among the central Californian tribes.

Angulo was visited in Berkeley by an Achomavi friend, who, soon after his arrival, pronounced the following *credo*:

All things have life in them. Trees are alive, so are stones, mountains, water; all is full of life. You believe a stone is a dead thing. But it isn't, it's full of life. When I came here to visit you, I took care to speak to everything there is around here. That tree at the corner of your house, I talked to it the first night before I went to bed. I went out on to the balcony and smoked and let my smoke rise to it. I spoke to it, I said 'Tree, don't harm me. I am not wicked, and I have not come here to harm anyone. Tree, be my friend.'

I spoke to your house too. Your house is alive, your house is somebody. You built it; well, you built it for a certain purpose. Your house is a person. It knows that. I am a stranger here. So I let my tobacco smoke rise towards it, to make friends with it. I spoke to it. I said: 'House, you are the house of my friend. You mustn't do me any harm. Don't let me fall ill while I am visiting my friend. I want to go back to my home without any harm coming to me. I haven't come to do anyone any harm; quite the reverse, I want everyone to be happy. House, I want you to protect me.' That is what I did. I went all round the house. I sent my smoke up to everything. This was to make friends with all the things. There must have been a lot of things looking at me in the night when I couldn't see them . . . they must have been talking to each other. Stones talk to each other just like we do, and trees and mountains talk to each other too. You can hear them if you listen carefully, especially out of doors at night. I am sure that all those people were watching me the other night, the first night I came here, probably they were saying to each other: 'Who is that man?' 'He's a stranger. We have never seen him before. But at least he is polite. He sends us his smoke. He greets us. He must be a good man. We must protect him so that no harm comes to him.'

That's what one ought to do. I tell you this so that you can learn because you are young. I am beginning to grow old. But I still have a long time to live, because I have a lot of friends out there in my own country. I often talk to them when I go outside at night. I send them smoke. I don't forget them. I take care of them and they take care of me.[4]

This man's intimate involvement with things near and far speaks for itself. His soul reacts positively to realities that civilized man regards as conveniences at best. This cast of mind is reflected in Achomavi mythology, and also in the immense importance of myth in the life of the tribe. People are positively infatuated with stories, and spend endless time telling them over and over again. If someone has a story to tell – the texts belong to everyone and do not exist in official or orthodox versions – old and young cast aside their work and listen with great reverence to the *tilasinii*, the 'old time stories'.[5]

The creation myth contains all the essential features of the central Californian cosmogonies.

In the beginning all was water. In all directions the sky was clear and pure. A cloud formed in the sky, gathered itself together and became Coyote. Then there rose a mist, gathered itself together and became Silver Fox. They became people. Then they thought. They thought up a boat and said: 'Let us stay here, let us make it our home'. Then they drifted round for many years. And the boat became old and mossy, and they wearied of this.

'Lie down to sleep,' said Silver Fox to Coyote, and he did so. While he slept Silver Fox combed him and kept the hair he combed out. When he had a lot, he rolled it in his hands, stretched it and beat it flat. Then he laid it on the water and spread it out until it covered the whole surface. Then he thought: 'Let there be a tree there,' and at once there was a tree. In the same way he created bushes and rocks. He weighted the surface with stones, to prevent the wind from raising waves. And so he made the world, so that it was as it should be. And then the boat gently touched land, and it was the world.

Now Silver Fox called out to Coyote: 'Wake up, we're sinking!' Coyote awoke and looked up. Above his head, as he lay, hung cherries and plums, and from the earth he heard crickets chirping. At once he began to eat the cherries and plums, and the crickets too. After a while Coyote said: 'Where are we? Where have we come to?' Silver Fox answered: 'I don't know, we are here. We struck land.' Of course he knew all the time, but he did not want Coyote to know that he had created the world. Then Silver Fox said: 'What shall we do? This is firm ground. I am going ashore and I shall live here.' So they landed, built a steam bath and lived in it.[6]

These two primordial beings, who created men and beasts from sticks of wood, continued to share control of the world, but the primacy of Silver Fox as Creator was maintained. An endless string of stories follows, most of them rather childish, cruel and obscene adventures of Coyote: an inexhaustible epic. Everything that Silver Fox plans for the good of mankind is thwarted by Coyote. Thus there was intended to be constant summer, but Coyote insisted on having a long winter. At first there was no death, because the dead always came back to life, but Coyote introduced the rule of final and inevitable death.

'Ah, what a Coyote! There was never anyone like him in the whole world!'

In the end Silver Fox tired of all this and slew Coyote. Then he travelled the earth and carefully scratched over every place where Coyote had urinated. Unfortunately he missed one place, and so his victim returned to life after three days, and Silver Fox was obliged to ply him with friendly words in order to calm his anger. Coyote was immortal.

This theme has already appeared, thousands of miles to the east, in the Iroquois myth of the hostile twin brothers. One of the twins rises to the status of a true supreme being, while the other remains in a minor (auxiliary or obstructive) role. The two primordial figures, although dominant, do not exist in isolation; there are numerous minor supernatural beings.

A rapid survey of those other central Californian tribes of whose mythology we know something should begin in the north with the inland Yuki. Their Creator, Taikomol, 'he who comes alone', floated as a down feather on the primeval sea, and took on human shape gradually as he sang. From his body he drew reeds, which he plaited together like a basket to make the earth. Coyote lived with him as his helper from the beginning, but there is no indication of how Coyote came into existence. Coyote helped in the creation of mankind, but insisted on the introduction of death.

The Wintun, who live to the east in the upper Sacramento valley, worship a truly dignified supreme being called Olelbis, 'he who is above', whose love of mankind is again thwarted at every turn by Sedit, the coyote. Here too Sedit by his wiles brings death into the world.[8]

The systematically ordered mythology of the northern Maidu on the eastern tributaries of the upper Sacramento begins with Wonomi, 'without death' (or Kodoyanpe, 'earth-namer') and Coyote sailing in a boat on the primeval sea. Kodoyanpe's body shines like the sun; his face is covered and can never be seen. By singing he called the earth into being, but Coyote at once made it hard and mountainous. They lived for a long time at the middle point, and the Creator Kodoyanpe tried to arrange everything as well as he can, but Coyote thwarted all his acts of benevolence, even destroying the hill with the lake of 'life-water' on its summit which preserved mankind from death.[9]

The pairing of the two primal deities reappears in the mythology of the eastern Pomo round Clear Lake. Marumda, a man-like being, and Kuksu, whom he addresses as 'brother', lived in houses of cloud and created the world together.

The western Pomo of the coast allot the role of Creator to Coyote. By thinking and wishing he formed the earth, the ocean, human beings and the six custodians of the cardinal points: north, south, east, west, zenith and nadir. We hear of no other mythological beings.[10] The Patwin, on the other hand, set Katit, the hawk, and Coyote against each other.[11] In the Miwok creation myth the supreme being, Coyote, shares his functions with Eagle and Hawk.[12]

A constant element in all these versions is the presence of a genuine Creator who produces the world by singing, thinking or wishing: this is something otherwise unknown in North America. Equally general is the presence of a companion god, usually an opponent of the Creator although sometimes his helper.

This raises once more the problem of dualism. This feature of religious belief is dominant in almost all areas east of the Rockies, usually in a stylized form (as with the Iroquois), appears in a different form among the Pueblo, and re-appears in a third version among the central Californians. This is therefore not a phenomenon restricted to farming cultures, but is present even at the hunting and gathering stage, along with the concepts of creation and a Creator. The absence of creation myths among farming peoples must be regarded as a consequence of their 'higher development'; the dual pattern of their practical life (woman and cultivation, man and hunting), ritual (winter and summer half-years) and mythology (twin gods or separate winter and summer gods), emphasized the idea of duality at the expense of that of a single supreme Creator.

This is the sort of fact which compels us to discard the crude idea that men first worshipped blocks and stones, then graven images, then a multitude of gods and finally one God. This notion of religious development is largely characteristic of European thought but it is totally inapplicable to the beliefs of primitive peoples. Even if attempts are made to modernize it by referring to 'supernatural powers' or even to 'one supernatural power', it remains completely useless as an approach to North American native religion.

There is a remarkable contrast between the poor and primitive material culture of the central Californians and the wealth of creative imagination revealed in their mythology, which is far richer and more interesting than that of their richer brethren in other parts of North America. Material poverty does not necessarily mean poverty of mind.

The mythology of the central Californians imposes the question of the part played by the two supreme gods in religious practice. Do they exist only as words and concepts, or do they govern religious action as well, prayer and ritual in particular? Foster has filled some of the gaps in our knowledge by his work among the inland Yuki.[13]

This tribe worships Taikomol, 'he who walks alone', whose other names mean 'he who sewed the earth together', or 'our language which he made in the beginning'. Taikomol dwells in the clouds, thunderstorms are manifestations of his displeasure. His voice is the thunder, and lightning darts from his eyes. When this happens the shamans or 'doctors' run out into the rain and pray with upraised hands:

Please stop. My people are afraid. Why are you doing this? Father be careful. We're living here. Be easy with us. We're doing the best we can.

226

But even apart from such exceptional occurrences as this the Yuki continually address prayers to their supreme God. They pray before meals, before hunting, and before building a fish dam, and never omit to request 'good hearts' for themselves. The breath of newborn children is Taikomol's gift. At the shaman initiation ceremony the 'doctors' address themselves to Taikomol as follows:

Our Father, give this boy a good way of talking [talking refers to conversation with the spirits] so that he will be able to save our people. I want you to promise this to me. Please take care of this boy from all dangers.[13]

Foster expressly refutes the idea that Taikomol is a product of civilized influence. 'The concept is too deeply ingrained in Yuki culture to be other than extremely ancient.'[14]

Taikomol also dominates the ritual life of the Yuki. As I said at the outset, Californian ceremonialism is at a lower level of development than those of the Iroquois, the Pueblo and the Pacific Coast fishing tribes, but these modest beginnings nevertheless bear the unmistakable mark of Californian culture: everywhere the supreme gods dominate the ritual, their cult alone is the pretext for dance, prayer and song.

California contains the whole range of North American ritual typologies in embryo. As we have seen, these can be very broadly divided into two categories of religious experience, individual and collective. The first category includes the medicine hut of the central Algonquin and the winter ritual of the Pacific fishermen, initiation rites which concentrate on the individual candidate. Alongside these individualistic rites we have noted the entirely differently-orientated Big House ceremony of the Delaware, and the somewhat similar rites performed by the Iroquois and the Pueblo. These ceremonies aim not at the good of the individual but at that of the world at large.[15] Just as initiation is a typical feature of individualistic cults, universalism is characterized by the presence of a festal calendar, a seasonal sequence or cycle of rites.

Central California can offer examples of both these patterns of ritual life. The *Kuksu* or 'big head' ceremony practised by the Kato, Yuki, Pomo, Miwok, Costano and Salina is both a tribal act of consecration or communion and a puberty initiation rite; and the *Hesi* ceremony among the Patwin and the northern Maidu is intended to procure rich harvests and the good of the world at large. The two patterns have a complex geographical distribution and often exist side by side, but it would seem that the *Hesi* originated in a narrow area in the Sacramento valley, and that the *Kuksu* has a wide distribution along the coast and extends inland to the north and south to encircle the *Hesi* territory.

Our fragmentary information suggests that the *Kuksu* is based on a death and rebirth myth of a very elementary type which nevertheless has many variants. The children are covered with straw, or mimically 'speared', or thrown out of the smoke hole of the dance house. One of the most important ways in which rebirth is celebrated is the recital of the creation myth, which is learned by heart as a symbol of the 'new creation' of the individual.

In most cases the puberty rite takes place in two stages, the first of which is for everybody, the second reserved to the *élite*, the next generation of shamans. Californian shamanism, it might be noted at this point, is very similar to that of the sub-Arctic forest Indians: there are various classes of shamans including the 'sucking doctors' who heal sickness by sucking, the 'singing doctors' who talk to the spirits and the 'bear doctors' who ward off enemies; just as in Canada, vocations are revealed in dreams, and the shamans possess spirit helpers and go on dream journeys to heaven.[16] And the *Kuksu* initiation, like shamanistic functions in so many other areas, is derived from the supreme god, who either appears in person with his huge feather headdress ('big head'), as does Taikomol among the Yuki, or is represented at the ceremony (known as the 'school') by his brother and helper, whose Pomo name is Kuksu.

The *Hesi* ceremony too draws its sanction from the creator god. He is formally invited by proclamations addressed to the four winds in turn, and an emissary in a voluminous feather mantle represents him during the rite. The *Hesi* is open to all, although the rites themselves are under the control of a religious fraternity. It is associated with a genuine festal calendar covering the period from 1 October to 1 May and incorporating a cycle of ceremonies which begins with the *Hesi* itself, and which is intended to bring rain, nourish the earth, increase the acorn harvest, and ward off epidemics, floods and earthquakes.[17] The Delaware Big House fulfils exactly the same functions, and among the Yurok and Karok of north-western California, both Algonquin tribes, there is an analogous rite known as the 'world renewal'.[18]

Whether the individualistic *Kuksu* or the universalistic *Hesi* is the older of the two rites, is difficult to say. In central California it looks as if the *Kuksu* gradually hemmed the *Hesi* in until only a small area in the Sacramento valley remained to it. Individualistic rites belong on the whole to the solitary north, and universalistic rites to the gregarious south. The Indians themselves believe the universalistic pattern, with its cosmic embrace, to be the older and more venerable; all other religions, as an Indian informant told Frank G. Speck, are but branches of this faith.[19] Even though the ethnographer cannot accept this claim without further examination, the study of Californian native rituals clearly reveals how deeply rooted in the most primitive stage of human life is a feeling of love for the whole world and everything that is in it.

CHAPTER FOUR

PRIMITIVE SOUTH AMERICA AND THE WEST INDIES

Otto Zerries

Introduction

No examination of the religious beliefs and practices of the native inhabitants of South America outside the zone of the Andean civilizations could afford to restrict itself to the narrow definition of religion as a belief in gods, transcendental beings on whom man feels himself to be dependent and who are the objects of prayer and worship. Quite apart from the presence of important *mythological* complexes intimately linked with and influencing theology and religious attitudes, religious practice is inextricably linked with a whole series of actions which are *magical* in the generally accepted sense of the word, and with the all-important figure of the witch doctor, medicine man or shaman.

This outline of the nature of the subject is that proposed by Alfred Métraux in the work of synthesis, published in 1949, from which I have borrowed the framework of my own account.

Primitive South America is by no means a single cultural unit. It is generally divided into the following large cultural areas:

1 The Circum-Caribbean culture, which possesses strong cultural as well as geographical links with advanced civilizations further west. We shall discuss its outposts in eastern Colombia and in Venezuela as well as the West Indies.

2 The Amazon basin, including the Guiana highlands and mainly occupied by agricultural peoples, some of whom belong to one or other of a number of large linguistic families (Tupian, Cariban, Arawakan, Tucanoan, Panoan, etc.), and many of whom are linguistically isolated. Individual or collectively, these tribes fall into a number of clearly defined cultural regions.

3 The mountains of eastern Brazil, mainly occupied by the old-established and archaic Ge tribes, and the regions of the Atlantic

hinterland that were formerly occupied by primitive hunters and gatherers.

4   The ethnic melting-pot of the Gran Chaco, where a hunting and gathering horizon has been overlaid by numerous influences from higher farming cultures.

5   The extreme south of the continent, with the long-extinct hunting peoples of the pampas and Patagonia, and the well-documented inhabitants of Tierra del Fuego.

6   The Araucanians of central and southern Chile, who came under the influence of Inca culture a few decades before the Spanish conquest after developing an extremely interesting independent culture of their own.

Even though any religious phenomenon may be more in evidence in one area than in the others, there are no such fundamental differences between the areas, from the point of view of our theme, as would demand a classification of the subject by regions. I have therefore dealt with the most important aspects of religious life separately, filling in the picture where necessary with local variations. No exhaustive treatment of the subject could, of course, be expected within the framework of this work.

I   *Supreme Being, Culture Hero and Ancestor*

The belief in a Creator, prime mover and teacher of mankind is universal in primitive South America, but in most cases this being is purely mythological, plays no part in the daily life of man, and is not worshipped. The remoteness and sublimity of such a figure sometimes leads to the idea of a purely spiritual supreme being. In addition, as Métraux remarks,[1] between a Creator who is worshipped, and therefore forms part of the religious system as such, and another who is purely a mythological figure, the distinction is more theoretical than practical.

Creator figures of both types are studied here in order to give some idea of the multiplicity of religious forms, as well as of the common elements which can be detected in spite of the fragmentary and even contradictory nature of our sources.

Belief in a supreme being seems to be one of the principal elements of the religion of the hunters and gatherers of Tierra del Fuego, as it appears in the reports of Martin Gusinde[2] and Wilhelm Koppers,[3] who carried out field work in the region in the early twenties at a time when these Indians already faced imminent extinction.

The Ona (or Selknam), the Yahgan (or Yámana) and the Alacaluf

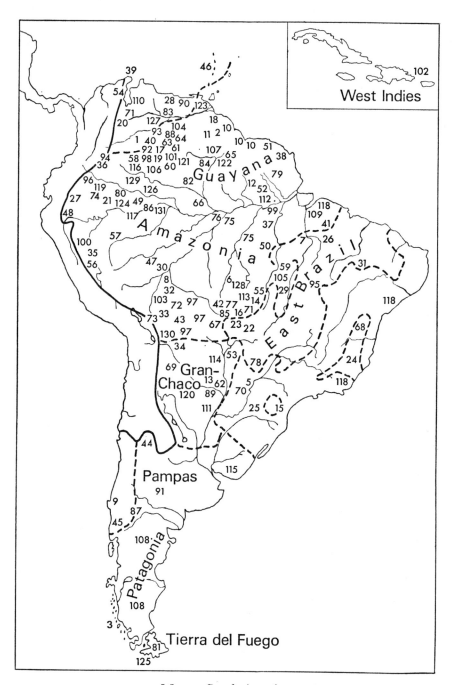

Map 4. South America

Key to Map 4

2	Acawai	61	Cunuana	91	Puelche
1	Achagua	37	Curuaya	92	Puinave
3	Alacaluf		East Tupi (see	93	Sáliva
4	Andoke		Tupinamba)	94	San Agustin
5	Apapocuva-Guarani	38	Galibi		Selknam (see Ona)
6	Apiacá	39	Goajiro	95	Sherente
7	Apinayé	40	Guahibo	99	Shipaya
8	Araona	41	Guajajara	100	Shipibo
9	Araucanians	42	Guaporé, tribes from	101	Shiriana (Guaharibo)
10	Arawakans of the		the right bank of	96	Sioni
	Guiana coast	43	Guarayu	97	Siriona
11	Arecuna	44	Huarpe	98	Siusí
12	Arikena	45	Huilliche		Surára (see Pakidái)
13	Ashluslay	47	Ipurina	103	Tacana
14	Auetö	46	Island Caribs	102	Taino
15	Aweikoma-Caingang		Itau-Tal (see	104	Tamanak
16	Bacairi		Chiriguano)	105	Tapirapé
17	Baniwa	48	Jivaro	106	Tariana
18	Barama River Caribs	49	Juri	107	Taulipang
19	Baré	50	Juruna	108	Tehuelche
20	Betoi	62	Lengua	109	Tembé
21	Bora	65	Macushi		Tenetehara (Tembé
22	Bororo, eastern	63	Maipure		and Guajajara)
23	Bororo, western	64	Makiritare		Timbira (see Canella,
24	Botocudo	66	Manao		Apinayé)
52	Cachuyana	67	Manasi	110	Timote
53	Caduveo		Mapuche (see	111	Toba-Pilaga
54	Cágaba		Araucanians)	112	Trombetas
25	Cainguá	68	Mashacalí	113	Trumai
51	Caliña Caribs	69	Mataco-Noctene	116	Tucano
55	Camayura	70	Mbyá (Guaranian)	117	Tucuna
56	Campa	71	Mehinacu		Tumupasa (see
26	Canella	72	Mojo		Caviña)
	(East Timbira)	73	Mosetene	118	Tupinamba
27	Canelos	74	Muinane		Tuyuca (see Tucano)
28	Caracas	75	Mundurucú	120	Vilela
29	Carajá	76	Mura	121	Waica
30	Caripuna	77	Nambicuara	122	Wapishana
31	Cariri	78	Ofaié-Chavante	123	Warrau
57	Cashinawa	80	Okaina	119	Witoto
58	Cáua	81	Ona	124	Yagua
32	Caviña	79	Oyana	125	Yahgan
59	Cayapó, northern	82	Pakidái	126	Yahuna
	Chama (see	83	Palenque		Yamana (see
	Shipibo, Conibo)	84	Paravilhana		Yahgan)
114	Chamacoco	85	Paressi-Cabishi	127	Yaruro
115	Charrua	86	Pasé	128	Yaulapiti
33	Chimane		Pau d'Arco (see		Yecuaná (see
34	Chiriguano		northern Cayapó)		Makiritare)
35	Conibo	87	Pehuenche	129	Yucuna
36	Correguaje	88	Piaroa	130	Yuracaré
60	Cubeo	89	Pilagá	131	Yurimagua
		90	Piritú		

all believed in an invisible, omniscient and omnipotent supreme spirit dwelling in the sky beyond the stars. He is disembodied and immortal, has neither wife nor children nor any material needs.

The Alacaluf creator god is called Xolas or Xelas ('star'); despite his remoteness from earth he takes a direct interest in the daily life of mankind.[4] At his behest, a soul enters the body of a newborn child and stays there until death, when it returns to Xelas. The Alacaluf abstained from any kind of worship of the supreme being, on the ground that his perfection made any attempt to influence his will pointless.

The Yahgan believed in a supreme being called Watauinewa, 'the ancient one' or 'the eternal one', who was also referred to as 'the mighty one' and 'the highest one' and addressed as 'my father'.[5] He was not regarded as the creator of the world, but as its ruler. He was the arbiter of life and death. Although Watauinewa was thought of as basically benevolent, he scrutinized the deeds of mankind with some care and requited breaches of his own moral code with the early death of the offender and often his children too.

The individual Yahgan prayed to Watauinewa in one of sixty or so fixed formulas, or in whatever other words were appropriate to the situation, imploring him, as owner of the wild animals and plants, to give food, to preserve health or heal sickness, or to give protection from the elements. If these prayers were answered, prayers of thanksgiving were frequently offered up.

In bad weather, sickness or other misfortune, complaints were addressed to Watauinewa. These were couched in strong language: when someone died the god was addressed as the 'murderer in the sky'.

As far as social life is concerned, Watauinewa played an important part in the initiation ritual for adolescent boys and girls, the Čiexaus, which according to Cooper was the focus of Yahgan religious life.[6] The laws laid down by Watauinewa, which included lofty moral precepts such as injunctions to selflesssness, industry and peaceableness, were impressed upon the young candidates by their instructors. The Čiexaus was instituted by Watauinewa himself;[7] and a breach of the laws which it enshrined was punished not only by the supreme being himself, but also by Yetaita, the highest of the evil spirits.[8] It is not therefore entirely surprising that in one version Watauinewa and Yetaita, as dominant figures in the Čiexaus, are treated as one,[9] and it is not entirely true, at least as far as this exoteric aspect of the rite is concerned, that Watauinewa was clearly distinct from all other good and evil spirits, 'as if he were alone', as Cooper postulates.[10]

In this connection, it should not be overlooked that according to

Gusinde[11] Watauinewa was described as *kespix*, 'a spirit', the word used for human and animal souls (a fact also noted by Snethlage).[12] Watauinewa is also the protector of all animals, especially the larger mammals and birds, which he grants to man for exploitation only insofar as they are needed for the maintenance of life; to destroy them wantonly would be to incur the wrath of the god.[13]

It also seems that Watauinewa, at some remote date and in circumstances which have not come down to us, created most of the animals;[14] and his role of creator and protector of the animals led me some time ago to detect in this supreme god the aspect of a 'lord of beasts', a form of deity characteristic of hunting cultures.[15] I was criticized for this by Haekel;[16] but those who believe in monotheism as the earliest form of religion should find support for their views in a hypothesis which would make Watauinewa a figure of great antiquity. Apart from this I think it is a good thing to subject even apparently firm conclusions to scrutiny from time to time in the light of new methods and new points of view. The concept of a supreme being and that of a lord of beasts are by no means identical – and a clear distinction is preserved in the present study – but as will be seen they do overlap both in Watauinewa and in other gods.[17]

My statement that some of the supreme gods of the primitive South American religions are purely mythological figures needs qualification: the term 'mythological' means in this context only that the deity in question is a purely theoretical entity who is not actually worshipped. It does *not* mean that the supreme being is associated with a particularly elaborate set of mythical events; on the contrary, the most rarefied of all 'supreme beings' are in this sense totally amythical. Watauinewa played no part whatsoever in the mythology or folklore of the Yahgan,[18] which was dominated by a cycle of myths about two brothers known as the Yoalox.[19] The Yoalox cycle was also closely linked with the Čiexaus, the communal adolescent rite; only initiates were allowed to share this very important sector of the Yahgan world view.[20]

The Ona (Selknam) of the main island of Tierra del Fuego called the supreme being Temaukel (untranslatable) but avoided using his name, preferring the circumlocution 'he up there in the sky'.[21] Temaukel existed from the very beginning; whether he also created the starless heavens and the formless earth is not clear, but he entrusted the first ancestor of the Ona, Kenos, with the final shaping of the cosmos and the establishment of the moral law. Although he takes no interest in day-to-day happenings on earth, Temaukel is the originator and custodian of the laws which govern the moral and social life of mankind.[22]

He punishes transgressors with serious illness and premature death. The soul of the dead individual goes beyond the stars to Temaukel, but has no further punishment to expect when he gets there.[23]

The Ona showed a deep feeling of reverence for Temaukel, but neither ritual nor priesthood had any connection with him. The Ona prayed to him, especially when someone was ill, but much less frequently than the Yahgan, and without the numerous formulas used in addressing Watauinewa. Prayers of thanksgiving were almost non-existent; but the Ona customarily threw the first pieces of meat of a nocturnal feast out of the hut as an offering, saying: 'this is for him up there'. During storms a woman would throw a mass of glowing coals outside for Temaukel, so that he might bring better weather.

All in all, the Yahgan supreme being, Watauinewa, was closer to mankind than the Ona god, Temaukel. It seems that among the Ona the idea of Kenos, the first ancestor, had pushed Temaukel rather into the background. This Kenos, in Jensen's and Gusinde's view a more recent concept than Temaukel,[24] was not the object of a cult; the fact that Kenos was thought to act only at Temaukel's behest is interpreted by Jensen as a secondary linking of two quite distinct parallel traditions;[25] Kenos is definitely the more active as a mythological figure. Temaukel finds his way into the mythology only by virtue of his connection with Kenos.

From our fragmentary and superficial knowledge of the religious life of the early inhabitants of Patagonia and the pampas, it is at least fairly clear that the Tehuelche of Patagonia recognized a supreme being who resembled the Temaukel of their southern neighbours the Ona, both in his role as lord of the dead and in his remoteness from earthly connections.[26] This *deus otiosus* was thought of as generally well-disposed towards mankind. Whether he was a creator or moral lawgiver is not clear, and we have no evidence of a public cult. Numerous names for him have been preserved, one of which, Soychu, may be a Puelche word; this was the name given by the Puelche of the pampas to the benevolent supreme being in whom they believed, and who was thought to give them anything they wished for.[27] They also believed in a supreme evil spirit, Gualichu, who was responsible for sickness and death. This concept was shared by the Tehuelche, who at the end of the nineteenth century offered the best morsel of rhea meat and the first bottles of spirits to Gualichu. After the Puelche and their neighbours had been almost entirely wiped out in wars with the Spaniards, the resulting vacuum was filled by an influx of members of the Araucanian Pehuenche tribe from the other side of the Andes. These new arrivals brought the belief in a supreme being with them from their former home.

Among the Araucanians west of the Andes, the cult of a supreme being can be traced back far into the eighteenth century.[28] His name was usually Ngenechen, 'lord of mankind' or Ngenemapun, 'lord of the land'. Among his many other appellations were a number of feminine ones which reveal his bisexual nature. Ngenechen was thought of as dwelling in the sky or in the sun. He was not only the creator of the world and the source of life and fecundity for men, beasts and plants, but was also directly responsible for the welfare of mankind. He was not, however, linked with the moral law, and the fate of the soul in the hereafter did not depend on his decision to reward or punish the individual. Nor was the 'lord of mankind' asked for forgiveness after a breach of tribal law. The individual had recourse to Ngenechen in times of purely material need, and propitiated him with prayer, blood sacrifice and first fruits. As a rule, a morsel of meat, a few drops of animal blood or a draught of drink were offered to the supreme being before meals, accompanied by a short prayer for a continued supply of food.

As far as the public cult of Ngenechen, the so-called *Ngillatun*, is concerned, we have a large number of accounts which often show marked discrepancies of detail and suggest the existence of local variants. This rite, which was under the direction of a master of ceremonies, centres on two objects; the *rewe*, a thick wooden post with branches of the tree *Drimys winteri* fastened to it, and a rectangular platform which served as a sacrificial altar. At the outset the worshippers circled these two objects several times; then came the sacrifice of animals, mainly lambs, whose blood was offered to the supreme being together with libations of *chicha* (maize beer); and then the master of ceremonies and the other participants in the *Ngillatun* prayed repeatedly to Ngenechen for food, long life, fair weather a good harvest, the well-being of the flocks and so on. The ritual ended with a banquet and a drinking session in which those present consumed large quantities of *chicha*.

The *Ngillatun* is still practised by the Araucanians in honour of their supreme god.[29] The female shaman (*machi*) still plays an important part in the rite in certain cases, performing the characteristic functions which I shall discuss in my chapter on shamanism in general.[30]

Many of the characteristics of Ngenechen suggest an origin in native Araucanian thought, but others show signs of Christian influence.[31] Before the middle of the eighteenth century the Spanish chronicles either denied that the Araucanians had a conception of a supreme god or referred to the thunder god Pillan as the main deity of the tribe,[32] and Pillan may indeed have been a forerunner and prototype for Ngenechen. A late eighteenth-century source, Juan Ignacio Molina, goes so far as to call Pillan 'the supreme being', the 'prime mover of all things', for the Araucanians.[33]

At the time of the Conquest in the middle of the sixteenth century the Cuyo area was inhabited by the Huarpe, a tribe influenced by the advanced Andean civilizations.[34] They believed that their god, Hunuc Huar, lived in the mountains; they held him in great fear and awe and made him offerings of *chicha*, maize and other things.

Métraux says of the tribes of the Gran Chaco that the missionaries were invariably unsuccessful in seeking among them for traces of a belief in a supreme being.[35] The god in the shape of a huge beetle who is believed by the Lengua to have created the world and peopled it with mighty spirits holds aloof from his creation and is not invoked in prayer.[36] The only mythological figure who comes close to the idea of a supreme being according to Métraux[37] is the great mother goddess Eschete-wuarha of the Chamacoco tribe.[38] She is the mother of countless forest spirits (*guarāō*), fathered by Pohichio, 'great spirit'.

She rules her consort and the whole world, and sees to it that mankind receives water, for she is the mother of the cloud bird Osasero. Prayers for rain are addressed to her, and she expects men to sing to her every night, even punishing with death those who neglect this duty. Métraux regards this information as insufficient to clarify the exact position of Eschetewuarha in Chamacoco religion.[39] But Baldus has compared Eschetewuarha with Gauteóvan, the mother goddess of the Cágaba of Colombia, and has made a good case for the existence of at least a phenomenological relationship.[40]

According to Haekel the chief characteristic of the religion of the Botocudo of eastern Brazil is the belief in a kind of supreme being in the sky.[41] Curt Nimuendajú heard about this from survivors of the tribe in 1939.[42] The supreme being is called Yekánkren Yirugn ('father white head') or 'old man' or 'big man'. He is the chief of the sky spirits (*maret*), but unlike them he never comes down to earth. When invoked by a shaman, who is the only man who can see them, the *maret* come to earth down a ten-foot pole, surmounted by a human figure, which is set up in the middle of the village. At the end of the ceremony they return to the sky by the same route.[43]

No one has ever looked on the face of Yekánkren Yirugn; but it is said that there were once people in direct contact with him. He has many tame animals about him, and like the other *maret* is well disposed towards mankind. The shaman prays to him in cases of sickness and other emergencies; and the *maret* act as intermediaries, escorting the souls of the departed to their celestial home. Yekánkren Yirugn punishes murderers and sends rain and storms.

According to an earlier report dating from 1915, he also kills enemies with invisible darts and causes the phases of the moon.[44] His head is white, and his face covered in red hair. This supreme *maret* is rather larger than an ordinary human being and has an enormous penis which is harmful to women. Nimuendajú's informants 24 years later were unable to offer any confirmation of this dual nature of Yakánkren Yirugn.

Most of the central and northern Ge tribes of eastern Brazil – the Apinayé, the Canella and the Sherente – regard the sun and moon as true gods, and not merely characters in myth; this is the conclusion reached by Robert H. Lowie.[45] The sun is the dominant figure; and all three tribes regard sun and moon as masculine and unrelated personalities. The primacy of the sun god among the Apinayé[46] leads Adolf E. Jensen to the conclusion that the mythical solar hero had undergone a secondary identification with a supreme god who originated in another culture.[47] Jensen points to the phrase 'my father' used in addressing the sun god as creator of mankind, the prayers which are addressed to him, and a number of extremely vivid accounts of dreams such as that in which an Apinayé chief told of an encounter with the sun father (in human shape) during a hunting expedition. Haekel too raises the question whether the relationship between sun god and moon god among the Ge tribes, and particularly the Apinayé, is based on that between the supreme being and his companion (the culture hero or 'trickster').[48] The Apinayé ascribe to the sun the establishment of the dual organization of the tribe and the allotment of specific localities to the two halves. In emergencies such as illness the Apinayé address the sun father in improvised prayers. Before the seed-sowing the sun is asked to protect the crops, and at the beginning of the harvest there is a four-day solar dance festival in which the dancers wear the red body paint appropriate to the sun. Although idols are absent, the circular Apinayé village and the round meat patties eaten at the festivals represent the sun disc. Prayers for the prosperity of the crops are also offered up to the moon; and each new moon is marked by special dances and songs which are said to have been taught by the moon god himself.

The Canella, unlike the Apinayé, do not refer to personal revelations vouchsafed by their astral deities, but they have public prayers for rain, for the safety of game animals, and for successful harvests of wild and cultivated plants, e.g.: 'May the great father (sun) protect all animals, so that they grow up and can be eaten by human beings.' Then the suppliant enumerates a long list of animal species which he seeks to place under the protection of the sun.[49] Improvised personal prayers are addressed to the sun and moon in such emergencies as the sickness of a child.

According to the Apinayé the sun and moon gods created mankind by throwing bottle gourds into a stream; and according to the Canella they did so by leaping into a stream themselves. The Sherente have no myth concerning the creation of mankind; but they nevertheless call the sun 'our Creator' and approach him with the same profound religious awe as do the Apinayé.

The Sherente sun and moon gods do not appear in person; divine instructions are conveyed to mankind by astral deities and are either acting on their own account or as emissaries of the two great gods. Such revelations are not the result of ritual preparations of any kind. The emissaries of the sun include the planets Venus and Jupiter; those of the moon include the planet Mars. All these luminaries appear only in human shape; the envoys of the sun visit only the members of the sun moiety of the tribe, and those of the moon visit only the moon moiety. The chosen individuals to whom these visions are granted also play an important part in the 'great feast', the principal ceremony of the Sherente, which was originally only performed when an angry sun had prolonged or intensified the dry season. A pole is set up, and the worshippers climb it in order to worship the sun. At the end of the rite the master of ceremonies climbs to the top himself, turns his head to the east, and receives a message by way of a star in the constellation Orion, usually to the effect that the sun is content with the rite and will send down rain providing that the ancient customs of the tribe are adhered to. Haekel draws attention to the obvious affinities between this Sherente custom and the Botocudo use of a ceremonial pole as a link with the celestial world.[50]

The echoes of a supreme being concept among the tribes of the Tupi-Guarani linguistic group are mentioned by Métraux.[51] The creator is often described here as a 'transformer' (culture hero), and he is usually also the lawgiver and tutor of mankind. After he has performed these tasks he departs westward to the end of the world, where he rules over the shades of the dead. Among the Tupinamba and Guarayu there are traces of a cult of the creator Tamoi. In Métraux's opinion the various Tupinamba culture heroes (Monan, Maira-Monan, Maira Potchy, Mairata, Sume) are all derived from a single mythical figure, the tribal grandfather Tamoi.[52] When there was an eclipse of the sun or moon, a phenomenon which the Tupinamba believed might herald the end of the world, the men sang a hymn to Tamoi while the women and children wailed and threw themselves to the ground in a paroxysm of despair. This eschatological turn of mind may be linked with the various messianic movements which swept the Tupinamba from the beginning of Portuguese colonization onwards and frequently led to mass migrations in search of the mythical land of Tamoi, which was thought of as a paradise whose inhabitants partook of immortality, eternal youth and other blessings. Among the Guarayu the Tamoi cult was seen in close association with a messianic movement at the beginning of the nineteenth century. Here too Tamoi is seen as the ruler of the celestial western kingdom of the dead, and his cult is linked with burial rites and beliefs about the hereafter.[53]

In the mid-nineteenth century the Apiacá worshipped a god who was the creator of heaven and earth and who gave vent to his wrath in thunder and lightning. His name Bahyra is linked by Nimuendajú with that of the Tupinamba culture hero Maira.[54]

The supreme deity of the Apapocuva-Guarani is the Creator Ñanderuvuçu, 'our great father', who has withdrawn to a remote region of eternal darkness illuminated only by the light of his breast.[55] There he has the means to destroy the world, and he delays their use only as long as he pleases. Day-to-day happenings on earth do not interest him, and there is no indication of an active cult of Ñanderuvuçu among the Apapocuva-Guarani. His wife is Ñandecy, 'our mother', who dwells in the 'land without evil', a paradise sometimes believed to be in the east, sometimes in the west, and which formed the goal of a number of migrations which took place under the influence of the messianic cults. According to the Mbyá (Guaranian) the supreme god Ñamandu dwells in the east and sends life to the world. The Mbyá pray to him for good health and success in the hunt in formulas such as the following:

O Ñamandu, permit us to kill an animal on your way. Lead the animals to us. Allow us then to return to our village, where our wives are. Lead the peccary to us too. May your sons watch over us and lead us to the tapir and the deer, and may we be able to kill them and take them home to our wives that we may all rejoice.[56]

These figures, with their strong affinity to the concept of a supreme being, bear the stamp of great antiquity; but the same cannot be said of the god of the ancient Tupi-Guarani tribes, Tupan. This deity started as a thunder spirit and was only elevated to the dignity of a supreme being by the early missionaries who likened him to the Christian God.[57]

Tupan is the term generally used for the Christian God among the Guarani-speaking population of Brazil and Paraguay; in some groups, notably the Tenetehara, he also appears in the guise of a native supreme god, a clear result of Christian influence on native religion.[58]

Not only the comparatively recently developed eastern Tupian cultures, such as that of the Tupinamba, but also the older culture of the central Tupians, display the belief in a supreme being. Among the Mundurucú in particular this belief has been recorded by several workers since the end of the nineteenth century. The most prominent figure in Mundurucú mythology is Karusakaibe, the 'father of the Mundurucú' as he is called by the Franciscan missionary Albert Kruse, whose work over many years is the best source of understanding on the subject.[59] Karusakaibe now has many features of a culture hero, but Gusinde,[60] in a sharply critical review of Robert F. Murphy's *Mundurucú Religion*,[61] has shown that Karusakaibe was originally regarded as a supreme being associated with a separate culture hero or 'trickster', and that he was transformed into a culture hero only at a later stage, a process which is by no means uncommon in the thought of South American Indians.

The available information may be summarized as follows: Karusakaibe once lived on earth and created human souls, the sky, the stars, game animals, fish and cultivated plants, together with all their respective guardian spirits; and he made the trees and plants fruitful.[62] Karusakaibe is omniscient; he taught the Mundurucú the arts of hunting and farming and such allied skills as tattooing and the roasting of manioc meal. He did not originate the whole of Mundurucú culture; but he is the lawgiver of the tribe and the originator of its dualistic structure. Although married, Karusakaibe has never slept with his wife. She conceived one son, Kurumtau, from a word spoken by her husband, and he carved another son from the wood of a tree. Karusakaibe is immortal; badly treated by the Mundurucú, he finally went to a place where there is no sky, only mist. It is also said of him that he transformed himself into the blazing sun of the dry season. When the end of the world comes Karusakaibe will incinerate mankind; but until then he looks after the well-being of the Mundurucú, his children; for he is basically well disposed towards them, although he punishes them when they infringe his laws. Prayers for success are addressed to him before hunting and fishing, and thanks are offered up to him afterwards; the same is done in cases of illness.

Donald Horton tells of a Mundurucú ceremony in which a tree is set up in the middle of the dwelling house, and the shaman, smoking tobacco, invokes the protection of Karusakaibe while the worshippers gather round the tree; a ritual also present among the Botocudo.[63]

The myth cycle which centres on Karusakaibe, as it has been accorded by Kruse, displays a whole series of Christian features which are consistent with the supposition that the Mundurucú have consciously identified Karusakaibe with the Christian God. So Karusakaibe has returned to his original function as a supreme being; but this obvious result of modern cultural influence can be discounted in dealing with the true original nature of this Indian deity.

Even more than the Tupians, the Caribans of the Guianas and elsewhere show signs of a tendency towards monotheism or rather henotheism, the primacy of one god among many. Here again, Albert Kruse is our principal source of information, in an illuminating paper on Purá, the supreme being in the religion of the Arikena or Warikyana, a Carib tribe in northern Purá.[64] This work has led Josef Haekel to discuss tendencies towards monotheism among the Caribans and other native ethnic groups in the Guianas and the territories to the west, in a paper on which the following brief account is based.[65]

Purá is the traditional name for 'god' among the Arikena. Purá and his servant Mura are little men with red faces and long beards. They have no parents, brothers, sisters or wives; they are immortal and ageless, and they shed their skins like snakes. They stand at the zenith, the peak of the sky mountain, to watch everything that happens. But only Purá is in control of everything. Mura has been known to do things wrong. Purá and Mura appeared at the beginning of the world together with the waters, the earth and the sky; but no one really knows how earth and sky came into being. At Purá's command the sky sends rain. The sky consists of mist and is inhabited by little men and women who do not, however, marry each other 'because it would not be proper in the presence of Purá' (!). The sky men are all servants of Purá and make the thunder and lightning. In the sky there are also various animals in holes; these are the constellations.

When Purá came down to earth with his servant, he carved pairs of human figures from the wood or certain trees, and they came to life and multiplied. He created the animals in the same way.

Purá wished to give mankind immortality; but as they failed to comply with his instructions, which included shedding their skins, they must die. Purá gave mankind a number of ethical precepts in song and then returned with Mura to the sky. When the human race were disobedient, Purá sent a great fire and a deluge. Some human beings survived the cataclysm, but Purá will set fire to the world again when man's wickedness brings it to an end; a belief strongly reminiscent of the eschatology of the Tupinamba and the Apapocuva-Guarani. According to Kruse's informant, prayers are offered up to Purá, and there is also a festival in his honour called the *Puráwokura*, at which an intoxicating liquor called *kashiri* is consumed and manioc cakes are offered up to Purá.

The foremost living authority on the Cariban tribes of Brazilian Guiana, another Franciscan, Fr Protasius Frikel, confirms this information on the Arikena and is able to complete or correct it on several points.[66]

According to Frikel, the Arikena identify the supreme being with the *Ursonne*, the primal sun. Purá is sometimes identified with this being, but is also sometimes said to be (or to have been?) the world on which the *Ursonne* poured out its blinding light. 'Purá' also signifies supernatural powers that are active everywhere; a belief that Frikel considers to be a comparatively recent accretion. Purá is often referred to as a 'primal man' (*Urmensch*) or culture hero. This idea of the god corresponds to the remarks made by many of Frikel's informants, who said that Purá had only 'connections' with the supreme godhead or the *Ursonne*, whose true name is unknown. However this may be, Purá lives in the sky and has authority over the elements, which he created in an unknown fashion. His servant and companion Mura has some connection with the moon and displays some features of a 'trickster'. After death the soul of the individual rises to heaven to join its other-world sib (patrilineal subdivision of tribe) before being reincarnated. The Cachuyana, as one section of the Arikena are called, say 'we die for the other world'. The model to which they liken human life is the eternal circling of the sun. As Kruse tells us, everyone, even the wicked, is finally believed to go to Father Purá in heaven.[67]

Haekel says that Purá as a name for the supreme being is not used by any Cariban tribe other than the Arikena, but reappears in a slightly different form in the western part of the Guianas among tribes belonging to other linguistic families.[68] According to Haekel the Surára and Pakidái, two tribes belonging to the isolated Waica and Shiriana linguistic family, which live on two tributaries on the left bank of the Rio Negro, say that Poré was the name given to the supreme being when he descended to earth.[69] This supreme being is identified by the Surára and Pakidái with the moon, and the sun is regarded as totally insignificant. Poré is also the name of a non-personal entity which is worshipped.[70] I have elsewhere called into question the assertion that the Poré of the Surára and Pakidái is a name for the supreme being.[71]

There is no room to repeat my arguments in detail here; but they are on the lines of Haekel's own remark that 'rather than a name for the supreme being, Purá is probably a descriptive term, perhaps meaning something like "holy" or "full of power".'[72]

Another similar name for the supreme being has been found by Haekel among the Sáliva, an isolated linguistic group in the savannahs of Colombia west of the middle reaches of the Orinoco.[73] The Sáliva believe in a supreme being called Purú.[74] Purú is believed to have existed long before the objects of the natural world. He is the creative power from which all things grow. A number of other supernatural powers, emanations of Purú, are regarded as persons (but not as entities independent of Purú?). In the beginning Purú, who is something like the air but cannot really be imagined, blew into the clouds and caused the first rain, thus causing the earth to grow fruitful and bring forth plants, animals and human beings. Purú rules over the members of the human race and sends them good or bad fortune according to their conduct. When he wishes to punish mankind for its sins he unleashes the elements. He once sent a deluge when men turned against him; and the survivors worshipped Purú and brought him offerings of fruit. The present-day Sáliva do not invoke Purú directly; their prayers reach him through the mediation of personified forces of nature, such as wind, fire, earthquake and thunder.

Haekel sees in these features of the Sáliva god Purú definite affinities with the Arikena conception of Purá.[75] One of the personified natural forces who emanate from Purú, Qurrama Minari, the hidden power of vegetation, seems to have a specially close link with the Creator, and re-appears among the neighbouring Achagua, an Arawakan tribe, as Gurrana Minari.[76] Haekel inclines to the supposition that the culturally younger tribe, the polytheistic Achagua, have exerted an influence on the older, monotheistic Sáliva.[77] The neighbouring Guahibo, another linguistically isolated group, have merged the words for two related concepts into one and called the god Purna Minali.[78] The Maipure, an Arawakan people of the Ventuari estuary, once knew this composite deity as Pura Minari, and in one of the myths of the Baré, another Arawakan tribe on the Casiquiare, Porona Minari (or Poronominare) is described as lord of all things and ruler of heaven and earth.[79] Porona Minari has a special link with animals, and it was he who gave them their allotted place on earth.[80]

Haekel draws further evidence from the work of C.H. de Goeje[81] and the Penard brothers[82] concerning the supreme being concept among the Cariban tribes of the coast of Surinam. The Caliña Carib myth runs more or less as follows: The universe has its source in Amana, a virgin mother and water goddess who has no navel (i.e. was never born), a beautiful woman whose body ends in a serpent. She is the essence of time, has borne all things, can adopt any shape, dwells in the waters of the heavens and exercises her power from the Pleiades. She is also called a serpent spirit and a sun serpent. Amana is a personification of 'eternity'. She renews herself continually, by sloughing her skin like a snake. She is also called Wala Yumu, 'spirit of the kinds', and is the ruler of all water spirits.[83]

Amana gave birth to twin brothers, Tamusi and Yolokan Tamulu: the first was born at first light, the second at dusk . . . Tamusi is the creator of all good things and the ancestor of the Caliña. He is visualized in human shape. Tamusi is present in the cold light of the moon. He is also lord of the celestial paradise, the 'land without evening', which he never leaves. The souls of the righteous go to his shining kingdom, but the light that surrounds him is too bright for them to see him. Tamusi has fought against the fiends. His constellation also that of his mother Amana, the Pleiades. The constellation of his adversaries, the fiends, is a celestial serpent which has already several times devoured the Pleiades and thus brought the world to an end. Each time Tamusi created the world anew, and he will do so once again.

Yolokan Tamulu is the lord, or alternatively the grandfather (tamulu), of the nature spirits (yolokan). De Goeje and Haekel both see him as the representative of the active but dark and hidden aspect of the mother goddess Amara. Yolokan Tamulu is the source of darkness and mischief. Like his brother, he lives in the sky; but his home is an island in the murkiest depths of the sky, in the 'land without morning'. Haekel considers the available evidence insufficient to class Yolokan Tamulu as a 'trickster' or adversary of Tamusi; he sees him as merely a necessary complement to Tamusi. Tamusi without his brother would be as unthinkable as light without darkness.

Haekel classifies both twins as gods because of their sovereign status. One of them, Tamusi, seems to outrank the other in many respects, so that in Haekel's view he has certain essential attributes of a supreme being. Tamusi is the 'grandfather of all grandfathers' and is described both by the brothers Penard and by de Goeje as 'God' in the Christian sense. His name has been connected not only with the word tamulu (grandfather) but with the Caliña adjective si (little).

There is an etymological and conceptual link between Tamusi and Tamoi, the mythical grandfather believed in by the ancient eastern Tupians; and this is not unexpected in view of the known close relationship between the Tupian and Cariban mythologies. The absence of a true proper name – Tamusi and Yolokan Tamulu are both mere periphrases – is interpreted by Haekel as an expression of the extremely elevated rank of these deities. He seeks to associate both the twins and their mother Amana with shamanism; shamans can contact Amana in their trance states.[85] Significantly, Tamusi and Yolokan Tamulu together are symbolized by one stone in the *maraca* of the shaman.[86]

The writings of the Renards and de Goeje on coastal Cariban religion must be approached with some caution, as the Renard brothers do not always fully distinguish between fact and interpretation. Nevertheless the beliefs recorded by them are shared in many respects by the various Carib neighbours of the Caliña in the northern Guianas. Roth rejects the idea that the Guianese natives believe in a supreme being at all,[87] but Lowie describes this as not strictly true.[88] He refers to the belief of the Barama River Caribs of northern Guyana that there is a supreme creator god, a *deus otiosus*, who as Haekel admits is rather vaguely defined.[89] The true name of this supreme being is unknown even to the shamans, and they are unable to communicate with him. He is referred to as Iopotari Akura, 'boss spirit', and considered to be a good entity on the whole. Iopatari Akuru established everything, created the universe and conversed in ancient times with mankind. He is distant and yet omnipresent, causes the phases of the moon, and controls the heavenly bodies in general. He has a number of associates, the most important of whom is Komanokaro, his 'executive arm', who concerns himself with more detailed matters, and who, although far removed from human concerns, can be reached by the most experienced shamans. John Gillin, who has made a detailed study of the religion of this Carib group, remarks that the Barama River conception of the supreme being cannot be derived from Christian influence, as it is present in the very earliest written sources which deal with Guianese Indians.[90] Elsewhere, however, he emphasizes that the supreme deity recognized, but not worshipped, by most Guianese Indians is *not* clearly visualized as the creator of the universe.[91]

Another Guianese Cariban tribe, the extinct Tamanac of the middle reaches of the Orinoco, believed that the earth and the Orinoco were created by Amalivaca and his brother Votchi.[92] Amalivaca is also linked with the tides. Once he dwelt among men; a certain steep cliff was his house. Before he departed he said that he was about to shed his skin and that men should do the same in order to grow young again. One woman seemed to doubt the efficacy of this procedure; and angered by her lack of faith, Amalivaca said that she would die. And

247

so death came into the world. This is strongly reminiscent of an Arikena tradition concerning Purá; and Amalivaca as creator is also a masculine variant of the Caliña mother goddess Amana. Important character-istics of Amalivaca are also present in the figure of Guanari, who accord-ing to Haekel is the supreme being of the Makiritare, another Cariban tribe.[93] Guanari has always existed and is immortal.[94] He created three other deities, and in ancient times came to a certain place on the Río Cunucunuma, a tributary of the Orinoco, where he fashioned human beings from earth, and left his footprint on a rock (just as Amalivaca carved glyphs in the rocky banks of the Orinoco).[95] The most powerful being known to the Cunuana, a branch of the Makiritare on the Río Cunucunuma, is Uanari, creator of all things, who created first the animals, then the plants and finally the first couple of human beings.[96] Uanari lives in a state of constant warfare with Káhû, the chief of the evil spirits, who in spite of his name is definitely unconnected with the sky (which in Cariban is *kahú*). The Makiritare of the upper Padamo (another tributary of the Orinoco) believe in a supreme god whose name is Uanadi. According to Koch-Grünberg the 'greatest god' of the Yecuana (another branch of the Makiritare) is called Uanali Hohoinye, and lives with his wife beyond the eastern sky.[97] The little information we have on this deity reveals civilized influence. There is also another figure called Uanali, who is the ancestor of the Makiritare and all other Indians, and who also lives in the east and is present in the rock crystal which the shamans use in their cures.

Haekel traces a further link between the supreme being *cum* ancestor Guanari (or Uanali) and Omaua (or Omayali), a supernatural figure in the mythology of the Waica of the upper Orinoco, a tribe linguistic-ally and culturally related to the Surára and Pakidái.[98] The Waica believe that Omaua created the earth and most living things. He also caused the deluge, and with his companion Yoaua still sends rain from the celestial rivers. Omaua dwells in the western sky and on the western earth, i.e. down the Orinoco, where he is linked, strangely enough, with foreigners, the white intruders and their evil influences. There is a basic resemblance here to what the Yecuana say about Uanali Hohoinye. Once Omaua lived with the Waica. As the most important figure in the magical-religious world he is invoked by the shamans both for black and white magic. Omaua is an ambivalent figure. Omayali, on the other hand, who lives with him, is a purely hostile cannibal being who nevertheless played an (unspecified) part in the creation of mankind.[99]

I would describe Omaua as a god; Haekel goes further and calls him a supreme being.[100] He accepts the probability, first mooted by me, that at least the names of Omaua and Omayali were borrowings from Carib or Arawak neighbours; but he also supposes that these neighbours had the conception of a supreme being – such as the Poré of the Surára and Pakidái – before the culturally 'older' Waica. In the absence of more detailed evidence, I cannot share this view. Omaua was described by American Protestant missionaries, working on the upper Orinoco in 1954–5, as *the* supernatural being believed in by the Waica who came closest to the idea of the Christian God, and it was debated whether the idea of 'God' should not perhaps be introduced under the name of 'Omaua'. This is a good and recent example of the process by which not a few of the conceptions of supreme beings found among South American Indians must have come into being. The supernatural being whose name is the most closely related etymologically to Omaua and Omayali happens to be an evil principle, the Umuauri of the (Cariban) Paravilhana and the (Arawakan) Manao.[101] The corresponding good entity is called Mauari; but in many places this name, said by Koch-Grünberg to be derived from the western Arawakan languages, has an ambivalent character.[102] The Baniwa, Arawakans of the upper Río Negro and Atapapo, use the name Mauari for the supreme so-called 'evil' spirit.[103] He appears masked at the puberty rites of the girls, and women are forbidden to look upon him on pain of death. Wilhelm Saake has published some previously unknown information on another figure in Baniwa mythology, which throws considerable light on the subject in hand;[104] although Fr Saake himself considers that it is not yet possible to fit the figure in question, Inapirikuri, into his proper place in Baniwa mythology.[105] Inapirikuri was the first living creature. His name indicates that he consisted entirely of bones; this is intended to confirm his permanent nature. He has no wife, but he made companions for himself out of clay. He drew the first human beings, all of them Baniwa, from a hole in the ground, and sent them to the places where they were to live as ancestors of the present-day groups within the Baniwa tribe. Inapirikuri left the early men a number of precepts, such as the laws of exogamy and monogamy. He is omniscient.

Somewhat earlier reports by Koch-Grünberg also refer to Yapericuli (i.e. Inapirikuri) as the tribal ancestor of the Arawakan tribes.[106] Here too he is described as the first man and the first Baniwa, but he is also *tupana* ('god', cf. Tupan).

A clearer supreme being concept than that of the Baniwa is found in Ribeiro de Sampaio's late eighteenth-century account of another Arawakan tribe, the Pasé.[107] They believed, we are told, in a creator and in a future life involving reward and punishment. This upper world was divided into several layers, and in the topmost layer lived God. His name is not given, but a version of the creation myth of the Paressi of Mato Grosso, another Arawakan tribe, refers to a supreme being called Enore, who is supposed to have carved the first man and woman from wood.[108] Enore shared his gifts between the two sons of this pair, one of whom took the Indian tools used by the Paressi and the other chose the achievements of European civilization, which made his descendants, the white men, rulers of the earth. This is the kind of obviously recent element which we frequently encounter in what the South American Indians say on the subject of the supreme being. The nomadic Nambicuara, who are less advanced than their neighbours the Paressi and linguistically distinct from them, nevertheless live in a sort of partial symbiosis with them. Lévi-Strauss tells us that the Nambicuara regard the thunder as a supreme being with whom every man (but usually a shaman) can make personal contact through revelations and visions.[109]

The Goajiro, a pastoral Arawakan tribe living on the Goajiro peninsula on the coast of Venezuela, believe in a creator god called Mareigua or Maleiwa, whom Armstrong and Métraux describe as a culture hero as well as a supreme being.[110] Maleiwa requires observance of certain moral laws; in former times he punished those who lived in incest. He drew the first Goajiro from the earth, taught them how to kindle fire with a fire drill, and saved them from the deluge by lifting up the mountain on which they had taken refuge. He still sends the rain and all the blessings of nature.

Our survey of the conceptions of a supreme being among the Arawakan tribes would be incomplete without some mention of the beliefs of the Arawakan inhabitants of the Greater Antilles. Irving Rouse says that the Taino, when asked about their supreme god, spoke of an immortal, invisible being called Yocahu Vague Maorocon.[111] Walter Krickeberg goes into greater detail.

The Taino believe in a supreme being dwelling in heaven, who is indifferent to mankind and cannot be reached by their prayers. His name perhaps has some connection with *yuca*, the Taino word for manioc; it was he who gave this staple food to mankind. In order to continue to enjoy rain and the other blessings which proceed from Yocahu, the human race must pray to the *zemi*, wooden or stone idols inhabited by the spirits of dead chiefs; these benevolent beings can influence Yocahu.[112]

We see that here as elsewhere acts of worship are addressed not to the supreme being himself but to intermediaries.

In the Orinoco delta there still exists a remnant of an older ethnic group which has been caught between Cariban elements on one side and Arawakans on the other. This linguistically isolated tribe is the Warrau. It was already known that they believed in a supreme being[113] when Johannes Wilbert[114] undertook a detailed study of this phenomenon. The supreme being Kanobo ('grandfather') is the creator and guardian of the world, and lives in heaven, attended by a hierarchy of spirits. He and most of his attendant spirits are powerful and benevolent protectors of man. God punishes the human race only when it is disobedient or lacking in respect. Kanobo is usually represented by anthropomorphic images made of wood, stone or clay, and sometimes also by a polished stone axe blade. The Warrau keep their idol in a temple set apart from the other houses and constructed rather differently, in which the priest (wisiratu) often makes his home.

Every year the Warrau perform a propitiatory ceremony at the time when Kanobo rises from his throne and causes the rivers to overflow their banks; this is a time of sickness and death, especially among the children.[115] Large quantities of starch flour from the moriche palm, and piles of fish, are placed in the temple as offerings to Kanobo. After several nights of singing and dancing Kanobo tells the priest that he has blessed the offerings and released them to the people for consumption. The ritual accompanying this festival includes a dance round the sacred central pole of a house, accompanied by prayers for the safety of the children, which Wilbert believes to belong to an archaic substratum of Warrau culture.[116] Temple worship as such, according to Wilbert, is a later borrowing from the Andean civilizations which has reached the Orinoco delta in way of the Circum-Caribbean culture.

Wilbert believes that the concept of a supreme being existed before there was temple worship; but he points not only to Andean theological influences (such as the hierarchical arrangement of the gods), but also to Christian influences in the actual beliefs concerning the supreme being himself. This has suggested to other workers that the Warrau supreme being concept may not be so old as Wilbert thinks.[117]

The temple worship addressed to a supreme being, which Wilbert found among the Warrau, also existed among the vanished Timote group of the Venezuelan Andes. This is a clear indication of the Andean origins of this religious feature as far as the Warrau are concerned. The Timote believed in a supreme being, Ches, dwelling in lakes and on the highest mountain tops and worshipped not only in temples in the middle of settlements, but on mountains and in caves as well.[118] The idols were made of cotton, clay, wood or stone. Votive offerings were of many kinds, and included the skulls and bones of deer whose flesh was burned. Before planting their fruit trees, one Timote tribe, the Miguri, carried out a nocturnal ceremony called the 'coming down of Ches' which involved miming the actions of sowing and harvesting.

In another ceremony the participants whipped each other. These features show that the Timote supreme being, at least as far as the Miguri tribe were concerned, had a close connection with the fruit-fulness of food plants, a feature shared by the Yocahu of the West Indian Taino. His designation Ches recalls the name Es applied by the neigh-bouring Betoi (a Chibchan tribe) to the sun, whom they regard as the creator and protector (of the world?).[119]

The gap between the Timote and the Warrau was once filled by a number of advanced Cariban tribes living north of the Orinoco. These peoples worshipped principally the sun and moon (as man and wife).[120] The tendency of these Orinoco tribes to concentrate on one of the two astral deities at the expense of the other leads Lowie to detect signs of a supreme being cult.[121]

One deity who has the unmistakable characteristics of a supreme being is the great goddess Kuma of the Yaruro, a tribe living along the Río Capanaparo in Venezuela. Kuma must originally have been a moon goddess and consort of a sun god who is now considered un-important. She created the world with the assistance of two brothers, the water serpent Puaná and the jaguar Itciai.[122] These in their turn created the earth and the water. The first human beings were the Yaruro, apparently created by Kuma herself. The culture hero or educator of mankind was Kuma's son Hatchawa, who had received his learning from the water serpent Puaná. When mankind turned to evil ways, Kuma sent a great flood. The human survivors of this flood divided the Yaruro tribe into the exogamous matrilineal moieties into which it is still divided, and which are named after Puaná and Itciai. Kuma has a kingdom far to the west, a happy land in which every terrestrial animal and plant species has a gigantic counterpart. The only members of the tribe who know anything about Kuma are the shamans. After long years of preparation they are able to see the land of Kuma in a dream or in a vision. The first chants in any shamanistic séance describe the journey of the shaman's soul to the land of Kuma. The shaman has a pole set up before him, and round this men and women dance in separate circles. This pole probably represents the link between this world and the other world; there is an obvious parallel here with Botocudo and Warrau ceremonies in honour of the supreme being. When the soul arrives at its destination the shaman rattles his *maraca* vigorously. It is incised with an anthropomorphic figure of Kuma with upraised arms – carved by the shaman as a record of what he sees during his visit to the beyond.

One informant quoted by Vincenzo Petrullo in the report, published in 1939, which is still our best source of information on Yaruro religion, summed up his ideas about Kuma in the words: 'Everything sprang from Kuma, and everything that the Yaruro do was arranged so by her – the other gods and culture heroes act according to her laws.' Métraux, who quotes these decisive words, draws attention to the typological affinities between Kuma and the Cágaba mother goddess Gauteóvan, which suggest definite links between the Yaruro and the advanced peoples of the northern Andes.[123]

Similar Andean connections are detectable in the religious ideas of the Witotoans, tribes living along the Río Putumayo on the borders of Columbia and Peru, as recorded by Konrad Theodor Preuss. Preuss was convinced that the creator god Moma ('father') was the dominant and indeed the only important deity.[124] Moma alone stands out from the complexities of Witotoan theology as the prime mover and maintainer of the world.[125] Among his many aspects, Moma is identified with the moon, and this leads Preuss to interpret the myths and religious practices of the Witotoans in terms of a lunar religion.[126] The only entity whom Preuss regards as solar is an immortal sky god, Husiniamui, who has many features in common with Moma, and who has a special concern with killing, headhunting and cannibalism. Jensen, who makes a thorough study of the concept of Moma and the religion and world view of the Witotoans in general, sees Husiniamui merely as a variant of Moma specifically concerned with his lunar (*not* his solar) aspect.[127] Jensen regards Moma as a culture hero or tribal benefactor of a special category for which he has coined the term *Dema-Gottheit*; he concedes that this father god does possess some of the characteristics of a supreme being.[128]

According to the Witotoan creation myth, Moma came into being without a father or mother; he was created by the 'word', by which is meant the supernatural powers attached to certain parareligious formulas and myths. He was also himself the personification of the word, and he transmitted it to the first human beings, who despite his title of 'father' are never referred to as his 'sons'. It was Moma who first instituted all religious ceremonies, but he is not directly worshipped; his religious importance lies in the belief that without him all chants and all rituals would be ineffective.[129] Moma created the world and all that it contains from the archetype, the 'seeming thing' (*naino*), the 'not-being substance' of each individual entity. In this connection his title is Nainuema, 'he who is (or has) what is not there (what is inexplicable, an illusion)'.[130]

This agrees with the fact that in a myth concerning the creation of the organic world, Moma is said to have drawn plants and animals from his own body. He is still present especially in the food plants (this passive element, linked with an active element in the same being, is one of the identifying characteristics of a *Dema-Gottheit* according to Jensen, who considers the *Dema-Gottheit* concept to have wholly different origins from the concept of a supreme being). When the trees on earth have no fruit, they go to the second lowest underworld, where as the first being ever to suffer death, Moma dwells as the lord of the dead; this is in addition to his celestial existence as the moon. In the fruit of the trees Moma returns to life again.

Preuss mentions the extraordinary parallel between this myth, in which Moma is both the possessor of 'the word' and actually identified with it, and the famous passage in the New Testament (St John 1:1) in which we read; 'In the beginning was the Word, and the Word was with God, and the Word was God.'[131] Preuss does not see this as a sign of Christian influence; the Witotoan sky god Huisiniamui, whom he regards as a separate concept, is much more likely to have come under the influence of missionaries, who selected him as a representative of the Christian God.[132] Métraux is inclined to see the abstract figure of Moma as the creation of a single brilliant metaphysical thinker; to my mind it suggests rather the tendency towards speculative thought common among the priests of many advanced cultures.[133]

Steward is unconvinced that Christian influence is present in Witotoan religion.[134] He can find little evidence of missionary activity, and cites the analogy of the supreme being believed in by the neighbouring Tucanoan tribes, a deity who seems to me rather pale by comparison with Moma-Huisiniamui.

Hömänihikö or Hümanihinkü, who according to Irving Goldmann is the supreme god of the Tucanoan tribes and especially of the Cubeo, has a house in heaven where he lives with his wife and receives the spirits of the dead, who offer gifts in return for permission to cross his threshold.[135] He created the earth and the rivers, but he does not intervene in human affairs. Goldmann considers Hömänihikö to be a product of Christian acculturation, and in this he has the support of many Indian informants.

More than thirty years before, Koch-Grünberg's informants had given him to understand that Hömänihikö was the tribal ancestor of the Cubeo, that he lived in a house on a high mountain range, and that he later went to heaven.[136] He is referred to as *tupána*. He was a great sorcerer who could change himself at will into an animal and back again. At his birth he sprang forth as a fully grown Cubeo warrior in full dance costume and slew all manner of animals and men. This may well be a reflection of the victories of the Cubeo over the earlier inhabitants of the upper Río Negro area. One of Hömänihikö's principal achievements was to wrest manioc, the staple vegetable food, from the vulture people; so he also sometimes appears in the guise of a fertility spirit.

Hömänihikö's brother Kuwai (Kúai, Koai), on the other hand, is a fertility spirit first and foremost. According to Koch-Grünberg he was a secondary addition to Cubeo mythology; originally he was one of the ancestors of the Arawakan tribes, and the son of Inapirikuri (Yapirikuli), the 'first Baniwa'.[137] Kuwai, unlike Hömänihikö, is the object of a cult, and is discussed in my chapter on vegetation spirits. According to Koch-Grünberg the ruler of the dead is the third of Hömänihikö's brothers, the deformed Mianikötöibo, who lives with his wife Wänio in a fine, spacious 'stone house' (i.e. mountain range) and is the overlord of all Cubeo souls and all macaws; this last suggests that the souls of the dead may actually be identified with macaws.[138] Of these three divine brothers, the two who are native to Cubeo mythology, Hömänihikö and Mianikötöibo, are reminiscent of the twin heroes so common in South American mythologies.

Among the tribes of the Panoan linguistic family in the western part of tropical South America, the Chama tribes of the Ucayali river in western Brazil have been stigmatized by Günter Tessmann as 'Men without God'.[139] But although Tessmann denies that they have any belief in a god, Izaguirre says of one Chama tribe, the Conibo, that they believe in a god called Mueraya, who rules the sky and the jaguars and who helps the shamans.[140]

Rafael Girard was told by an old member of the Shipibo (a Chama tribe) that his people believed in an omnipotent supreme god, Iba,[141] who was invisible to ordinary mortals.[142] Iba lives in the mist of the heavens and is consequently also called Kanarawa, 'lord of the sky'. Iba created the earth and the sky as well as the human race. Snakes and lizards are his servants, and through their agency he sends rain when the shaman prays for it. Iba's hammock is woven of water serpents; his seat is a turtle; and among his retainers is a ferocious jaguar which lies down in the path of the dead and forces them to make a detour in order to reach the kingdom of Iba.

The Cashinawa, a Panoan tribe of the Jurua-Purus region, believe in an 'old father' who dwells with his wife the 'old mother' in the sky. He is also the thunder god and ruler of the 'lightning people' whose principal function is to carry the souls of the dead to heaven and provide them with all kinds of food and possessions. Capistrano de Abreu, the best authority on the Cashinawa, identifies the 'old father' with another, purely mythological figure, Poka, the 'good one' who once wanted to make mankind immortal. Métraux sees the 'old father' as a parallel figure to the creator god and 'great ancestor' of other South American tribes.[143]

Civilized influence from the Andean peoples is apparent in the true pantheons and temple cults possessed by certain tribes. The religion of the Araona, a Tacana tribe, showed particularly strong signs of this influence when the Franciscan missionary Nicolas Armentia visited them in the late nineteenth century.[144] The principal deity was Baba-Buada, a wind god, who possessed the status of a Creator. He was the lord of the seasons, and determined the times for sowing and harvesting the crops. Many other deities were subordinate to him. The gods were often represented by small wooden idols decorated in feather mosaic, which were set up in rectangular temple buildings in the forest and tended by special priests (*yanacona*). There were major festivals at seed-time and harvest.

K. Hissink now confirms the existence of a supreme deity in Tacana religion.[145] In addition, Métraux cites the testimony of the priest Lucas Caballero, who in 1706 visited the now extinct (Chiquitoan) Manasi.[146] Their principal deity was Omequituriqui ('father god') also known as Oracozorico, who begat the god Urasaña on the goddess Quipozi. These three, together with the associated thunder god Urapo Stiquitetu, were the 'higher gods' (Stinimaaka). Omequituriqui, who spoke in a loud voice, performed the functions of judge and avenger of the tribe. Disease and death were sent by him, and he appeared in person to sick people in order to lash them and torment them. However, Urasaña, Urapo Stiquitetu and above all Quipozi were on the side of the patient. The goddess Quipozi seems to have been especially popular. She was customarily addressed as 'our mother' and visualized as a gigantic lady with billowing white garments who protected the people from the anger of the other deities. When a sick votary invoked her name she came to his bedside and ordered the shamans to heal him.

The gods themselves were believed to 'descend' to earth at the ceremonies held in their honour. These took place in the large cabins which served as places of assembly for the Manasi and dwellings for their chiefs. Inside these was a sanctuary for the four Stinimaaka, partitioned off with mats, to which only the ceremonial priests (*mapono*), members of a class superior to the ordinary shamans, were admitted.

Offerings of *chicha* were made to the god. Then a high priest questioned him as to the outcome of future activities such as wars, hunting and fishing, and the harvest. The loud dialogue between them was conducted in a special liturgical language but was understood by almost all those present. Then game and fish were offered to the god. Finally the gods soared upwards, taking the priest (or shaman) with them; after a certain lapse of time he was returned to the temple, asleep, by the goddess Quipozi. Before returning to the heavenly kingdom, the goddess received offerings of food and *chicha*.

Belief in a supreme being takes many forms in South America. The wide variations of emphasis apparent in the versions of this concept discussed in this section is partly a result of my having cast my net rather wider than Métraux felt able to do.[147] In the majority of cases the deities concerned are celestial: personifications of the sky, the heavenly bodies or atmospheric phenomena. Many of them combine this cosmic aspect with that of a Creator, culture hero or ancestor. The supreme being also often has links with the staple food plant, and with plant fertility in general; and he also frequently rules the larger game animals.

The dominant god also often combines a number of aspects which would otherwise have belonged to a variety of inferior deities; but it is more common for these other gods to play a more prominent part than their nominal superior both in ritual practice and in religious thought. A specific *cult* of the supreme being is found almost exclusively in areas directly influenced by the advanced Andean civilizations, but *belief* in such a being is present at all levels of cultural development in South America. Its most perfect development is among the most primitive people of all, the pre-agricultural tribes of Tierra del Fuego. Wilhelm Koppers has once more argued that the supreme being concept is indigenous to the Yahgan of Tierra del Fuego.[148] Métraux too considers Fuegian religion to be essentially uninfluenced by Christianity in spite of a long period of contact with white people; he does however point to the remarkable affinities between the Fuegian conception of the supreme being and the Christian idea of God.[149] Métraux goes on to say that many details of the native supreme being tradition may well have been lost in the course of time, and that statements collected at the very last moment may consequently give the impression that this deity was conceived in much more abstract and theoretical terms than he really was. In my opinion, however, the striking example of the religions of Tierra del Fuego, and the other approximations to monotheism which have been discussed here, do not make it possible to conclude with any certainty that the belief in a supreme being was the *oldest* form of religion in primitive South America, nor that it was the *only* form of religion at the earliest stage of cultural development, that of the hunters and gatherers. On the contrary, in hunting societies as in more advanced cultural groups, the religious emphasis is on other themes. Nor is the belief in culture heroes and tribal ancestors, which I have discussed here together with the supreme being concept, commonly reflected in actual worship despite its profound social significance.[150] This is especially true of the twin heroes who so often appear as patrons of the dual organization of the tribe; but the mythical and ritual consequences of this are far too complex to discuss here in any detail.

The religious life of the tribes of primitive South America is dominated not by gods or heroes but by nature spirits.[151] Métraux draws a distinction between two classes of nature spirits: personalized 'daemons', entities with individual names, and nameless 'spirits' who are members of a collective.[152] However, the Indians themselves are not always able to distinguish between the two categories, or between nature spirits and 'ghosts' (the spirits of the dead).

All over South America natural objects and phenomena are personified or regarded as manifestations or dwelling places of supernatural beings; but there are great variations in the degree of individuality displayed by these beings and in their relationships with mankind.[153] Two broad categories may be distinguished: spirits connected with animals, whose importance is greatest for hunters and fishermen, and spirits connected with the plant world, whose importance is greatest for gatherers and agriculturalists.

II   *Spirits and Rituals of the Hunt*

The patrons or protectors of the game animals are among the most personalized of nature spirits.[1] Agricultural peoples often preserve many of the religious attitudes of a hunting and gathering culture;[2] but this section, which is based largely on my own detailed account of the subject,[3] is intended as a general picture of the thought and religious practice of the pure hunting tribes.

The concept of a 'lord of beasts', a ruler of all the animal species, is best exemplified in South America by the forest spirit Korupira or Kaapara believed in by the vanished Tupinamba of eastern Brazil and by the modern Tupian tribes, the Lingua Geral-speaking population of the Amazon basin.

The myths collected by Barbosa Rodrigues in 1890 reveal Korupira as the guardian spirit of the forest as well as of the game animals. He punishes those who try to exterminate the game, and rewards those who obey his commandments or on whom he takes pity;[4] he can conceal the quarry from the hunter, or bring it within his reach, just as he pleases. He guards the secrets of the forest, teaches the virtues of medicinal plants, and dispenses all the products of the forest. He appears in many aspects, sometimes weird, remote and imperious, sometimes fierce and crude. In his more forthcoming moods he is often sympathetic to the point of weakness. He is often grateful for what is done for him, but he always imposes conditions which it is dangerous not to fulfil. He usually appears as a little man, hardly three feet tall, bald-headed but with the rest of his body covered by long hair, one-eyed and with blue or green teeth, large ears, jointless legs, and feet turned backwards; he possesses great physical strength. He lives in hollow trees deep in the forest. He can deceive the hunted by imitating any animal or bird. To get lost in the forest is to be bewitched by Korupira. The sound of old trees falling, the noise made by woodpeckers extracting food from the bark – every sudden noise – is caused by Korupira kicking the roots of the trees or striking them with his hatchet, to test whether they will last out the next storm. As lord of beasts Korupira will give permission to hunt in return for an offering of tobacco; but he also has magic hunting equipment of his own, a magic cord, arrow or trap, which he lends to those whom he favours.

Whether the tobacco offering to Korupira actually takes place, and if so how, is not clear, but Anchieta reported in 1550 that at certain spots,[5] especially along paths and on mountain tops, the natives left flowers, feathers and other offerings to propitiate the Korupiras (in the plural).[6]

Korupira is usually pictured riding on a game animal; sometimes his mount is a deer or rabbit, but usually he rides a peccary (wild pig) and acts as a swineherd.[7]

The Tembé, one of a closely-linked group of present-day Tupian tribes of eastern Brazil, see Korupira as an avenger of the animals slain in the hunt.[8] Wagley and Galvão, in their study of the Tembé and Guajajara (known collectively as the Tenetehara),[9] describe Mara-nauwa (identified with Korupira) as the owner of the forest and of all the forest animals (in particular the white-lipped peccary) who punishes men who kill these animals wantonly.[10] The Shipaya, a Tupian tribe on the lower Xingú, use the name Korupira to denote a forest monster;[11] they call the 'lord of beasts' Tumacha. Tumacha's authority extends to all the game animals except the jaguar, which is subject to a special dispensation.[12] He is friendly to the human race and always ready to help the unfortunate.

Figures similar to Korupira appear also in the Gran Chaco; the mixed population of the Itau valley, as well as the Chiriguano, an isolated Tupian tribe, believe in a spirit called Coquena who protects the animals of the forest.[13] When the female deer gives birth he looks after the young.

It is said that once a number of men were hunting when their dogs ran away. A little later the hunters were bewildered to find the missing animals tethered. A little man came forward; it was Coquena. He said that he would kill the men if they did not stop hunting his animals, and showed them three large enclosures, one full of peccary, one of deer and another full of tapir. They never dared to go hunting again. When a wild animal has a mark on its ear, it is said that it bears Coquena's sign. There is no mention of worship in these cases, so that they are not strictly speaking religious phenomena. The Mundurucú, on the other hand, starting from the belief, common to all Tupian tribes, that each object in nature has its 'mother' (cy),[14] worship Putcha Ši ('mother of game'), an entity who protects her 'children' from destruction by mankind.[15] Although clearly defined, she has no constant external form. She manifests herself in two principal aspects; a stone object called the wirakuá, and particular tortoises and coatá monkeys. Her presence can be detected only by the shamans.

The concept of the wirakuá is not very clearly defined; it is vaguely thought of as a supernatural power; just as Putcha Ši is thought of more as a 'power' than a person. In the guise of the wirakuá, Putcha Ši dwells in the eternal springs in the upper parts of the river valleys. The hunter who goes there never comes home empty-handed, because the animals have a tendency to congregate around their 'mother'. The shamans can move Putcha Ši to springs nearer to their village, where she remains unless she is stolen by the shamans of another village. When the shaman moves her, she emits a thunderous roar which can only be heard by the animals, and they follow her to her new home.

Putcha Ši's manifestation in certain individuals of two species, tortoise and *Ateles ateles* (coatá monkey), is temporary. But she takes her revenge on anyone who kills one of these individual animals, or fails to eat all the flesh of an animal he has killed, or fails to treat the dead animal with due respect. Sometimes tortoises in which Putcha Ši is believed to reside are kept by the shamans in secret places near the villages, where they are fed with *möri*, a sweet paste made of manioc, and washed with water scented with liana. This is believed to ensure success in the hunt. The feeding of Putcha Ši with *möri*, now discontinued, was the responsibility of the most powerful shaman (*mamú*) in the village, who went into a trance state for this purpose and for no other.[16] As he lay covered in a hammock and fortified by three magical implements (*naneh*), supposed to be inserted into his neck and knee joints, the other shamans blew tobacco smoke over him until he passed into a trance in which he could sense a supernatural presence. Then he leaped out of his hammock, grasped a bowl of *möri*, and guided by a magic object called a *borombö* stormed off to feed Putcha Ši. Not far from the village he jumped into a hole in the ground which only he could see and ran on underground, with loud cries, to another hole not far distant, where he emerged and continued his journey above ground. He visited the various manifestations of Putcha Ši and gave them all *möri* to eat. When he returned to the men's house in the village the other shamans removed the three *naneh*, which would otherwise have turned him into an animal. His colleagues blew more tobacco smoke over him, and washed and dried him, thus withdrawing him from his dangerous trance state. Only the very strongest shamans could go in person to feed Putcha Ši; their weaker brethren would send *naneh* to call the various manifestations of Putcha Ši together in the land of the game animals, where the soul of the shaman would go and feed them.

The Tupian Korupira, lord of beasts, who has definite physical 'trade marks' and even character traits, is obviously very different in many ways from the far more abstract, immanent power of Putcha Ši. But the two concepts spring from basically similar conceptions of the world; both have deep roots in hunting and gathering culture.

The 'lord of beasts' is much more obviously zoomorphic in the beliefs of certain Guianese tribes. According to Koch-Grünberg, the Taulipang, a Cariban tribe, invest the water spirit Keyeme with the attributes of a lord of beasts.[17] In the guise of a gigantic anaconda he was killed by the birds as a punishment for dragging down to his abode all the creatures he could find. His many-coloured skin was then distributed among the birds and other creatures; and this was how they acquired the characteristic colours and patterns of their fur and feathers, and also their own individual sounds. This myth of the great snakeskin is also current among the Warrau and Arawakans of the Guianas;[18] but here only the waterfowl acquired their characteristic plumage in this way. Keyeme too has a special connection with these birds.[19] Caribans, Arawakans and Warrau also have in common the belief that the magic plants (*bina*), mostly varieties of caladium, which are used to procure success in the hunt, sprang from the ashes of the great anaconda.[20] The Barama River Caribs still grow their *bina* from the ashes of a cremated anaconda.[21]

When the Cashinawa of the Jurua-Purus region see an anaconda, they gather round it and each man points in turn to a different golden patch on its skin and pronounces the name of the game animal he wants to kill.[22] Then they kill the snake, and from its skin they make headbands which will bring them success in the hunt. Similarly the Carajá have a myth in which a hunter receives from a snake a bundle of arrows which will never miss their mark.[23]

In Guianese myth the animal which bestows magic arrows is more often a frog. The Arawakans tell of a tree frog, Adaba, who is a 'spirit helper' rather than a lord of beasts. He once appeared to three huntsmen in the guise of a man with narrow stripes running down his thin legs, and showed them how to shoot arrows into the air in such a way that they would come down and strike the animals in the back. From that time forward the three men never missed an animal, and Abada lived with them as their brother-in-law. But one day he came into contact with water and turned into a frog once more.[24]

In many parts of the Guianas the frog is used as a hunting charm; the Arawakans rub frog spawn and parts of the animal's body into the sense organs or scarified skin of the hunter; members of other hunting peoples actually swallow living toads.[25] Among the Barama River Caribs, when a youth is old enough to go hunting he is set to catch a specimen of a particular type of tree frog which is said to imitate in its croaking the noises made by various beasts of prey, and which is therefore a potent aid in hunting all kinds of quarry. The hunter rubs its slime and later its ashes into his scars, and summons the spirit of the dead frog to help him in the hunt, saying for example: 'Make me as you are yourself. Let me catch all kinds of game.'[26]

Among the Canelo of Ecuador a type of tick (garrapata) is believed to be a way of attracting all the species on which it lives as a parasite.[27] Significantly, the tick is called Aischa Mama, 'mother of game'. Success in the hunting field depends on the possession of this insect.

The Taulipang believe that the hunter is assisted by a *kamayuag*, a monstrous supernatural wasp as big as a man's hand.[28] Accordingly Taulipang hunters cause wasps to sting their arms to ensure good fortune, and submit to being bitten by a huge ant (tocandeira).[29] Koch-Grünberg[30] believes that the wasp and ant ordeals which are so common in the Guianas are basically hunting rituals, and that their function as initiation ceremonies is secondary. They are not confined to adolescents; older men submit to them periodically in order to ensure success in hunting or fishing. A wicker container used by the Oyana for the wasp ordeal represents the water spirit Ka-Jum, the father of fish,[31] whose name and functions are obviously the same as those of the Taulipang water spirit and lord of beasts, Keyeme. The intimate connection between myth and magical practice is apparent in all these cases.

As we have seen, the lord of beasts, Korupira, Maranauwa, Keyeme or Coquena, often has particular links with one species, usually a large game animal. From this it is only a step to the idea that each species has its own proprietor or 'boss spirit'. Thus one tribe of the Amazon headwaters, the Sioni of the Río Putumayo, believe that the peccary live in a house under the earth and are governed by an *uatti* (spirit), to whom the *curaca* (shaman) must apply if there is to be a good 'bag' of these animals.[32] The Shipaya too believe in a peccary boss spirit;[33] in one of their myths, Kumãphari, the culture hero and tribal ancestor, punishes his cousin, who has misused the magic formulas employed in peccary hunting, by sentencing him to live with the peccary as their ruler. Kumãphari's cousin is now a little man who rides on the back of one of the animals in the herd and gives an alarm call to warn them of the arrival of the hunt.

A Mura myth tells how a young husband who killed a sow peccary was carried off by her indignant companions and placed under the care of the 'pig mother', a small red animal.[34] The Ofaié-Chavante of eastern Brazil believe that one must never exterminate a peccary herd, but must always let two or three animals get away; one hunter who failed to obey this law, and who shot and maltreated many animals, came face to face one day with the boss spirit of the herd, a huge, misshapen peccary with no face but with great fanged jaws, which told him severely that when he needed meat, he should ask and it would be given to him; if he continued to kill and wound peccary indiscriminately it would be the worse for him.[35]

In the Gran Chaco of Bolivia the lowlanders who live along the Río Pilcomayo and the Río Confuso believe in a boss spirit in the shape of a gigantic rhea who protects the rhea herds.[36] The Toba-Pilaga call this being Dawaik;[37] he permits no one to kill more of the birds than is necessary.

Fishing plays an important part in the economy of South American tribes, and many of them believe in a spirit who rules over fish and all aquatic animals. The Taulipang, for example, believe in a water daemon called Rató, who is enough of a personalized entity to have a wife.[38] On the eve of a fishing expedition, the tribesmen invoke Rató and ask him to grant them fish, and he warns them not to let his grandchildren (the fish) go rotten. Against the evil eye of the fish he recommends that the fishermen should paint themselves with *genipapo* and *urucú*.[39] Naturally enough, belief in an aquatic boss spirit is especially frequent among the riverine tribes of the Amazon basin. The Manasi (Chiquitoan) of Eastern Bolivia honour the river god Ysituu as ruler of the fish and other aquatic creatures.[40] The priests used to go down to the river, blow tobacco smoke over the water, and recite the following magic formula: 'Ysituu, let them poison and shoot the fish and fill their pouches.' During the thanksgiving ceremony the god would say, 'I have given fish to my children.'

The Araucanians have a prayer which is addressed by a fisherman to Sompallwe, the ruler of water: 'Look favourably on me, Sompallwe, send up your beasts to me, here I invoke you with a pitcher from which you shall drink. Sompallwe, give me your beasts, do me this favour, lord of the water, great man...'[41] According to Latcham, Sompallwe is an elemental lake spirit who sometimes takes on the shape of a tiny manikin ('Tom Thumb') with dark skin and curly hair, and is more feared than reverenced.[42]

In the Gran Chaco the Toba-Pilaga believe in a fish spirit called Soinidi, who does not permit unnecessary fishing or wastefulness.[43]

The Yahgan of Tierra del Fuego cause their shamans (*yekamush*) to invoke the *čovanni*, the spirits ruling the beach and the marine animal, and the next day the *čovanni* send the hunters and fishermen schools of herrings, crabs, sea birds and other creatures.[44] An Ona woman, looking for fish along the shore, turns to the sun and says: 'Kran, give me some fish, I am hungry. I have been standing here for a long time waiting for something but not one fish has come.' Hardly has she finished her little speech when the fish rise. The woman takes as many as she wants and goes home content.[45]

Many of the instances quoted here show clearly that many South American tribes believe that in theory every animal species has its own boss spirit. Some tribes possess definite systems of boss spirits of all kinds. As I have mentioned, the Tupians believe that every animal and plant species has its 'mother' (*cy*).[46] The Mundurucú too believe not only in the 'mother of game', Putcha Ši, but in separate mothers for all the animal species. These 'mothers' or boss spirits are much less important than Putcha Ši; but there are ceremonies at which offerings are made to a chosen few among them as well as to Putcha Ši. These chosen few are the mothers of the tapir, the peccary, the deer and the monkey *Cebus macrocephalus*.[47]

Another, less important category of mothers is linked with life in the water. Putcha Ši has a counterpart in Asima Ši, the alligator-borne 'mother of fish' and mother of aquatic reptiles, amphibians and mammals. The individual fish species have no separate mothers or boss spirits, although there are separate mothers for the two varieties of turtle, the tartaruga and the tracaja (*Emys emys*). The shamans can detect the presence of these 'mothers' in their individual 'children'; and the mothers of the tapir and the peccary can even be 'synthesized'.[48] All that is necessary is to kill a gravid female, take out the foetus and dry it over a fire in the men's house. It is 'soothed' with tobacco smoke, 'fed' with sweet *möri* and finally placed near the source of a river, where it will grow into a young tapir which will contain the 'mother of the tapir'.

The ceremonies held by the Mundurucú at the beginning of the wet season to propitiate the boss spirits or 'mothers' of the fish and game species have been recorded by several independent observers since the end of the nineteenth century. According to Donald Horton they are dedicated to the game and fish 'mothers' in alternate years.[49] Murphy describes two almost identical ceremonies, the *Araiarai* and the *Dajearuparip*, both dedicated to the mothers of game.[50] One of the elders of the village initiates the preparations for the ceremonies and also acts as master of ceremonies (*piwat*). After food and drink has been made ready, the participants foregather and dancers in palm-leaf mantles go from house to house playing bamboo pipes. The climax of the ceremony is the invocation of the boss spirits and their arrival. A large number of animal skulls, classified according to species, are laid in parallel rows under shelters built on to the men's house. Before being placed in position, they are washed in *möri* and water perfumed with liana. A dish of *möri* is set down for the spirits. Then two singers, who know the chants proper to each animal species, sit down in front of the rows of skulls and invoke the various 'mothers'. The arrival of the spirits is announced by a shaman who blows tobacco smoke over the skulls and goes through the motions of sucking out of them the arrowheads and bullets which are thought to have penetrated and injured the spirits. Mollified, the 'mothers' then eat the *möri* and depart. Earlier sources tell of ventriloquial dialogues between a shaman, alone in a hut, and the animal 'mothers'.[51] These propitiatory rites are of course designed to induce the 'mothers' to grant success in the hunt.

According to Murphy the propitiation ceremony is followed by animal dances in which the men give very realistic imitations, first of the peccary, then of the tapir, and finally of other game animals.[52] The tapir dancers form a special society called the *biu ši* or 'mother of the tapir'. During the ceremonies they must sing tapir songs, and they are subject to a number of special taboos. Their solemn entry into the village takes place at night and may not be seen by the women.

Finally, C. von Strömer's description of the *Araiarai-At* ceremony mentions ritual sexual intercourse and a heap of peccary hair on which the participants dance while invoking the supreme god Karusakaibe, presumably to ask his help in the peccary hunt.[53]

The Mbyá, a Guaranian tribe, believe that each variety of animal has a boss spirit or chieftain who is called its 'real father'.[54] Thus the tapir (*mborevi*) obey Mborevi Ru Ete, ('real father of the tapir'), the deer (*guachui*) obey Guachui Ru Ete, and the birds of passage too have their own 'real father'.

The Bacairi, a Cariban tribe of the upper Xingú, believe that the ghosts of the dead become boss spirits of the animal species. The more volatile of the two souls possessed by each human being, the *kagatopuri*, leaves the body at death and wanders as a disembodied spirit (*kadopa*) until it comes to the village of the culture hero Nakoeri (who is also the creator of animals and men), where it becomes an *iamüra* and goes to dwell in a living creature.[55] Properly speaking, animals and plants are nothing more than external manifestations of the *iamüra*, and the masks worn by Bacairi ritual dancers represent not the animals themselves but their *iamüra*. When an animal or fish is killed, the Bacairi leave offerings for the *iamüra*; and the whole business of hunting and cultivation is hedged round with precautions and propitiatory rites intended to ward off the anger of the *iamüra* who have been deprived of their animals and plants.

The Caviña and Tumupasa of north-eastern Bolivia, on the other hand, believe that the animal boss spirits or *ishauva*, clearly distinguished from the *chokihua* or ghosts of the dead, are personalized daemons with individual attributes.[56] They are usually preternaturally large and oddly shaped individuals of the species concerned. There is an *ishauva* for every important species: eel, frog, alligator, turtle, anteater, monkey, deer and jaguar. They are mostly hostile to mankind. In their hands lies the power to accord success in the hunt.

The Aweikoma-Caingang of eastern Brazil, a pure hunting tribe, believe that the boss spirits freely grant permission to kill some of their animal protégés, but that they become angry if the hunter kills indiscriminately or rejects an animal which is offered to him.[57]

The Caduveo of the Gran Chaco believe that everything in the world, including of course the animals, has its lord and owner.[58] Each animal 'owner' or boss spirit sends his charges out in a given direction with instructions to return on a certain day. A hunter can kill only a limited number of animals during his career, and at the end of a certain time he must retire; if he does not his life is in danger. It is even forbidden for a superannuated huntsman to rear dogs; if he does so they will die as soon as they are old enough to hunt.

In the Guianas the boss spirit concept often reaches a great degree of specialization. The Caliña Caribs of the north coast refer to a species boss spirit either as *yumu* ('father') or *tamulu* ('grandfather'). As I have already said, the 'grandfather of all grandfathers', Tamusi, is a kind of supreme being. At the other end of the scale are the spirits of individual animals, *yana*. Each 'grandfather' (*tamulu*) rules one variety of animals or objects, which he has created and which he propagates. According to Penard the word *yumu*, 'father' signifies the life cycle linking one generation with another, and the Caribs say 'If there were no spirit to cause everything to be as it is, there would be nothing'.[59] This leads Penard and de Goeje to formulate the following basic principle of the Caliña world view: 'The world is the spirit in substance. The essence of every material object lies in its psychic being. Every animal is the materialization of a passion, an instinct; and man unites all these passions within himself.' 'We believe,' say the Caliña, 'that the *aula* [word, speech] of every *wala* [species] has existed from the very beginning, and that it created the physical aspect. Every *wala* in the visible world is the physical counterpart of a flowing *wala* [melody] which gives it life. The sound which a creature makes is the expression of its vital principle. All creatures which emit the same sound are embodiments of the same vital principle.'

This formulation is certainly influenced by the European mentality; but it undoubtedly contains an authentic echo of the unique and highly sophisticated native philosophy of this remarkable tribe.

The intimate connection between animal and plant boss spirits and shamans in Guianese tribes is discussed in my chapter on shamanism. Our principal concern here is with the part played by boss spirits in hunting ritual. The Makiritare of the Cuntinama river believe in an array of boss spirits whom the shaman must ask before the hunt and thank afterwards. The first generation of these spirits, who were half-human, half-animal, were the 'natural parents of the first animals'.

The Taulipang and Arecuna also recognize individual boss spirits apart from the 'lords of beasts' Keyeme and Rató. These boss spirits are either incarnated in particular individuals of the species concerned or take the form of preternaturally large specimens of the same creatures.[60] These animal prototypes bear the title *Podobe* 'father'. Thus there is a lizard father, a toad father, a crab father, a pacu fish father, a curassow father, a macaw father, an alligator father, a king vulture father, a wolverine father and a dog father. Two other 'fathers', the peccary father Zauelazali and the fish father Moro-Pódole, who were both once human shamans,[61] play a specially important part in hunting ritual. In the *Parishera* and *Tujui*, the two Taulipang magic hunting dances, figures representing Zauelezali and Moro-Pódole lead the dance. The *Parishera* is intended to ensure a good bag of foor-footed game, while the *Tukui* is concerned with birds and fish.[62] The long chain of dancers in the Taulipang, Macushi and Acawai *Parishera*, dancing in palm-leaf masks to the booming of cane trumpets, represent a grunting peccary herd. The dance songs of the *Parishera* rite all deal with the story of the shaman Eteto, and how he became the peccary father; and the humming bird dance in the *Tukui* rite, accompanied by shrill pipes, concerns the deeds of the hero Wazamaime, later metamorphosed into the 'fish father' in the shape of the humming bird Sekei. The Arawakan Goajiro have an interesting set of beliefs concerning the underworld, Pirauri, and the spirits, also called the *Pirauri*, who live there, and who are the 'fathers' or boss spirits of various wild mammalian species.[63] The underworld is the place of origin and the home of the game animals, and they return there every night. At dawn each *pirauri* opens one of the gates and releases his own variety of animals. Men have as yet discovered only a few of these openings into the underworld. The *pirauri* knows each of his animals, and is angry when one of the herd is missing at the end of the day. He retaliates by kidnapping one or two human beings, teaching them that it is wrong to kill animals, and releasing them through another door.

South American Indians often picture the stars and the constellations as mythical animals.[64] I have studied this phenomenon in some detail elsewhere,[65] and shown that in most cases these celestial animals are regarded as representatives or even as boss spirits of their species. On the whole the preoccupations reflected in astronomical names are those of the hunter, although the names of a few food plants occur as well. The constellations are not worshipped, as they were in civilized Peru, but beliefs concerning them often, especially among the Caliña Caribs and the Guianese Arawakans, often go far beyond the realm of pure myth.[66] There are numerous myths telling how the animals were once treated badly by man and escaped to the sky, where they became constellations. This took place when the primal age of the world came to an end and the world became what it is today. The animals mentioned in the myth are now the boss spirits of the various species. The Caliña Carib names for the constellations are accordingly those of the animals concerned, with the addition of the same suffix, *yumu* ('father'), as is used to designate the boss spirits. The Arawakans, for their part, use either the suffix *oyo* ('mother') or *kuyu* or *kuyuha* ('wildness or shyness of an animal'). When a given constellation appears in the sky the appropriate animal species breeds.[67] The Arawakans of the Guianas refer to the breeding places of the animals, where the *kuyuha* go to breathe life into their charges, by the same names as the constellations or stars.[68] Thus *Kamma-Kuyuhu* is the star which is thought of as the home of the tapir spirits; and a very similar name is given to an inlet on the left bank of the Demerara River, which, at the season when *Kamma-Kuyuhu* reaches a certain point in the heavens, is or was a favourite tapir breeding-place. The individual *kuyuha* descends from the sky to the breeding-place, where he joins others of his kind and enters a living organism. He will leave it at death to return to his celestial home. It will be seen that besides the 'lord of beasts' and the boss spirits of individual species, there is also a third class of spirits dwelling in individual animals. Especially in the case of large animals, the hunters carry out propitiatory rites whenever they make a kill in order to escape the revenge of the spirit.

The Ona of Tierra del Fuego carry out a propitiatory ritual whenever they catch a fox. This cunning creature is always on the alert for some trick to play on mankind; so while the hunter skins a fox he has killed, he addresses it as follows:

Dear fox, I wish you no harm. I love you and have no wish to harm you. But I need your flesh because I am hungry, and my children need your soft fur. Do not be angry with me. One day I shall probably catch one or other of your kinsfolk. I shall take his skin off as well, and make a beautiful coat, and we shall eat the flesh when we are hungry. Do not be angry; I love you really, dear fox.

The Ona justify this remarkable little speech as follows:

The whole brotherhood of foxes must be pacified when one of them has been killed. If the hunter treats it well, it will be content with its fate and not complain to the other foxes. This is the only way the hunter can have a chance of catching another fox in the near future.[69]

When the Aweikoma-Caingang of eastern Brazil have killed a tapir, they prop up its head and squeeze over it crushed green plants, which the tapir likes very much, and address the spirit (*kupleng*) of the animal in a friendly manner so that he may tell his brethren that he has been treated well and that they ought to let themselves be shot too.[70] The same takes place when they kill a deer or a howler monkey.

Among the eastern Brazilian Bororo, when a game animal is killed, the shaman goes into a trance and blows on the dead creature (tapir, capybara, cayman, wels, dorado) and spits in its mouth. This custom was interpreted by K. von den Steinen, when he observed it in 1893, as a 'blessing' of the game;[71] but I agree with Rafael Karsten that it is a propitiatory rite addressed to the spirit of the dead animal.[72]

There is a narrow area in the north of the continent, along the Venezuelan coast from the Gulf of Paria to Cape Codera and in the hinterland, where the Cariban tribes combine advanced (Circum-Caribbean) cultural features with relics of an archaic horizon. In the province of Piritú, when a hunter comes home, his wife pours a drink of *chicha* into the mouth of the animal he has killed, so that its 'soul' may tell the other animals how well it has been treated.[73] The Caracas Indians do the same.[74] The Palenque use water instead of alcohol.[75]

A special place among propitiation rites belongs to the jaguar ritual. This cat is not, of course, a source of meat but a beast of prey, almost invariably thought to be endowed with supernatural powers.[76] I quote from Frazer:

> The ounce, a leopard-like creature, is dreaded for its depredations by the Indians of Brazil. When they have caught one of these animals in a snare, they kill it and carry the body home to the village. There the women deck the carcass with feathers of many colours, put bracelets on its legs, and weep over it, saying, 'I pray thee not to take vengeance on our little ones for having been caught and killed through thine own ignorance. For it was not we who deceived thee, it was thyself. Our husbands only set the trap to catch animals that are good to eat: they never thought to take thee in it. Therefore, let not thy soul counsel thy fellows to avenge thy death on our little ones.'[77]

According to Métraux, this refers to the Tupinamba;[78] but it also tallies with Julio Koslowsky's account of the jaguar ritual of the western Bororo near Descalvados.[79] When a hunter brings back a jaguar, there is a dance during which the women weep and wail in great agitation to propitiate the soul of the beast. If the soul of the jaguar is not mollified, it causes the death of the hunter. In the dance the part of the vengeful jaguar is played by the man who has killed it. The shaman and other old men also invoke the jaguar in a monotone chant, dancing round the hunter facing him and shaking *maracas*. The shaman renews the dance again and again with his chanting. When the dancers are eventually overcome with fatigue, the jaguar's soul is deemed to be satisfied, and they fear it no more. The jaguar dance is also danced on other occasions, with men and women in a line behind a masked, feather-crowned man disguised in the pelt of the cat and adorned with its teeth and claws.[80] It is believed that the soul of the dead jaguar has passed into the body of the man, who manifests its presence by his wild gestures and leaps.

Nearly forty years after Koslowsky, when Vincenzo Petrullo visited Laguna, a village inhabited by the Bororo da Campanha, a western Bororo tribe, and watched a similar dance, the tribesmen were unable to explain its significance to him.[81] He does however give a detailed description of the costume of the jaguar dancer himself, as well as a good illustration. In a cubicle screened with palm leaves, which women were forbidden to enter, the dancer is painted with *urucú*, his face is covered with a mask of woman's hair, and he is dressed in a girdle of palm-leaf strips and a mantle of jaguar skin. Snakeskins of every kind hang round his head. The inside of his jaguar mantle is painted with red and black geometrical patterns of unknown significance. The costume is completed by a magnificent headdress made of the feathers of many birds.

Among the eastern Bororo, the Orarimugudoge, the jaguar ritual has a different significance, connected with the ritual hunt which takes place after someone has been killed.

The special position occupied by the jaguar as a big game animal in western Bororo thought has a parallel far to the west in Bolivia, where the ancient Mojo had a jaguar cult, which Métraux has reconstructed from a number of original sources.[82] In this cult the killing of a jaguar gives a hunter great prestige and is marked by elaborate and lengthy rites. These take place outside the village, as there would be an epidemic if the carcass were brought inside. The villagers dance all night round the dead animal to the sound of the drum. Only those who have killed the cat may skin it. The flesh is eaten on the spot. The skull is cleaned and ornamented with cotton, and placed together with the paws and other trophies in the temple, where the jaguar-slayers retire for several days of fasting and continence; the temple is forbidden ground for women. The jaguar shaman offers a libation to the jaguar god on behalf of the hunters, and tells them the jaguar's secret name, which now becomes theirs. The fast and the retreat are concluded by a drinking party in the course of which each hunter cuts off some of his hair.

When anyone is killed by a jaguar, another special ritual takes place. All the possessions of the dead person are stacked in front of his house, and are sacred to the jaguar which killed him, and which is now the rightful owner. Anyone who has escaped alive from the clutches of a jaguar is admitted to the guild of jaguar shamans, who are in charge of all rites connected with the jaguar, and can conjure these animals as well as propitiating them. These jaguar shamans also claim to be able to change themselves into jaguars; this may be an explanation of the belief, current throughout South America, that shamans in general have this ability.[83]

All the propitiatory rites I have mentioned have one basic aim: to pacify or to ward off the vengeful spirit of an animal killed in the hunt. How would the unpropitiated animal take its revenge? One way is to prevent its fellow-creatures from allowing themselves to be killed by the individual hunter in question; and many tribes, especially in eastern Brazil, have a custom whereby this hunter is permitted to eat nothing (or only a ritually circumscribed portion) of his quarry.[84] An Aweikoma-Caingang hunter who has killed a tapir may not eat any of the meat until he has ritually consumed premasticated tapir flesh and the charred remains of the animal's trachea wrapped in grass.[85] Among the Bororo the hunter never roasts the meat he has shot himself, but gets someone else to do it for him.[86] Failure to observe this taboo, as well as failure to carry out the propitiatory ceremony (the so-called 'blessing'), causes the vengeful animal spirit to send sickness and death to the hunter and all those who eat of its flesh.[87] This idea of a dangerous power residing in animals is especially well developed among the Mundurucú, who call this power *chewoi*.[88] This vengeful power is embodied in two baleful objects called *yakib* and *wirakuá*.[89] We have already encountered the *wirakuá* as a manifestation of Putcha Ši, the 'mother of game'. The *yakib* is described as a kind of louse. *Yakib* and *wirakuá* can be emanations of the animal's own soul or of Putcha Ši; they are sent to punish injuries done to the animal kingdom by men who fail to observe the hunting ritual. They work by penetrating the body of the victim and causing suffering and death. The shaman has the task of removing the *yakib* and *wirakuá*; this is particularly difficult when they have been sent by Putcha Ši directly.

Another practice closely linked with propitiation is the preservation of the bones of the dead animal, which have a special significance in connection with future success in the hunt. Behind this custom lies the belief that the animal may one day be resurrected from its bones; but the significance of most present-day 'bone rituals' has been forgotten. Thus the Waica of the upper Orinoco, who carefully preserve the bones of game animals, birds and fish, were unable to tell me why. A definite link between bone rituals and the idea of resurrection has however recently been shown to exist among another Cariban group, the

Makiritare of Guiana. Members of one tribe, the Yecuaná, keep the bones of hunted animals, and in particular the breastbones of the larger birds, in the roofing above the doors of their houses; while another tribe, the Cunuana, have a myth concerning this subject. The supreme being and culture hero, Uanári, had a brother-in-law, a great peccary hunter, who used to throw the picked bones of these animals into a celestial spring called Akuena to bring them back to life. So Uanári sent for the charred bones of his mother, took them to Akuena, and threw them in, thus bringing them to life.[90]

In the legend of the divine twins, current in many parts of South America, one of the twins, in the shape of an animal, is killed by a hostile forest spirit, and the other brother brings him back to life from his bones, blood or dismembered corpse.

The Mosetene of eastern Bolivia, a region prolific in hunting lore, believe that a dead peccary can be brought to life not from its bones but from its liver. The bones are taken into the forest lest they prevent the species from being killed in the future.[91] The neighbouring Chimane cut off the feet of game animals, to prevent their spirits from leaving the district and taking the rest of the game with them.[92] The rest of the bones are suspended in great baskets from the roof of the hut, for the same reason.[93] The Yuracaré take great pains to collect all the bones of the animals, birds and fish that they eat and to throw them into a river, or hide them in the depths of the forest, 'that the animals of the species killed may not become angry and may continue to allow themselves to be killed.'[94]

The Siriono, hunters of eastern Bolivia, suspend the skull near the place where the animal is eaten.[95] The Jivaro of Ecuador believe that the bones and especially the skulls of game animals have the power to attract living animals of the same species.[96] Most Jivaro huts accordingly contain a number of these relics of past hunting expeditions. Often, when a Jivaro tribesman has caught and eaten a monkey in the forest, he cleans the skull and hangs it on a liana between two trees near the place where the animal was shot; the idea is that it will attract other monkeys to the same place.

The Betoi of eastern Colombia seek an intimate personal contact with the spiritual powers contained in animal bones: an individual wounds his legs with ray fish spines in order to catch more fish and scratches his left arm with a bird's femur and his right arm with a peccary bone in order to enjoy good fortune in the hunt.[97]

The most important piece of information on this theme dates from 1706, when Martin de Nantes observed that the Cariri of northern

Brazil rubbed a mixture of charred fish and animal bones into incisions made in the bodies of boys at puberty, and also compelled them to drink a concoction of the same ingredients. Concurrently with this rite the adolescents were given practical training in hunting. On their return from these training expeditions they gave the game to their elders and contented themselves with maize and manioc.[98]

Other parts of the animal are also used as hunting talismans. The Wapishana of Guiana have a custom which strongly recalls the Pariri initiation ceremonies; parts of the bird or animal which the hunter wishes to kill, the head of a curassow (*Crax alector*) or the heart of an acouri, are burned, crushed and mixed with wild honey. Then incisions are made in the hunter's arms and the mixture rubbed into the wounds.[99]

In other cases the link between the hunter and the animal relics is less intimate; it is sufficient for him to carry them with him. The Pilaga of the Gran Chaco use as a hunting amulet a necklace hung with little leather pouches full of down, hair and scraps of various kinds.[100] When the hunter sees game in the distance he takes one of these pouches and rubs it vigorously round his mouth. The animal is thereby robbed of all its strength and collapses. An alternative kind of charm is a girdle, made from the skin from the necks of two rhea, which contains two twists of similar relics. When the Ashluslay go rhea hunting, they carry scraps of skin from the breasts of birds they have already killed.[101]

No Ona tribesman of Tierra del Fuego goes hunting guanaco without wearing his *kočel*, a scrap of skin from the forehead of a guanaco.[102] As soon as the guanaco sees the *kočel*, it does not run away but either continues to browse or simply gazes at the man, even if it sees his whole body. The hunter is thus enabled to approach and kill it. The *kočel* is formally awarded to the young man at his initiation (*Kloketen*).

The Jivaro and Canelo have other hunting charms consisting of stones, gravel, hairballs and pieces of wood that have been found in the gizzards of birds or the stomachs of quadrupeds.[103] The pebbles are taken mainly from the crops of toucans, geese and wild turkeys, the three species most valued as sources of food. Before setting out on a hunting expedition the Indian takes one of these little round pebbles, together with the powder which collects round it when it is dried, and uses it to paint certain ornamental patterns on his face. These almost invisible patterns are believed to have a miraculous power to attract the species of bird from which the stone was taken.

When the Canelos hunt tapir, they rub the fur of their dogs with a little hairball of the kind frequently found in the stomach of their quarry; this gives them a better nose for the hunt. Similarly, the round pieces of wood sometimes found in the stomachs of deer are used as charms to attract other deer. Stones and other objects from the stomachs of fish are similarly used to rub on fish hooks before casting.[104]

A later development from the use of parts of animals as hunting charms is the use of effigies for a similar purpose. The Lengua of the Gran Chaco use wax figures as hunting charms,[105] probably, as Karsten suggests, hoping to catch the souls of the beasts in the effigies.[106] The Bororo of eastern Brazil sing a hymn of praise on the eve of every hunting expedition, to tell the animal concerned how well it will be treated, and then make sand drawings (especially if their intended enemy is a tapir), to bring it within their power.[107]

The Bororo hunting hymn leads us to another important branch of hunting magic: the use of the spoken word addressed not to a presiding spirit but to the animal itself.

When the time comes for the peccary and certain fish (piranha and morocobo) to migrate, the Piaroa of the Orinoco decorate themselves with feathers, teeth and fishbones and assemble for a nocturnal 'liturgy' in which they cast hunting spells. On the eve of the day set aside for the hunting or fishing expedition, they gather round the hut of the most experienced hunter among them. The chief sings a song in honour of the desired beast, tells its story and praises its virtues.[108]

Three days before the *Yawapani* or 'dog feast' of the Jivaro there is a magical dance, the *Wuimchi*, in which, as the dancers circle the centre post of the house, they intone the names of the animals and birds they wish to catch, including the toucan, the guan, the wild turkey, a species of parrot, the peccary, and various species of monkey which are hunted for their flesh, their teeth and their fur. The purpose of the dance is to give the host good fortune with his new dog.[109]

In the Cashinawa animal dance the dancers dance in a line like a great serpent, each man holding the arms of the man in front. The line is led by the chief, carrying a whip in his hand. He recites all the animal names he can think of (agouti, peccary, etc.) plus those of sun, moon, fire, rain, and so on until he runs out of breath. The others answer him, repeating each name as many as twenty times.[110]

On the night before a hunting expedition the Lengua of the Gran Chaco sing to the rhythm of their *maracas* to entice the game to come to certain areas.[111] H. von Becker gives the following account of a dance which takes place during the seasonal festivals (*Keaya*) of the Leagua:

The leader of the dance, usually the shaman, steps into the middle of the circle with an assistant. The rhythm beats faster. The two dancers in the

centre execute a number of figures which are unmistakably stylized imitations of the movements of game animals. One especially remarkable variation
represented the behaviour of two male rhea. The dancers swing their rattles
in their left hands and a feathered stick in their right. The number of figures
executed varies according to the inventive capacity or the specific needs of
the individual dancer. A shaman confirmed to me that these animal dances
are a part of hunting magic.[112]

The Mataco-Noctene of the Chaco dance their *Vuocoi*, 'dance of the
fish', especially in the months of May and June, before they set out
fishing. The dance is thought to cause the fish to gather in large numbers
in the part of the river in which they intend to fish.[113]

Other animal mask dances in South America, those of the Carajá, the
Upper Xingú tribes and the tribes of the north-west of the Amazon
basin, are not directly concerned with hunting, and are therefore
discussed elsewhere.

III *Vegetation Gods and Fertility Rites; Headhunting and Cannibalism*

Among certain tribes the same rites that are used by hunters to attract
or to propitiate game animals have been taken over and applied to the
cultivation of food plants. The Bororo propitiatory rite or 'blessing'
ritual is applied not only to game animals but also to piki, mangave and
maize.[1] The Mundurucú have an annual ceremony to propitiate the
'mothers' of maize and manioc in which the shaman invokes the
manioc mother in the following terms:

Mother of manioc, show favour to us. Let us suffer no famine; we call on
you each year with our prayers. We have not forgotten you.[2]

The Piaroa too 'sing' to manioc, maize and banana just as they sing to
the game animals.[3] The Cashinawa ask the anaconda for good harvests
as well as for abundant game; they also dance special dances to induce
the maize spirit to grant them a plentiful crop.[4]

Thus alongside agrarian rites which are closely modelled on the
ceremonial patterns of a hunting culture we find others, such as the
Cashinawa maize dances, which have their origin in an entirely
different conception of the nature of supernatural beings.

A further distinction can be made between rites connected with cultivated cereals and root crops, such as maize and manioc, and rites
concerning (usually wild) fruit trees.

I have already referred to the important part played in the further-
ance of crop growth by supreme beings such as the Ngenechen of the

Araucanians, the sun father of the Ge tribes, the Purú of the Sáliva and Achagua, the creator god Baba-Buada of the Araona, the Moma of the Witotoans, the Ches of the Miguri and the Yocahu of the Taino. The emphasis in this chapter will, however, lie on specialized agricultural deities, and on those subordinate spirits which are delegated to deal with agricultural matters by the supreme being.[5]

It can hardly be accidental that the most significant piece of information we have on this aspect of religion comes from an area bordering on the territory of the Andean civilizations. According to Rafael Karsten the Jivaro worship an earth goddess, Nungui;[6] Tessmann however, demotes this Nungui to the status of a simple vegetation daemon.[7] Her sphere is restricted to those plants considered to be feminine. When manioc is planted for consumption at a 'tobacco feast' in honour of a woman, the woman and her companions squat by the seedlings and chant an incantation. Then they invoke Nungui, who is embodied in a strangely shaped stone, the *nantára*, which can be used to summon Nungui herself but also contains the female soul of the manioc plant. The first manioc cutting is painted red, and the woman to be honoured places it against her groin. Each woman who plants the cutting sits on a manioc tuber. The connection between the fertility of women and the growth of food plants could hardly be more clearly expressed. After the field has been planted, a ceremonial digging stick is stuck into the ground and the people pray to Nungui. For five successive nights after planting their fields Jivaro women dance and beg Nungui to allow their manioc to grow.[8]

When the Jivaro men plant banana shoots they observe a number of taboos and pray to Nungui's husband Shakaema. The masculine vegetation deity corresponds here to the masculine souls of the banana plants, which are cultivated only by men.

As we have already seen, the most important aspect of the Witotoan father god Moma or Naimuema is his role as provider of food plants. He drew both plants and animals from his own body – an echo of the belief common to many agricultural tribes of the Old and New World tropics, that the food plants originally sprang from parts of the human body. His most conspicuous manifestation, as we shall see, is in tree fruit; he is also responsible for cultivated plants, manioc, maize and peanuts. The 'words' of the festival which concerns these plants were handed down by Father Moma through the intermediacy of the tribal ancestor Nofuyemi.[9] This festival, the *Okima*, is described by Preuss as the 'festival of *yuca* (manioc) and the ancestors'.[10] The linking of the two ideas is particularly revealing, as Moma is not only identified with the moon but also lives in the underworld as ruler of the dead; 'the father died, although the word ["death"] did not yet exist'.[11] The *Okima* which Preuss attended was held in honour of a dead chief by his son. The ancestors, who live just under the surface of the earth, celebrate the festival at the same time as their descendants, using the 'right words'. The living make contact with the dead by stamping their feet or beating rhythmically on the ground with 'stamping sticks' fitted with rattles.[12] In other sections of the *Okima*, dancers carry torches and manioc plants. Their chants refer to events in mythical antiquity. Flute players play in pairs. The men stage a mock combat, in which they 'fence' with spears, and the women mimic the gait of the moon woman as she leans on her staff made of a food plant 'like *ñame* [yam]'.

The most important Witotoan myth concerning the origin of manioc concerns not Moma but a young girl whose name means 'dark' or 'blind one', and who is impregnated by a spirit while sitting on a trough.[13] The 'dark one' brings the child into the world in a pot without looking at it. She returns to the spot later to find a manioc tree growing there. Its roots thereafter become the staple diet of the Indians. The manioc is thus born of woman, an idea which irresistibly recalls the custom of the Jivaro women who place manioc cuttings against their pudenda or seat themselves on manioc tubers.

The Witotoan fertility rite is similar in many respects, notably the use of stamping sticks, to the equivalent rite among the Guarayu of eastern Bolivia.[14] Early in the nineteenth century Alcide d'Orbigny recorded the belief that 'God', under the name of Grandfather Tamoi, once lived among the Guarayu, taught them agriculture and promised them his future aid.[15] Tamoi then ascended one day before dawn, while 'angels' beat on the ground with lengths of thick bamboo.

To commemorate the promises once made by Tamoi, the Guarayu assemble round the octagonal sacred hut. The men sit naked in a circle, each with a bamboo stamping tube in his hand. The oldest begins a dirge, beating on the earth with his bamboo, and the others follow suit. Behind them the women sing and genuflect, praying for a plentiful harvest. The ceremony ends with libations.

Here Tamoi, whom we have already encountered as a supreme being, plays a part comparable with that of the Father Moma of the Witotoans. The possibility of a link cannot be excluded despite the great distance separating the two tribes; the Witotoan languages show marked affinities with the Tupi-Guarani group, to which the Guarayu language belongs.

The most important of the ceremonies held by the Apapocuva-

Guarani is celebrated by the whole tribe shortly before the harvest. Cultivated plants, wild fruits and game are exhibited beside candles, and after four days of ritual dancing they are sprinkled with holy water.[16] The Cainguá offer cakes baked from the first fruits of the ripe green maize to the god Tupã; no one may eat any of the maize before it has been offered to the god. The chants which accompany the ensuing dances have a pronounced erotic character which clearly connects with the theme of fertility.[17]

The unique fertility rite of the Tupinamba, in which a bottle-gourd idol with movable jaws symbolically masticated the seed corn, is dealt with in a later chapter. The agrarian rites of the north-western and central Ge tribes of eastern Brazil have been touched on in connection with their cult of sun and moon.

On the upper Xingú the most significant ritual is the *Ole* (manioc ceremony) of the Trumai. This takes place between the middle of August and the end of September, before cultivation begins. Its purpose is to ensure a good harvest. A week after the opening songs and dances of the festival, the *Ole* posts are set up. A number of stripped tree trunks are rubbed with clay, painted in bright colours and otherwise ornamented before being erected in the centre of the village. Offerings of food (fish laid on manioc cakes) are placed before them every day. One of the poles, which is called 'Nukekerehe', and is thought of as hostile, is also soaked in manioc gruel, as is the fiercely gesturing man who in the course of a dance scene identifies himself with Nukekerehe. It is clear from this that the other *Ole* posts must also represent various spirits; but the linguistically isolated Trumai, the oldest-established ethnic group on the upper Xingú, can provide no further details.[18]

Murphy accordingly supposes that the whole *Ole* ritual complex was taken over from culturally more advanced neighbours such as the Camayura, whose *Kwarup* ceremony closely resembles it.[19] The *Kwarup* seems more like a ceremony in honour of the dead than a fertility rite; the posts represent not only those recently dead but the four mythical first ancestors of the tribe. A direct connection with fertility becomes apparent only in the dances which follow the *Kwarup*, and which are intended to promote the growth of plants, and in particular the piquí tree (*Caryocar villosum*) with its oil-bearing edible seeds.[20] On the other hand, the Camayura regard the *Ole* spirits of the Trumai as identical with their own *mama'é* or 'mothers', the boss spirits of the animal and vegetable species, which are such a characteristic feature of Tupian religion.[21] Manioc has no less than three *mama'é*, all of which are represented by symbolic posts which are often models of the implements used for the cultivation and preparation of manioc: the dibber, the T-shaped digging stick, and a half-moon shaped spatula used for turning manioc cakes. A number of general features indicate that these ritual implements represent the fish-like *mama'é* which originally gave the Camayura both manioc itself and the articles used in its preparation.[22] Unfortunately no observer has seen the manioc fertility ritual itself.

The Barama River Caribs of Guyana recognize a special manioc spirit by the name of Piuku, who watches over every manioc field. He has been described as a god,[23] but there is no sign that he is worshipped. Piuku is directly linked with the manioc plants; where they are absent, as in a field after the harvest, Piuku is absent too, and the land comes under the protection of the *ume* or hill spirits. When a new field is planted, the *ume* withdraw in their turn and Piuku takes over. Propitiatory sacrifices are made on these occasions not to the *ume* themselves but to the spirits of the trees that are felled. A mouthful of *kashiri* (manioc beer) is spat out on every stump to appease the resentment of the tree spirit. If this is not done he will spoil the manioc crop.

Just as the Jivaro link the fertility of manioc with female sexuality, the Cáua (Arawakan) and Cubeo (Tucanoan) of the Uaupés region of the north-west Amazon associate the fruitfulness of the fields with the potency of the human male. Both tribes have a phallic dance (*nóädö*) in which all the mask dancers take part together, irrespective of the roles they play in the other mask dances. In this phallic dance fertility is symbolized unequivocally by mimic representations of coitus.

In front of their bodies the dancers hold large phalluses made of bast, and testicles made of the red cones of a certain tree. First they dance in a line one behind the other, in quick time, their bodies bent forward, stamping their right feet on the ground and singing . . . suddenly they spring forward with vigorous coital movements and loud groans, and finally halt in an irregular group. They stroke the phalluses gently with their right hands, tap them with their fingers, making loud clicking sounds, and blow upon them, making wafting movements with their hands as if scattering something in the air. They carry the spurting semen everywhere, to every corner of the house, to the edge of the forest and the adjoining cultivated area, and leap in among the women and girls, who scatter screaming and laughing . . . Nevertheless, this is a serious, and, as it represents a natural process, a perfectly decent dance in the eyes of people in a state of nature.[24]

The mask spirits are here thought of as fertility daemons who perform the sexual act in order to promote growth, development and prosperity in the whole of nature. The Cubeo believe that the forest spirit Popäli and the culture heroes Hömänihikö and Kuwai, like certain other supernatural beings, have huge phalluses. Koch-Grünberg accordingly describes them as fertility daemons; and the two last-named, at least, show other features which confirm this.[25]

The phallic dances of the Cubeo and Cáua are concerned with the fertility of wild edible fruits as well as cultivated plants; and it is to vegetation rituals belonging to gathering (as distinct from farming) cultures that we now turn.

The most spectacular religious festivals among the lowland Amazon tribes are those held in the north-western part of the area, usually (and wrongly) referred to as Yurupary ceremonies, after the fierce daemon Yurupary believed in by the old Tupinamba.[26] Among the Tucanoan and Arawakan groups of the upper Río Negro and the basin of the Rio Cairí-Uaupés the Yurupary rites take place at the time when certain palm fruits are ripe. At the beginning of the festivals baskets of these fruits are ceremonially escorted into the village by men blowing giant trumpets. These sacred instruments, which represent the vegetation daemons, are kept some way from the village in hiding places where women and children may not see them on pain of death. During the first part of the ceremony, in which the men scourge each other with long rods, the women remain closed in a hut; but they join with the men in the several days of fasting and drinking which follow.

At the end of the nineteenth century the French traveller Henri Coudreau recorded some interesting details on the part played by Yurupary in the mythology of the Tariana (Arawakan) and other tribes of the Rio Uaupés region.[27] Yurupary was believed to be the son of a virgin who had no genital organs and who conceived him through drinking *kashiri*. A fish slit open her abdomen while she was bathing so that the birth could take place. The body of the child emitted light; when he moved his finger he produced a strange sound; his whole body made a noise like thunder. Yurupary grew rapidly. One day he killed and devoured some boys who had disobeyed his dietary laws; and the men then intoxicated him with *kashiri* and threw him into a fire. From his ashes there grew a paxiuba palm; paxiubas are the 'bones of Yurupary'. In the course of the same night the soul of Yurupary climbed up the trunk of one of these trees to heaven. Before daybreak, to prevent the women seeing these living relics of Yurupary, the men felled them and made their trunks into the sacred trumpets which now represent the voice of Yurupary himself. And as the virgin-born Yurupary went clothed in the skin of a monkey, his holy symbol is now the *macacaraua*, a mask and costume made of monkey and human hairs.

One version of the myth says that after Yurupary's death the women at first appropriated the trumpet and *macacaraua*, but that Yurupary, who did not like women, descended from heaven, retrieved his attributes from them, and decreed that women must henceforth have no access to them or to the mysteries which he then instituted, the *Dabucuri* or scourging rites. In the Cairí-Uaupés basin there were according to Coudreau six *Dabucuri* in every year to mark the ripening of various forest fruits.[28]

When Koch-Grünberg visited the same area between 1903 and 1905, the black monkey-hair costume, the *macacaraua*, was not (or was no longer?) in use. He learnt from the Siusí of the Río Cairí that the Lingua Geral name Yurupary conceals the figure of none other than Kuwai, son of Yapericuli, the tribal ancestor-hero of the Arawakan tribes of the area.[29] His image, a male figure with heavily emphasized genitals, was incised in a rock at the Bokoepana rapids. The great paxiuba-wood trumpets, which are really open megaphones without a sound generator of their own, are also known as *koai* or *kuai*. They are played when the fruit of two varieties of palm, the assai (*Euterpe oleracea Mart.*) and the bacába (*Oenocarpus bacaba Mart.*), is brought into the village. The Siusí chief Mandu told Koch-Grünberg that men danced to these instruments all along the Río Içana and its tributaries; along the Río Guainia and the northern tributaries of the Orinoco, a kind of long single-note horn was played instead. The continued existence of the Yurupary myth and ritual among the Baniwa of the lower Içana is confirmed by recent reports.[30]

A festival celebrated by the tribes of the upper Orinoco, the Atabapo and the Inirida, in honour of the good spirit Cachimana who rules the seasons and causes the fruit to ripen, was reported by Alexander von Humboldt in the early nineteenth century.[31] The sacred trumpets used in these rites were tubes of fired clay, three to four feet long with globular swellings at intervals along their length. They were in the custody of a number of old men versed in the mysteries, and were blown under the palms to make these trees bear well. The initiates submitted to scourging, fasts and other ordeals. Sometimes Cachimana blew the trumpet himself; sometimes he let his will be known through the individual who had charge of the instrument. The women were not permitted even to see the sacred instrument, and were excluded from every aspect of the festival. If one of them had the misfortune to catch sight of the trumpet she was put to death without fail.

In the late 1930s, two anthropologists visited the Puinave of the lower Inírida and witnessed a *fiesta del Diablo*, identical with the Yurupary festivals of the lower Inírida, from which it was obviously derived.[32]

Even the musical instruments, or some of them at least, bore the same name of *cuhay*. Not only did a fruit-bearing palm tree – in this case the moriche (*Mauritia flexuosa*) – spring from the ashes of the 'devil' (Yopinai), but his bones became the musical instruments in which he manifests himself. The mythological theme underlying so many vegetation rituals – the idea that food plants first sprang from parts of a human body – here finds one of its most revealing expressions.

The Waica of the upper Orinoco have an annual festival which I was able to observe in 1955.[35] It has an unmistakable direct link with the ripening of the fruit of the peach palm (*Guilielma gasipaes*), which is eaten raw in many parts of the Amazon basin.[33] The ceremonial entry of men bearing fruit is strongly reminiscent of the Yurupary ritual reported by Koch-Grünberg, but the Waica have no musical instruments, and I detected no reference to a mythological origin for the festival. The male participants struck each other on the chest or back with their fists or palms, a practice which clearly takes its origin from the scourging customary in the north-west Brazilian Yurupary festivals. A remarkable dance of the women with great bundles of red and yellow peach-palm fruit, and the way in which the children pelt each other with single fruit, confirmed my impression that this was basically a fruit-gathering celebration which had accumulated other elements in the course of time.

We have discussed the Yurupary festivals of the Arawakan tribes of the north-west Amazon basin; those of the Tucanoans have also been studied by Koch-Grünberg, who describes and illustrates the festival as practised by the Tuyuca of the Rio Tiquié.[34] Here the paxiuba-wood pipes are joined by huge trumpets made of bark (also used in a similar ritual far away in the south of the Amazon basin). Curiously, the pipes are identified with cujubim birds and the bark trumpets with armadillos, an indication of the immense importance of the relationship between mankind and animals in primitive South American thought.

Koch-Grünberg finds confirmation for his thesis, that the presiding spirit of the Yurupary festivals, and hence the provider of wild fruit, is a solar hero, in the myth in which the Yahuna of the Río Apaporis seek to explain the origin of the festival itself.

Many years ago there came from the great water house, the home of the sun [the sea], a small boy who sang so beautifully that people came from far and near to hear him. His name was Milómaki. But when the people who had heard his voice went home and ate fish, they all fell down dead. Their relatives took hold of Milómaki, who had grown into a youth by now, and burned him on a great pyre because he had killed their brothers. But he went on singing beautifully up to the last. When the flames were already licking

283

up his body, he sang: 'Now I die, my son, now I leave this world.' When his body started to swell up with the heat, he sang on in his loveliest tones: 'Now my body breaks, now I die.' And his body burst. He died and was consumed by the flames; but his soul rose to heaven. On the very same day there rose from his ashes a long green leaf. It grew bigger and bigger, spread itself out, and by the next day it was a lofty tree, the first paxiuba palm, for there were no paxiubas before that time. People made great flutes from its wood, and these played the same beautiful melodies which Milómaki had sung. The men play them to this day when the forest fruits (ingá, peach palm fruit, castanha, umari, etc.) are ripe, and they dance in honour of Milómaki who created all kinds of fruit.[35]

At this festival too the participants scourge one another until the blood flows. The flogging of the young men to the sound of a flute – the sound which the late seventeenth-century traveller Peter Samuel Fritz found unendurable[36] – was the climax of the Yurimagua festival in honour of the 'devil' Guaricana. Another festival classed by Métraux among the Yurupary festivals is the initiation ceremony of the adolescent girls among the Tucuna,[37] at which the bark trumpets still used today are probably identical with those formerly played by the Yurimagua; they still bear the name of the Yurimagua 'devil' Guaricana (uaricana).[38]

The nineteenth-century traveller Martius, in his account of the Pasé, tells us that all females fled to the depths of the forest as soon as the great magic trumpets sounded the signal for the 'forest devil dance', the *Gurupira-Cau*.[39] Although Martius alludes here to the *botuto* played by the Orinoco tribes, as described by Humboldt, he does not mention any direct connection with plant fertility. The flagellation ritual, too, is absent, as it is among the Tucuna. The ritual taking of snuff has a clear link with the sacred musical instruments of the Tucuna.[40] It is practised by the men who are the players and custodians of the *uaricana*. From the age of seven onwards, boys are allowed to enter the sacred enclosure in which the instruments are kept, after they have first taken snuff. Among the Mura too, the first sniff of a narcotic powder was the sign of man's estate, but it was accompanied by a ritual whipping.[41] The excessive consumption, as snuff, of the powdered seeds of the pariaca tree (*Mimosa acacioides*) was the occasion, among the Mura, of a special annual festival from which women were excluded, and which took place at the time of the (seed?) harvest.[42] It began with what Martius calls the 'act of love', in which pairs of men lashed each other with whips made of tapir hide,[43] and its climax came when the same pairs knelt blowing pariaca powder into each other's nostrils through pairs of foot-long hollow bones. As in the Amazonian Yurupary festivals and elsewhere, whipping among the

Mura was clearly a fertility ritual. It was also practised when a new patch of forest was burned prior to planting.[44] It was administered to all the children of the village, with a whip made of a vegetable material, by one of the very old men. The conceptual link between the ripening of the food plants and the adolescence of the human child is clear. The sixteenth-century traveller Thevet, in his *Cosmographie universelle*, summarizes a highly revealing Tupinamba myth; once, during a time of great famine, the creator himself, Maire Monan, changed himself into a child, and was *beaten* by a group of starving children who were desperately searching for food themselves and who wanted to drive him away. Thereupon all manner of edible plants rained down upon them, and their hunger was relieved.[45]

Other festivals to celebrate the ripening of the forest fruit trees, especially the peach palm, are found among the Uainuma[46] and Yucuna (both Arawakan tribes),[47] the Bora, Muiname and Okaina (Witotoan),[48] the Correguaje[49] and the Jivaro.[50] We have enough detailed information concerning the Bora peach-palm festival to show that sacred trumpets are used to represent the voices of spirits. Tessmann accordingly classifies the Witotoan peach palm festivals with the Yurupary festivals of the Arawakan and Tucanoan tribes,[51] and suggests that the participants in the Witotoan ceremony, as in the others named, engaged in ritual flagellation.[52]

These three Witotoan tribes use the sacred trumpets, aside from the peach-palm festival, in certain ceremonies held by the men's secret societies. Indeed, there are many instances in which the role of the ritual trumpets as esoteric cult objects overshadows their role in the promotion of fertility.

The Witoto themselves do not seem according to Preuss to have had a peach-palm rite as such; but the *Uike* or ball game festival seems to have served much the same function.[53] In it special emphasis is laid on the bringing in of the fruit of the peach palm; and one of the three origin myths associated with the festival is linked with this tree in particular. The first peach palm was stolen as a seed and brought into the world by a woman who lived under water as the wife of a fish spirit;[54] this is a clear example of the widespread mythical theme of the theft of grain from the spirit world. The Witoto *Uike* festival is celebrated every two years in March and September, the dry season when fruit is plentiful. It lasts for some weeks, but is interrupted by intervals of several days at a time.[55] *Chicha* is brewed, supplies of game – and of fish above all – are laid in, and these are given to people from other villages in payment for the fruit and edible roots of all kinds which they contribute to the feast. Before the participants go off to the ball game, they request the master of ceremonies to tell them the origin of the particular tree or plant to which the ceremony is sacred, and he recounts the myth of its appearance from the 'seeming thing' (*Scheinding*) *no* or *naino*.[56] Preuss himself thinks that the *Uike* game is primarily a tree-fruit festival; root crops have their own separate festival, the *okima*.[57] The rubber ball itself, which must be kept off the ground with the players' knees,[58] has clear symbolic affinities with the ripe fruit dangling from the branches. The name of the ball, *uike*, means 'fruit', and the fruit of the rubber tree in particular. The ball embodies all the fruits which are brought to the festival; symbolically speaking they are its food. The ball is also referred to as a child of Father Moma, and it is also said that his soul dwells in it. The game is punctuated with loud cries, including the injunction 'kill him!'. One Witoto myth speaks of decapitating a person with a ball in order to eat him.[59] This recalls the cannibal feast, the *Bai*, which is also mentioned by Preuss in his account of the Witoto, and which incorporates masks very like those worn by the related Bora and Okaiba tribes during the peach-palm festival.[60]

The very strong link between plant fertility and the cannibalism formerly practised by the Witoto is expressed in a myth according to which Moma, under his alternative name of Father Buneima (father of the 'tribe' of food-plants and fish, the Bunesai) ate his fellow tribesmen the plants and fish.[61] The Bunesai are regarded as conquered enemies whose teeth and other relics are kept as trophies. 'Buneima', the singular of Bunesai, is a name given to individual ancestors and creatures of the underworld.[62]

In the oration delivered on the eve of the cannibal *Bai* feast, four varieties of fish and sixteen of tree fruit and tubers are mentioned; they are then eaten one by one as enemies (of Moma), and their 'teeth' and 'heads' are kept as trophies in the hut.[63] Moma is known as the bringer of vegetation, and so is Husiniamui (the being most closely concerned with cannibalism as such among the Witoto), who is probably no more than an aspect of Moma.[64] His deeds are glorified in the cannibal feast which takes place some time after the warriors have returned from a battle, eaten a little of the flesh of their slain or captured foes, and subsequently vomited. Preuss says that at the *Bai* festival itself only animal flesh is eaten.[65]

This form of cannibalism is a re-enactment of a mythical event, Moma's devouring of the Bunesai, and of the happenings in the night sky which are thought of as cannibalistic; the moon eats the stars and the rising sun eats the moon.

Ritual cannibalism springs from an identification of man with plant, and is thus characteristic of farming peoples;[66] Boglár carries this idea one stage further and shows that endocannibalism, the eating of the ashes of the dead, is found almost exclusively among peoples which practise slash-and-burn agriculture.[67] The ashes which remain after the forest has been cleared are necessary for the growth of cultivated plants; and the dead can have new life only by being ingested by the living. The same practice was intended to ensure the continued vigour of the food plants themselves. The ashes of the dead were most frequently consumed in a drink made from plants. The best example of this attitude is provided by the Arawakan Tariana, who practised endocannibalism and possessed a myth in which a sorcerer is burned and the first paxiuba palm grows from his ashes, an obvious variant of the Yurupary myths of the Rio Uaupés.[68]

Quite apart from the narrower question of the link with the introduction of slash-and-burn agriculture, the idea of a connection between plant ashes as a source of fertility and the consumption of human ashes as a resurrection ritual is extremely important; it helps us to understand the world view of the forest Indians of the north-west of the Amazon basin and their tendency to interpret human life in terms of the growth cycle of plants.

In a Witoto myth already mentioned in connection with the *uike* festival, in which a person is decapitated (with a ball) before being eaten, the connection between cannibalism and headhunting is manifest. Headhunting is quite common in South America, but it is not often linked, as it is in South-east Asia, with the fertility of the fields. The most important exception to this lies in the rites and beliefs which the warlike Jivaro of Ecuador connect with the acquisition of *tsantsa*, shrunken heads.[69]

The impulse to go on headhunting expeditions comes from the much feared spirits of dead ancestors, *arutama*, 'the old ones', who manifest themselves in many natural phenomena, and especially in wild beasts; on these ancestral spirits the success of the harvest depends. The shrinking of a head to make a *tsantsa*, a process accompanied by many rituals and taboos, bestows on these trophies a magical power known as *tsarutama*, (obviously an allusion to the ancestors, *arutama*), which is of great advantage to the owner of the trophy. The *tsarutama* is also communicated to the soil. This explains why during a victory celebration the 'counsellor' of the women working in the fields – a role which only a woman may undertake at other times – is the successful headhunter himself with his *tsantsa* hung round his neck. He visits not only the manioc fields and other cultivated areas but also the paddock containing the domesticated peccary pigs, whose increase is also connected with the *tsantsa*. At victory feasts a number of pigs are ceremonially slaughtered. This festival also formerly incorporated one feature which may be a sign that the Jivaro were once cannibals.[70] Before finally taking possession of the *tsantsa* of his victim, the headhunter had to swallow a piece of skin from the back of the head in order to make it appear that he had 'eaten his enemy'.

The cannibalism formerly practised by the Shipaya on the middle Xingú shows no detectable link with the growth of food plants or the fertility of the fields; but it is very definitely linked with the idea of a supernatural being. Until about fifty years ago the Shipaya and their neighbours the Yurupa, both Tupian tribes, had an autonomous cult of a tribal god called Kumãphari, who combines the aspects of tribal ancestor, culture hero and cannibal jaguar god. Kumãphari is the son of a deceased god of the same name, and is without doubt the dominant figure in Shipaya religion.[71]

The elder Kumãphari was mild and sociable; he is also called Señã, 'our dead one' and appears only in certain myths in which he transforms primeval human beings into animals. The younger Kumãphari, on the other hand, had the alternative name of Sekárika, 'our creator', because he created the first Shipaya Indians out of arrow reeds; and as the father of the twin brothers Kuñarima and Arubiata he bears the name Marušawa, which perhaps means 'chief'.[72] One of his first acts was the stealing of fire. Ultimately Kumãphari became angry with mankind, left this world and departed northwards down the Xingú valley to the end of the world, where earth and sky meet. He is now invisible to human eyes; his whole sib lineage dwells with him, and so do the great shamans who conversed with him in their lifetimes. He originally looked like a man, but now looks like a jaguar. He hears everything that is said about him. Three women are continually employed in collecting the saliva which drips from his open mouth in *cuias* (bottle gourds); for whenever a drop touches the earth misfortune comes upon the Shipaya: a person cuts himself, or is bitten by a snake, or something of the sort. Kumãphari sits with his face turned to the north; if he turns round and looks up the valley, the Indians must die. With him sits a gigantic toad, Kududú, which carries the sky on its back. If Kumãphari wishes to destroy the world he has only to walk round the toad to the outside of the sky and pull the creature out from under its burden, which will then collapse. His food to this day is still the roasted flesh of the Adji, the wild men with no anuses, whom his son Kuñarima once killed. When he has eaten all the flesh he blows on the bones and they are clad in flesh as before. Thus Kumãphari's staple diet is human flesh. From time to time through the medium of the shaman, he would request a meal of fresh meat. When this happened the Shipaya would set out on the warpath against another tribe with a view to taking a prisoner alive. If they succeeded the captive was bound with a special type of cord and brought back to the village. He was well treated until the preparations for the feast were complete, the drinks prepared and the guests present. Then he was handed over to the men of the tribe, who shot him to death with arrows. Part of the body was eaten by the participants in the rite; the rest was placed in a large covered pot, with some *chicha*, on a rock by the river as an offering to Kumãphari. On the next morning the pot was empty.

The shamans and their helpers were consecrated to the service of Kumãphari; in addition there were a number of young girls, the wives of the god, who lived chastely and had to perform certain religious duties, such as decorating the statues of Kumãphari and holding the great bamboo trumpets which were blown in front of these images at the *Zetábia* ceremony. No one was allowed to dance at this ceremony who had had sexual intercourse since the preceding day ... Anyone who wished to be admitted to the so-called *Maituma* fraternity had to go up to the statue of Kumãphari during this ceremony and make his desire known. The shaman answered in the name of the god, and blew tobacco smoke over the candidate, who then joined with the other new *Maituma* in drinking *kashiri*. They were henceforth expected to honour and assist each other all the rest of their lives, and never to quarrel among themselves.[73]

The cannibal ritual of the Shipaya preserved several conspicuous elements of the ritual cannibalism of the old Tupinamba, such as the cord of many-coloured threads of cotton with which the captive was bound. However, whereas Shipaya cannibalism definitely constituted a sacrifice to the god Kumãphari, as far as we know the Tupinamba ritual was not connected with a cult.

IV *The Soul and Ancestor Worship*

Most of the primitive peoples of South America believe that a human individual has several souls, which reside in various parts of his body and are responsible for the various manifestations of life. After death these several souls meet with different fates. One of the most interesting examples of this idea is found among the Apapocuva-Guarani.[1] One soul, called the *ayvucué* ('breath'), comes from the dwelling place of a deity in the zenith (Ñanderyquey, the tribal hero), in the east (Ñandecy, 'our mother') or in the west (Tupã, the thunder god). In its place of origin the *ayvucué* already exists in a finished state; at the moment of birth it enters the body. It is the task of the shaman to determine the place of origin of each soul. Soon after birth the *ayvucué* (vegetable soul?) is joined by another element, the *acyiguá* (animal soul); *acyiguá* means 'lively, vigorous, strong'.[2] This animal soul resides in the back of the neck. The good and gentle impulses in human nature, the appetite for vegetables, and repose are manifestations of the *ayvucué*; the evil and violent impulses, the appetite for meat and unrest are manifestations of the *acyiguá*.

The character of the individual human being depends on that of the particular animal which, as *acyiguá*, forms part of his psyche. A patient, good-natured person may for instance possess a butterfly soul; a jaguar soul – the fiercest *acyiguá* of all – makes a man cruel and violent. Immediately after death the two souls part company.[3] The *ayvucué* of a little child goes to paradise, the 'land without evil'. The *ayvucué* of an adult cannot travel as far as this; it finds its way to another afterworld which lies before the entrance of the land without evil, and where conditions are much as they are on earth. But the *ayvucué* does not always get so far without complications, especially if its possessor has died a violent death. In such a case it haunts its former home and endangers the surviving relations. There is, however, a special dance through which it can be caught and handed over to the storm god Tupã for final transference to the land of the *tavycué* (adult dead). Meanwhile the animal soul, the *acyiguá*, transforms itself into a much feared ghost called an *anguéry*, which persecutes mankind and must therefore be fought and destroyed.[4]

Like the Apapocuva, the Shipaya believe that the soul divides into two at death;[5] the impalpable breath soul, the *isãwi*, issues from the mouth of the dying person and goes to a kingdom of the dead situated inside hills and rocks; the *ãwá*, the 'shell' of the soul, becomes a ghoul. The Cariban Taulipang of Guiana say that each person has five souls.[6] All these souls resemble human beings, except that they are insubstantial, like shadows. Three of them are transformed after death into birds of prey. At the back of the knee, where a vein can be felt beating, there dwells a fourth soul called the *olozán*, which remains in the grave with the corpse. The fifth soul is the one that speaks. This is the most important. It is called the 'shadow', *yekatón*. During sleep it leaves the body, and after death it travels over the Milky Way to the world beyond.

The island Caribs of the West Indies believed that the individual had one soul for each part of his body where he could feel his pulse; one word was used to mean both heart and soul.[7] Only the most important of the souls, that of the heart, passes after death into the beyond. Some of the other souls repaired to the seashore and were called *umeku*; they caused shipwrecks. Others went into the woods and became evil spirits called *maboya*. They often resided in the bones of the dead, which were kept in the huts in which people lived.

The careful preservation of the remains of the dead is a custom reported from many tribes in the Amazon basin.[8] Although the idea that the soul dwells in the bones does not seem to be universal, it seems safe to assume that this belief is present in all the cases where we hear of endocannibalism, the eating of the bone ashes of the dead. This is not the place to embark on a discussion on the disposal of the dead among South American tribes; I have myself published a paper on the practice of endocannibalism in general.[9]

The Waica of the upper Orinoco hold beliefs concerning the soul which merit close attention. The soul of the individual has no independent existence during his lifetime, and emerges only in the smoke of his funeral pyre. Its name, *nobolebe*, is the word used to mean 'cloud', and obviously refers to the clouds of smoke in which the soul rises to heaven. The *nobolebe* exists only in human beings, not in animals, and is thought by many to be absent in children below the age of six. It follows that small children do not join the community of souls in heaven. Instead they rove the earth in the guise of malevolent spirits called *bole*, seeking for some way other than the smoke of a funeral pyre by which they can rise to heaven.[10]

The same fate, that of roaming the earth as *bole*, befalls those who have not been properly cremated, and whose ashes have not been consumed by members of their families. This category includes all those who have died an accidental death in the forest, or have been killed by wild beasts, or by human enemies. To say to someone that he will not be cremated after his death is the worst insult known to the Waica. Enemies killed in war are tossed into the forest unburnt; only if fear of the *bole* is stronger than hatred of the dead foe are his remains handed over to his family for cremation.

Apart from the 'immortal' indwelling soul, the *nobolebe*, the Waica believe that each individual has another, the *nonish* or *noneshi* ('shadow'), which is united with the *nobolebe* only at the moment of death. This *nonish*, although linked with the human shadow, usually dwells outside the body, sojourning in various parts of the forest in the shape of an animal. The forest-dwelling *nonish* of Waica men are identical with the *mohóme*, eagles of the species *Morphnus guianensis* (crested harpy). If any-one accidentally kills one of these birds, he observes the same taboos as a warrior who has killed a man: it is likely that the *mohóme* was the bearer of a man's *nonish* and that the man concerned fell dead at the moment the bird was shot. The *nonish* of the women dwell in another kind of wild creature which from the descriptions given by the Waica themselves seems to be a small rodent.

The concept of the *alter ego*, rare in South America, appears also in the beliefs attached to the third variety of soul, the *noúdibe* or image soul. Each child possesses an *alter ego* in the shape of a small brown lizard with black markings which is known as *ihilu noúbide*, 'image soul of the child'. If the lizard dies, the child dies too; and *vice versa*. The *noúdibe* is more substantial than the *nonish*; effigies of human beings, animals and plants are referred to as their *noúdibe*. Animals and plants thus possess a *noúdibe* but not a *nonish*.

The *alter ego* concept undoubtedly has its origins in the close affinity between man and beast which a hunting culture inevitably establishes in the human consciousness. Numbers of small stone figures which have been found by archaeologists in the Amazonian lowlands near the mouth of the Trombetas river, and which represent the beast-on-man motif, are generally regarded as expressions of the *alter ego* concept.[11]

Most of the available ethnographical evidence for the existence of this idea in South America belongs to the realm of shamanism. The Araucanian female shaman (*machi*) possesses an *alter ego* in the shape of a tree, usually a canelo tree (*Drimys winteri*), a magnoliacea which she tends in the forest, and whose fate is intimately linked with her own.[12] If someone discovers this tree and damages or destroys it, the *machi* in-variably becomes sick and dies. Among the Mataco of the Gran Chaco the shaman's *alter ego* is the mighty tree in the sky.[13] This tree is always present as an apparition while the shaman is engaged in ritual; nor-mally it is covered with leaves, but if it is dry and leafless the shaman knows that he must die within the year. The tree disintegrates as he draws his last breath. The replacement of the animal *alter ego* by a plant, as in these two examples, does not indicate a fundamental difference in the nature of the *alter ego* concept itself; it is merely a derivative variant of the original form.

Among the Ona of Tierra del Fuego the shaman possessed a guardian spirit called a *waiyuwen*, the soul of a deceased colleague.[14] The *waiyuwen* replaced the shaman's own soul for the purposes of his activities as a shaman. Hostile shamans did battle through the medium of their *waiyuwen*. If a *waiyuwen* was injured in one of these duels, the shaman concerned became ill; and if his *waiyuwen* was severely hurt the man died, and himself became the *waiyuwen* of another shaman. The *waiyuwen* took on the guise of an animal in certain special circumstances. In time of war the shaman used the *hahmaen*, an aspect of the *waiyuwen*, as a scout; this was normally an animal the size and shape of a guanaco, but sometimes took on the shape of a fox or a tuco tuco, a rodent of the species *Ctenomys magellanicus*. Although to some extent it shares the fate of its possessor, the *waiyuwen* is not strictly an *alter ego*; it is an independent entity, the soul of another shaman, and is thus better called a guardian spirit. The Yahgan shamans too had guardian spirits, *yefačel*, which came to them in a dream, and were either animal spirits (*čovanni*) or spirits of a special class who lived in old rotten stumps.[15] In order to keep his *yefačel* by him, the novice shaman slept with the short thick piece of spongy wood in which the *yefačel* was thought to dwell under his neck as a pillow. There is no sign that the *yefačel* was believed to share the fate of its possessor; nor was it a ghost like the *waiyuwen* of the Ona. It was a guardian nature spirit.

It is probably no accident that the belief in a personal guardian spirit, so widespread in North America, is found in South America principally in the tribes of the extreme south. This concept is deeply rooted in the way of life of nomadic hunters and gatherers. The best example of a technique for finding a guardian spirit, of the kind that is widespread in North America, is reported of the extinct Charrua of Uruguay.

Some men went on top of a solitary hill where there was a pile of stones to fast in order to find a companion. There they inflicted on themselves many wounds and suffered a rigorous penance until in their mind they saw a living being whom they invoked in times of peril as their guardian angel.[16]

Unfortunately, we have no information as to the exact nature of this 'guardian angel'.

The propitiation of the spirits of the dead is a major function of the funeral rites of the primitive South American peoples. Linked with this is the desire to prevent their return and to ease their journey to the realm of the dead. The worship of the dead, on the other hand, which is a consequence of the belief that they have a direct influence on the welfare of their descendants, is a much rarer phenomenon in all parts of South America outside ancient Peru.[17] A few significant examples of a cult of the dead in primitive South America are exemplified by the *Ianai-Kariá*, the ghost dance of the Shipaya, referred to by Métraux as the most important religious celebration of this tribe.[18] It is described in detail by Nimuendajú.[19]

The souls of the dead, the *isāwi*, are referred to by the collective honorific *i-ánāi*. They are well disposed towards mankind, and through their chief Wuba they often make known to the shaman their desire to hold a feast together with the living. In the course of the *Ianai-Kariá* the souls of the dead are believed to take possession of his body in order to dance and drink with the living in the village square. Meanwhile the shaman's own soul lies idle in his hut.

The festival itself takes place only at night and goes on for a week or more. The shaman, enveloped in a white cotton mantle called the *azabata*, is the first to dance on to the village square; he then retires to his hut. The performers representing the other *i-ánāi* then dance into the circle of men and women, who greet them with loud cries and the sound of two flutes. Each soul sings a short verse, in a nasal voice, a few times, and joins the round dance for a while before withdrawing to make room for the next soul. The proceedings end in a drinking bout in which the *i-ánāi* take part. At its conclusion the shaman restores to the mortal dancers their own souls (*isāwi*) which the *i-ánāi* have supplanted (as they have his), for the duration of the ceremony.

There is no evidence of the existence of a cult of the dead among the Indians of Tierra del Fuego; and there is little enough evidence of such a cult in the Gran Chaco. In eastern Brazil, on the other hand, ancestor worship plays an important part in native religion. The Bororo in particular have a highly developed ancestor ceremonial. They are among the few South American tribes which make a clear distinction between nature spirits (*bope*) and the spirits of the dead.[20] Like the Shipaya, the Bororo believe that the souls of their ancestors, the *aroe*, maintain close links with mankind, influence daily life and often visit the villages to eat, drink and dance. The link between the living and the *aroe* is provided by a special class of shamans, the *aroettawarari*, who are sharply distinguished from the other shamans, the *bari*, whose concern is with the nature spirits (*bope*).[21] On certain special occasions, such as baptisms, initiation rites and funerals, the spirits of the dead are ceremonially invoked by their medium, the *aroettawarari*, whom they 'possess or enlighten in dreams' (Lowie). Each *aroe* is also represented in two distinct concrete forms; the individual who impersonates it in the funeral rite, and the little flute (*poari*), with a bottle-gourd resonator, which constitutes its voice. This instrument, adorned with the appropriate clan insignia in feather mosaic and other ornaments, is carefully preserved by the fellow-clansmen of the deceased as a memorial to him.[22] Not surprisingly, considering the importance attached to the spirits of the dead, the funeral rites of the Bororo are highly developed.[23]

First there is a ceremonial hunt, after which the successful hunter takes the part of the dead man in the funeral ceremony proper, which incorporates a complex series of rites including the *mariddo* dance, in which the dancers carry large disc-shaped bundles, and another dance involving a mythical beast whose voice is represented by bullroarers. During the fourteen days or so that elapse between the death of an individual and his funeral, the body has undergone a primary burial, its flesh has been removed from its bones to the sound of dirges, the bones have been painted red with *urucú*, and feathers in the clan colours have been stuck to them, and particularly to the skull, which is displayed to the mourners. Then all the bones are put in a basket which is then suspended next to the house of the deceased. Subsequently the hunter who is to impersonate the dead man in the dance leads the way to a river, where the basket is thrown into deep water and the place is marked by a post stuck in the ground.

Ancestor worship was a prominent feature of the religion of the old Taino of the West Indies; the great *zemis* (idols) of the *caciques* (rulers) were believed to be the abode of the souls of their ancestors. Certain cotton and wooden *zemis* also contained the skulls and other bones of dead kinsmen.[24] We have already encountered these *zemis* as intermediaries between man and supreme being; and in addition the word *zemi* was applied, as we shall see, to other ideas and objects in Taino religion which are unconnected with the ancestor cult.

The religion of the (Tucanoan) Cubeo is based on the cult of the ancestors and founders of the patrilinear sibs within the tribe.[25] These ancestors are known in general as the *beküpwanwa* ('the ancients'); but each sib worships its own ancestor. These benevolent beings are invoked at each assembly of the sib and are normally represented by large trumpets which women are forbidden to see. The ancestors are the guardian spirits of the sibs and lend the men strength. Men and boys who wish to acquire strength and courage bathe every morning to the sound of the ancestor trumpets, which are also played at the boys' puberty rite while the boys are being whipped in order to make them grow to the great stature of the ancestors themselves.[26] When a man dies, his soul travels after a number of false starts to the dwelling place of the ancestors of his sib, which is not far from its earthly dwelling.[27] At the funeral ceremonies the ancestors are present, in the shape of trumpets, to console the mourners. There are also mask dances which I shall discuss in another connection; these do not involve the representation of ancestral ghosts but of gods.

The representation of the Cubeo sib ancestors by sacred musical instruments belongs to the wider category of Yurupary rites, basically connected with fertility. It does not present the same direct personal contact with individual and still-remembered ancestors as does the ancestor cult of the Shipaya and Bororo. There is no unbroken link between the anonymous mass of those dead in 'historic' times – which means within living memory – and the remote ancestors who are considered to belong to a legendary past. The newly dead are forgotten as soon as the funeral is over.[28] The first ancestors of mankind emerged from the boulders of the rapids in the form of anacondas, and became human beings only after they had sloughed their skins.[29]

A combination of a memorial service for the recently dead and a commemoration of the legendary tribal ancestors can be seen in the *Kwarup* ritual of the Camayura of Mato Grosso.[30] The *Kwarup* (*kuat*, 'sun'; *yerup*, 'my ancestor') centres on a number of posts with human faces and ornaments each about three feet high and carved from the same camayuva wood (*Guadua sp.*) from which the creator Mavutsine created the first Camayura. The chant which is raised as the people dance round the posts is the same one that Mavutsine sang as he created mankind. Thus not only do the ancestors return to welcome the newly-dead into their midst, but the dramatic re-enactment of the act of creation ensures the survival of the tribe.[31]

A remarkable parallel to the ancestral trumpet cult of the Cubeo is found in the great wind instruments, the *kaduke*, of the Mundurucú, also embodiments of the sib ancestors, which may not be seen by women.[32] At the conclusion of the ceremony a drink made of manioc is poured down the *kaduke*, caught in a bottle-gourd dish, and drunk by the men present. In this way the ancestors are induced to look with favour on their descendants.[33]

The few examples I have given cover virtually all the known instances of ancestor worship as such in primitive South America; as we have seen, however, the role of ancestral spirits in fertility rituals is an extremely important one.

V *Representations of Supernatural Beings*

Idols of wood, stone, clay and other materials are relatively uncommon in South America away from the Andes; although isolated archaeological finds, and the reports of early travellers, suggest that the position may have been somewhat different in former times.

The region which offers the most material is the West Indian area formerly inhabited by the Arawakan Taino tribe. Taino religion centred on the cult of the images and sacred objects known as the *zemi*. These included stone and wood idols; images made of cotton and other textiles enclosing human bones; prepared skulls; masks and frontal amulets; body ornaments; rock paintings or engravings in caves and on exposed surfaces.[1] Most *zemis* were grotesque anthropormorphic figures, frequently provided with exaggerated male or female genital organs. Many were regarded as repositories of the souls of ancestors; others were concrete representations of nature deities. A minority of the figures were in the shape of birds, quadrupeds or even plants. Some *zemis* were in geometrical shapes; there exist three-pointed stone carvings, oval stone rings and other stone objects of unknown significance. The numerous *zemis* that have been found, in natural and artificial caves, make it easy to understand the deep impression made on the first *conquistadores* by Taino religion. Certain *zemis* belonging to the chief were worshipped by the whole tribe; but every man had at least one personal *zemi* of his own. A number of the most famous images were credited with miraculous powers; they were believed to be able to speak, walk, cause amputated limbs to grow again and perform other feats. To give even the briefest account of the whole range of beliefs and practices connected with the *zemis* would be impossible here; a number of their functions have been described under other headings in this book.

The extraordinary wealth of religious and parareligious sculpture and other sacred objects in the West Indies has often, and probably correctly, been traced to mainland influences. Similar features are indeed to be found in the mainland areas of Circum-Caribbean culture. I have already referred to the idols in the temples of the Timote of the Venezuelan Andes; a similar example of so-called 'sub-Andean' influence is the religion of the Araona of eastern Bolivia, centred on wooden idols adorned with feather mosaic and on round stones representing the gods of food plants.[2] The image of the god Epymará ('father of the gods') was an oval piece of wood.

The Arawakan Paressi of the western Mato Grosso were even less ambitious in the design of their images of the gods. At the beginning of the present century one of their most sacred objects was an unhewn block of wood bearing the name Johôhô.[3] When it became rotten and wormeaten, a shaman would go with his assistant into the forest and fetch another. To the accompaniment of a monotone chant which women were forbidden to hear, the new sacred object was carried back to the village.

In the middle of the nineteenth century, the Paressi had special huts set aside in which they kept what Pires de Campos called 'terrifying' idols.[4] They were accompanied by ritual trumpets, so it is supposed that they were connected with the serpent god Nukaima. The Arawakan Mojo too, were observed by the seventeenth-century Franciscan missionary Francisco de Rosario to have rough-hewn posts in their temples as representations of their gods.[5] We recall the analogy with the *ole* posts of the Trumai, representations of manioc spirits, and the *kwarup* figures of the Camayura, embodiments of ancestors.

At the bidding of their principal deity Kumãphari or of his sons Kunãrima and Arubiata, the Shipaya, Curuaya and Yuruna made statues (*upáši*) representing Kumãphari himself and other mythical figures.[6] These were cylindrical wooden posts with carved and painted human heads, and formed the focal point of the Shipaya *Zetábia* dance.[7] Métraux connects these figures of Kumãphari with the posts which the ancient Tupinamba used to erect in places frequented by spirits, and at the foot of which they used to lay offerings.[8] There was sometimes a transverse beam from which were suspended human likenesses painted on palm leaves. The Botocudo have ten-foot-high wooden posts, sacred to the *maret* spirits, the upper third of which is carved as a human figure whose face is turned to the east.[9] This is virtually the only example of native religious sculpture in the whole of eastern Brazil; while the Gran Chaco and the south provide no examples at all, apart from the wooden idols of the Caduveo, which are now used as children's playthings although they may well once have had religious significance.[10] The sacred ladders (*rewe*) used ritually by the Araucanian female shamans occasionally bear human faces whose significance is unknown.[11]

On the upper Amazon the chronicler of the 1542 Orellana expedition, Gaspar de Carvajal, saw in the village of the chief Omagua two idols

woven out of feathers of divers sorts . . . and on their arms, stuck into the fleshy parts, they had a pair of discs resembling candlestick sockets, and they also had the same thing on their knees; their ears were bored through, like those of the Indians of Cuzco, and larger.[12]

In the middle of the seventeenth century another traveller, the priest Cristobal de Acuña, mentions that the Amazonian tribes worshipped idols which they had made with their own hands. He singles out two small Arawakan tribes on the right bank, near the confluence with the Río Negro, as the most proficient woodcarvers. The idols were kept in huts and only removed from their resting-places when their presence in the human world was necessary to give assistance in the department of life in which they specialized, whether fishing, seedtime or war.[13]

In the sands of a small tributary of the Río Casiquiare there has been found a wooden female figure, some twenty inches high, which was probably the work of these old Arawakan woodcarvers; the find was made in territory occupied by the Baré, a once numerous Arawakan tribe which formerly inhabited the whole Río Negro area.[14] The figure probably represents a goddess. Much cruder wooden figurines are still made by the Witoto and Yagua in memory of the dead;[15] similarly, the Arawakan Huilliche formerly erected wooden posts carved to represent human figures.[16] These were not worshipped, and were therefore not true idols.

From time to time stone sculptures have also been found in the Amazonian jungles; in the seventeenth century a crouching human figure 46 inches high, carved from sandstone, was found in the head-waters of the Río Uauapés. In the middle of the nineteenth century it was taken to Europe by the French traveller Francis de Castelnau, and it is now in the Musée de l'Homme in Paris.[17] We know nothing of the cult that was associated with this statue. We are better informed as to the small stone figures which have been found along the lower Amazon in the vicinity of its confluence with the Rió Trombetas; they show the beast-on-man motif which is almost certainly a reflection of the concept of an animal *alter ego*.[18] On the basis of this motif Konrad Theodor Preuss postulates cultural links between inhabitants of this region and the people responsible for the monumental stone figures of San Agustín in Colombia.

Roughly the same area along the lower Río Trombetas is the probable source of a number of startlingly well-executed wood carvings which represent another aspect of the *alter ego* concept, the bird-on-quadruped motif. Their significance is probably parareligious; they were all carved at least a hundred years ago. One example is a stamping-stick in the National Museum in Copenhagen; another is a large wooden trumpet in the Rijksmuseum voor Oudheiden in Leiden; and there is a ceremonial axe in the British Museum and a ceremonial stave in the Staatliches Museum für Völkerkunde in Munich.[20] The present-day Cashuena of the Trombetas area carve figures similar in subject but much cruder in execution on the sticks used by their shamans; the older wood carvings from the same area presumably served the same purpose. They formed part of the equipment of the shamans and represented their animal *alter egos* or familiar spirits.[21] There is no lack of evidence to suggest that shamans everywhere in South America use clay wooden figures in their activities, but it is by no means always clear that these figures are true idols. The old Tupinamba of the Maranhão region kept small wax figures in huts built in the bush, into which the shamans retired from time to time to burn sweet-smelling resin and make offerings to the nature spirits.[22]

The most important piece of the shaman's equipment in South America was and is the *maraca*, the bottle-gourd rattle, which is regarded as a sacred object by many tribes. The rattling of the stones or seeds within the *maraca* is interpreted as the voice of the spirits, and the stones themselves are seen as their manifestation. But even without the rattling stones which make it into a *maraca*, the bottle gourd or calabash is often revered as an idol in itself. Gourd idols mounted on handles are often almost indistinguishable from *maracas*. Early travellers such as Nobrega and Vasconcellos report that the *pajes*, the shamans of the old eastern Tupian tribes, always carried with them gourds carved to represent human faces, and that they took these with them into a dark hut where they allegedly conversed with them.[23] There was another way in which the *pajes* could make contact with the spirits; they burned tobacco leaves inside the gourd and inhaled the smoke which issued from its mouth, eyes and ears until they relapsed into a trance state. In this state they were possessed by the spirits, and the words they spoke were regarded as oracles. The same procedure was observed a hundred years ago among the Manao, an Arawakan tribe living at the confluence of the Río Negro and the Amazon;[24] a woodcut in the famous account of the travels of the sixteenth-century German soldier of fortune Hans Staden[25] shows a Tupinamba *maraca* with a mouth carved on it. Even the modern *maracas* of South American Indian tribes often carry mysterious incisions which may be rudimentary facial features. I have tried in another work to make clear the connection between *maracas* or gourd idols and the disembodied 'head spirits' which appear in South American mythology.[26]

The old Tupinamba sometimes gave their gourd idols an even more elaborate form. At the beginning of the seventeenth century, Yves d'Evreux saw shamans putting grains of maize and other plant seeds into the mouths of gourd idols which were fitted with movable lower jaws to imitate chewing. This was believed to ensure that the spirit which dwelt in the gourd would allow reproductive power to enter the seeds, and the seeds thus blessed were sown in the fields.[27]

The representation of supernatural beings by ritual masks is confined to certain clearly defined areas of South America. The tribes of the right bank of the Río Guaporé, the Amniapä and Macurap, have gourd masks which are referred to as 'gods';[28] and there are isolated instances of the same use of masks in various other parts of the continent, notably the north-western Amazon area.[29] I have already mentioned the funerary mask dances which take place among the Tucanoan Cubeo and the Arawakan Cáua and Siusí along the Río Uaupés and the Río Içana. Besides propitiating the spirit of the dead person and keeping it away, the dances also serve the purpose of bringing fruitfulness and plenty to the village and its inhabitants, to the crops and to nature in general.[30]

The Cubeo and Cáua masks are knee-length hooded garments made of bark cloth painted with geometrical designs and provided with sleeves. They represent all kinds of animals, including insects, as well as evil forest spirits, giants and dwarfs.[31] The dancer mimes the characteristic movements of the creature concerned and identifies himself wholly with it. The mask and its wearer represent not an ordinary representative of the species but a spirit; this is indicated by the fact that many of the animal masks have human faces.[32] The only signs of the animal in question that appear on the masks are certain conventional attributes and certain ornamental motifs. There is a special concern with using mask and mime to bring the enemies of the hunter within his power; the forest spirit Makukö (Cubeo) and the jaguar (but not important game animals such as the tapir and peccary), and agricultural pests such as caterpillars and beetle larvae. The funerary mask dance begins with a mock attack on the communal house (maloka) by the group of mask dancers who emerge from the forest. They overcome the resistance of two other masked men and force their way in, while the mother and widow of the dead man weep and wail.[33] The climax of the ceremony, among both Cubeo and Cáua, is the phallic dance already described. At the end of the dancing the masks are usually burned, while their 'souls', the spirits dwelling within them, go to the world of dead masks, just as the human soul goes after death to its own after-world.

According to Koch-Grünberg the true Cáua equivalent of the Yurupary of the old eastern Tupians is not Kuwai but Iyäimi, an evil spirit who is represented by a mask costume of a unique pattern; a large piece of bast has been cut out and sewn together to make trouser legs, but the dancer's arms remain bare.[34] He pulls another bast garment, painted with a face and pierced with eye holes, over his head.[35]

The macacaraua, the mask costume which represents Yurupary himself in the whipping dances, has already been described in the section dealing with vegetation gods. At the beginning of the present century, Koch-Grünberg was able to acquire two very old macacaraua from an old Tariana chief at Yauarete on the middle Uauapés. They were sleeveless hooded garments made of brown monkey-hair cords sewn together and intertwined with hair cut from girls at their first menstruation (a clear sign of the connection between masks and puberty rites). There were holes for eyes, mouth and arms; a long drape of tucumã fibres covered the legs of the dancers. The chief called the larger of the two masks 'man' and the smaller 'woman'. According to Koch-Grünberg they always appeared in pairs and represented the presiding spirit of the Yurupary festival and his wife. As a rule each tribe possessed only one pair of masks, which were in the custody of the supreme head of the tribe, who issued it to the various *molokas*, single-house villages, as and when required.[36]

Among other north-western Amazonian tribes, such as the Witotoans (Witoto, Bora, Muinane, Okaina) and the Yagua, hood-shaped masks and mantles of bark cloth are used to represent animal spirits (among the Witotoans) or the souls of the dead (among the Yagua). However, in most cases we do not possess detailed descriptions of the individual entities portrayed or of the functions and significance of the masks.[37]

However, we do have a comprehensive description of the adolescence ceremony of a young girl among the Tucuna of the upper Amazon, in which bark cloth masks are used.[38] The girl's hair is torn out, a painful variant of the common practice of cutting the hair of a girl at puberty. This is a symbolic death, as the hair is the seat of the life force. About six months later, when the hair has grown again, there is another ceremony, and the girl enters upon a new life as a full member of the community. During the puberty rites, which begin with her first menstruation, she is kept closely confined and is thought to be in great danger from animal spirits. The most spectacular part of the ceremony is that in which the invited guests – sometimes forty or fifty of them – appear in the grotesque masks of the animal and forest spirits, demand drink, and disappear once more into the forest. The most important of the mask spirits are the storm daemon Oma, with his enormous penis, the female butterfly daemon Beru (equivalent in meaning to the Lingua Geral name Yurupary), the water spirit Dyëvaë, a tree daemon called Mavi, the maize spirit Čavi, and two monkey daemons.[39] The masks made by the Tucuna today show a marked artistic decline from those made by the same tribe and their long-extinct neighbours, the Yuri, which the Bavarian naturalists Johann Baptist Spix and C. F. Phil. von Martius took back to Germany after their remarkable voyage up the Amazon in 1819–20. These unique examples of South American religious sculpture now adorn the collections of the Staatliches Museum für Völkerkunde in Munich. They include grotesque anthropomorphic masks representing forest spirits, and a number of highly realistic heads of birds, beasts and fish, made from reeds, covered with bark cloth, and painted. The subjects include tapir, jaguar, wildcat, squirrel, deer, vulture, piranha fish and tick. They are utterly different stylistically from the masks made by the Tucuna of today, and from the geometrically stylized animal masks made by the neighbouring Arawakan and Tucanoan tribes to the north; and this very marked contrast has not yet been satisfactorily explained. Spix and Martius say of these Tucuna and Yuri masks:

The birth of a child gives rise to a singular masquerade in which the evil spirit Yurupary, the storm wind, and the various beasts of the forest are represented by masks made of bark. A procession passes through the village, and to the sound of a monotone chant and the clatter of a tortoise shell gong, the infant's hair is torn out.[40]

Nimuendajú confirms that small children as well as girls at puberty have their hair torn out (although this does not normally take place until the age of two or three), and that this ceremony, still practised in 1952, closely resembles the more important puberty ceremony.[41] However, he has several criticisms of the report of the nineteenth-century travellers and of the illustration in their volume of plates which purports to show a 'ceremonial procession of the Tucuna' and which depicts most of the masks now in Munich.

South of the Amazon the most important mask rituals were those of the tribes of the upper Xingú;[42] and among the Camayura at least they have not yet died out.[43] Although the masks are basically anthropomorphic, they are regarded as representations of wild creatures, especially birds and aquatic animals. Each animal is represented by a symbol painted in the middle of a human face. The commonest form of mask is a roughly square board with a forehead and nose carved out of it. All the masks incorporate the so-called *mereshu* pattern,[44] which represents a mereshu fish in a net and recalls the common origins of the pattern and of the mask.[45]

Another type of mask consists of an oval frame covered with a cotton tissue bearing human features moulded from wax or painted on the surface. From the frame hang palm straw fibres which conceal the body of the dancer; the wooden masks, too, have a long 'beard' or fringe, and probably a mantle of leaves or straw.

According to von den Steinen, the dances in which the masks are used have their origin in hunting ceremonies;[46] and it is true that the fish dance and the guan dance danced by the Tupian Camayura and Auetö have a proven link with the desire for good fishing and hunting.

But we know little of the true religious significance of the masks or of the function of the dance.

The same is true of the mask dances of the Carajá and their neighbours the Tapirapé in the middle Araguaya region. The first detailed account was written by Paul Ehrenreich, who established that all the masks used in the dance represent animals or animal spirits, whether game animals or animals which play a part in myth.[47] Here too the animals or spirits are characterized only by certain obvious attributes or by conventional motifs. Ehrenreich distinguishes between several groups of masks. The most typical are cylindrical hats, covered with an elaborate feather mosaic pattern which represents the animal prototype in a way which is often hard for the uninitiated to recognize.[48] The dancer's costume was completed by long hangings of buriti fibre which were placed round his shoulders and hips. As well as these cylindrical hats there were simple basketwork structures which were placed over the head and the upper part of the body; one of these, twelve feet long and funnel-shaped, represented the long pointed snout of an anteater. This type of mask sometimes evolves into complete plaited mask suits with trousers, sleeves and a hood. The famous dolphin mask is an example of this; its outsize phallus corresponds not to the nature of the animal itself but to its Amazonian reputation as a priapic daemon. The Bacairi of the upper Xingú, too, have straw mask suits with an attached phallus made of a maize cob or something similar; but these represent an insect, the imeo, the larva of the palm borer beetle.[49]

The third type of mask used by the Carajá consists of a half-gourd hung with strips of leaves. Again, a human face is used to represent a wild creature; an individual species of bird, for instance, is denoted by feathers hung on the mask. Each mask is associated with a chant which imitates the call of the creature concerned. As in the upper Xingú area, the mask dances coincide with the ripening of certain fruits and with hunting and fishing expeditions. The Carajá women may neither see the masks without their wearers nor enter the men's house where they are stored. The mask dancers enter the village from the forest, mostly in pairs, and throw pieces of wood about in all directions. There are also mendicant mask dancers who collect food. At the conclusion of the festivities the masks are discarded or burned.

The neighbours of the Carajá, the north-western and central Ge tribes, the Canella, the Apinayé, the Sherente and some of the northern Cayapó, also have mask dances, but only in a much corrupted form.[50] The procession of the Great Anteater among the Sherente, Apinayé and Pau d'Arco strongly recalls the use by the Carajá of their anteater mask.[51] The masks are made in secret in the bush; they appear at the ceremony in which girls are given names by the men's fraternities, a ceremony which is based on an origin myth. Their original ritual significance is apparent in the custom of dumping them in the river at the end of the proceedings. Men in anteater masks demand food from the women, as do the Canella mask dancers. These latter do not, however, represent anteaters, but water monsters in which the Canella still firmly believe.[52] The Canella masks consist of a wide plaited headpiece with a face painted on it and with wooden projections like horns on either side. They are not sacred, unlike the straw masks of the Mashacali, which are used in initiation rites and represent the dead. They are kept in the men's house, which like the masks is taboo for all those who have not been initiated. At all events, this was the state of affairs when Curt Nimuendajú visited the last survivors of the tribe in eastern Brazil in 1938 and 1939.[53]

The two main centres of mask ritual are north-western Amazonia and the Xingú-Araguaya region; but isolated examples of mask dances appear in the Gran Chaco, and this practice has spread from the advanced agricultural tribes of the Amazon basin as far afield as Tierra del Fuego.

Like the Tucuna of the upper Amazon, the Lengua of the Gran Chaco use a mask dance to symbolize the supernatural dangers which threaten a girl at the onset of puberty. At the girl's puberty ritual a line of masked youths clad in rhea-feather girdles thrust their way through the festive crowd, swinging bundles of deer-hoof rattles and uttering shrill cries. They represent evil spirits; they attempt to approach the girl but are driven back by the women.[54]

The Chamacoco have a boys' adolescence rite which ends with the so-called Anãpösö feast. The anãpösö are forest spirits whose ruler, the dog daemon Pohichio, was born from a tree and is the consort of the great mother Eshetewuarha. Three or four days after the beginning of the festival the performers impersonating the anãpösö come out of the forest into the camp. They have bags with eye holes over their heads, in place of the elaborate feather masks which were formerly worn, and have hammocks wrapped round them. They are decorated all over with feathers, and the exposed parts of their skin are painted. The women hide behind a screen of matting and turn their backs on the dancers, whom they may not see on pain of death. It is believed that the whole tribe would perish if the women were ever to find out that the dancers were not spirits but men. This secret is revealed to the candidates for initiation, with strict instructions never to tell it to the women.[55]

Another ritual reserved for the men and adolescent boys of the tribe was the initiation ritual of the Ona of Tierra del Fuego, the *Kloketen*, which corrresponded to the *Kina* of the Yahgan and the *Yinchihaua* of the Alacaluf.[56] Among the Ona the spirits made their appearance at the outset of the initiation ceremony in order to frighten off the women. Grown men and already-initiated youths represented various spirits, wearing conical bark or skin masks and painting their bodies with patterns in black, white and pink. They emerged from the initiation hut and danced and postured in full sight of the women, calling to them that they would be punished if they did not obey their husbands. The women are supposed to have believed in the reality of the spirits; the young men were let into the secret at their initiation.

The presiding spirit at the *Kloketen* was the female being Xálpen, who made only one appearance in the course of the ritual. She was a huge worm crawling on the earth. Her consort, Soorte, passed through the village at least once every day, threw a few huts into disorder, shifted a few articles of property, beat a few women and returned whence he had come.[57] There were a number of other spirits as well.

The shaman played an important part in the *Kloketen* of the Ona; the equivalent ritual among the Yahgan, the *Kina*, was directed by him. The *Kina* was reserved for men who had twice undergone the compulsory tribal initiation ceremony, the *Ciexaus*. The entry of the spirits took a very similar form to the equivalent part of the ceremony among the Ona; both tribes based the whole ritual on an origin myth. The number of spirits – Gusinde describes them as extramundane beings – was much greater among the Yamana than among the Ona, but the feminine supreme spirit, the counterpart of Xálpen, whose name was Tanuva, was not impersonated.[58] A spirit called Kalampasa made his appearance in much the same way as Soorte; and there were also a sea spirit, a forest spirit and a number of animal spirits.[59]

Another religious element which, as we have seen, is very closely linked with mask dances in general is the representation of the voices of supernatural beings by sacred wind instruments. The use of these spread over large portions of tropical South America largely as a consequence of the expansion of the mainly agricultural Arawakan peoples. North of the Amazon the instruments are usually played in connection with the cult of vegetation deities; south of the Amazon they form the focal point of an esoteric cult of their own. This is the case among the Shipaya of the middle Xingú, who play spirit flutes before the images of the jaguar god Kumãphari; and an even closer link between visual and auditory divine symbols is found among the Tucuna. In this case the bark trumpet (*bu/bu*) does no more than provide an accompaniment to the more important of the two *uaricana* instruments, the *toki*, a kind of wooden megaphone, which takes precedence because it represents the voice of the spirit itself.[60] In former times the *toki* was always close to two statues of muirapiranga wood which the shades of the daemons would enter in order to sing through the *toki*, which they did without any human assistance. Curt Nimuendajú saw two of these crudely carved figures, one rather more and the other rather less than three feet high, which obviously represented man and wife. Nimuendajú was unable to find out the names of the beings represented; but he says that the *toki* were named after wild creatures (king vulture, otter, etc.). The *toki* was invented by the culture hero Dyoi.

The esoteric all-male ritual of the type which is common in regions south of the Amazon is represented by one excellent example in the north. The ancient Maipure, an Arawakan tribe which lived on the middle Orinoco, were visited towards the end of the eighteenth century by an Italian missionary, Filippo Gilij,[61] who reported that in their *Cheti* (animal dance) spiral bark trumpets were played. The men asserted that serpents had come into the village to dance and drink with them; while the women were afraid both of the serpents and of the trumpets in which they manifested themselves.

The Arawakan Ipurina of the middle reaches of the Río Purus dedicate a flute dance ceremony to the *kamutshi* or *kamatsha*, spectral beings, said to be covered with feathers or fine hair, whose dwelling place in a certain lagoon is known to none but a few shamans. Ehrenreich links the name *kamutshi* with the Arawakan word *kamu*, meaning 'sun'.[62] The sight of the *kamutshi* is fraught with dangers for any uninitiated person; for women it means certain death. When the ceremony is about to take place the shaman fetches the flutes and the magic trumpets of spiral jutahy bark from the lake where they lie. In them dwell the *kamutshi* themselves. When the procession of fifteen or twenty players approaches the village, all the women take refuge in one of the houses. The men circle this house, blowing their instruments for all they are worth, until the women, with averted gaze, hand out food which is immediately eaten by the men. The women ritualistically manifest fear of the 'animal' which howls round their house; and the two leaders of the instrumentalists are known as the 'peccaries'.

The Paressi-Cabishi, an Arawakan tribe of the western Mato Grosso, have an esoteric cult centring on the figures of the snake spirit Nukaima and his wife Kamuteriro.[63] The name Nukaima is considered by Max Schmidt to have some connection with the Paressi word *kaimare*, which means 'moon': and to me the link between Kamuteriro and the Arawakan word *kamu* ('sun') seems more apparent still. The two entities are represented by two instruments, a large trumpet with a gourd resonator and a small flute which the women may on no account see. Women are forbidden on pain of death to enter the men's house, which is also a dance house and is the dwelling-place of Jararaca, as the snake spirit is known (the name is that of a common venomous snake of the genus *Bothrops*). On the evening of the ceremony the women keep to their huts. The two spirits appear in the shape of two dancers, who play on the *jararaca* instruments in the open space between the houses.

There are knocks on all the doors, and everyone is told that Jararaca himself has come and demands *chicha*. This and food are prepared by the women, who may not leave their huts or even look out, and are taken to the men's house by the master of ceremonies, the *arume*, ostensibly to feed the hungry Jararaca, but really to feed the men assembled there. Snake patterns and other figures decorate the two uprights supporting a horizontal bar which the young men seek to break with their shoulder during *chicha* festivals as a test of strength.

Among the Mojo of eastern Bolivia the equivalent of the serpent spirit Jararaca of the Paressi was the alligator spirit, and the ritual dedicated to it was called the 'Alligator Spring', as we are told by the Jesuit Franz Xaver Eder who visited them at the end of the eighteenth century.[64] The climax of the festival consisted of a procession of the participants, all men, with trumpets and other musical instruments which the uninitiated believed to be the voices of spirits. If the women and children saw the musicians they would be eaten up by alligators. The core of the procession consisted of twelve men each of whom blew a nine-foot-long trumpet which was carried by another man. Eder's description makes it clear that these trumpets were of the familiar conical type made of spirally wound bark. To this day, at Christian festivals, the Mojo and their neighbours the Caviña and the Itonama play huge panpipes made of no less than eleven of these bark trumpets put together.[65]

In the upper Xingú region to the east of Paressi territory, the use of musical instruments is mainly found among Arawakan tribes. The Mehinacu, for example, have a mask ritual during which a sacred flute of great length is played; again, this is taboo to women, as is the house in which the masks and musical instruments are kept.[66] In the men's house of the Yaulapiti, another Arawakan tribe, Vincenzo Petrullo saw three men dancing with flutes which the women were forbidden to see.[67] The same taboo was in operation among the Bacairi.[68] This Cariban tribe had a myth according to which Kame, the ancestor of the neighbouring Arawakan groups, built the first flute house and carved the first flutes. Then he and the ancestor of the Bacairi, Keri, held the first mask dance.[69] Kame and Keri are the mythical twin culture heroes of the upper Xingú, Keri being linked with the moon and Kame with the sun.

More recent information concerning the neighbouring Tupian tribe, the Camayura, tells roughly the same story.[70] The flute house, the *jacuí*, is the centre of the village. *Jacuí* is also the name of the three sacred flutes, 35–40 inches long, which are linked with a powerful *mama'é* or mother spirit which appears in the shape of a guan (*jacuí*).[71] These flutes and four other ritual implements kept in the flute house were originally donated by the sun (*kuat*); again, they may not be seen or touched by women.

The use of sacred wind instruments in men's rituals to represent the voices of spirits has not spread any further north than the upper Xingú; and in this area we find it in close proximity to another and probably older form of sound-production bearing the same ritual significance, the bullroarer swung on the end of a cord.[72]

In 1894, when von den Steinen visited the Mehinacu, there hung in the flute house, alongside the masks used in cayman dance, a two-foot-long red wooden bullroarer shaped like a sword blade.[73] The bull-roarers of the neighbouring Nahukwa are fish-shaped, and some of them are ornamented with serpent patterns; they are not concealed from the women. The Bacairi call their bullroarers, which are also usually fish-shaped, *yélo* or *iyelo*;[74] the same word also means thunder and lightning.[75] The fish shape of the Camayura bullroarer is linked with the mythical belief that this instrument was originally given to mankind by the dog-fish.[76] The bullroarer is used in order to bring rain; it also belongs to the piqui fruit tree and is used at the piqui harvest ceremony at which the *jacuí* flutes are also heard. Like the *jacuí*, it is kept in the flute house as a sacred object.

The great centre of the religious use of the bullroarer lies in eastern Brazil. Among the Sherente, those votaries of the personified planet Mars who wish to become shamans or good huntsmen invoke him by means of bullroarers, which represent his own 'roar'.[77]

Among the Bororo, bullroarers are used alongside flutes in the con-text of funeral rites. Von den Steinen plausibly interprets the sound of these instruments as representing the voices of the dead in general;[78] Colbacchini-Albisetti[79] tells us, more circumstantially, that the sound represents the voice of a mythical underwater beast, which is impersonated by one of the dancers at the funeral ritual and which is itself classified among the spirits of the dead.[80] The bullroarers are kept strictly concealed from the uninitiated; the youths of the tribe are shown them for the first time at a funeral. In the initiation ceremony of the eastern Timbira the bullroarer is used to keep the candidates awake; its role was formerly more prominent, and it possessed an intrinsic sacred significance.[81] At the young men's puberty ceremony of the Mashacali, masked dancers represent the dead and bullroarers are swung to represent their voices.[82]

The Apinayé (north-western Ge) who use the bullroarers as a mere plaything, still call it 'soul of the dead';[83] and the Caduveo of the Gran Chaco, who also give it to their children to play with, nevertheless use it in the course of funeral ceremonies.[84] The Caripuna of the upper Río Madeira, on the other hand, who use it to mourn the dead, regard it as a sacred object which one must never be without.[85]

In the esoteric *Zetábia* ritual which the Shipaya men held in honour of the god Kumãphari, the sound of the *pari* flutes mingled, after midnight with that of a new instrument called the *wari wari sami*. Its name (*wari wari*: 'whirl', *sami*: 'elder male kinsman', i.e. ancestor) recalls the epithets 'our dead one' and 'our creator', which belong to the elder and the younger Kumãphari. If Nimuendajú has correctly understood the scanty information he was given and the mysterious sketch drawn by his informant, the *wari wari sami* was a roughly elliptical bullroarer. This was a powerful and terrible object which might cause sickness and bad luck; no women or children were allowed to approach it.[86] The bullroarer is also present among a number of other tribes which possess sacred wind instruments, the Ipurina,[87] the Tucuna,[88] the Bora[89] and the Baniwa,[90] but in these cases its function is either unknown or known to be non-religious. It does, however, play a part in the mask dance of the Piaroa of the middle Orinoco, a northern extension of the Yurupary festival, as one of the instruments which embody the voices of gods.[91] It is not clear which god is represented by the bullroarer.

In the hands of the shaman of the Caliña Caribs of Surinam it serves to exorcize the evil spirit, not to invoke him.[92]

VI *Shamanism*

In the course of this account we have repeatedly come across the figure of the shaman, medicine man or witch doctor. In the whole area of South America outside the sphere of the Andean civilizations he is the centre of religious life in the widest sense of the word, and his role merits a chapter to itself.

The term 'shaman', borrowed from the ethnography of Siberia, means a magician, healer and spirit medium combined, a person who is able to put himself into trance states in which he is thought to travel in heaven or in the underworld or to be possessed by spirits from these places. Its use in a South American context stems from the leading authority on South American shamanism, Alfred Métraux,[1] on whose work this section of my account is especially closely based.[2]

Contact with supernatural beings is the principal source of the shaman's power; and this, rather than the more obvious process of inheritance, is frequently the means by which the shaman's office is passed on from one generation to the next. The necessary qualifications to be a shaman are thus basically a matter of psychological makeup; it is only in exceptional cases, notably among the Araucanians, that physical abnormalities play a part in determining a shaman's vocation. One important physical attribute which is considered by the inhabitants of the Putumayo area (east of the Peruvian Andes) to be important for a shaman is hairiness; unlike his fellow-tribesmen, he does not depilate himself. The Andoke have a particularly strong prohibition in this respect.[3] Métraux makes the point that nature spirits in tropical forest areas 'often were pictured as hairy men', and that these are precisely the beings with whom the shamans have the closest contacts.[4]

Shamanism in South America is predominantly a masculine activity, but women are by no means totally excluded. The female shamans (*machi*) of the Araucanians have completely displaced their male colleagues, who were nearly all *berdache* (transvestites). Métraux plausibly suggests that the disappearance of these male shamans took place under the influence of the Spaniards, who particularly detested the homosexuality which was comparatively common among the Indians.[5]

The process by which shamans are directly 'called' to their profession by the agency of supernatural beings belongs principally to the southern half of the continent. The *machi* of the Araucanians frequently assert that they have been forced to become shamans against their will by the power of a nature spirit or of the supreme being Ngenechen, whose aid they consequently invoke. In the Gran Chaco, too, the new shaman is told of his vocation by a nature spirit which appears to him in a vision. He then passes into an abnormal state of excitement, trembling and behaving in an eccentric way. The shamans of the Ona and Yahgan of Tierra del Fuego learned of their vocations from their guardian spirits, the *waiyuwen* and *yefačel* respectively; Sherente shamans were recruited among those who had been vouchsafed a vision of one of the personified planets Mars, Jupiter and Venus.[6]

A Bororo tribesman who is to become a *bari* (shaman) receives a mystic summons to go hunting in the bush and there encounters a *bope*, a nature spirit in the shape of an animal, which demands his obedience.[7] As a sign of assent the man gives the *bope* his bow and arrows, whereupon it disappears. The man thus called to be a *bari* must henceforth give unconditional obedience to the commands of his *bope* on pain of losing his powers and developing an incurable illness.

The marginal areas of the tropical forest belt provide few instances of a supernatural call of this kind; here the initiative is usually taken by the young man himself, who inflicts various mortifications on himself in order to make contact with the spirit world.[8] The Guianese tribes, especially the Caribs of Surinam, have schools for shamans in which everything possible is done to induce trance states in which the students see hallucinations. They fast, dance and drink tobacco juice until they finally see spirits who teach them the magical incantations which can be used for conjurations in time of need.[9] The new shaman passes through a novitiate varying in length from a few months to several years; in the latter case the new shaman has presumably been with his teacher from early childhood, always supposing that he has a flesh-and-blood teacher at all. If his education is in the hands of a spirit, as in many cases he himself claims, the period of instruction is considerably shorter. A Campa shaman, for instance, received instructions from the soul of his dead predecessor in a series of nightly visits which continued until he was versed in all the arts necessary to his calling.

The novice shamans of the old Araucanians were shut up for long periods in caves or other secret places and then ceremonially inaugurated in their new office. The present-day *machi* is not recognized as a fully-fledged shaman until she has had a thorough grounding in her profession which involves submitting to the medical treatment which she will have to administer to her own patients.[10]

The equipment of the South American shaman is simple. The emblem of his office is usually his *maraca*; its sound is the voice of the spirits who are embodied in the tiny pebbles inside it. Sometimes the *maraca* is replaced by a bundle of leaves which rustles to indicate the presence of the spirits; this is the case among the Taulipang and the Jivaro.[11] The flat skin drum used by the Araucanian *machi* in order to put herself into a trance state is not paralleled anywhere else in South America. This instrument represents a direct cultural link between southern Chile and North America and Siberia, where drums of the same type are typical attributes of shamans.

Alongside the rare instances in which the shaman uses a sort of doll to manipulate his spirits, we should mention the spirit bench in use in Guiana, a seat carved to represent the shaman's animal guardian spirit. If a Caliña Carib shaman sits on a seat carved with a cayman head, he is able to control the spirits of all the animals which are eaten by the cayman; the bench represents the 'grandfather of the cayman', the ruler of all aquatic creatures.[12]

In order to make contact with the supernatural world, shamans go into a trance state in which they can either send their own souls away or invite possession by a guardian spirit. This trance state may be attained either by massive doses of tobacco smoke from huge cigars (the old Tupinamba) by drinking tobacco juice (the Taulipang[13] and most other Guianese tribes), or by ingesting *caapi* or *ayahuasca*, a powerful narcotic prepared from a liana of the genus *Banisteriopsis* (the Jivaro and other northern Amazonian tribes). The sniffing of a narcotic powder made from seeds of a tree of the genus *Piptadenia* is practised by many shamans in the Gran Chaco, including those of the Mataco and Vilela. I also encountered this practice among the Waica of the upper Orinoco, where it is an indispensable preliminary of the *hekulamo* or conjuration rites.

'The shaman's power', writes Métraux, 'rested on his ability to summon a spirit that could perform tasks beyond the capability of ordinary people.'[14] In some cases the shaman detaches his own soul and sends it to consult the souls of the dead, the nature spirits or the gods in their remote dwelling-places; the Mataco shamans send their souls in the guise of birds to consult the sun, which is regarded as a great and sagacious shaman.[15] There is also a widespread belief that the soul of the shaman can enter the body of a jaguar or change itself into a jaguar, during the shaman's lifetime and especially after his death. In other cases the shamans are assisted in their work by the spirits of the dead, especially dead shamans (as with the Ona).[16] The spirits of the shamans occupy a special status among dead souls, as the Bororo[17] and the Taulipang[18] believe.

More frequently, however, the shaman's spirit helpers are nature spirits; and many of the animal spirits which assist the shaman are species boss spirits of the kind which have so much importance in the life of the hunter.[19] When a Taulipang shaman sets out to heal a sick person he first drinks tobacco juice, and his soul (*piasan*) rises aloft and calls upon the spirit of a dead shaman, who then undertakes to carry out the cure in place of the living one.[20] Then the harsh voice of the river monster Rató is heard, followed by the grunting of another spirit, Zauelezali, the 'father of the peccary', who was himself once a shaman.

Finally Ayug appears, the spirit of a magic tree, who is one of the most powerful of the shaman's helpers, and who puts even Rató to flight.

The power of the shaman is often linked with his breath or tobacco smoke, both of which possess cleansing and reinvigorating properties which play an important part in healing and in other magic practices.

In some cases the magical power is described as a mysterious tangible but invisible substance which the shaman carries within his body. He receives it periodically from the spirits and can transmit it to other people. The so-called intrusive bodies which are believed to cause disease, and which the shaman claims to extract from the bodies of his patients, are similarly invisible. In many cases, too, the shaman himself has invisible magic objects such as arrows, crystals and thorns embedded in his body; these correspond to the objects of the same kinds which he wears as material embodiments of his magic power. Métraux considers that 'magic substance, pathogenic objects, and guardian spirits are three different aspects of the same fundamental but vaguely conceived notion of magic power'.[21]

The Cubeo shaman is believed to insert small rock crystals into the head of the candidate for initiation; these eat up the existing eyes and brain and replace them with a much more potent psychic substance. The Barama River Caribs regard rock crystal and a number of other minerals as representatives of spirits; by acquiring stone of a certain type the shaman also acquires power over the appropriate class of spirits.[22] Towards the end of the initiation period, stones are supposed to be driven through the novice's body from his mouth into his arms in order to clear a path for a magic missile.[23]

The South American shaman is primarily a 'witch doctor', a healer, whose principal task is to heal sicknesses which are very rarely believed to have a natural cause. It is assumed that the patient has been struck by a supernatural missile discharged by a hostile spirit or sorcerer, or that his soul has been kidnapped by one of these 'evil' powers, or that it has abandoned him for some reason of its own, perhaps because of a sudden shock. If a spirit has caused the sickness, this may either be an independent action on its part or one undertaken on behalf of a hostile sorcerer. Plant and animal spirits above all are liable to revenge themselves in this way for injuries received; mankind cannot survive without continually running the risk of their vengeance.

The methods used to deal with intrusive pathogenic objects in the human body are the same all over primitive South America: suction, massage and blowing. When the intrusive object has been 'extracted' it is shown to the patient in the shape of a twig, thorn insect, etc., thus meeting the patient's psychological need to see for himself.

In cases of soul loss the shaman dispatches his own soul to catch that of the patient and return it to the body. North of the Amazon, above all, healing is accompanied by spirit consultations.[24] Deep in a trance, the shaman travels to the land of spirits to ask them about the causes and specific remedies of the sickness in question, or to issue a challenge to the soul of the hostile sorcerer responsible. Often he consults the very spirits which caused the sickness, and which are therefore in the best position to know the remedy.[25]

In the case of the Taulipang – very exceptionally for South America – we possess a large number of spells which may be used in cases of all possible diseases.[26] These spells which may be used by ordinary people as well as shamans, begin with a short mythological narrative which leads into an incantatory formula. According to Jensen the mythical events recounted in this introductory narrative are the most important aspects of the whole; he sees them as purely religious rather than magical acts.[27] The spells often refer to the mythical animals which also appear in the conjurations of the shamans. The animals invoked in the healing spells have a direct link with the sickness concerned;[28] in order to be rid of ulcers, which are believed to be the result of eating certain game (tapir, deer, peccary), various kinds of jaguar are invoked on the grounds that they can 'frighten the ulcers away'; for jaguars can eat all these varieties of game and still not get ulcers.

The shaman is more than a healer, however; in almost all cases he is also a black magician.[29] One side of his nature would be unthinkable without the other. Here, as in so many other departments of primitive South American thought, 'good' and 'evil' are largely synonymous with 'friendly' and 'unfriendly' to the person or community from whose point of view one is speaking. The same magical substance which the shaman employs to heal the sick becomes a deadly weapon when he turns it against his enemies.

The shaman presides over the birth, puberty and death of each person in the tribe, but his duties extend far beyond his role in the life of the individual; and perhaps the most important of his activities are those connected with hunting, which concern the community as a whole. He is also in charge of sacrifices, and he organizes religious festivals and leads the dances. He is the custodian of the purity of religious traditions of belief and behaviour. He is consulted before a warlike expedition, and uses his magical arts to promote its success; he also has a hand in the judgment of disputes. He seeks to influence the weather and other natural occurrences as well as to defend the village against hostile spirits. His authority and prestige are thus considerable, and he is nearly always well paid for his work.

As a rule the functions of the shaman are distinct from those of the chief; but many cases are known in which chiefs have been powerful shamans. This was often the case among the old Tupi-Guarani peoples; their famous shamans were the objects of a veneration which by no means came to an end when they died. Their bones were set up in a place of honour, where offerings were made to them, and they became oracles.[30] The Tupinamba shamans had one function which has been performed by no other shamans in South America: to hear the confessions of young women who had transgressed against tribal morality in some respect connected with marital relations or sexual life in general, and to give them absolution.[31]

The shaman's only qualification is his intrinsic magic power; he does not become what he is by virtue of a formal initiation or investiture. His acts are always spontaneous, conditioned rather by the immediate circumstances than by traditions of belief or ritual. His relationship with the spirits, which is his most essential characteristic, is always purely personal. Nevertheless, in primitive cultures which lack a priesthood, he is the only person qualified by his special abilities to act as an intermediary between the community and the supernatural world;[32] and in those parts of South America where the influence of the Andean civilizations is felt, among the Mojo and Mansi of eastern Bolivia, the Araucanians of Chile, and the Taino of the West Indies, the shaman has begun to evolve into a priest.

NOTES

Introduction: Walter Krickeberg

1   N.C.Nelson, 'The Antiquity of Men in America in the Light of Archeology', in Jenness, *The American Aborigines*, Toronto 1933, pp. 87–130.

2   Rivet, in A.Meillet and M.Cohen, *Les Langues du monde*, Paris 1924, pp. 597–707. Swanton, *The Indian Tribes of North America*, Bureau of American Ethnology *Bulletin*, No. 145, Washington 1952, pp. 8–9. Mason, 'The Native Languages of Middle America', *The Maya and Their Neighbours*, New York 1940, pp. 52–87. Loukotka, 'Klassifikation der amerikanischen Sprachen', *Zeitschrift für Ethnologie*, LXXIV, Berlin 1944.

3   Thor Heyerdahl, 'The Voyage of the Raft Kon-Tiki', *Geographical Journal*, vol. CXV, 1950; *American Indians in the Pacific. The Theory behind the Kon-Tiki Expedition*, Oslo 1952. Robert von Heine-Geldern, 'Some Problems of Migration in the Pacific', *Kultur und Sprache*, vol. 9, Vienna 1952.

4   Robert von Heine-Geldern and Gordon Ekholm, 'Significant Parallels in the Symbolic Arts of southern Asia and Middle America', *Proceedings of the 29th International Congress of Americanists*, Chicago 1951. Heine-Geldern, 'Chinese Influences in Mexico and Central America', 'Chinese Influences in the Pottery of Mexico, Central America and Colombia', 'Representations of the Asiatic Tiger in the Art of the Chavín culture', *Actas del XXXIII. Congreso*

Internacional de Americanistas, San José, Costa Rica 1959. See p. 26 of the present volume (El Tajín).

5   Carl Hentze, *Objets rituels, croyances et dieux de la Chine antique et de l'Amérique*, Antwerp 1936; *Die Sakralbronzen und ihre Bedeutung in den Frühchinesischen Kulturen*, Antwerp 1941; *Bronzegeräte, Kultbauten, Religion im ältesten China der Shang-Zeit*, Antwerp 1951. Cf. also Walter Krickeberg, 'Ostasien-Amerika', *Sinologica*, vol. II, no. 3, Basle 1950.

6   See the chronological tables in Miguel Covarrubias, *Indian Art of Mexico and Central America*, New York 1957, p. 16, and H.D.Disselhoff and Sigvald Linné, *Ancient America*, London 1961, pp. 254–5.

Mesoamerica   Walter Krickeberg

I. MEXICO

1   Covarrubias 1957, pp. 76, 110. They are also found on the Pacific slopes of Guatemala.

2   Haekel 1960, p. 5.

3   Drucker, Heizer and Squier 1959, pp. 152–61.

4   Stirling 1943, p. 19.

5   Covarrubias 1957, p. 77 note.

6   Caso and Bernal 1952, pp. 113–15 and fig. 184 a–e.

7   Krickeberg 1949, pp. 199–206.

8   Caso 1942.

9   Armillas 1945, pp. 56–8; Armillas 1947, pp. 171–8.

10 Armillas 1945, pp. 36–51; Covarrubias 1957, pp. 60–3, fig. 22.

11 Krickeberg 1948.

12 Covarrubias 1957, p. 151.

13 Illustrated in Krickeberg 1956, p. 477; *Codex Borgia* ff. 56 and 73.

14 Ellen Spinden 1933, pp. 246–58.

15 Génin 1928.

16 Covarrubias 1957, p. 177, fig. 76.

17 Seler 1902/23, vol. III, pp. 541–2.

18 Covarrubias 1957, fig. 78.

19 Formerly named after the site Ranchito de la Animas (Strebel).

20 The original of his *Antigüedades Mexicanas* (1543) has disappeared, but there is a French translation by the cosmographer André Thevet (*Histoyre du Mechique*, 1605).

21 The contents of a lost pictographic manuscript incorporating interesting information on Aztec mythology are partly known to us through its Spanish commentary (*Historia de los Mexicanos por sus pinturas*, 1891).

22 Thompson 1956, p. 110.

23 Seler 1902/23, vol. II, pp. 778–82.

24 Thompson 1943b.

25 Moedano 1942/4, pp. 159–60.

26 Lothrop 1952, pp. 67–71, figs. 54–5.

27 See the illustration in Marquina 1951, p. 858.

28 Ce Ácatl (1 Reed) was the calendar name of the morning star god. According to Sahagún, the priest-king of Tula did not set sail across the eastern sea but burned himself on a pyre on the Gulf Coast, and his soul became the morning star.

29 Illustrated in Seler 1902/23, vol. V, p. 367.

30 Kirchhoff 1950.

31 Hvidtfeldt 1958, pp. 77 sqq.

32 Haekel 1952.

33 *Codex Borbonicus*, f. 34 (right).

34 *Codex Borgia*, f. 27 (lower right).

35 *Histoyre du Mechique* (Krickeberg 1928, pp. 5–6).

36 *Historia de los Mexicanos por sus pinturas* (Krickeberg 1928, pp. 8–10).

37 Sahagún (Krickeberg 1928, pp. 15–17).

38 *Historia de los Reynos de Colhuacan y de Mexico* (Krickeberg 1928, pp. 10–12); Haekel 1959, p. 139.

39 Haekel 1959; Dietschy 1941/2.

40 *Historia Tolteca-Chichimeca*, vol. II, pp. 40–2.

41 Seler 1902/23, vol. IV, pp. 157–67; Haekel 1959, pp. 140–2.

42 *Codex Borgia*, ff. 27–8; *Historia de los Mexicanos por sus pinturas* (Krickeberg 1928, pp. 34–5).

43 Krickeberg 1960, pp. 15–23.

44 Krickeberg 1960, pp. 8–15.

45 Beyer 1955.

46 Palacios (Tenayuca 1935, pp. 232–63).

47 Krickeberg 1949, pp. 126–32.

48 Seler 1902/23, vol. II, pp. 978, 983.

49 Seler 1904/9, vol. I, p. 101.

50 *Codex Selden*, f. 12 (Beyer 1921, p. 1).

51 Caso 1927.

52 Seler 1904/9, vol. I, pp. 170–5.

53 Preuss 1930b, pp. 67–81.

54 Noguera 1937.

55 Sahagún 1952, pp. 83 sqq.

56 Marquina 1951, pp. 252–60.

57 Villagra Caleti 1954.

58 On Zapotec religion see Seler 1895, pp. 17–18, 23–9.

59 On Totonac religion see Krickeberg 1918/25, I, pp. 47–8; II, pp. 4–5.

60 On Tarascan religion see Seler 1902/23, vol. III, pp. 116–27 and 133–54.

61 Covarrubias 1957, pp. 98–101.

II. MAYA TERRITORY

1 There exist two rival correlations of the Maya and Gregorian calendars; as in most modern works on Mesoamerica, the one adopted here is that proposed by Thompson, Goodman and Martínez Hernández. The Spinden correlation places all dates some 260 years earlier.

2 The terms 'Old Empire' and 'New Empire' do not refer to political units of any kind but to successive phases of cultural development. The only period at which there was a Maya state of any size was between 1194 and 1441; at all other times the Maya world was a patchwork of city-states like those of ancient Greece and Renaissance

Italy, united only by a common artistic culture.

3 Illustrated in Krickeberg 1949, pl. 39.
4 Herbert Spinden 1913, pp. 17–18.
5 Illustrated in Morley 1947, pl. 54c.
6 Illustrated in Seler 1915, pp. 84–6; Herbert Spinden 1913, p. 55; Trik 1939, pl. 12–13.
7 Illustrated in Herbert Spinden 1913, p. 50.
8 Illustrated in Herbert Spinden 1913, p. 51, fig. 47.
9 Ruz Lhuillier 1952, pp. 7–10.
10 Morley 1947, p. 425 and pl. 89b.
11 Krickeberg 1949, pp. 166–8 and ill. 68b.
12 Trik 1939, frontispiece.
13 Seler 1917, pp. 41–3, pls. V and VIII; pp. 140–3, pl. XXVIII.
14 Morley 1947, pp. 231–2 and 288; Thompson 1960, pp. 12 and 208–12.
15 Seler 1901b, pp. 28–31.
16 Thompson 1956, pp. 99–100. We have already mentioned this hypothesis in connection with Chichén-Itzá.
17 On the island of Cozumel off the north-eastern coast of Yucatán, there was an oracle of Itzamná-Ixchel which was dispensed by a priest inside a hollow clay figure. No doubt the same procedure was adopted at the oracular cave near Chaculá in the north-west of the state of Chiapas (Seler 1901a, pp. 146–85) near which Seler found an incense burner decorated with the mask of the sun god.
18 Seler 1902/23, vol. III, p. 619.
19 Seler 1902/23, vol. I, pp. 367–82.
20 Landa 1941, pp. 102–6.
21 Ruz Lhuillier 1953; Covarrubias 1957, pl. 51.
22 Landa 1941, pp. 130–1.
23 Tozzer 1907, p. 163.
24 The 'Observatory' at Chichén-Itzá (the Caracol), the oldest building of the Toltec period at the site, was probably designed by Maya priests.
25 Lothrop 1921. These include: fig-

ures with bird bills (resembling the jade Tuxtla statuette which is the second oldest dated relic of the La Venta culture, AD 162); figures with an *alter ego* crouching on their shoulders; and 'chacmools'.
26 Kidder, Jennings and Shook 1946, p. 255.
27 Kidder, Jennings and Shook 1946, pp. 210–11, fig. 207g.
28 Kidder, Jennings and Shook 1946, pp. 86–97; Krickeberg 1949, pp. 235–6, ill. 94.
29 Thompson 1943a.
30 For the following see Thompson 1948 and Krickeberg 1958.
31 Krickeberg 1958, pp. 508–9.
32 Termer 1930, pp. 450–2.

South Central America and the Central Andes
Hermann Trimborn
1 Cieza 1853/80, ch. 28.
2 Martyr 1907, III, 4.
3 Martyr 1907, VII, 10.
4 Martyr 1907, VII, 10.
5 Vadillo 1884, p. 408.
6 Martyr 1907, VII, 10.
7 Arriaga (1621) 1920, pp. 28–9.
8 Tschudi 1891, p. 120.
9 Arriaga (1621) 1920, pp. 28–9.
10 Polo de Ondegardo 1916, p. 21.
11 Avila 1939, p. 77.
12 Avila 1939, p. 101.
13 Avila 1939, p. 109.
14 Avila 1939, p. 116.
15 Avila 1939, p. 137.
16 Avila 1939, p. 83.
17 Avila 1939, p. 101.

North America   Werner Müller
I. NORTH AMERICA IN 1600
1 Champlain 1922, vol. I (1599–1607), pp. 46, 56 sq., 67 sqq., 74 sq., 82 sqq., 88, etc. The page numbers are those of the French original edition, given in the inside margin of the 1922 reprint.

II. THE LONELY DRUM
1 Keith's letters to Roderick Mackenzie, in Masson 1889–90, vol. 2.

2   Cf. Wallis 1954.
3   Osgood 1932, p. 42, says that the Great Bear Lake Indians simply have no adequate equipment for this type of hunting.
4   Wallis 1954, pp. 184 sqq.
5   Petitot 1876, pp. xxxii sq.; Goddard 1916, pp. 299 sq.; Osgood 1932, p. 86.
6   Speck 1935, pp. 18 sqq.
7   For Labrador see Speck 1935, p. 48; for Athapascans see Osgood 1932, p. 83, and Mason 1946, p. 38. The Passamaquoddy of Maine also engage in ascetic training with a view to obtaining miraculous powers; see Prince 1900–1, p. 385. The dream fast of the novice shamans of the Micmac is described in Hagar 1896, p. 172.
8   Honigmann 1949, p. 220.
9   Osgood 1932, p. 83.
10 There is a synopsis of definitions of shamanism in Park 1938.
11 Osgood 1932, pp. 83–4; Mason 1946, pp. 38 sqq.
12 See the notes on this subject in Speck 1919, pp. 241 and 256; Speck 1935, pp. 169 sqq. The scantiness of first-hand information makes it impossible to gain as clear an idea of the North American shaman as we have of his Asian counterpart; see Eliade 1957.
13 Drums with two heads do exist, but they are rare; see Speck 1935, p. 170.
14 Speck 1935, p. 171.
15 Original in Prince 1900/1, pp. 385–6.
16 This is one of the few accounts of a shaman's journey into the beyond to have been recorded among the Canadian forest Indians; it is taken from Petitot 1876, p. xxxi.
17 For Micmac see Rand 1894, p. 110, note 2; for the Narraganset see Williams 1643, Foreword [f. 7] and p. 70.
18 Petitot 1876, pp. xxi–xxii.
19 Mason 1946, p. 37.
20 Osgood 1932, pp. 85–6.
21 Speck 1935a, pp. 12 sqq.; Speck

1935b, pp. 71 sqq.; Osgood 1932, p. 86.
22 On the boss spirit concept see Speck 1935b, pp. 82, 95.
23 A detailed description of one of these bear feasts in Speck 1935b, pp. 103–4.
24 Speck 1935b, p. 105.
25 Cf. an account of a bear feast in honour of the Great Manito on the south shore of Lake Superior in 1765, in Henry 1901, pp. 192 sqq.
26 Jenness 1935, p. 30.
27 Speck 1935a, p. 4; Rand 1894, p. xliii.
28 Speck 1935b, pp. 36–7.
29 Osgood 1932, p. 83. Petitot 1876, XXIII, mentions another name or title, Tit'sé, 'father of mankind'.
30 Speck 1935a, p. 4; Speck 1935b, p. 37.
31. Petitot 1876, p. xxxii; Wallis 1954, pp. 142–3.
32 Penobscot mythology in Speck 1935a, pp. 5 sqq.; the three eras of the world, *ibid.* pp. 17–18. Micmac mythology in Rand 1894, pp. xliv sqq.; Wallis 1954, pp. 317 sqq. Naskapi in Speck 1935b, pp. 53 sqq. Athapascans in Goddard 1916, pp. 232 sqq.; eras of the world, *ibid.* p. 262, Mason 1946, pp. 41–2, Osgood 1932, pp. 87 sqq.
33 Wentzel mentions in a letter to Mackenzie (27 March 1807) that the central Athapascans believe in reincarnation. Cf. Masson 1889–90, vol. 1, p. 88; Speck 1935b, p. 47. According to the Naskapi the soul or spirit appears as a shadow, or as a spark or little flame which issues from the mouth. Speck 1935b, pp. 48, 50.

III. SUPREME BEING AND BIG HOUSE

1   For Oklahoma Delaware see Harrington 1921; Speck 1931 and 1937. For Ontario Delaware see Speck 1945. A survey of all the forms of the Big House ritual is to be found in Müller 1956, pp. 256 sqq.

2   The evidence in favour of the identification of the images on the centre post with the supreme being is as follows: the Oklahoma Delaware, Speck 1931, pp. 22 and 30 ('the visible symbols of the supreme power ... represent the supreme *manitu*, the Creator'); the Ontario Delaware, Speck 1945, p. 40 ('the icons represent, as I was told, the Creator alone' ... 'the father and Creator looks down on his people during the ritual, and his votaries look up to him through his carven images'); pp. 41–2 ('the images on the east and west sides of the centre post are representations of the countenance of the Creator carved in wood').

3   Harrington 1921, pp. 87 sqq.

4   Harrington 1921, p. 112.

5   Speck 1945, p. 32.

6   Dankers and Sluyter 1867, pp. 267–8.

7   Hallowell 1926.

8   Speck 1945, pp. 27 sqq.

9   Speck 1931, pp. 43–4; Speck 1937, pp. 49 sqq.

10   Speck 1937, pp. 61 sqq.

11   Speck 1937, pp. 70 sqq.

12   Speck 1937, p. 78.

13   For the dream fast among the Delaware see Harrington 1921, pp. 61 sqq. For a treatment of this subject in general see Blumensohn 1933.

14   The concept of soul among the Delaware is discussed in Harrington 1921, pp. 52 sqq. and Speck 1931, pp. 25–6.

15   Brainerd 1822, p. 346; Harrington 1921, p. 53.

16   Brainerd 1822, *loc. cit.*

17   Kohl 1859, vol. 2, pp. 186–7, refers this anecdote to the Ojibwa, but it is characteristic of all the Algonquin tribes.

18   Harrington 1921, p. 24. A great authority on the Ojibwa comes to a similar conclusion; 'This doctrine of two great spirits, one good and one evil, undoubtedly gained much

of its prominence through Christian teaching. It must have been rather vague and tenuous in earlier times, since it appears to have exerted little influence on religious practices' (Jenness 1935, p. 30).

IV. DREAM, VISION AND TRADITION

1   Two vols., Bremen 1859.

2   Kohl 1859, vol. 1, pp. 102, 177, 281, 303–4; vol. 2, pp. 33–4, 70–1, 75, 165, 185–6, 198, 207–8, 241, 243, 264–5.

3   Kohl 1859, vol. 1, pp. 276 sqq., 315 sqq.

4   Copway 1850, pp. 39–40.

5   Kohl 1859, vol. 1, pp. 59 sqq., 63; Hoffman 1891, pp. 143 sqq.; the medicine society ritual in general and its offshoots among the Sioux are discussed in Müller 1954.

6   The evidence is recorded in Müller 1956, pp. 219–20.

7   Brainerd 1822, p. 349.

8   Speck 1935b, pp. 185 sqq.

9   Kohl 1859, vol. 1, pp. 322–3; vol. 2, pp. 1 sqq.

10   Speck 1931, p. 21.

11   Müller 1956, pp. 197–8.

12   Coleman 1937, p. 38.

13   On the *wabeno* and *jossakid* among the Ojibwa see Hoffman 1891, pp. 156 sqq.; Jenness 1935, pp. 62 sqq. The Menomini: Hoffman 1896, pp. 138 sqq.

14   Jenness 1935, pp. 40 sqq.

15   Jenness 1935, pp. 68, 87–8.

16   Jenness 1935, p. 21.

17   Jenness 1935, p. 108.

V. TWIN GODS AND A DUAL WORLD

1   Among the older accounts of the subject Morgan 1851 still deserves to be read. A new general work is Speck 1945.

2   Hewitt 1903, pp. 127–339; Hewitt 1928, pp. 449–819. These are not popular versions known to every member of the tribe but sacred texts belonging to the officials of the long house and couched in an archaic metaphorical idiom which is not always fully understood by

the priests themselves; see Hewitt 1903, pp. 134, 137.

3 My summary follows first the Onondaga version, then the Mohawk version; see Hewitt 1903, pp. 141 sqq., 285 sqq.

4 Descriptions of the long houses in Converse 1891, p. 72 (Newtown on Catteraugus, Seneca); Beauchamp 1895, p. 209 (Onondaga reservation near Syracuse); Speck 1949, p. 21 (Sour Springs, Cayuga).

5 For an account of the Iroquois festal calendar and ritual see Müller 1956, pp. 129 sqq.

6 Morgan 1851, pp. 226 sqq.; Parker 1912.

7 The material is assembled in Müller 1956, pp. 132–3. For the dish and dice games see also Fenton 1936, p. 16.

8 For the white dog sacrifice see Hale 1885, pp. 7 sqq.; Beauchamp 1885, 235 sqq.; Converse 1888, pp. 83 sqq.; Hewitt 1912, pp. 939 sqq.

9 Descriptions of the great feather dance and the war dance in Morgan 1851, pp. 269 sqq.; Converse 1891, pp. 74 sqq.

10 Parker 1912, pp. 102–3.

11 Smith (1799) 1870, pp. 96–8.

12 For the false faces see Fenton 1937, pp. 215 sqq.; Fenton 1941, pp. 397 sqq. For the secret societies see Parker 1909 (an essential work), pp. 161 sqq. For the ritual of one such society, the 'Guardians of the Little Waters', see Parker 1908, pp. 149 sqq.

13 Wallace 1952, pp. 22, 24–5, 27, 37.

VI. THE KINGDOM OF THE GODS IN THE MIDDLE

1 Douglass 1917, pp. 344 sqq.

2 For a general introduction to the environment, culture and religion of the Indians of the South-West see Goddard 1927.

3 See the big plan in Kroeber 1917, map 6. Zuñi is well over six and a half thousand feet above sea level.

4 Cushing 1896, p. 367.

5 The clan lists given by our sources show no major discrepancies if we bear in mind that Cushing 1896 mentions three clans (Antelope, Sky and Water) which were already almost extinct in his day, and which naturally do not appear in later lists. See Kroeber 1917, table 2.

6 Kroeber 1917, pp. 103 sqq., maps 2, 3, 4.

7 Cushing 1896, pp. 369–70. The Zuñi also possess a special word for 'religion': tewusu, which embraces the whole of their ritual life. See Bunzel 1932, p. 489. The ritual 'compass' is discussed in Parsons 1939, pp. 365 sqq.; but the author fails to mention the links between the cardinal points and qualities other than colour.

8 Stevenson 1904, pp. 25 sqq.; Parsons 1939, pp. 218 sqq.

9 Bunzel 1932, p. 534; Parsons 1939, p. 570 note.

10 Stevenson 1904, p. 108.

11 On the pekwin see Stevenson 1904, pp. 109, 148, 166, 169; Bunzel 1932, p. 512.

12 Stevenson 1904, p. 166.

13 Stevenson 1904, pp. 108–9, 148–9; Bunzel 1932, pp. 512, 534; Parsons 1939, pp. 570 sqq.

14 Bunzel 1932, pp. 499–500; Parsons 1939, pp. 270 sqq.

15 Bunzel 1932, pp. 511 sqq.; Parsons 1939, pp. 292 sqq.

16 Stevenson 1904, pp. 22 sqq.; Cushing 1896, p. 379.

17 Bunzel 1932, p. 486, note 12. The missionaries use the word as the Zuñi equivalent for 'God'. Cf. also the remark of a Zuñi informant in Parsons 1939, p. 169: 'In Zuñi not one boss but many', and Parsons' gloss: not one god but many gods.

18 Bunzel 1932, p. 622 and note 5, pp. 636, 644, 648, etc.

19 Fishler 1953, pp. 9 sqq.; Goodwin 1938, p. 25; Russell 1908, pp. 206 sqq.

20 Stirling 1942, p. 3; Stevenson 1894, pp. 26 sqq.

21 Bunzel 1932, p. 483; for the following see Parsons 1939, pp. 170 sqq.: 'Spirits'.

22 For the war gods see Stevenson 1904, pp. 24 sqq.; Bunzel 1932, pp. 325 sqq.; Parsons 1939, p. 183.

23 For the mask gods see Stevenson 1904, pp. 32 sqq.; Bunzel 1932, pp. 516 sqq., 843 sqq., 905–8 (a list of all the known mask gods of Zuñi).

24 Stevenson 1904, pp. 111, 129, 132, 141, 171, etc.

25 For the animal gods see Stevenson 1904, p. 49; Bunzel 1932, pp. 528 sqq.

26 Bunzel 1932, pp. 482, 517.

27 Bunzel 1932, pp. 509, 621.

28 Bunzel 1932, p. 480.

29 Kroeber 1917, p. 177.

30 In this case the usual order of precedence, north–west–south–east, does not apply.

31 In 1896 Mrs Stevenson was admitted to the winter retreat of the *shiwanni* of the nadir; Stevenson 1904, pp. 173 sqq. Concerning the rainmakers in general see Stevenson 1904, pp. 163 sqq.; Bunzel 1932, pp. 513 sqq.

32 For the *ettone* (plural *ettowe*) see Stevenson 1904, pp. 163–4; Kroeber 1917, pp. 166 sqq.

33 Stevenson 1904, p. 176.

34 For the medicine societies see Stevenson 1904, pp. 409 sqq.; Bunzel 1932, pp. 528 sqq.; Parsons 1933, pp. 16 sqq.

35 For the *Koko* dance societies see Stevenson 1904, pp. 62 sqq.; Bunzel 1932, pp. 517 sqq., 874 sqq., Parsons 1939, pp. 730 sqq.

36 In fact the *kivas* are now all in the western half of the *pueblo*; see Kroeber 1917, map 8.

37 Stevenson 1904, pp. 154–5.

38 Ruth Bunzel makes a distinction between the true gods, personated by *katcina* (*Koko*) priests, and the shadowy group or dance *Koko*. On the mask gods as ancestors see the interesting quotations in Bunzel 1932, p. 844, note 4.

39 Bunzel 1932, p. 540.

40 E.g. Bunzel 1932, pp. 508, 534: 'The solstice ceremonies are all nicely synchronized. They are fitted into a period of twenty days and so neatly arranged that there are no conflicts even for a man with varied ceremonial affiliations.'

41 The following account of the winter solstice ritual is based on Stevenson 1904, pp. 108 sqq.; Bunzel 1932, pp. 534 sqq., 908 sqq.

42 Bunzel 1932, p. 912.

43 Stevenson 1904, p. 130.

VII. DEATH AND REBIRTH

1 Cf. the introductory sections in Müller 1955.

2 See the day-to-day festal calendar in Parsons 1939, pp. 514 sqq.

3 Boas 1889, p. 826; Boas 1890, p. 608. The tribe itself, on the other hand, is a territorial unit; it consists of the descendants of all those clan ancestors who entered the world at a given spot.

4 The Kwakiutl carefully distinguish between clan legends (or family histories) and myths (*nuyam*). As we shall see, the myths are set in an antediluvian world, on Crooked Beach; the clan legends belong to the age after the Flood, when the first human being appeared. Texts of both kinds appear in Boas 1902–5 and Boas 1906.

5 Concerning Baxbakwalanuxsiwae see Boas 1897, pp. 394, 396 sqq., 405–6.

6 For a detailed description of the sacred land and its role in Kwakiutl myth and legend see Müller 1955, pp. 41 sqq. Crooked Beach is on Tournour Island, north of Johnstone Strait.

7 For the cosmology see Müller 1955, pp. 15 sqq. The cosmic significance of the post or pole has been discussed by Josef Haekel (Haekel 1958).

8 For further details see Müller 1955, pp. 68 sqq.

9 Pinkerton 1940, p. 135.

VIII. CREATOR AND ADVERSARY

1 For the Californian Indians in general see Kroeber 1925, pp. 898 sqq.; Krause 1921, map 1 (ethnic and linguistic map).

2 Kroeber 1925, p. 395.

3 A general survey of religion in California is to be found in Kroeber 1907; a slightly different account in Loeb 1926. Important photographs illustrating religious features like the *Kuksu* (big head) masks in Merriam 1955.

4 Angulo 1928, pp. 150–1.

5 Angulo 1928, pp. 582–3.

6 Dixon, Achomawi and Arseqewi tales, *Journal of American Folk-Lore*, vol. 21 (1908), pp. 159–60.

7 Kroeber 1907, pp. 183 sqq.; Kroeber 1925 (HB), pp. 182–3; Kroeber 1932, pp. 905 sqq.; Angulo 1928, p. 585.

8 Extraordinarily beautiful Wintun myths in Curtin 1899, No. 1, pp. 3–48: 'Olelbis'. See also Du Bois and Demetrocopoulou 1931, 287, 290.

9 Dixon 1903, pp. 32 sqq.; Dixon 1902, pp. 39 sqq.; Dixon 1912, pp. 4 sqq.; Loeb 1933, pp. 157, 203 sqq.

10 The eastern Pomo in Loeb 1926, pp. 489 sqq.; western Pomo, *ibid.* pp. 475 sqq.

11 Kroeber 1925, 362. The southern Wintun mentioned by Kroeber are the Patwin. See also Kroeber 1932, pp. 304 sqq.

12 Gifford 1917, pp. 310 sqq.; Merriam 1910, p. 18.

13 Foster 1944, pp. 204 sqq., 213.

14 Foster 1944, p. 213.

15 *Kuksu*; see Kroeber 1925 (HB), pp. 364 sqq., 855 sqq.; Loeb 1932; Loeb 1933. A lucid exposition of these rites, with special reference to their two-stage structure, in Schmidt 1934 (vol. 5), pp. 17 sqq., 41–2, 46 sqq., 52–3, 65 sqq., 78

sqq., etc. *Hesi:* see Barrett 1919, pp. 438 sqq. See also the illuminating discussion of the relationship between the two cults in Kroeber 1925, pp. 381–2.

16 Cf. the instructive account of a shaman's dream in Kroeber 1925, p. 197.

17 Kroeber 1925, pp. 383–4; Loeb 1933, pp. 194 sqq.; Barrett 1919, p. 468.

18 Kroeber and Gifford 1949.

19 Speck 1931, p. 21.

Primitive South America and the West Indies
Otto Zerries

I. SUPREME BEING, CULTURE HERO AND ANCESTOR

1 Métraux 1949, HB 5, p. 562. The initials HB refer to the seven volumes of the *Handbook of South American Indians* (ed. Steward 1946–57).

2 Gusinde 1931; Gusinde 1937.

3 Koppers 1926.

4 Bird 1946, HB 1, p. 79; Gusinde 1925, pp. 137–40.

5 Cooper 1946a, HB 1, pp. 102–3.

6 Cooper 1946a, HB 1, pp. 98–9.

7 Gusinde 1937, p. 883.

8 Cooper 1946a, HB 1, p. 99.

9 Gusinde 1937, pp. 884, 897–8.

10 Cooper 1946a, HB 1, p. 10.

11 Gusinde 1937, p. 1054.

12 Snethlage 1938, p. 506.

13 Gusinde 1937, pp. 1050–1.

14 Gusinde 1937, p. 1337.

15 Zerries 1954, pp. 35–6.

16 Haekel 1954, p. 235.

17 Cf. Jensen 1951, pp. 172–3.

18 Cooper 1946a, HB 1, p. 103.

19 Cooper 1946a, HB 1, p. 105.

20 Cooper 1946a, HB 1, p. 99.

21 Cooper 1946a, HB 1, p. 123.

22 Gusinde 1931, p. 504.

23 Cooper 1946a, HB 1, p. 161.

24 Jensen 1951, p. 127.

25 Jensen 1951, pp. 125 sqq.

26 Cooper 1946a, HB 1, pp. 157–8.

27 Cooper 1946a, HB 1, pp. 167–8.

28 Cooper 1946b, HB 2, pp. 742 sqq.

29 Titiev 1951, pp. 130 sqq.
30 Cooper 1946b, HB 2, p. 743.
31 Métraux 1949, HB 5, p. 561.
32 Cooper 1946b, HB 2, p. 745.
33 Cooper 1946b, pp. 748–9; Latcham quoted in Krickeberg 1939, p. 156.
34 Canals Frau 1946, HB 1, pp. 169 sqq.
35 Métraux 1946b, HB 1, pp. 350–1.
36 Cf. Grubb 1911, pp. 114 sqq.
37 Métraux 1946b, HB 1, pp. 350–1.
38 Cf. Baldus 1931a, pp. 777 sqq.
39 Métraux 1949, HB 5, p. 563.
40 Baldus 1931b, pp. 285 sqq.
41 Haekel 1952, pp. 972–3.
42 Nimuendajú 1946b, pp. 105–6.
43 Métraux 1946b, HB 1, p. 539.
44 Manizer quoted in Métraux 1946b, HB 1, p. 539.
45 Lowie 1946, HB 1, pp. 396, 509 sqq.
46 Nimuendajú 1939, p. 133.
47 Jensen 1951, pp. 156–9.
48 Haekel 1952, p. 989.
49 Nimuendajú 1946a, pp. 71–2.
50 Haekel 1952, p. 989.
51 Métraux 1949, HB 5, p. 560.
52 Métraux 1948b, HB 3, p. 131.
53 Métraux 1948b, HB 3, pp. 436–7.
54 Nimuendajú 1948, p. 319.
55 Métraux 1948b, HB 3, p. 90; Nimuendajú 1914, pp. 316 sqq.
56 Vellard 1939, pp. 169 sqq.; Métraux 1948a, p. 90.
57 Métraux 1949, HB 5, p. 564.
58 Wagley and Galvão 1948, HB 3, pp. 145, 147.
59 Kruse 1952.
60 Gusinde 1960, p. 304.
61 Murphy 1958.
62 Kruse 1951, pp. 921 sqq.; Kruse 1952, pp. 1013 sqq.
63 Horton 1948, HB 3, p. 280.
64 Kruse 1955.
65 Haekel 1958.
66 Frikel 1957; see also the information supplied by him to Haekel, in Haekel 1960, pp. 28–9.
67 Kruse 1951.
68 Haekel 1959, pp. 39 sqq.
69 H. Becher, personal communication in Haekel 1959, p. 40.
70 Becher 1960, pp. 91 sqq.

71 Zerries 1960, pp. 504–5.
72 Haekel 1959, p. 35.
73 Haekel 1959, pp. 44 sqq.
74 Walde-Waldegg 1936, pp. 40 sqq.
75 Haekel 1960, pp. 46 sqq.
76 Cf. Hernandez de Alba 1948, HB 4, p. 410.
77 Haekel 1959, p. 46.
78 Cf. Zerries 1956a, p. 232.
79 Haekel 1958, p. 48.
80 Baldus 1958, pp. 25 sqq.
81 De Goeje 1943.
82 Penard 1907–8.
83 Haekel 1959, pp. 30–5.
84 De Goeje 1943, p. 4.
85 Haekel 1959, pp. 32–5.
86 The Caliña Carib shaman carries with him a number of small pebbles, each of which is the dwelling-place of a spirit.
87 Roth 1915, p. 117.
88 Lowie 1948, HB 3, p. 46.
89 Haekel 1959, p. 29.
90 Gillin 1936, pp. 155 sqq.
91 Gillin 1948, HB 3, p. 855.
92 Haekel 1959, pp. 33 sqq.; de Goeje 1943, p. 116.
93 Haekel 1959, p. 341.
94 Cruxent 1953, p. 325.
95 De Goeje 1943, p. 116.
96 Civrieux 1959, pp. 111–12.
97 Koch-Grünberg 1923, p. 379.
98 Haekel 1959, p. 41.
99 Zerries 1958; Zerries 1960, pp. 495 sqq.
100 Haekel 1959, pp. 40–2.
101 Martius 1867, p. 632.
102 Koch-Grünberg 1923, p. 183.
103 Matos Arvelo 1908, pp. 11 sqq.
104 Saake 1958a; Saake 1958b, p. 90.
105 Saake 1958a, p. 279.
106 Koch-Grünberg 1909, pp. 113, 203; Koch-Grünberg 1910, p. 55.
107 Quoted in Métraux 1948b, HB 3, p. 711.
108 Roquette Pinto, quoted in Métraux 1948b, HB 3, p. 360.
109 Lévi-Strauss 1948, HB 3, p. 369.
110 Armstrong and Métraux 1948, HB 4, p. 382.
111 Rouse 1948, HB 4, p. 538.
112 Krickeberg 1939, p. 162.
113 Cf. Kirchhoff 1948a, HB 3, p. 879.

114   Wilbert 1956, pp. 239 sqq.
115   Wilbert 1956, p. 242.
116   Wilbert 1956, p. 20.
117   Cf. Kirchhoff 1948a, HB 3, p. 879.
118   Kirchhoff 1948b, HB 4, pp. 367–8.
119   Hernandez de Alba 1948, HB 4, p. 46.
120   Kirchhoff 1948b, HB 4, p. 491.
121   Lowie 1948, HB 3, p. 46.
122   Cf. Kirchhoff 1948b, pp. 462–3.
123   Métraux 1949, HB 5, p. 563.
124   Preuss 1921, p. 32.
125   Preuss 1921, p. 153; cf. also Lowie 1948, HB 3, p. 46.
126   Preuss 1923, p. 667.
127   Jensen 1948, pp. 108–18; cf. Girard 1958, p. 68.
128   Jensen 1951, p. 130.
129   Cf. Métraux 1949, HB 5, p. 562.
130   Preuss 1921, p. 27.
131   Preuss 1921, p. 25.
132   Preuss 1921, pp. 30–1.
133   Métraux 1949, HB 5, p. 562.
134   Steward 1948, HB 3, p. 760.
135   Goldmann 1948, HB 3, p. 794.
136   Koch-Grünberg 1910, pp. 159 sqq.
137   Koch-Grünberg 1910, p. 162.
138   Koch-Grünberg 1910, p. 164.
139   Tessmann 1928.
140   Quoted in Steward and Métraux 1948, HB 3, p. 592.
141   Girard 1958, p. 249.
142   According to Girard 1958, *moeraya* is the Shipibo word for 'shaman'.
143   Métraux 1948b, HB 3, p. 681.
144   Métraux 1948b, HB 3, p. 447.
145   Personal communication.
146   Métraux 1942a, p. 129; Métraux 1948b, HB 3, pp. 389, 340.
147   Métraux 1949, HB 5, p. 563.
148   Koppers 1960, pp. 205 sqq.
149   Métraux 1949, HB 5, p. 561.
150   Cf. Métraux 1946a.
151   Cf. Krickeberg 1939, p. 146.
152   Métraux 1949, HB 5, p. 566.
153   Métraux 1949, HB 5, p. 563.

II. SPIRITS AND RITUALS OF THE HUNT

1   Métraux 1949, HB 5, p. 565.
2   Cf. Krickeberg 1922, p. 276.
3   Zerries 1954.
4   Cf. Koch-Grünberg 1920, pp. 323–4.
5   Quoted in Barbosa Rodrigues 1890, p. 12.
6   Cf. Métraux 1928, pp. 64 sqq.
7   Barbosa Rodrigues 1890, pp. 8 sqq.
8   Nimuendajú 1915, pp. 290 sqq.
9   Wagley and Galvão 1948, HB 3, p. 145.
10   Wagley and Galvão 1948, HB 3, p. 137.
11   Nimuendajú 1919/20, p. 1038.
12   Nimuendajú 1919/20, pp. 1034–5.
13   Nordenskiöld 1924, p. 33.
14   Barbosa Rodrigues 1890, p. 93.
15   Murphy 1958, pp. 13 sqq.
16   Murphy 1958, p. 40.
17   Koch-Grünberg 1916, pp. 72 sqq.
18   Roth 1915, pp. 225–6.
19   Koch-Grünberg 1923, p. 177.
20   Roth 1915, pp. 283–4.
21   Gillin 1936, pp. 193–4.
22   Tastevin 1926, p. 167.
23   Ehrenreich 1891, p. 42.
24   Roth 1915, p. 215.
25   Roth 1915, pp. 278–9.
26   Gillin 1936, p. 181.
27   Karsten 1935, p. 165.
28   Koch-Grünberg 1923, p. 189.
29   Koch-Grünberg 1923, pp. 123–4.
30   Koch-Grünberg 1923, p. 127 note.
31   De Goeje 1907, pp. 12–13, pl. II, 1.
32   Galella 1941, p. 743.
33   Nimuendajú 1919/20, pp. 1013–4.
34   Nimuendajú 1948, HB 3, pp. 265–6.
35   Ribeiro 1951, pp. 132–3.
36   Belaieff 1946, p. 379.
37   Métraux 1937, p. 175.
38   Koch-Grünberg 1923, p. 177.
39   Koch-Grünberg 1923, p. 179.
40   Métraux 1943, pp. 22 sqq.
41   F. de Augusta, in Gerdts-Rupp 1937, p. 136, note 6.
42   Latcham, in Gerdts-Rupp 1937, p. 136, note 6.
43   Métraux 1937, p. 175.
44   Gusinde 1937, p. 1422.
45   Gusinde 1931, p. 711.
46   Magalhães 1876, pp. 136 sqq.; Barbosa Rodrigues 1890, p. 93.
47   Murphy 1958, p. 16.
48   Murphy 1958, pp. 40–1.

49 Horton 1948, HB 3, p. 279.
50 Murphy 1958, pp. 58 sqq.
51 Horton 1948, HB 3, p. 279.
52 Murphy 1958, pp. 60–1.
53 Strömer 1932, pp. 119–20.
54 Cadogan 1950, pp. 331–2.
55 Altenfelder-Silva 1950, pp. 264 sqq.
56 Nordenskiöld 1924, pp. 274 sqq.
57 Métraux 1946b, HB 1, p. 470.
58 Ribeiro 1950, pp. 37–8, 165.
59 De Goeje 1943, p. 4.
60 Koch-Grünberg 1923, p. 187; Koch-Grünberg 1916, p. 20.
61 Koch-Grünberg 1923, p. 159.
62 Koch-Grünberg 1923, pp. 422–3.
63 Wilbert 1959, pp. 166 sqq.
64 Métraux 1949, HB 5, pp. 564–6.
65 Zerries 1952, pp. 220–35; cf. Zerries 1954, pp. 128–33.
66 De Goeje 1943, p. 17.
67 Roth 1924, p. 715 sqq.
68 De Goeje 1943, pp. 17–18.
69 Gusinde 1931, pp. 280, 707.
70 Henry 1941, pp. 84–5.
71 Steinen 1894, pp. 492–3.
72 Karsten 1926, p. 484.
73 Kirchhoff 1948b, HB 4, p. 491.
74 See Roth 1915, p. 285.
75 Hernandez de Alba 1948, HB 4, p. 412.
76 Walter 1956.
77 Frazer 1933, p. 235. The prayer is quoted from Thevet 1575, f. 937 R°.
78 Métraux 1928, pp. 174–5.
79 Koslowsky 1895, pp. 12–13.
80 Koslowsky 1895, pp. 3 sqq.
81 Petrullo 1932, p. 122.
82 Métraux 1942a, pp. 74–5; Métraux 1943, pp. 12–14; Métraux 1948b, HB 3, pp. 422–3.
83 Walter 1956, p. 94.
84 Cf. Baldus 1955.
85 Henry 1941, pp. 84–5.
86 Steinen 1894, p. 491.
87 Steinen 1894, p. 512.
88 Murphy 1958, p. 16.
89 Baumann 1950.
90 Civrieux 1959, p. 112.
91 Métraux 1948b, HB 3, p. 512.
92 Wegner 1936, p. 232.
93 Nordenskiöld 1924, p. 123.

94 Orbigny 1844, p. 201.
95 Holmberg 1950, p. 91; Wegner 1936, pp. 137, 145, 178.
96 Karsten 1935, pp. 167 sqq.
97 Hernandez de Alba 1948, HB 4, p. 398.
98 Quoted in Métraux 1949, HB 5, pp. 377–8.
99 Farabee 1918, p. 49.
100 Palavecino 1933, p. 318.
101 Bonnerjea 1934, p. 184.
102 Gusinde 1931, pp. 215, 705–6.
103 Karsten 1935, pp. 164 sqq.
104 Karsten 1935, p. 180.
105 Grubb 1911, p. 138.
106 Karsten 1926, p. 212.
107 Cook 1907, p. 58.
108 Chaffanjon 1889, pp. 203 sqq.
109 Karsten 1935, p. 171.
110 Tastevin 1926, pp. 160–1.
111 Métraux 1944b, p. 283.
112 Becker 1944, p. 400.
113 Karsten 1913, p. 210.

III. VEGETATION GODS AND FERTILITY RITES

1 Steinen 1894, p. 493.
2 Tocantins 1877; see also Horton 1948, HB 3, pp. 279–80.
3 Chaffanjon 1889, p. 204.
4 Métraux 1948, HB 3, p. 681.
5 For this aspect of South American religion I have drawn freely on Poduschka 1955.
6 Steward and Métraux 1948, HB 3, p. 620.
7 Tessmann 1930, pp. 356, 746.
8 Métraux 1949, HB 5, p. 620.
9 Preuss 1921, pp. 129 sqq.
10 Preuss 1921, pp. 124 sqq.
11 Preuss 1923, p. 645; Preuss 1921, p. 29.
12 Preuss 1921, pp. 126–7; Poduschka 1955, p. 95.
13 Jensen 1948, p. 112.
14 Poduschka 1955, p. 94.
15 Martius 1867, p. 218.
16 Métraux 1948b, HB 3, p. 91.
17 F. Müller 1934, pp. 191, 195.
18 Murphy and Quain 1955, p. 67; Lévi-Strauss 1948, HB 3, p. 246.
19 Murphy and Quain 1955, p. 67.
20 Oberg 1953, pp. 56–7.

21 Oberg 1953, pp. 54–5.
22 This is a good example of the widely-held belief that the first cultivated plants were given to mankind by the animals; an echo of hunting culture.
23 Gillin 1936, p. 160.
24 Koch-Grünberg 1909, pp. 137–8; 1910, pp. 194–5.
25 Koch-Grünberg 1910, pp. 157–8, 166.
26 Métraux 1949, HB 5, pp. 576–7.
27 Coudreau 1887, pp. 184–7.
28 Coudreau 1887, pp. 187 sqq.
29 Koch-Grünberg 1909, pp. 186 sqq., 201.
30 Cf. Saake 1958b, pp. 83 sqq.
31 In Koch-Grünberg 1909, p. 189.
32 Walde-Waldegg 1942, pp. 193 sqq.; Rozo 1945, pp. 242 sqq.
33 Cf. Zerries 1955b.
34 Koch-Grünberg 1909, pp. 314 sqq.
35 Koch-Grünberg 1910, pp. 292–3.
36 In Nimuendajú 1952, p. 78.
37 Métraux 1948b, HB 3, p. 704; Métraux 1949, HB 5, p. 576.
38 Nimuendajú 1952, pp. 77–8.
39 Martius 1867, p. 513.
40 Nimuendajú 1952, p. 79.
41 Nimuendajú 1948, HB 3, p. 261.
42 Nimuendajú 1948, HB 3, pp. 263–4.
43 Martius 1867, pp. 410–11.
44 Nimuendajú 1948, p. 264.
45 In Métraux 1948a, pp. 22–3.
46 Martius 1867, p. 502.
47 Patino 1958, pp. 188 sqq.
48 Tessmann 1930, pp. 276, 335, 555; Girard 1958, pp. 108 sqq.
49 Preuss 1921, p. 22.
50 Tessmann 1930, p. 359.
51 Tessmann 1930, p. 604.
52 Tessmann 1930, pp. 275, 335, 554–5.
53 Preuss 1923, p. 656; Preuss 1921, p. 75; cf. Girard 1958, pp. 110 sqq.
54 Preuss 1921, p. 215; cf. the Okaina myth in Girard 1958, pp. 109–10.
55 Preuss 1921, p. 133.
56 Preuss 1921, pp. 166 sqq.; Preuss 1923, pp. 647, 734.
57 Preuss 1921, p. 135.
58 Preuss 1921, pp. 133–4.

59 Preuss 1921, p. 75.
60 Preuss 1921, pp. 143 sqq.; cf. Tessmann 1930, pp. 276, 324, 555.
61 Volhard 1939, pp. 472–3.
62 Preuss 1921, p. 29.
63 Preuss 1923, pp. 670 sqq.
64 Preuss 1921, p. 29.
65 Preuss 1921, p. 143.
66 Volhard 1939, p. 485.
67 Boglár 1958.
68 Boglár 1958, p. 82.
69 Karsten 1923, pp. 23, 46–7; Stirling 1938, pp. 75–6.
70 Karsten 1923, p. 48.
71 Nimuendajú 1948, HB 3, p. 241.
72 Nimuendajú 1919/20, pp. 1013 sqq.
73 Nimuendajú 1919/20, pp. 1022–8.

IV. THE SOUL AND ANCESTOR WORSHIP

1 Nimuendajú 1914, pp. 301 sqq.
2 Nimuendajú 1914, p. 305.
3 Nimuendajú 1914, pp. 308 sqq.
4 Nimuendajú 1914, pp. 311 sqq.
5 Nimuendajú 1922, p. 367.
6 Koch-Grünberg 1923, pp. 170 sqq.
7 Rochefort, in Koch-Grünberg 1923, p. 171.
8 Cf. Métraux 1949, HB 5, p. 569.
9 Zerries, ms. 1.
10 Zerries 1958; for the Surára and Pakidai see Becher 1960, pp. 64–5.
11 Cf. Haekel 1952, pp. 141–2.
12 Gerdts-Rupp 1937, p. 74.
13 Métraux 1939, p. 94.
14 Gusinde 1931, pp. 744 sqq.
15 Gusinde 1937, pp. 1397 sqq.
16 Gomez Haedo in Métraux 1949, HB 5, p. 568.
17 Métraux 1949, HB 5, p. 569.
18 Métraux 1949, HB 5, p. 570.
19 Nimuendajú 1921/2, pp. 373 sqq.
20 Lowie 1946, HB 1, p. 433.
21 Métraux 1949, HB 5, pp. 567, 570.
22 Cf. Colbacchini and Albisetti 1942, p. 156.
23 Lowie 1946, HB 1, pp. 430–1.
24 Métraux 1949, HB 5, p. 570.
25 Goldmann 1948, HB 3, p. 795.
26 Goldmann 1948, HB 3, p. 783; cf. Girard 1958, pp. 42 sqq., on the *Mayantu* festival of the Yagua.
27 Goldmann 1948, HB 3, p. 796.

28 Goldmann 1948, HB 3, p. 789.
29 Goldmann 1948, HB 3, p. 781.
30 Oberg 1953, p. 56.
31 Cf. Oberg 1953, p. 56.
32 Horton 1948, HB 3, p. 280; Kruse 1934, pp. 55 sqq.
33 Murphy 1958, pp. 22 sqq., 63 sqq.

V. REPRESENTATIONS OF SUPER-
    NATURAL BEINGS

1 Métraux 1949, HB 5, p. 572; Rouse 1948, pp. 535 sqq.
2 Métraux 1949, HB 5, p. 573. This recalls the *nantara*, the stone which for the Jivaro embodies the earth mother Nungui.
3 Roquette-Pinto, in Métraux 1942a, p. 168.
4 In Métraux 1942a, p. 168.
5 In Métraux 1942a, pp. 75–6.
6 Nimuendajú 1948, HB 3, pp. 241, 243.
7 Nimuendajú 1919/20, pp. 1027–8.
8 Métraux 1928, p. 72.
9 Métraux 1946b, HB 1, p. 539.
10 Métraux 1949, HB 5, p. 573.
11 Cooper 1946b, HB 2, pl. 153; Titiev 1951, p. 119, pl. X, 1.
12 Métraux 1948b, HB 3, p. 706.
13 Cf. Roth 1915, pp. 139–40.
14 Zerries 1956b, pp. 191 sqq.
15 Steward 1948, HB 3, p. 578, pl. 82; Steward and Métraux 1948, pp. 734–5, pl. 78.
16 Cooper 1946b, HB 2, p. 735, pl. 153.
17 Nordenskiöld 1930, pp. 62–3, pl. LVI.
18 At the beginning of the seventeenth century a Carib (?) told the English traveller Harcourt that his tribe on the headwaters of the Oyapock River worshipped a stone idol in a special temple or house of worship; Gillin 1948, HB 3, pp. 824, 856; Harcourt 1928.
19 Preuss 1929.
20 Cf. Gerbrandts 1955.
21 Zerries ms. 2.
22 Métraux 1949, HB 5, p. 573.
23 In Métraux 1928, pp. 72–3.
24 Martius 1867, p. 588.
25 Staden 1927, part 2, chapter 22.

26 Zerries 1953a.
27 In Métraux 1928, pp. 73, 171.
28 Snethlage 1937, pp. 104–6.
29 Haekel 1953, pp. 131–2.
30 Koch-Grünberg 1909, p. 139; Koch-Grünberg 1910, p. 196.
31 Koch-Grünberg 1910, pp. 176 sqq.
32 Koch-Grünberg 1910, p. 176.
33 Koch-Grünberg 1909, pp. 133–4.
34 Koch-Grünberg 1909, p. 113.
35 Koch-Grünberg 1910, p. 180, ill. 106.
36 Koch-Grünberg 1910, pp. 252 sqq., ill. 174.
37 Haekel 1953, pp. 134–5; but cf. Girard 1958, pp. 110 sqq.
38 Nimuendajú 1952, pp. 73–92.
39 Nimuendajú 1952, pp. 82–3.
40 Martius 1831, p. 1088.
41 Nimuendajú 1952, pp. 70–1.
42 Lévi-Strauss 1948, HB 3, pp. 342 sqq.; Métraux 1949, p. 574.
43 Oberg 1953, p. 54.
44 Steinen 1894, pp. 320 sqq.
45 Steinen 1894, p. 319.
46 Steinen 1894, p. 298.
47 Ehrenreich 1891, pp. 34 sqq.; Haekel 1953, p. 126.
48 Cf. Krause 1910, pp. 101–2.
49 Steinen 1894, pp. 301–2. It is not proven, but it is strongly to be suspected that the ornamentation of the mask costumes of the Caraja and the Bacairi has the same significance as the phalluses used in the mask dances of the Caua and Cubeo.
50 Haekel 1952, pp. 983–4.
51 Nimuendajú 1942, pp. 67 sqq.
52 Nimuendajú 1946a, pp. 201 sqq., pls. 37–9.
53 Métraux and Nimuendajú 1946, HB 1, pp. 544–5.
54 Grubb 1913, p. 178.
55 Baldus 1931, pp. 77–8, 93 sqq.; Métraux 1946b, HB 1, pp. 358 sqq.
56 Cooper 1946a, HB 1, pp. 120–21, 104–5, 76.
57 Gusinde 1926, pp. 274 sqq.
58 Gusinde 1926, pp. 284 sqq.
59 Koppers 1924, pp. 121, 124.
60 Nimuendajú 1952, p. 77.
61 In Izikowitz 1934, p. 223.

22

62 Ehrenreich 1891, pp. 70–1.
63 Max Schmidt 1914, pp. 238 sqq.
64 In Métraux 1942a, p. 76.
65 Cf. Izikowitz 1934, pp. 224–6.
66 Haekel 1953, p. 129.
67 Petrullo 1932, pp. 139–40.
68 Steinen 1894, p. 59.
69 Steinen 1894, pp. 297–8.
70 Oberg 1953.
71 Cf. 'Dance of the guan' (*jacu*).
72 Zerries 1953b.
73 Steinen 1894, pp. 104, 307, ill. 121.
74 Max Schmidt 1905, p. 418.
75 Steinen 1894, pp. 327–8, ill. 122.
76 Oberg 1953, pp. 23–4, 53 sqq.
77 Nimuendajú 1942, p. 85.
78 Steinen 1894, pp. 497 sqq.
79 Colbacchini and Albisetti 1942, pp. 162–3.
80 Colbacchini and Albisetti 1942, p. 408.
81 Nimuendajú 1946a, p. 186.
82 Métraux and Nimuendajú 1946, HB 1, p. 545.
83 Nimuendajú 1939, pp. 108, 140.
84 Métraux 1946b, p. 343.
85 Keller-Leuzinger 1874, p. 104.
86 Nimuendajú 1919/20, pp. 1027–8.
87 Ehrenreich 1891, p. 71.
88 Nimuendajú 1952, p. 72.
89 Tessmann 1930, p. 273.
90 Izikowitz 1934, p. 209.
91 Gheerbrandt 1953, pp. 121–2.
92 Ahlbrinck 1931, p. 405.

VI. SHAMANISM

1 Métraux 1944a; Métraux 1944b.

2 Métraux 1949, HB 5, p. 588.
3 Whiffen 1915, pp. 181–2.
4 Métraux 1949, p. 589.
5 Métraux 1949, pp. 588–9.
6 Lowie 1946, HB 1, pp. 513–14.
7 Colbacchini and Albisetti 1942, p. 111.
8 Métraux 1949, p. 590.
9 Cf. Andres 1938.
10 Métraux 1949, HB 5, p. 591.
11 Koch-Grünberg 1923, p. 196; Tessmann 1930, p. 359.
12 De Goeje 1943, p. 48.
13 Koch-Grünberg 1923, pp. 196 sqq.
14 Métraux 1949, HB 5, p. 592.
15 Métraux 1946b, HB 1, p. 361.
16 Cf. Nimuendajú 1946a, pp. 234 sqq.; Nimuendajú 1939, pp. 140 sqq.
17 Colbacchini and Albisetti 1942, p. 92.
18 Koch-Grünberg 1923, p. 192.
19 Cf. Zerries 1955a.
20 Koch-Grünberg 1923, pp. 196 sqq.
21 Métraux 1949, HB 5, p. 593.
22 Gillin 1936, p. 158.
23 Métraux 1949, HB 5, p. 593.
24 Métraux 1949, HB 5, p. 595.
25 Cf. Zerries 1955a, *passim*.
26 Koch-Grünberg 1923, pp. 2199 sqq.
27 Jensen 1951, pp. 275 sqq.
28 Cf. Koch-Grünberg 1923, p. 220.
29 Métraux 1949, HB 5, pp. 597–8.
30 Métraux 1949, HB 5, p. 597.
31 Métraux 1928, p. 90.
32 Métraux 1949, HB 5, pp. 598–9.

BIBLIOGRAPHY

Mesoamerica

Armillas, Pedro
Los dioses de Teotihuacán. *Anales del Instituto de Etnología Americana* VI. S. Luis, Mendoza, S. Juan (Argentina) 1945.
La serpiente emplumada. Quetzalcoatl y Tlaloc. *Cuadernos Americanos* VI. Mexico D.F. 1947.
Teotihuacán, Tula y los Toltecas. *Runa* III 1/2. Buenos Aires 1950.

Beyer, Hermann
El llamado 'Calendario Azteca'. Mexico D.F. 1921.
La 'procesión de los señores', decoración del primer teocalli de piedra en México–Tenochtitlán, *El México Antiguo* VIII. Mexico D.F. 1955.

Caso, Alfonso
El teocalli de la guerra sagrada. Monografías del Museo Nacional de Arqueología, Historia y Etnografía. Mexico D.F. 1927.
Las estelas Zapotecas. Mexico D.F. 1928.
El paraiso terrenal en Teotihuacán. *Cuadernos Americanos* VI. Mexico D.F. 1942.

Caseo, Alfonso and Bernal, Ignacio
Urnas de Oaxaca. *Memorias del Instituto Nacional de Antropología e Historia* II. Mexico D.F. 1952.

(Chilam Balam)
The book of Chilam Balam of Chumayel. Carnegie Institution of Washington, Publication 438. 1933.

Codices Mexicanos (Duc de Loubat)
Codex Borgia (Rome) 1898.
Codex Borbonicus (Paris) 1899.
Codex Telleriano-Remensis (Paris) 1899.
Codex Fejérváry-Mayer (Paris) 1901.

Covarrubias, Miguel
Indian art of Mexico and Central America. New York 1957.

Dietschy, Hans
Mensch und Gott bei mexikanischen Indianern. *Anthropos* XXXV/XXXVI. Fribourg 1940/41.
Vom Charakter des höchsten Gottes der Azteken. *Bulletin der Schweizer Gesellschaft für Anthropologie, Archäologie und Ethnologie*. Basle 1941/42.

Drucker, Philip, Heizer, Robert F. and Squier, Robert J.
Excavation at La Venta, Tabasco, 1955. *Bur. of American Ethnology, Bull.* 170. Washington 1959.

Génin, Auguste
Note sur les objets précortéziens nommés indûment yugos ou jougs. *Atti del XXII Congr. Intern. degli Americanisti*, Roma 1926. 1928.
Groth-Kimball, Irmgard
Maya-Terrakotten. Tübingen 1946.
Guías oficiales del Instituto Nacional de Antropología e Historia. Mexico D.F.
Teotihuacán (Jorge Gurría Lacroix) 1956.
Uxmal (Alberto Ruz Lhuillier) 1956.
Tula (Pablo Martínez del Río and Jorge Acosta) 1957.
El Tajín (José Gracía Payón) 1957.
Monte Albán, Mitla (Jorge Gurría Lacroix) 1957.
Haekel, Josef
Die Vorstellung vom Zweiten Ich in den amerikanischen Hochkulturen. *Kultur und Sprache* (Wiener Beiträge zur Kulturgeschichte und Linguistik). 1952.
Hochgott und Götter im alten Mexiko. *Kairos* 3. Salzburg 1959.
Der 'Herr der Tiere' im Glauben der Indianer Mesoamerikas. *Mitteil. aus dem Museum für Völkerkunde in Hamburg* XXV. 1960.
Historia de los Mexicanos por sus pinturas
Ed. García Icazbalceta. *Nueva Colección de Documentos para la Historia de México* III. Mexico D.F. 1891.
(Historia de los Reynos de Colhuacán y de México)
Die Geschichte der Königreiche von Colhuacan und Mexico. Text and translation by Walter Lehmann. Quellenwerke zur alten Geschichte Amerikas, hsrg. vom Ibero-Amerikanischen Institut Berlin I. 1938.
Historia Tolteca-Chichimeca
Translated and edited by Konrad Theodor Preuss and Ernst Mengin. I: Die Bilderschrift nebst Übersetzung. II: Der Kommentar. Baessler-Archiv Beiheft 9 and Bd. XII. Berlin 1937/38.
Histoyre du Mechique
Ed. Edouard de Jonghe. *Journal de la Soc. des Américanistes*. N.S.II. Paris 1905.
Hvidtfeldt, Arild
Teotl and *ixiptlatli. Some central conceptions in ancient Mexican religion. Copenhagen 1958.
Kidder, Alfred V., Jennings, Jesse D. and Shook, Edwin M.
Excavations at Kaminaljuyú, Guatemala. Carnegie Institution of Washington, Publ. 561.
Kirchhoff, Paul
The Mexican calendar and the founding of Tenochtitlan-Tlatelolco. *Transactions of the New York Academy of Sciences*, Ser. II, Vol. 12, 4. 1950.
Krickeberg, Walter
Die Totonaken. Ein Beitrag zur historischen Ethnographie Mittelamerikas. *Baessler-Archiv* VII (I) and IX (II). Berlin 1918/25.
Märchen der Azteken und Inkaperuaner, Maya und Muisca. Jena 1928.
Das mittelamerikanische Ballspiel und seine religiöse Symbolik. *Paideuma* III. Bamberg 1948.
Felsplastik und Felsbilder bei den Kulturvölkern Altamerikas mit besonderer Berücksichtigung Mexicos I. Berlin 1949.
Bauform und Weltbild im alten Mexico. *Paideuma* IV. Bamberg 1950.
Altmexikanische Kulturen. Berlin 1956.
Bemerkungen zu den Skulpturen und Felsbildern von Cozumalhuapa. *Miscellanea Paul Rivet*. Mexico D.F. 1958.
Xochipilli und Chalchiuhtlicue. *Baessler-Archiv* N.F. VIII. Berlin.

Landa, Diego de
Relación de las cosas de Yucatán (1566). A translation, edited with notes by Alfred M. Tozzer. *Papers of the Peabody Museum of American Archaeology and Ethnology, Harvard University*, XVIII. Cambridge (Mass.) 1941.

Linné, Sigvald
Archaeological researches at Teotihuacan, Mexico. The Ethnogr. Museum of Sweden, New Series, Publ. I. Stockholm 1934.
Mexican highland cultures. The Ethnogr. Museum of Sweden, New Series, Publ. VII. Stockholm 1942.

Lothrop, Samuel Kirkland
The stone statues of Nicaragua. *American Anthropologist* N.S. XXIII. Lancaster (Pa.). 1921.
Metals from the Cenote of Sacrifice, Chichen Itzá, Yucatan. *Memoirs of the Peabody Museum of American Archaeology and Ethnology, Harvard University*, X 2. Cambridge (Mass.) 1952.

Marquina, Ignacio
Arquitectura prehispánica. Mexico D.F. 1951.

Maudslay, Alfred Percival
Archaeology I–IV. *Biologia Centrali-Americana*, edited by Godman *and* Salvin. London 1889/1902.

Moedano Koer, Hugo
A quién estuvo dedicado el Edificio B [de Tula]? *Revista Mexicana de Estudios Antropológicos* VI 3. Mexico D.F. 1942/44.
El friso de los cariques [Tula]. *Anales del Instituto Nacional de Antropología e Historia* II. Mexico D.F. 1947.

Morley, Sylvanus Griswold
The Ancient Maya. 3rd ed. Stanford (Calif.). 1947.

Noguera, Eduardo
El altar de cráneos esculpidos de Cholula. Mexico D.F. 1937.

Popol Vuh
Edited and translated by Leonhard Schultze Jena. *Quellenwerke zur alten Geschichte Amerikas*, Ibero-Amerikanischen Institut Berlin II. 1944.

Preuss, Konrad Theodor
Die Nayarit-Expedition. I Die Religion der Cora-Indianer. Leipzig 1912.
(a) *Mexikanische Religion.* Bilderatlas zur Religionsgeschichte, edited by H. Haas, XVI. Leipzig 1930.
(b) *Der Unterbau des Dramas.* Vorträge der Bibl. Warburg 1927/28. Leipzig 1930.

Proskouriakoff, Tatiana
An Album of Maya architecture. Carnegie Institution of Washington, Publ. 558. 1946.
A Study of Classic Maya Sculpture. Carnegie Institution of Washington, Publ. 593. 1950.

Ruz Lhuillier, Alberto
Estudio de la cripta del Templo de las Inscripciones en Palenque. *Tlatoani* I 5/6. Mexico D.F. 1952.

Sahagún, Bernardino de
Einige Kapitel aus dem Geschichtswerk des Fray Bernardino de Sahagún. Nahuatl text, translated by Eduard Seler. Stuttgart 1927.
Gliederung des alt-aztekischen Volkes in Familie, Stand und Beruf. Nahuatl text, translated by Leonhard Schultze Jena. 1952.
Quellenwerke zur alten Geschichte Amerikas, hrsg. vom Ibero-Amerikanischen Institut Berlin V. 1952.

Schellhas, Paul
Die Göttergestalten der Maya-Handschriften, 2. Aufl. Berlin 1904.

Schultze Jena, Leonhard
Indiana. I. Leben, Glaube und Sprache der Quiche von Guatemala. II. Mythen in der Muttersprache der Pipil von Izalco in El Salvador. Jena 1933/35.

Seler, Eduard
Wandmalereien von Mitla. Eine mexikanische Bilderschrift in Fresko. Berlin 1895.
(a) *Die alten Ansiedlungen von Chaculá im Distrikt Nenton des Dep. Huehuetenango der Republik Guatemala.* Berlin 1901.
(b) *Codex Fejérváry-Mayer.* Eine altmexikanische Bilderhandschrift des Free Public Museums in Liverpool. Berlin 1901.
Gesammelte Abhandlungen zur Amerikanischen Sprach- und Altertumskunde I–V. Berlin 1902/23.
Codex Borgia. Eine altmexikanische Bilderschrift der Bibliothek der Congregatio de Propaganda Fide. Berlin 1904/9.
Beobachtungen und Studien in den Ruinen von Palenque. *Abh. der Kgl. Preußischen Akademie d. Wiss.*, Jg. 1915, Phil.-Hist. Klasse Nr. 5. Berlin 1915.
Die Ruinen von Uxmal. *Abh. der Kgl. Preußischen Akad. d. Wiss. Jg.* 1917, Phil.-Hist. Klasse Nr. 3. Berlin 1917.

Smith, A. Ledyard
Uaxactun, Guatemala. Excavations of 1931–1937. Carnegie Institution of Washington, Publ. 588. 1950.

Spence, Lewis
The Gods of Mexico. New York 1923.

Spinden, Ellen S.
The place of Tajin in Totonac archaeology. *American Anthropologist* N.S. XXXV. Menasha 1933.

Spinden, Herbert J.
'A study of Maya art'. *Memoirs of the Peabody Museum of American Archaeology and Ethnology, Harvard University*, VI. Cambridge (Mass.) 1913.

Stirling, Matthew W.
Stone monuments of southern Mexico. *Bureau of American Ethnology*, Bull. 138. Washington 1943.

Strebel, Hermann
Studien über Steinjoche aus Mexico und Mittelamerika. *Intern. Archiv. für Ethnographie* III. Leiden 1890.
Über Tierornamente auf Tongefäßen aus Alt-Mexico. *Veröff. aus dem Kgl. Museum für Völkerkunde* VI 1. Berlin 1899.

Tenayuca
Estudio arqueológico de la pirámide de este lugar. Mexico D.F. 1935.

Termer, Franz
Zur Ethnologie und Ethnographie des nördlichen Mittelamerika. Berlin and Bonn 1930.

Thompson, J.Eric S.
(a) A trial survey of the southern Maya area. *American Antiquity* IX 1. Menasha 1943.
(b) Representations of Tlalchitonatiuh at Chichen Itzá, Yucatan, and El Baúl, Escuintla. Carnegie Institution of Washington, *Notes on Middle American Archaeology and Ethnology* 19. 1943.

An archaeological reconnaissance in the Cotzumalhuapa region, Escuintla, Guatemala. *Carnegie Institution of Washington*, Publ. 574. 1948.
The rise and fall of Maya civilization. London 1956.
Maya hieroglyphic writing. An introduction. Univ. of Oklahoma Press. Norman 1960.

Toscano, Salvador, Rubín de la Borbolla, D.F. and Kirchhoff, Paul
Arte precolombino del occidente de México. Mexico D.F. 1946.

Tozzer, Alfred M.
A comparative study of the Mayas and the Lacandones. Archaeolog. Institute of America. New York 1907.

Trik, Aubrey S.
Temple XXII at Copan. Carnegie Institution of Washington, *Contributions to American Anthropology and History* 27. 1939.

Vaillant, George C.
Early cultures of the Valley of Mexico. *Anthrop. Papers of the Amer. Museum of Natural History* XXXV 3. New York 1935.

Villacorta, J.Antonio *and* Villacorta, Carlos A.
Codices Mayas. Guatemala, C.A. 1930.

Villagra Caleti, Agustín
Bonampak, la ciudad de los muros pintados. *Anales del Instituto Nacional de Antropología e Historia* III, Supl. México D.F. 1949.
Pinturas rupestres. Ixtapantongo, Edo. de México. Mexico D.F. 1954.

South Central America and the Andean Civilizations

Ackerknecht, Erwin H.
Medical Practices. In: *Steward*, Vol. 5. Washington 1949.

Acosta, Joaquín
Compendio histórico del descubrimiento y colonización de la Nueva Granada en el siglo décimosexto. Paris 1848.

Acosta, José
Historia natural y moral de las Indias (1590). *Biblioteca de Autores Españoles*, Vol. 75. Madrid 1954.

Aguilera, Miguel
La antropofagia de las tribus americanas. In: *Boletín de Historia y Antigüedades.* Bogotá 1937.

Andagoya, Pascual de
Relación de los sucesos de Pedrarias Dávila en las provincias de Tierra firme ó Castilla del oro, y de lo occurrido en el descubrimiento de la mar del Sur y costas del Perú y Nicaragua. In: Martín Fernández de Navarrete, *Colección de los viages y descubrimientos que hicieron por mar los españoles desde fines del siglo XV*, Vol. 3. Madrid 1929.

Anónimo
Idolatrías de los Indios Wankas. In: *Inca*, Vol. I, No. 3. Lima 1923.
Varias noticias curiosas sobre la provincia de Popayán. In: *Colección de documentos inéditos relativos al descubrimiento, conquista y colonización de las posesiones españolas en América y Oceanía*, Vol. 5. Madrid 1866.

Arriaga, Pablo José de
La Extirpación de la Idolatría del Perú (1621). In: *Colección de libros y documentos referentes a la historia del Perú*, Vol. I, 2nd Serie. Lima 1920.

(Augustinos)

Relación de la Religión y ritos del Perú hecha por los primeros religiosos Augustinos que allí pasaron para la conversión de los naturales. In: *Colección de documentos inéditos relativos al descubrimiento, conquista y colonización de las posesiones españolas en América y Oceanía,* Vol. 3. Madrid 1865.

Avila, Francisco de

Dämonen und Zauber im Inkareich. Translated from Quechua into German and introduced by Hermann Trimborn. *Quellen und Forschungen zur Geschichte der Geographie und Völkerkunde,* Vol. 4. Leipzig 1939.
Dämonen und Zauber im Inkareich. Nachträge zum Khetschuawerk des Francisco de Avila. Herausgegeben von Hermann Trimborn. In: *Zeitschrift für Ethnologie,* Jahrgang, Berlin 1941.

Bandelier, A.F.

The Islands of Titicaca and Koati. New York 1910.
The Ruins at Tiahuanaco. In: *Proceedings of the American Antiquarian Society,* Vol. 21, 1911.

Bastian, Adolf

Die Culturländer des alten America, 3 vols. Berlin 1878/89.

Baudin, Louis

L'Empire socialiste des Incas. Paris 1928.
So lebten die Inkas vor dem Untergang des Reiches. Stuttgart 1957.

Bennett, Wendell C.

Excavations at Wari, Ayacucho, Peru. *Yale University Publications in Anthropology,* 49. New Haven 1953.

Bennett, Wendell C. and Bird, Junius B.

Andean Culture History. *American Museum of Natural History. Handbook Series,* 15. New York 1949.

Bernal Villa, Segundo

Aspectos de la cultura Paez. Mitología y cuentos de la parcialidad de Calderas, Tierradentro. In: *Revista Colombiana de Antropología, Seg. ép.,* Vol. I, 1. Bogotá 1953.
Medicina y magia entre los paeces. In: *Revista Colombiana de Antropología, Seg ép.,* Vol. II, No. 2. Bogotá 1954.

Betanzos, Juan de

Suma y narración de los Incas. *Biblioteca Hispano-Ultramarina,* Vol. 5. Madrid 1880.

Beuchat, Henri

Manual de Arqueología Americana. Madrid 1918.

Brinton, Daniel G.

American Hero-Myths. Philadelphia 1882.
The American Race. A linguistic classification and ethnographic description of the native tribes of North and South America. New York 1891.

Brühl, Gustav

Die Culturvölker Alt-Amerikas. New York 1875–87.

Bry, Johann Dietherich de

Zwölffter Theil der Newen Welt. Das ist: Gründliche volkommene Entdeckung aller der West Indianischen Landschaften usw. . . . beschrieben durch Antonium de Herrera. Frankfurt 1623.

Buchwald, Otto von
  Leyendas americanas. El Diluvio. *Publicaciones del Museo de Etnología y Antropología de Chile*, Vol. 4, No. 3 and 4. Santiago de Chile 1927.

Bushnell, Geoffrey H.S.
  Peru. 2nd edn. London 1969.

Cabello de Balboa, Miguel
  Histoire du Pérou, in: Ternaux-Compans, *Voyages, relations, et mémoires originaux pour servir à l'histoire de la découverte de l'Amérique.* Paris 1840.

Calancha, Antonio de
  Coronica Moralizada del orden de San Agustín en el Perú. Barcelona 1638.

Carrión Cachot, Rebeca
  La Luna y su Personificación Ornitomorfa en el Arte Chimú, in: *Actas del XXVII. Congreso Internacional de Americanistas. Lima 1939,* Vol. 1, Lima 1940.
  Cultura Chavín. Dos Nuevas Colonias: Kuntur Wasi y Ancón, in: *Revista del Museo de Antropología y Arqueologia,* Vol. 2, No. 1. Lima 1948.

Carrión Cachot de Girard, Rebeca
  Revisión del Problema Chavín, in: *Proceedings of the XXXII. International Congress of Americanists, Copenhagen 1956.* Copenhagen 1958.

Casas, Bartolomé de las
  Breuissima relacion de la destruycion de las Indias. *Colección de documentos inéditos para la historia de España,* Vol. 71. Madrid 1879.

Castellanos, Juan de
  Elegías de varones ilustres de Indias. *Biblioteca de Autores Españoles,* Vol. 4. Madrid 1852.

Cieza de León, Pedro de
  La Crónica del Perú. *Biblioteca de Autores Españoles,* Vol. 26. Madrid 1853.
  Segunda parte de la Crónica del Perú. *Biblioteca Hispano-Ultramarina,* Vol. 5. Madrid 1880.
  Guerra de Las Salinas. *Colección de documentos inéditos para la historia de España,* Vol. 68. Madrid 1877.
  Guerra de Chupas. *Colección de documentos inéditos para la historia de España,* Vol. 76. Madrid 1881.
  La guerra de Quito. *Nueva Biblioteca de Autores Españoles,* Vol. 15. Madrid 1909.

Cobo, Bernabé
  Historia del Nuevo Mundo, 4 vols., Sociedad de Bibliófilos Andaluces. Sevilla 1890–95.

Coreal, François
  Voyages de F.C. aux Indes Occidentales, 3 vols. Amsterdam 1722.

Cuervo Márquez, Carlos
  Orígenes etnográficos de Colombia. Estudio presentado ante el II. Congreso Científico Panamericano 1915–16. Washington 1917.
  Estudios arqueológicos y etnográficos, 2 vols. Madrid 1920.

Dapper, Olfert
  Die Unbekante Neue Welt, oder Beschreibung des Weltteils Amerika, und des Sud-Landes. Amsterdam 1673.

Dávila Briceño, Diego
  Descripsion y relacion de la provincia de los Yauyos toda, Anan Yauyos y Lorin Yauyos, hecha por D.D.B., corregidor de Guarocheri, in: *Relaciones Geográficas de Indias.* Publícalas el Ministerio de Fomento. Perú, Vol. 1. Madrid 1881.

Disselhoff, Hans Dietrich
Geschichte der altamerikanischen Kulturen. Munich 1953.

Eckert, Georg
Die Kopfjagd im Caucatal, in: *Zeitschrift für Ethnologie,* Vol. 71. Berlin 1939.
Die Menschenhauttrommeln in Alt-Peru, in: *Zeitschrift für Ethnologie,* Vol. 73. Berlin 1943.
Totenkult und Lebensglaube im Caucatal. *Kulturgeschichtliche Forschungen,* Vol. 1. Braunschweig 1948.

Escobar, Jerónimo de
Relación sobre el carácter y costumbres de los indios de la provincia de Popayán, in: *Colección de documentos inéditos relativos al descubrimiento, conquista y colonización de las posesiones españolas en América y Oceanía,* Vol. XLI. Madrid 1884.

Fernández de Oviedo y Valdés, Gonzalo
Historia general y natural de las Indias, islas y tierrafirme del mar-océano, 4 vols. Madrid 1851–5.

Fernández Piedrahita, Lucas
Historia general de las conquistas del Nuevo Reyno de Granada. Antwerp 1688.

Fettweis, Ewald
Berührungspunkte der pythagoreischen Zahlenlehre mit dem Totemismus, in: *Zeitschrift für Philosophische Forschung,* Vol. 5, No. 2. Meisenheim 1950/51.

Frederici, Georg
Die Ethnographie in den 'Documentos inéditos del Archivo de Indias', in: *Globus,* Vol. 90. Braunschweig 1906.
Über die Behandlung der Kriegsgefangenen durch die Indianer Amerikas. *Festschrift Ed. Seler.* Stuttgart 1922.

Garcilaso de la Vega
Comentarios Reales, Part 1. Lisbon 1609.

Graebner, Fritz
Alt- und neuweltliche Kalender, in: *Zeitschrift für Ethnologie,* Vol. 52. Berlin 1921.

Guaman Poma de Ayala, Felipe
El Primer Nueva Coronica i Buen Gobierno. La Paz 1944.

Hernández Príncipe, Rodrigo
Mitología Andina, in: *Inca,* Vol. 1, No. 1. Lima 1923.

Herrera, Antonio de
Historia general de los hechos de los Castellanos en las islas y tierra firme del mar Océano. Madrid 1726–30.

Herrera, F.L.
Fitolatría Indígena. Plantas y flores simbólicas de los Incas, in: *Revista Universitaria,* Vol. 16, No. 52. Cuzco 1926.

Hissink, Karin
Motive der Mochica-Keramik, in: *Paideuma,* Vol. 5, No. 3. Bamberg 1951.

Horkheimer, Hans
El Perú precolombino. Lima 1950.

Idolatrías de los indios Wancas (unnamed author), in: *Inca,* Vol. 1. Lima 1923.

Jensen, Adolf E.
Mythos und Kult bei Naturvölkern. Wiesbaden 1951.

Jijón y Caamaño, Jacinto
  La religión del Imperio de los Incas. Quito 1919.
  Sebastián de Benalcázar, Vol. 2. Quito 1938.

Jiménez de la Espada, Marcos (editor)
  Tres Relaciones de Antigüedades peruanas. Madrid 1879.
  Relaciones Geográficas de Indias. Perú, 4 vols. Madrid 1881–1897.

Joyce, Thomas A.
  South American Archaeology. London 1912.

Karsten, Rafael
  *The Civilization of the South American Indians. With Special Reference to Magic and
  Religion.* London–New York 1926.
  Die altperuanische Religion, in: *Archiv für Religionswissenschaft,* Vol. 25. Leipzig–
  Berlin 1927.
  Das altperuanische Inkareich und seine Kultur. Leipzig 1949.
  A Totalitarian State of the Past: the Civilization of the Inca Empire in Ancient Peru.
  Helsinki 1949.

Kirfel, Willibald
  Ist die Fünfzahl der symbolische Ausdruck einer bestimmten Kultur? in: *Geistige
  Arbeit, Zeitung aus der Wissenschaftlichen Welt,* 6 vols., No. 4. Berlin 20 Jan. 1939.

Koch, Theodor
  Die Anthropophagie der südamerikanischen Indianer, in: *Internationales Archiv für
  Ethnographie,* vol. 12. Leiden 1899.

Krause, Fritz
  Maske und Ahnenfigur. Das Motiv der Hülle und das Prinzip der Form. Ein
  Beitrag zur nichtanimistischen Weltanschauung. *Ethnologische Studien,* Vol. 1,
  1931.

Krickeberg, Walter
  Märchen der Azteken und Inkaperuaner, Maya und Muisca. Jena 1928.
  Amerika, in: *Bernatzik, Die Grosse Völkerkunde,* Vol. 3. Leipzig 1939.
  Felsplastik und Felsbilder bei den Kulturvölkern Alt-Amerikas, Vol. 1. Berlin 1949.

Kroeber, A.L.
  Paracas, Cavernas and Chavín, in: *University of California Publications in American
  Archaeology and Ethnology,* Vol. 40, No. 8. Berkeley 1953.

Kubler, George
  The Quechua in the Colonial World, in: Steward, *Handbook,* Vol. 2. Washington
  1946.

Kunike, Hugo
  El Jaguar y la Luna en la Mitología de la Altiplanicie Andina, in: *Inca,* Vol. 1,
  No. 3. Lima 1923.
  Die Herkunft der amerikanischen Flutsagen, in: *Der Erdball,* Vol. 2. Berlin 1928.

Kutscher, Gerdt
  Chimú, eine altindianische Hochkultur. Berlin 1950.
  Nordperuanische Keramik. *Monumenta Americana,* Vol. 1. Berlin 1954.

Laet, Johannes de
  Beschrijvinge van West-Indien door J.d.L. Leiden 1630.

Larco Hoyle, Rafael
  Los Mochicas, 2 vols. Lima 1938–1939.

Las Casas, Bartolomé de
  De las antiguas gentes del Perú. Madrid 1892.

Latcham, Ricardo E.

The Totemism of the Ancient Andean Peoples, in: *Journal of the Royal Anthropological Institute*, Vol. 57. London 1927.

Las creencias religiosas de los antiguos peruanos, in: *Anales de la Universidad de Chile*, 2nd series, vols. 7/8. Santiago de Chile 1929–30.

Lehmann-Nitsche, Robert

Coricancha, el Templo del Sol en el Cuzco, y las imágenes de su altar mayor, in: *Revista del Museo de La Plata*, Vol. 31. La Plata 1928.

Studien zur südamerikanischen Mythologie. Die ätiologischen Motive. Hamburg 1939.

Lehmann, Walter *and* Doering, Heinrich

Kunstgeschichte des Alten Peru. Berlin 1924.

Leicht, Hermann

Indianische Kunst und Kultur. Ein Jahrtausend im Reiche der Chimu. Zurich 1944.

Lenoir, Raymond

Les fêtes de boisson en Amérique du Sud, in: *Journal de la Société des Américanistes de Paris*, N.S., Vol. 17. Paris 1925.

López de Gómara, Francisco

Hispania victrix. Primera y segunda parte de la historia general de las Indias. *Biblioteca de Autores Españoles*, Vol. 22. Madrid 1852.

López de Velasco, Juan

Geografía y descripción universal de las Indias, recopilada por el cosmógrafo-cronista . . . desde el año de 1571 al de 1574.

Mackenzie, Donald A.

Myths of Pre-Columbian America. London 1924.

Markham, Clements Robert

The Incas of Peru. London–New York 1910.

Martyr, Petrus

De orbe novo de Pierre Martyr Anghiera. Les huit décades traduites du latin, avec notes et commentaires par Paul Gaffarel. Paris 1907.

Means, Philip Ainsworth

Ancient Civilizations of the Andes. New York 1931.

Mejía Xesspe, Toribio

Mitología del Norte Andino Peruano, in: *América Indígena*, Vol. 12, No. 3. Mexico 1952.

Métraux, Alfred

Religion and Shamanism, in: Steward, *Handbook*, Vol. 5. Washington 1949.

Minnaert, Paul

Les Institutions et le droit de l'impire des Incas. Ostend 1925.

Le Culte des pierres au Pérou, in: *Bulletin de la Société des Américanistes de Belgique*, Brussels, August 1930.

L'Adoration dans la Religion Péruvienne, in: *Bulletin de la Société des Américanistes de Belgique*, Brussels, December 1931.

Mishkin, Bernard

The Contemporary Quechua, in: Steward, *Handbook*, Vol. 2. Washington 1946.

Molina (de Cuzco), Cristóbal de

Relación de las fábulas y ritos de los Incas. *Collección de libros y documentos referentes a la historia del Perú*, Vol. 1. Lima 1916.

Montesinos, Fernando de
  Memorias antiguas historiales y políticas del Perú. *Colección de libros raros o curiosos que tratan de América*, Vol. 16. Madrid 1882.

Müller, J.G.
  Geschichte der amerikanischen Urreligionen, 2 vols. Basel 1867.

Muñiz, César Augusto
  Del Folk-Lore Indígena, in: *Revista Universitaria*, vol. 16, No. 52. Cuzco 1926.

Murúa, Martín de
  Historia del origen y genealogía de los reyes incas de Perú. Madrid 1946.

Nachtigall, Horst
  Shamanismo entre los Indios Paeces, in: *Revista Colombiana de Folklore*, Seg. ép., No. 2. Bogotá 1953.
  Kolumbianische vorgeschichtliche Tempel und Gottheiten, in: *Atlantis*, No. 2. Freiburg 1954.
  Tierradentro. Archäologie und Ethnographie einer kolumbianischen Landschaft. Zürich 1955.

Nieuwenhuis, A.W.
  The difference between the conception of soul (animus) and of spirit (spiritus) among the American Indians, in: *Proceedings of the XXI. Congress of Americanists*. The Hague 1924.

Orbigny, Alcide d'
  Voyage dans les deux Amériques. Paris 1867.

Pachacuti Yamqui Salcamayhua
  Juan Santa Cruz: Relación de antigüedades deste reyno del Pirú, in: Jiménez de la Espada, *Tres Relaciones*. Madrid 1879.

Pérez de Barradas, José
  Arqueología y Antropología de Tierra Adentro. Bogotá 1937.
  Arqueología Agustiniana. Bogotá 1943.
  Los Muiscas antes de la conquista, 2 vols. Madrid 1950–51.

Pittier de Fábrega, Henry
  Ethnographic and linguistic notes on the Paez Indians of Tierra adentro, Cauca, Colombia, in: *American Anthropological Association, Memoir* 1. Lancaster 1907.

Pizarro, Pedro
  Relación del descubrimiento y conquista de los reinos del Perú, in: *Colección de documentos inéditos para la historia de España*, Vol. 5. Madrid 1844.

Podewils-Dürnitz, Gertrud, Gräfin v.
  Legenden der Chibcha. Stuttgart 1930.

Polo de Ondegardo, Juan
  Relación de los adoratorios de los Indios en los cuatro caminos (zeques) que salían del Cuzco, in: *Colección de libros y documentos referentes a la historia del Perú*, Vol. 4. Lima 1917.
  Los errores y supersticiones de los indios, in: *Colección de libros y documentos referentes a la historia del Perú*, Vol. 3. Lima 1916.

Posada Arango, Andrés
  Essai ethnographique sur les aborigènes de l'Etat d'Antioquia en Colombie. *Mémoires de la Société d'Anthropologie de Paris*, 2 sér., Vol. 1. Paris 1873.

Preuss, Theodor
Die Begräbnisarten der Amerikaner und Nordostasiaten. Königsberg 1895.
Forschungsreise zu den Kágaba. Beobachtungen, Textaufnahmen und sprachliche Studien bei einem Indianerstamm in Kolumbien, Südamerika. Mödling bei Wien 1928.

Preuss, Konrad Theodor
Monumentale vorgeschichtliche Kunst, 2 vols. Göttingen 1929.

Raimondi, Antonio
El Perú, 6 vols. Lima 1874–1913.

Reichlen, H. *and* P.
Recherches Archéologiques dans les Andes de Cajamarca, in: *Journal de la Société des Américanistes de Paris*, N.S., Vol. 38. Paris 1949.

Reiss, Wilhelm *and* Stübel, Alphons
The Necropolis of Ancon in Peru, 3 vols. Berlin 1880–1887.

Restrepo Tirado, Ernesto
Estudios sobre los aborígenes de Colombia. Bogotá 1892.
Ensayo etnográfico y arqueológico de la provincia de los Quimbayas en el Nuevo Reino de Granada. Bogotá 1912 (First impression 1892).

Robledo, Jorge
Descripción de los pueblos de la provincia de Ancerma, in: *Colección de documentos inéditos relativos al descubrimiento, conquista y colonización de las posesiones españolas en América y Oceanía*, Vol. 3. Madrid 1865.

Rochereau, Père
Nociones sobre creencias, usos y costumbres de los Catíos del occidente de Antioquia, in: *Journal de la Société des Américanistes de Paris*, N.S., Vol. 21. Paris 1929.

Román y Zamora, Jerónimo
Repúblicas de Indias; idolatrías y gobierno de México y Perú antes de la conquista, in: *Colección de libros raros o curiosos que tratan de América*, Vols. 14, 15. Madrid 1897.

Rowe, John Howland
Inca Culture at the Time of the Spanish Conquest, in: Steward, *Handbook*, Vol. 2. Washington 1946.

Rowe, John H., Collier, Donald *and* Willey, Gordon R.
Reconnaissance Notes on the Site of Huari, near Ayacucho, Peru, in: *American Antiquity*, Vol. 16, No. 2. Salt Lake City 1950.

Rydén, Stig
Archaeological Researches in the Highlands of Bolivia. Göteborg 1947.

Saavedra, Bautista
El ayllu. La Paz 1913.

Santillán, Fernando de
Relación del origen, descendencia, política y gobierno de los Incas, in: Jiménez de la Espada, *Tres relaciones de antigüedades peruanas*. Madrid 1879.

Sardella, Juan Baptista
Relación del descubrimiento de las provincias de Antiochia por Jorge Robledo, in: *Colección de documentos inéditos relativos al descubrimiento, conquista y colonización de las posesiones españolas en América y Oceanía*, Vol. 3. Madrid 1865.

Sarmiento, Pedro
  Relación del viaje del capitán Jorge Robledo a las provincias de Ancerma y
  Quimbaya, in: *Colección de documentos inéditos relativos al descubrimiento, conquista y
  colonización de las posesiones españolas en América y Oceanía,* Vol. 2. Madrid 1864.

Sarmiento de Gamboa, Pedro
  Geschichte des Inkareiches. *Abhandlungen der Kgl. Gesellschaft der Wissenschaften
  Göttingen. Philologisch-historische Klasse,* Vol. 6, No. 4. Berlin 1906.

Schaedel, Richard P.
  Mochica Murals at Pañamarca, in: *Archaeology,* Vol. 4. 1951.

Schmidt, Max
  Kunst und Kultur von Peru. Berlin 1929.

Seler, Eduard
  Gesammelte Abhandlungen zur amerikanischen Sprach- und Altertumskunde, Vol. 5. Berlin
  1915.
  Die buntbemalten Gefässe von Nasca im südlichen Peru und die Hauptelemente
  ihrer Verzierung, in: Seler, Ed., *Ges. Abh. z. amer. Sprach- u. Altertumskunde,* Vol. 4.
  Berlin 1923.

Simón, Fray Pedro
  Noticias historiales de las Conquistas de Tierra Firme en las Indias Occidentales, 5 vols.
  Bogotá 1891/92.

Soustelle, Jacques
  Observations sur le symbolisme du nombre cinq chez les anciens Mexicains, in:
  Actes du XXVIIIᵉ Congrès International des Américanistes Paris 1947. Paris 1948.

Squier, E. George
  Peru. Reise- und Forschungs-Erlebnisse in dem Lande der Incas. Leipzig 1883.

Steward, Julian H. (editor)
  Handbook of South American Indians. Bureau of American Ethnology, Smithsonian
  Institution, Bulletin 143, 6 vols. Washington 1946–50.

Stöpel, Karl Theodor
  Südamerikanische prähistorische Tempel und Gottheiten. Ergebnisse eigener Ausgrabungen
  in Ecuador und Südkolumbien. Frankfurt 1912.

Stübel, Alphons *and* Uhle, Max
  Die Ruinenstätte von Tiahuanaco. Leipzig 1892.

Tello, Julio C.
  Los antiguos cementerios del valle de Nasca. Washington 1917.
  El uso de las cabezas artificialmente momificadas en el antiguo arteperuano. Lima 1918.
  Los descubrimientos del Museo de Arqueología Peruana en la península de Paracas,
  in: *Atti del XXII Congresso Internazionale degli Americanisti Roma 1926.* Roma 1928.
  Las primeras edades del Perú por Guaman Poma. Lima 1939.
  Wira Kocha, in: *Inca,* Vol. 1. Lima 1923.
  Antiguo Perú. Primera época. Lima 1929.

Tello, Julio C. *and* Miranda, Próspero
  Wallallo, in: *Inca,* Vol. 1. Lima 1923.

Torquemada, Juan de
  Segunda parte de los veinte i un libros rituales i Monarchia Indiana. Madrid 1723.

Trimborn, Hermann
  Das Recht der Chibcha in Kolumbien, in: *Ethnologica,* Vol. 3. Leipzig 1930.
  Quellen zur Kulturgeschichte des präkolumbischen Amerika. Stuttgart 1936.

343

Zwei Gebetsformeln aus präkolumbischer Zeit, in: *Forschungen und Fortschritte*, 1936, No. 7.

Francisco de Avila. Dämonen und Zauber im Inkareich. Aus dem Khetschua übersetzt und eingeleitet von H.T. *Quellen und Forschungen zur Geschichte der Geographie und Völkerkunde*, Vol. 4. Leipzig 1939.

Der Kannibalismus im Caucatal, in: *Zeitschrift für Ethnologie*, Vol. 70. Berlin 1939.

Dämonen und Zauber im Inkareich. Nachträge zum Khetschuawerk des Francisco de Avila, in: *Zeitschrift für Ethnologie*, Vol. 73. Berlin 1941.

Die Gewittergöttin Dobaiba, in: *Actes du XXVIIIᵉ Congrès International des Américanistes Paris 1947*. Paris 1948.

Vergessene Königreiche. Kulturgeschichtliche Forschungen, Vol. 2. Braunschweig 1948.

Señorío y Barbarie en el Valle del Cauca. Madrid 1949.

Herrentum und Herrengestalten im vorkolumbischen Caucatal, in: *Paideuma*, Vol. 4. Bamberg 1950.

Die Erotik in den Mythen von Huarochirí, in: *Jahrbuch des Linden-Museums* 1951. Heidelberg 1951.

Mehrfaltige Götter in den Mythen von Huarochirí, in: *Ethnologica, Neue Folge*, Vol. 2. Cologne 1960.

Tschudi, Joh. Jak. v.
Reisen durch Süd-Amerika. Leipzig 1896.
Culturhistorische und sprachliche Beiträge zur Kenntnis des alten Peru, in: *Denkschriften der Kaiserlichen Akademie der Wissenschaften in Wien. Philosophisch-Historische Klasse*, Vol. 39. Vienna 1891.

Uhle, Max
Pachacamac. Univ. of Pennsylvania, Department of Archaeology, Philadelphia 1903.
Zur Deutung der Intihuatana, in: *Verhandlungen des 16. Internationalen Amerikanisten-Kongresses Wien 1908.* Vienna and Leipzig 1908.
Die Ruinen von Moche, in: *Journal de la Société des Américanistes de Paris*, Vol. 10. Paris 1913.

Uribe Angel, Manuel
Geografía general y compendio histórico del Estado de Antioquia en Colombia. Paris 1885.

Vadillo, Juan de
Carta a Su Magestad dándole quenta de su vysita a la Gobernación de Cartagena, in: *Colección de documentos inéditos relativos al descubrimiento conquista y colonización de las posesiones españolas en América y Oceanía*, Vol. 41. Madrid 1884.

Valcárcel, Luis E.
Historia de la cultura antigua del Perú, 2 vols. Lima 1943–1949.
Del ayllu al Imperio. Lima 1925.

Valera, Blas
Relación de las costumbres antiguas de los naturales del Perú, in: Jiménez de la Espada. *Tres Relaciones de Antigüedades Peruanas.* Madrid 1879.

Vega Toral, Tomás
Historia del reino de Quito, 3 vols. Quito 1841–44.

Velasco, Juan de
Historia del Reino de Quito en la América meridional, 3 vols. Quito 1841–44.

Villagomes, Pedro de
Exortaciones e Instrucción acerca de las Idolatrías de los indios del Arzobispado de Lima, in: *Colección de libros y documentos referentes a la historia del Perú*, Vol. 12. Lima 1919.

Waitz, Theodor
Anthropologie der Naturvölker, Vol. 4. Leipzig 1864.

Wassén, Henry
An Archaeological Study in the Western Colombian Cordillera. *Etnologiska Studier*, No. 2. Göteborg 1936.

Wiener, Charles
Pérou et Bolivie. Paris 1880.

Willey, Gordon R. *and* Corbett, John M.
Early Ancon and Early Supe Culture. Chavín Horizon Sites of the Central Peruvian Coast, in: *Columbia Studies in Archaeology and Ethnology*, No. 3, Columbia University Press. New York 1954.

Wrigley, G.M.
The Travelling Doctors of the Andes, the Callahuayas of Bolivia, in: *Geographical Review*, 1917, No. 4.

Xerez, Francisco de
Verdadera relación de la conquista del Perú y provincia del Cuzco llamada la Nueva Castilla, in: *Colección de libros y documentos referentes a la historia del Perú*, 1st series, Vol. 5. Lima 1917.

Zárate, Agustín de
Historia del descubrimiento y conquista de la provincia del Perú, in: *Biblioteca de Autores Españoles*, Vol. 26. Madrid 1853.

Zerda, Liborio
El Dorado. Estudio histórico, etnográfico y arqueológico de los Chibchas, habitantes de la antigua Cundinamarca y de algunas otras tribus. Bogotá 1883.

Zerries, Otto
Wild- und Buschgeister in Südamerika. Wiesbaden 1954.

North America

Angulo, Jaime de
La Psychologie religieuse des Achumawi. *Anthropos XXIII*, 1928, 141–66, 561–89. With an introduction by Wilhelm Schmidt.

Barrett, Samuel Alfred
The Wintun Hesi Ceremony. *University of California Publications in American Archaeology and Ethnology* XIV, 1919, 437–88.

Beauchamp, William Martin
The Iroquois White Dog Feast. *The American Antiquarian and Oriental Journal* VII, 1885, 235–39.
Onondaga Notes. *Journal of American Folk-Lore* VIII, 1895, 209–16.

Blumensohn, Jules
The Fast among North American Indians. *American Anthropologist* N.S. 35, 1933, 451–69.

Boas, Franz
First General Report on the Indians of British Columbia. *Report of the British Association for the Advancement of Science* 1889, 801–93.

Second General Report on the Indians of British Columbia. *Ibid. Report* for 1890, 562–715.

The Social Organization and the Secret Societies of the Kwakiutl Indians. *Report of the U.S. National Museum for 1895*, Washington 1897, 311–738.

Boas, Franz *and* George Hunt

Kwakiutl Texts. *Memoirs of the American Museum of National History* III, 1902–5. (Publication of the Jessup North Pacific Expedition).

Boas, Franz *and* George Hunt

Kwakiutl Texts Second Series. *Ebenda* X, pt. 1, 1906.

Bois, Cora Alice du *and* Dorothy Demetrocopoulou

Wintu Myths. *University of California Publications in American Archaeology and Ethnology* XXVIII, 1931, 279–403.

Brainerd, David

Memoirs of the Rev. David Brainerd, Missionary to the Indians on the Borders of New York, New Jersey and Pennsylvania: chiefly taken from his own diary by Jonathan Edwards. New Haven 1822.

Bunzel, Ruth Leah

Introduction to Zuñi Ceremonialism. *47th Annual Report of the Bureau of American Ethnology 1929–30*. Washington 1932, 467–544.

Zuñi Ritual Poetry. *Ibid.* 611–835.

Zuñi Katcinas. An analytical study. *Ibid.* 837–1086.

Champlain, Samuel de

The Works. Reprinted, translated and annotated under the General Editorship of H.P.Bigger. Vol. I (1599–1607), translated and edited by H.H.Langton and W.F.Ganong. Toronto 1922.

Coleman, Bernard

The Religion of the Ojibwa of Northern Minnesota. *Primitive Man* X, 1937, 33–57.

Converse, Harriet Maxwell

The Festival of the Sacrifice of the White Dog as now Practised at the Onondaga Reservation. *Journal of American Folk-Lore* I, 1888, 83–5.

Über das Grünkorn und den Großen Federtanz der Seneca. *Ibid.* IV, 1891, 72–8.

Copway, George

Recollections of a Forest Life. London, Edinburgh and Dublin 1850.

Curtin, Jeremiah

Creation Myths of Primitive America. London and Edinburgh 1899.

Cushing, Frank Hamilton

Outlines of Zuñi Creation Myths. *13th Annual Report of the Bureau of Ethnology 1891–1892*, Washington 1896, 321–447.

Dankers, Jaspar *and* Peter Sluyter

Journal of a Voyage to New York in 1679–80. Translated from the Original Manuscript in Dutch and edited by Henry C.Murphy. Brooklyn 1867. (*Memoirs of the Long Island Historical Society* I.)

Dixon, Roland Burrage

Maidu Myths. *Bulletin of American Museum of Natural History* XVII, 1902, 33–118.

System and Sequence in Maidu Mythology. *Journal of American Folk-Lore* XVI, 1903, 32–6.

Maidu Texts. *Publications of American Ethnological Society* IV, 1912.

Douglass, William Boone
  Notes on the Shrines of the Tewa and Other Pueblo Indians of New Mexico. *Proceedings of the Nineteenth International Congress of Americanists 1915*, Washington 1917, 344–78.
Eliade, Mircea
  Schamanismus und archaische Ekstasetechnik. Zürich and Stuttgart 1957.
Fenton, William Nelson
  An Outline of Seneca Ceremonies at Coldspring Longhouse. *Yale University Publications in Anthropology* IX. New Haven 1936.
  The Seneca Society of Faces. *The Scientific Monthly* XLIV, 1937, 215–38.
  Masked Medicine Societies of the Iroquois. *Smithsonian Report* 1940. Washington 1941, 397–429.
Fishler, Stanley A.
  In the Beginning. A Navaho Creation Myth. *Utah University Department of Anthropology, Anthropological Papers*, No. 13, 1953.
Foster, George McClelland
  A Summary of Yuki Culture. *Anthropological Records*, Vol. 5, No. 3. Berkeley and Los Angeles 1944, 155–244.
Gifford, Edward Winslow
  Miwok Myths. *University of California Publications in American Archaeology and Ethnology* XII, 1917, 283–338.
Goddard, Pliny Earle
  The Beaver Indians. *Anthropological Papers of the American Museum of Natural History* X, pt 4, 1916, 201–93.
  Indians of the Southwest. New York 1927. *American Museum of Natural History, Handbook Series*, No. 2.
Goodwin, Grenville
  White Mountain Apache Religion. *American Anthropologist.* N.S. 40, 1938, 24–37.
Haekel, Josef
  Kosmischer Baum und Pfahl in Mythus und Kult der Stämme Nordwestamerikas. *Wiener völkerkundliche Mitteilungen* VI, 1958 (Neue Folge I), 33–81.
  Der Hochgottlaube der Delawaren im Lichte ihrer Geschichte. Völkerkundliche Forschungen. Martin Heydrich zum 70. Geburtstag überreicht. Hrsg. von W. Fröhlich. *Ethnologica* Neue Folge , Vol. 2. Köln 1960, 439–84.
Hagar, Stansbury
  Micmac Magic and Medicine. *Journal of American Folk-Lore* IX, 1896, 170–7.
Hale, Horatio
  The Iroquois Sacrifice of the White Dog. *The American Antiquarian and Oriental Journal* VII, 1885, 7–14.
Hallowell, Alfred Irving
  Bear Ceremonialism in the Northern Hemisphere. *American Anthropologist* N.S. XXVIII, 1926, 1–175.
Harrington, Mark Raymond
  Religion and Ceremonies of the Lenápe. *Indian Notes and Monographs.* New York 1921.
Henry, Alexander
  Travels and Adventures in Canada and the Indian Territories, between the Years 1760 and 1776. Edited by James Bain. Toronto 1901.

Hewitt, John Napoleon Brinton
  Article White Dog Sacrifice in Handbook of the American Indians North of
    Mexico. *Smithsonian Institution Bureau of American Ethnology Bulletin 30*, Washington
    1912, Vol. II, 939–44.
  Iroquoian Cosmology, First Part. *21st Annual Report of the Bureau of American
    Ethnology 1899–1900*. Washington 1903, 127–339.
  Iroquoian Cosmology, Second Part. *43rd Annual Report 1925–1926*. Washington
    1928, 449–819.
Hoffman, Walter James
  The Midē'wiwin or Grand Medicine Society of the Ojibwa. *7th Annual Report
    1885–1886*. Washington 1891, 143–300.
  The Menomini Indians. *14th Annual Report 1892–1893*. Washington 1896, 3–328.
Honigmann, John Joseph
  Culture and Ethos of Kaska Society. *Yale University Publications in Anthropology* 40.
    New Haven 1949.
Hultkrantz, Ake
  Conceptions of the Soul Among North American Indians. A Study in Religious
    Ethnology. Stockholm 1953. *The Ethnographical Museum of Sweden, Stockholm,
    Monograph Series Publication* No. 1.
Jenness, Diamond
  The Ojibwa Indians of Parry Island, Their Social and Religious Life. *Canada
    Department of Mines National Museum of Canada, Bulletin 78, Anthropological Series* 17.
    Ottawa 1935.
Kohl, Johann Georg
  Kitschi-Gami oder Erzählungen vom Oberen See., Vols. 1–2. Bremen 1859.
Krause, Fritz
  Die Kultur der kalifornischen Indianer in ihrer Bedeutung für die Ethnologie. Leipzig 1921.
Kroeber, Alfred Louis
  Indian Myths of South Central California. *University of California Publications in
    American Archaeology and Ethnology* IV, 1907, 167–250.
  The Religion of the Indians of California. *Ebenda*, 319–56.
  Zuñi Kin and Clan. *Anthropological Papers of the American Museum of Natural History*
    XVIII, 1917, 39–204.
  Handbook of the Indians of California. *Smithsonian Institution Bureau of American
    Ethnology Bulletin* 78. Washington 1925.
  Yuki Myths. *Anthropos* XXVII, 1932, 905–39.
  The Patwin and their Neighbors. *University of California Publications in American
    Archaeology and Ethnology* XXIX, 1932, 252–423.
Kroeber, Alfred Louis *and* Edward Winslow Gifford
  World Renewal, a Cult System of Native Northwest California. *Anthropological
    Records of the University of California* 13, 1949.
Loeb, Edwin Meyer
  The Creator Concept among the Indians of North Central California. *American
    Anthropologist* N.S. XXVIII, 1926, 467–93.
  The Western Kuksu Cult. *University of California Publications in American Archaeology
    and Ethnology* XXXIII, 1932, 1–137.
  The Eastern Kuksu Cult. *Ebenda* 1933, 139–232.
Mason, John Alden
  Notes on the Indians of the Great Slave Lake Area. *Yale University Publications in
    Anthropology* 34. New Haven 1946.

Masson, Louis-François Rodrigue
  Les Bourgeois de la Compagnie du Nord-Ouest, Vols. 1–2. Quebec 1889–90.

Merriam, Clinton Hart
  The Dawn of the World. Myths and weird tales told by the Mewan Indians of
  California. Cleveland 1910.
  Studies of California Indians. Edited by the Staff of the Department of Anthropology
  of the University of California. Berkeley and Los Angeles 1955.

Morgan, Lewis Henry
  League of the Ho-de'-no-sau-nee or Iroquois. Rochester 1851.

Müller, Werner
  Die blaue Hütte. Zum Sinnbild der Perle bei nordamerikanischen Indianern.
  Wiesbaden 1954. (*Studien zur Kulturkunde* XII.)
  Weltbild und Kult der Kwakiutl-Indianer. Wiesbaden 1955. (*Studien zur Kultur-
  kunde* XV.)
  Die Religionen der Waldlandindianer Nordamerikas. Berlin 1956.

Osgood, Cornelius B.
  The Ethnography of the Great Bear Lake Indians. *Canada Department of Mines,
  National Museum of Canada, Bulletin* No. 70. Ottawa 1932, 31–92.

Park, William Zerbe
  Shamanism in Western North America. A Study in Cultural Relationships. Evanston
  and Chicago 1938. (Northwestern University Studies in the Social Sciences
  No. 2).

Parker, Arthur Caswell
  Neh Hoh-no-tci-noh-gah, the Guardians of Little Waters, a Seneca Medicine
  Society. *New York State Museum Bulletin* 125. Albany 1908, 149–183.
  Secret Medicine Societies of the Seneca. *American Anthropologist* N.S. 11, 1909,
  161–85.
  The Code of Handsome Lake, the Seneca Prophet. *New York State Museum Bulletin*
  163. Albany 1912, 1–80.
  Outlines of the Cornplanting and the Maple Thanksgivings. *Ibid.* 101–4.

Parsons, Elsie Clews
  Hopi and Zuñi Ceremonialism. *Memoirs of the American Anthropological Association* 39,
  1933.
  Pueblo Indian Religion, Vols. 1–2, Chicago 1939. (*The University of Chicago Publications in Anthropology, Ethnological Series.*)

Petitot, Emile
  Monographie des Dènè-Dindjié, in: Petitot, *Dictionnaire de la langue Dènè-Dindjié.*
  Paris 1876, pages XIX–XXVI.
  Essai sur l'origine des Dènè-Dindjié. *Ibid.*, pages XXVII–XLV.

Prince, John Dyneley
  Notes on Passamaquoddy Literature. *Annals of the New York Academy of Sciences* XIII,
  1900–1, 381–6.

Rand, Silas Tertius
  Legends of the Micmacs. New York and London 1894.

Russell, Frank
  The Pima Indians. *26th Annual Report of the Bureau of American Ethnology 1904–1905.*
  Washington 1908, 3–389.

Schmidt, Wilhelm
    Die Religionen der Urvölker Amerikas. Münster i. W. 1929.
    Nachträge zu den Religionen der Urvölker Amerikas, Asiens und Australiens.
    Münster i. W. 1934. (*Der Ursprung der Gottesidee,* Vols. II and V.)
Smith, James
    An account of the remarkable occurrences in the life and travels of Colonel James
    Smith during his captivity with the Indians, in the years 1755, 1756, 1757, 1758
    and 1759. Lexington Kentucky 1799. Printed in Samuel Drake: *Indian Captivities
    or Life in the Wigwam.* New York 1859, 178–264.
Speck, Frank Gouldsmith
    Penobscot Shamanism. *Memoirs of the American Anthropological Association* VI, 1919,
    237–88.
    A Study of the Delaware Indian Big House Ceremony. *Publications of the Penn-
    sylvania Historical Commission* 2, Harrisburg 1931.
    Penobscot Tales and Religious Beliefs. *Journal of American Folk-Lore* 48, 1935, 1–107.
    Naskapi. The Savage Hunters of the Labrador Peninsula. Norman 1935.
    Oklahoma Delaware Ceremonies, Feasts and Dances. *Memoirs of the American
    Philosophical Society* VII, 1937.
    The Celestial Bear Comes Down to Earth. *Reading Public Museum and Art Gallery
    Scientific Publications* 7, Reading, Pa., 1945.
    The Iroquois, a Study in Cultural Evolution. Bloomfield Hills, Michigan 1945.
    Midwinter Rites of the Cayuga Long House. Philadelphia 1949.
Stevenson, Matilda Coxe
    The Sia. *11th Annual Report of the Bureau of Ethnology of the Smithsonian Institution
    1889–1890.* Washington 1894, 1–157.
    The Zuñi Indians. Their Mythology, Esoteric Fraternities, and Ceremonies. *23rd
    Annual Report of the Bureau of American Ethnology 1901–1902.* Washington 1904,
    1–634.
Stirling, Matthew Williams
    Origin Myth of Acoma and Other Records. *Smithsonian Institution Bureau of American
    Ethnology Bulletin* 135. Washington 1942.
Wallace, Anthony Francis Clarke
    The Modal Personality Structure of the Tuscarora Indians. *Smithsonian Institution
    Bureau of American Ethnology Bulletin* 150. Washington 1952.
Wallis, Wilson Dallam *and* Ruth Sawtell Wallis
    The Micmac Indians of Eastern Canada. Minneapolis 1954.
Williams, Roger
    A Key into the Language of America. London 1643.

Primitive South America and the West Indies

Ahlbrinck, W.
    Encyclopaedie der Karaïben. *Verhandelingen der Koninklijke Akademie van Wetenschappen
    te Amsterdam, Afdeeling letterkunde,* N.S. Vol. 27, No. 1. 1931.
Altenfelder-Silva, F.
    O estado de uanki entre os Bakairi. *Sociologia,* Vol. XII, No. 3. São Paulo 1950.
Andres, F.
    Die Himmelsreise der caraibischen Medizinmänner. *Zeitschr. f. Ethnol.* Vol. 70,
    Heft 3/5. Berlin 1938.

Armstrong, J. M. *and* Métraux, A.
  The Goajiro. Handbook of South American Indians, Vol. 4, Bull. 143. *Bur. Amer. Ethnol. Smiths. Inst.* Washington 1948.

Baldus, H.
  a: Indianerstudien im nordöstlichen Chaco. *Forschungen zur Völkerpsychologie und Soziologie*, Vol. XI. Leipzig.
  b: Die Allmutter in der Mythologie zweier südamerikanischer Indianerstämme (Kagaba und Tumereha). *Archiv. f. Religionswiss.* Vol. 29. 1931.
  Supernatural relations with animals among Indians of Eastern and Southern Brazil. *Proc. 30th Intern. Congr. of Americanists, Cambridge 1952.* 1955.
  Die Jaguarzwillinge. Kassel-Eisenach 1958.

Barbosa Rodrigues, João
  Poranduba amazonense. Rio de Janeiro 1890.

Baumann, Hermann
  Nyama, die Rachemacht. *Paideuma* Band IV. 1950.

Becher, Hans
  Die Surára und Pakidái. *Mitt. Mus. f. Völkerkunde in Hamburg*, XXVI. 1960.

Becker, H. (von)
  Lengua und Kaiotugui. Indianerstudien im Chaco Boreal. *Zeitschr. f. Ethnol.* Vol. 73 and Vol. 74. Berlin 1944.

Belaieff, J.
  The present-day Indians of the Gran Chaco. Handbook of South American Indians, Vol. 1, Bull. 143, *Bur. Amer. Ethnol. Smiths. Inst.* Washington.

Bird, J.
  The Alacaluf. Handbook of South American Indians, Vol. 1, Bull. 143, *Bur. Amer. Ethnol. Smiths. Inst.* Washington 1946.

Boglar, Luis
  Ein endokannibalischer Ritus in Südamerika. *Miscellanea Paul Rivet Octogenario Dicata II.* Mexico 1958.

Bonnerjea, Biren
  Hunting Superstitions of the American Aborigines. *Int. Archiv. f. Ethnogr.* Vol. 32. 1934.

Cadogan, Leon
  El Culto al arbol y a los animales sagrados en el Folklore y las tradiciones Guaranies. *America Indigena*, Vol. X, No. 4. Mexico 1950.

Calella, Placido de
  Apuntes sobre los Indios Siona del Putumayo. *Anthropos.* Vols. XXXV/VI. 1940–1.

Canals Frau, Salvador
  The Huarpe. Handbook of South American Indians, Vol. 1, Bull. 143. *Bur. Amer. Ethnol. Smiths. Inst.* Washington 1946.

Chaffanjon, Jean
  L'Orénoque et le Caura. Paris 1889.

Civrieux, Marc de
  Datos antropológicos de los Indios Kunuhana. *Antropológica*, No. 8. Caracas 1959.

Colbacchini, A. *and* Albisetti, C.
  Os Bororos Orientais Orarimugudoge do planalto oriental do Mato Grosso. *Bibl. Pedag. Brasil.* ser. 5 a, Vol. 4. Rio 1942.

Cook, W. A.
   The Bororo Indians of Matto Grosso, Brazil. *Smithsonian Miscellaneous Collections,*
   Vol. 50, Part 1. 1907.
Cooper, John M.
   (a) The Yahgan. – The Ona. – The Patagonian and Pampean Hunters. Handbook
   of South American Indians, Vol. 1, Bull. 143. *Bur. Amer. Ethnol. Smiths. Inst.*
   Washington 1946.
   (b) The Araucanians. Handbook of South American Indians, Vol. 2, Bull 143.
   Bur. Amer. Ethnol. Smiths. Inst. Washington.
Coudreau, Henri A.
   La France équinoxiale. Voyage a travers les Guayanes et l'Amazonie, Vol. II. 1887.
Cruxent, José M.
   Guanari, Dios Bueno Maquiritare. *Boletín Indig. Venezolano,* Año I, Tomo I, No. 2.
   Caracas 1953.
Ehrenreich, Paul
   Beiträge zur Völkerkunde Brasiliens. *Veröff. Königl. Mus. f. Völkerkunde,* 2 vols.,
   Nos 1/2. Berlin 1891.
Farabee, William C.
   The Central Arawak. *Univ. Pennsylvania, Anthr. Publ.* Vol. IX. Philadelphia 1918.
Frazer, James G.
   The Golden Bough, Part V, 'Spirits of the corn and the wild', Vol. II. 1933.
Frikel, Protasius
   Zur linguistisch-ethnologischen Gliederung der Indianerstämme von Nord-Pará
   (Brasilien) und den anliegenden Gebieten. *Anthropos.* Vol. 52, Fasc. 3/4. 1957.
Gerbrands, A. A.
   Masterpieces of Woodcarving from the Amazon Basin (Ms.). Abstract in: *Anals do*
   XXXI Congr. Intern. Americanistas, Vol. I. São Paulo 1955.
Gerdts-Rupp, Elisabeth
   Magische Vorstellungen und Bräuche der Araukaner. *Ibero-Amerikanische Studien,*
   Vol. 9. Hamburg 1937.
Gillin, John
   The Barama River Caribs of British Guiana. *Pap. Peabody Mus. Arch. Ethnol.*
   Harvard Univ., Vol. 14, No. 2. 1936.
   Tribes of the Guianas. Handbook of South American Indians, Vol. 3, Bull. 143,
   Bur. Amer. Ethnol. Smiths. Inst. Washington 1948.
Girard, Rafael
   Indios selváticos de la Amazonia Peruana. Mexico 1958.
Goeje, C. H. de
   Beiträge zur Völkerkunde von Surinam. *Int. Archiv. f. Ethnogr.* Vol. XIX. Leiden
   1908.
   Philosophy, Initiation and Myths of the Indians of Guiana and adjacent countries.
   Int. Archiv. f. Ethnogr. Vol. XLIV. Leiden 1943.
Goldmann, Irving
   Tribes of the Uaupés – Caquetá region. Handbook of South American Indians,
   Vol. 3, Bull. 143. *Bur. Amer. Ethnol. Smiths. Inst.* Washington 1948.
Grubb, Wilfred
   An unknown people in an unknown land, an account of the life and customs of the Lengua
   Indians of the Paraguayan Chaco . . . London 1911.

Gusinde, Martin
  Elemente aus der Weltanschauung der Ona und Alakaluf. *Proc. 21st Intern. Congr. Americanists*, 2. Part. Göteborg 1925.
  Männerzeremonien auf Feuerland und deren kulturhistorische Wertung. *Zeitschr. f. Ethnol.* Vol. 58. Berlin 1926.
  Die Feuerland-Indianer. Vol. 1. Die Selknam. Mödling bei Wien 1931.
  Die Feuerland-Indianer. Vol. 2. Die Yamana. Mödling bei Wien 1937.
  Review by Murphy, R.: 'Mundurucu Religion'. *Anthropos.* Vol. 55, Fasc. 1/2. 1960.

Haekel, Joseph
  Die Vorstellung vom Zweiten Ich in den amerikanischen Hochkulturen. *Wiener Beiträge z. Kulturgesch. u. Linguistik*, Vol. IX. Vienna 1952.
  Neue Beiträge zur Kulturschichtung Brasiliens. *Anthropos.* Vol. 47, Fasc. 5/6; Vol. 48, Fasc. 1/2. Fribourg 1952–3.
  Bespr. Zerries, Otto: 'Wild- und Buschgeister in Südamerika'. *Mitt. Anthrop. Gesellschaft*, Vol. LXXXIII, Heft 3. Vienna 1954.
  Purá und Hochgott. Probleme der südamerikanischen Religionsethnologie. *Archiv. f. Völkerkunde*, Vol. XIII. Vienna 1958.

Henry, Jules
  Jungle people, a Kaingáng tribe of the Highlands of Brazil. New York 1941.

Hernandez de Alba, Gregorio
  The Betoi and their neighbors. – The Achagua and their neighbors. Handbook of South American Indians, Vol. 4, Bull. 143, *Bur. Amer. Ethnol. Smiths. Inst.* Washington 1948.

Holmberg, Allan R.
  Nomads of the Long Bow. The Siriono of Eastern Brazil. *Inst. Soc. Anthr. Smiths. Inst.* Publ. No. 10. Washington 1950.

Horton, Donald
  The Mundurucu. Handbook of South American Indians, Vol. 3, Bull. 143, *Bur. Amer. Ethnol. Smiths. Inst.* Washington 1948.

Izikowitz, Karl Gustav
  Musical and other sound instruments of the South American Indians. *Göteborgs Kungl. Vetenskap och Vitterhets Samhäller Handlingar, Femte Följden.* Ser. A, Vol. 5, No. 1. 1934.

Jensen, Adolf E.
  Das religiöse Weltbild einer frühen Kultur. *Studien zur Kulturkunde*, Vol. 9. Stuttgart 1948.
  Mythos und Kult bei Naturvölkern. *Studien zur Kulturkunde*, Vol. 10. Wiesbaden 1951.

Karsten, Rafael
  La religion de los Indios Mataco-Noctenes de Bolivia. *Anales del Museo Nac. de Hist. Nat. de Buenos Aires*, Tomo XXIV. 1913.
  Contributions to the sociology of the Indian tribes of Ecuador. *Acta Academiae Aboensis Humaniora*, I/3. Abo 1920.
  Blood revenge, war and victory feasts among the Jibaro Indians of Eastern Ecuador. Bull. 79, *Bur. Amer. Ethnol. Smiths. Inst.* Washington 1923.
  The Civilization of the South American Indians. London 1926.
  The headhunters of Western Amazonas, the life and culture of the Jibaro Indians of eastern Ecuador and Peru. *Soc. Sci. Fennica, Commentationes Humanarum, Litterarum*, Vol. 7, No. 1. Helsingfors. 1935.

Keller-Leuzinger, Franz
Vom Amazonas und Madeira. Stuttgart 1874.

Kirchhoff, Paul
(a) The Warrau. Handbook of South American Indians, Vol. 3, Bull. 143, *Bur. Amer. Ethnol. Smiths. Inst.* Washington 1948.
(b) Food-gathering tribes of the Venezuelan Llanos. – The Tribes north of the Orinoco River. Handbook of South American Indians, Vol. 4, Bull. 143, *Bur. Amer. Ethnol. Smiths. Inst.* Washington 1948.

Koch-Grünberg, Theodor
Zwei Jahre unter den Indianern. Reisen in Nordwestbrasilien, Vol. I. Berlin 1909.
Idem, Vol. II. Berlin 1910.
Vom Roroima zum Orinoco, Vol. II, Mythen u. Legenden. Berlin 1916.
Idem, Vol. III, Ethnographie. Stuttgart 1923.
Indianermärchen aus Südamerika. Jena 1920.

Koppers, Wilhelm
Unter Feuerländern. Stuttgart 1924.
Die Originalität des Hochgottglaubens der Yamana auf Feuerland. *Tribus,* No. 9. Stuttgart 1960.

Koslowsky, Julio
Algunos datos sobre los Indios Bororos. *Revista del Museo de La Plata,* Tomo VI. 1895.

Krause, Fritz
Tanzmaskennachbildungen vom mittleren Araguaya (Zentralbrasilien). *Jahrbuch des Städtischen Museums f. Völkerkunde, Leipzig,* Vol. 3. 1910.

Krickeberg, Walter
Amerika. G. Buschan, *Illustr. Völkerkunde,* Vol. I. Stuttgart 1922.
Amerika. H. A. Bernatzik, *Die grosse Völkerkunde,* Vol. III. Leipzig 1939.

Kruse, Albert
Mundurucu Moieties. *Primitive Man,* Vol. VII, No. 4. 1934.
Karusakaybë, der Vater der Munduruku. *Anthropos.* Vols. 46/47. 1951–2.
Purá, das Höchste Wesen der Arikena. *Anthropos.* Vol. 50. 1955.

Lévi-Strauss, Claude
Tribes of the upper Xingu River. – The Nambicuara. Handbook of South American Indians, Vol. 3, Bull. 143, *Bur. Amer. Ethnol. Smiths. Inst.* Washington 1948.

Lowie, Robert H.
Eastern Brazil: An Introduction. – The Bororo. – The Northwestern and Central Ge. – Handbook of South American Indians, Vol. 1, Bull. 143, *Bur. Amer. Ethnol. Smiths. Inst.* Washington 1946.
The Tropical Forests: An Introduction. Handbook of South American Indians, Vol. 3, Bull. 143, *Bur. Amer. Ethnol. Smiths. Inst.* Washington 1948.

Magalhães, Couto de
O Selvagem. Rio de Janeiro 1876.

Martius, C. F. Phil. von
Beiträge zur Ethnographie und Sprachenkunde Amerikas, Vol. I. Leipzig 1867.

Matos Arvelo, Martin
Algo sobre etnografía del Territorio Amazonas de Venezuela. Ciudad Bolivar 1908.

354

Métraux, Alfred

La religion des Tupinamba et ses rapports avec celle des autres tribus Tupi-Guarani. Paris 1928.

Etudes d'ethnographie Toba-Pilaga (Gran Chaco). *Anthropos*, Vol. 32. 1937.

Myths and tales of the Matako Indians. *Ethnol. Studier*, Vol. 9. Göteborg 1939.

(a) The native tribes of eastern Bolivia and western Matto Grosso, Bull. 134, *Bur. Amer. Ethnol. Smiths. Inst.* Washington 1942.

(b) Le shamanisme araucan. *Rev. Inst. Antropologia Univ. Nac. Tucuman*, Vol. 2, No. 10. 1942.

Mojo and Manasi society and religion. *Primitive Man*, Vol. XVI, No. 1/2. Washington 1943.

(a) Le shamanisme chez les Indiens de l'Amérique du Sud tropicale. *Acta Americana*, Vol. II, No. 3/4. Mexico 1944.

(b) Estudios de etnografia chaquense. *Anales Inst. Etnografia Americana*, Vol. V, Univ. Nac. de Cuyo. Mendoza 1944.

(a) El Dios Supremo, los creadores y héroes culturales en la mitologia Sud-americana. *Americana Indigena*, Vol. VI. 1946.

(b) Ethnography of the Chaco. – The Caingang. – The Botocudo. *Handbook of South American Indians*, Vol. 1, Bull. 143, Bur. Amer. Ethnol. Smiths. Inst. Washington 1946.

(a) Ensayos de mitologia comparada Sudamericana. *America Indigena*, Vol. VIII, No. 1. Mexico 1948.

(b) The Guaraní. – The Tupinamba. – The Paressi. – Tribes of eastern Bolivia and the Madeira Headwaters. – Tribes of the eastern slopes of the Bolivian Andes. – Tribes of the Juruá-Purús Basins. – Tribes of the middle and upper Amazon River. *Handbook of South American Indians*, Vol. 3, Bull. 143, Bur. Amer. Ethnol. Smiths. Inst. Washington 1948.

Boys' initiation rites. – Religion and shamanism. *Handbook of South American Indians*, Vol. 5, Bull. 143, Bur. Amer. Ethnol. Smiths. Inst. Washington 1949.

Métraux, A. *and* Kirchhoff, P.

The northeastern extension of Andean culture. *Handbook of South American Indians*, Vol. 4, Bull. 143, Bur. Amer. Ethnol. Smiths. Inst. Washington 1948.

Métraux, A. *and* Nimuendaju, C.

The Mashacalí, Patashó, and Malalí linguistic families. *Handbook of South American Indians*, Vol. 1, Bull. 143, Bur. Amer. Ethnol. Smiths. Inst. Washington 1946.

Müller, Franz

Beiträge zur Ethnographie der Guarani-Indianer im östlichen Waldgebiet von Paraguay. *Anthropos*, Vols. 29/30. 1934–5.

Murphy, Robert F.

Mundurucu Religion. *Univ. Calif. Publ. Amer. Archeol. Ethnol.*, Vol. 49, No. 1. Berkeley-Los Angeles. 1958.

Murphy, Robert F. *and* Quain, Buell

The Trumai Indians of Central Brazil. *Monographs of the American Ethnological Society*, XXIV. New York 1955.

Nimuendaju, Curt

Die Sagen von der Erschaffung und Vernichtung der Welt als Grundlagen der Religion der Apapocuva-Guarani. *Zeitschr. f. Ethnol.*, Vol. 46. Berlin 1914.

Sagen der Tembe-Indianer. *Zeitschr. f. Ethnol.* Vol. 47. Berlin 1915.

Bruchstücke aus Religion und Überlieferung der Šipaia-Indianer. *Anthropos*, Vols. XIV/XV *and* XVI/XVII. 1919–20 *and* 1921–2.

The Apinayé. The Catholic Univ. of America, Anthropological Series No. 8. Washington 1939.
The Šerente. *Publ. Frederick Webb Hodge Anniv. Publ. Fund,* Vol. IV, The South-West Museum, Los Angeles 1942.
(a) The Eastern Timbira. *Univ. Calif. Publ. Amer. Archaeol. Ethnol.,* Vol. 41. Berkeley-Los Angeles 1946.
(b) Social organization and beliefs of the Botocudo of Eastern Brazil. *South-Western Journal of Anthrop.,* Vol. 2, No. 1. 1946.
Tribes of the lower and middle Xingú River. – The Mura and Pirahá. – The Cayabí, Tapanyuna and Apiacá. *Handbook of South American Indians,* Vol. 3, Bull. 143, Bur. Amer. Ethnol. Smiths. Inst. Washington 1948.
The Tukuna. *Univ. Calif. Publ. Amer. Archaeol. Ethnol.,* Vol. XLV. Berkeley and Los Angeles 1952.

Nordenskiöld, Erland
Forschungen und Abenteuer in Südamerika. Stuttgart 1924.
L'Archéologie du Bassin de l'Amazone. *Ars Americana* I. Paris 1930.

Oberg, Kalervo
Indian Tribes of Northern Mato Grosso, Brazil. *Inst. Soc. Anthrop. Publ.* No. 15, Smiths. Inst. Washington 1953.

Orbigny, Alcide d'
Voyage dans l'Amérique meridionale, Vol. 3, Part 1. Paris 1844.

Palavecino, Enrique
Von den Pilagá-Indianern im Norden Argentiniens. *Anthropos,* Vol. XXVIII. 1933.

Patiño, Víctor
El cachipay o pijibay (Guilielma gasipaes Bailey) y su papel en la cultura y en la economía de los pueblos indígenas de América tropical. *América Indígena,* Vol. XVIII, No. 3/4. Mexico 1958.

Penard, F. P. *and* A. P.
De menschetende aanbidders der zonneslang, I–III. Paramaribo 1907–8.

Petrullo, Vincenzo
Primitive peoples of Matto Grosso, Brazil. *The Museum Journal, Univ. Mus. Philadelphia,* Vol. XXIII, No. 2. 1932.
The Yaruros of the Capanaparo River, Venezuela, Bull. 123, *Bur. Amer. Ethnol. Smiths. Inst. Anthrop. Papers,* No. 11. Washington 1939.

Poduschka, Walter
Ackerbauriten in Südamerika, Diss. Vienna 1955.

Preuss, Konrad Th.
Religion und Mythologie der Uitoto, Vol. I, II. Göttingen 1921, 1923.
Die Darstellung des Zweiten Ich unter den Indianern Amerikas. *In memoriam Karl Weule.* Leipzig 1929.

Ribeiro, Darcy
Religião e mitologia Kadiueu. *Serviço do Proteçao aos Indios,* Publicação No. 106. Rio de Janeiro 1950.
Noticia dos Ofaié-Chavante. *Revista Museu Paulista,* N. S. Vol. V. São Paulo 1951.

Roth, Walter E.
An inquiry into the animism and folk-lore of the Guiana Indians. *30th Ann. Rep. Bur. Amer. Ethnol. Smiths. Inst. (1908/9).* Washington 1915.
An introductory study of the arts, crafts, and customs of the Guiana Indians. *38th Ann. Rep. Bur. Amer. Ethnol. Smiths. Inst. (1916/17).* Washington 1924.

Rouse, Irving
The Arawak. *Handbook of South American Indians*, Vol. 4, Bull. 143, Bur. Amer. Ethnol. Smiths. Inst. Washington 1948.

Rozo, José M.
La fiesta del Diablo entre los Puinave. *Boletín de Arqueología*, Vol. I, No. 3. Bogotá 1945.

Saake, Wilhelm
(a) Die Juruparilegende bei den Baniwa des Rio Issana. *Proc. 32nd Intern. Congr. Americanists, Copenhagen (1956)*. 1958.
(b) Aus der Überlieferung der Baniwa. *Staden-Jahrbuch*, Vol. 6. São Paulo 1958.

Snethlage, Emil H.
Atiko y. Meine Erlebnisse bei den Indianern des Guaporé. Berlin 1937.
Review of M. Gusinde, Die Feuerland-Indianer, Vol. 2, Die Yamana. *Zeitschr. f. Ethnol.*, Vol. 70. Berlin 1938.

Spix, Joh. Bapt. von, *and* Martius, C. F. Phil. von
Reise in Brasilien, Vol. III. Munich 1831.

Staden, Hans
Wahrhaftige Historia und beschreibung eyner Landtschafft der wilden nacketen grimmigen Menschenfresser-Leuthen in der Newenwelt America gelegen. 1557. (Facsimile Marburg and Frankfurt 1927).

Steinen, Karl v. d.
Unter den Naturvölkern Zentral-Brasiliens. Berlin 1894.

Steward, Julian H.
Western Tucanoan tribes. – The Witotoan tribes. *Handbook of South American Indians*, Vol. 3, Bull. 143, Bur. Amer. Ethnol. Smiths. Washington 1948.

Steward, Julian H. *and* Métraux, Alfred
Tribes of the Peruvian and Ecuadorian Montaña. – The Peban tribes. *Handbook of South American Indians*, Vol. 3, Bull. 143, Bur. Amer. Ethnol. Smiths. Inst. Washington 1948.

Stirling, Matthew W.
Historical and ethnographical material on the Jivaro Indians. *Bull. 117, Bur. Amer. Ethnol. Smiths. Inst.* Washington 1938.

Strömer, C. von
Die Sprache der Munduruků. *Anthropos: Coll. Int. de Monographies Linguistiques*, Vol. XI. Vienna 1932.

Schaden, Egon
Der Paradiesmythos im Leben der Guarani-Indianer. *Proc. 30th Intern. Congr. Americanists, Cambridge (1952)*. 1955.

Schmidt, Max
Indianerstudien in Zentralbrasilien. Berlin 1905.
Die Paressi–Kabiši. *Baessler-Archiv*, Vol. 4. Berlin 1914.

Tastevin, Constant
Le Haut Tarauacá. *La Géographie*, Vol. XLV. Paris 1926.

Tessmann, Günter
Menschen ohne Gott. Stuttgart 1928.
Die Indianer Nordost-Perus. Hamburg 1930.

Thevet, André
Cosmographie universelle. Paris 1575.

Titiev, Mischa
Araucanian culture in transition. *Occ. Contrib. Mus. Anthrop. Univ. Michigan*, No. 15.
Ann Arbor 1951.

Vellard, Jean
Une civilisation du miel. Paris 1939.

Volhard, Ewald
Kannibalismus. *Studien zur Kulturkunde*, Vol. 5. Stuttgart 1939.

Wagley, Charles *and* Galvão, Eduardo
The Tenetehara. *Handbook of South American Indians*, Vol. 3, Bull. 143, Bur. Amer.
Ethnol. Smiths. Inst. Washington 1948.

Walde-Waldegg, Hermann von
Notes on the Indians of the Llanos of Casanare and San Martin (Colombia).
Primitive Man, Vol. IX, No. 3. 1936.
Indians of the upper Orinoco. *Proceedings 8th American Scientif. Congress*, Vol. 2. 1942.

Walter, Heinz
Der Jaguar in der Vorstellungswelt der südamerikanischen Naturvölker. Diss. Hamburg
1956.

Wegner, Richard N.
Zum Sonnentor durch altes Indianerland. Darmstadt 1936.

Whiffen, Thomas W.
The north-west Amazon: notes of some months spent among cannibal tribes. London and
New York 1915.

Wilbert, Johannes
Rasgos culturales circuncaribes entre los Warrau y sus inferencias. *Mem. Soc.
Ciencias Naturales La Salle*, Vol. XVI, No. 45. Caracas 1956.
Puertas del averno. *Mem. Soc. Ciencias Naturales La Salle*, Vol. XIX, No. 54.
Caracas 1959.

Zerries, Otto
Sternbilder als Ausdruck jägerischer Geisteshaltung in Südamerika. *Paideuma*,
Vol. V, No. 5. 1952.
(a) Kürbisrassel und Kopfgeister in Südamerika. *Paideuma*, Vol. V, No. 6. 1953.
(b) The bullroarer among South American Indians. *Revista do Museu Paulista*,
Vol. VII. São Paulo 1953.
Wild- und Buschgeister in Südamerika. *Studien zur Kulturkunde*, Vol. 11. Wiesbaden
1954.
(a) Krankheitsdämonen und Hilfsgeister des Medizinmannes in Südamerika.
Proc. 30th Intern. Congr. Americanists, Cambridge (1952). 1955.
(b) Das Lashafest der Waika-Indianer. *Umschau* 55, No. 21. Frankfurt 1955.
(a) Beiträge zur Ethnographie der Guahibo-Indianer des Territorio Amazonas,
Venezuela. *Paideuma*, Vol. VI, No. 4. Frankfurt 1956.
(b) Eine seltene Holzstatue aus Venezuela. *Baessler-Archiv* N.F. No. 2. Berlin 1956.
Die Vorstellungen der Waika-Indianer des oberen Orinoco (Venezuela) über die
menschliche Seele. – Schöpfung und Urzeit im Denken der Waika . . . *Proc. 32nd
Intern. Congr. Americ. Copenhagen (1956)*. 1958.
Medizinmannwesen und Geisterglaube der Waika-Indianer des oberen Orinoco.
Ethnologica N.F. Vol. 2. Cologne 1960.
El endocannibalismo en la América del Sur. *Revista Museo Paulista*, N.S. Vol. XI.
Ms. 1.
Der Zeremonialstab der Erlanger Sammlung aus Brasilien im Staatl. Mus. f.
Völkerkunde zu München. 34*th Int. Amer. Kongr. Wien (1960)*. Ms. 2.

INDEX